DIAMOND AND JUBA

DIAMOND AND JUBA

THE RAUCOUS WORLD OF 19TH-CENTURY CHALLENGE DANCING

APRIL F. MASTEN

UNIVERSITY OF ILLINOIS PRESS
Urbana, Chicago, and Springfield

© 2025 by the Board of Trustees
of the University of Illinois
All rights reserved
Manufactured in the United States of America
c 5 4 3 2 1
♾ This book is printed on acid-free paper.

Cataloging data available from the Library of Congress

ISBN 978-0-252-04679-7 (hardcover)
ISBN 978-0-252-04834-0 (ebook)

For Vince, Cara, and my father, Ric Masten, the writers in my life

Yes!
let it be a dance
let life be a dance
because we dance to dance
not to go anywhere
and let it be a dance
let life be a dance
because within the dance
we move easily
with the paradox
knowing
that for every step forward
there must be a step back
and anything else
would have us marching
away from the music

—Ric Masten
   "Dance Benediction"

CONTENTS

Introduction: Purely American Dance 1

Part I Rising from the Streets

1. Out of the Mix 13
2. Humbug's Apprentice 32
3. Trials of Skill and Servitude 56
4. Master Rattler 76

Part II Champions of the World

5. North and South 93
6. Under Canvas 122
7. A Sensation in Print 143
8. Partners in Time 169
9. Gross Imitators 189

Part III Falling Giants

10. Juba Abroad 217
11. Assertions of Independence 244
12. Above All Puny Rivalry 273

Conclusion: Forgotten Legacies 293

Acknowledgments 301

Notes 305

Index 357

INTRODUCTION
Purely American Dance

In January 1843 readers of the *New York Sporting Whip* spotted an odd announcement among the turf reports, ring results, and brothel reviews that dominated the newspaper's columns. The *Whip*, one of several salacious illustrated "flash" weeklies that aided the growing ranks of young clerks and workingmen in their quest to sample the city's many commercial pleasures, promoted a new kind of athletic contest for the betting crowd: a jig-dancing match between the young Irish American John Diamond and a "colored boy" identified only as Juba.

Publicized trials of skill between Black and white people were rare in this era when most of the nation's almost three million African Americans were enslaved in the cotton South. Slavery had been abolished in New York State for sixteen years, but the number of free Black people living in Northern cities was small and shrinking due to out-migration. New York City counted sixteen thousand African Americans out of a total population of almost four hundred thousand. A few prominent community members headed Black churches and abolition societies, but most African Americans scraped by as domestic servants, waiters, street hawkers, or in other so-called degraded occupations.[1] Most Black Northerners lived side by side with poor white people. Indeed, the color line dividing the races was faintest in the lowlier wards, saloons, and theaters of the city, where the latest fad among entertainers of all hues was to perform in blackface and parody "Negro" singing, dancing, and storytelling traditions. These acts blurred and reinforced the existing racial hierarchies.

There would be no "corking up" at the match advertised in the *Whip*, but the dancers' names laid bare their ethnoracial origins. Many a Diamond had disembarked from the packed emigrant ships that carried thousands of impoverished and often despised Irish fleeing economic and political oppression in the Emerald

Isle.² And "Juba" was the name of a river in the Horn of Africa as well as a lively slave dance developed on Southern plantations. Promoters of the challenge, *Whip* editor George B. Wooldridge among them, no doubt hoped that the differing races of the contestants would increase interest in the match. "The stake is large and an unparalleled display will be the result," promised the paper, which nevertheless predicted that Diamond would "conquer" his opponent.³

While equally small in stature and talented as dancers, Diamond and Juba are otherwise studies in contrast. Diamond was born John Dimond to Irish immigrant parents, probably in New York City in 1823. He was short, lithe, and muscular. No portrait of him survives, but written descriptions suggest that he was not handsome. By all accounts, he was pugnacious, intemperate, impulsive, and vain. He had little formal education and never married. He moved between circuses, theaters, and minstrel troupes, billing himself as the "original John Diamond" to ward off impersonators. He asserted his superiority by issuing dance challenges at the end of his shows. Trouble followed him everywhere: He stabbed a man in New Orleans, was jailed for brawling in Massachusetts, and shot a man in Kentucky. In 1847, at the height of his career, he joined the Mexican War, injuring his health and pocketbook. After the war, he called himself an artist-athlete and ended his career dancing matches against newcomers and amateurs, including clog dancers, Native Americans, and boxers.

Juba, by contrast, was comely, gentlemanly, abstemious, self-confident, and reliable. He was born William Henry Lane to free Black parents in either New Jersey or New York around 1824. He was "about 5 feet 3 inches in height" and "tightly, trimly built," with pleasing good looks and a "happy cast of countenance."⁴ He was more educated and clever than his Irish counterpart and took advantage of opportunities for advancement. He headed to New England, where Black performers were safer, founded his own minstrel troupes, billed himself as the dancer "who beat John Diamond," and demonstrated his superiority by imitating his blackface rivals. In 1848 he traveled with a blackface minstrel troupe to the United Kingdom, where he danced in royal gardens, Theatres Royal, and mechanics institutes as "Boz's Juba." Lane took over his own career after two years abroad and experienced a kind of liberty unattainable in the United States. He married a white woman and never returned.

The 1843 dancing match took place at African American Pete Williams's cellar tavern in New York's Sixth Ward before a rowdy, mixed-race crowd of dancers, gamblers, and pugilists. No judge presided, as it was agreed that the spectators would determine the winner by acclamation according to who danced the longest with the greatest vigor and variety of steps. Juba hit the floor first. He "shuffled, and twisted, and walked around" for over an hour, recalled one eyewitness interviewed years later. But when Diamond's turn came, he "outstepped" Juba. He "kept on puttin' in all the fancy touches and the funny business" until he had surpassed Juba's time.[5]

Diamond won the purse that night. The amount is not known, but it probably exceeded the dollar-a-day wage that he and other white male laborers in the city typically earned. Juba likely got only a small cut, but he gained such a following that night that the rivalry continued. He and Diamond, their names destined to remain linked in the public's mind, would exchange more boastful challenges in print and "can't touch this" steps on stage over the next few years in an effort to capitalize on their extraordinary prowess and popularity—and to determine not just the best jig dancer in the house but the "champion dancer of the world."[6]

Diamond and Juba takes this celebrated rivalry as its subject in order to rescue challenge dancing from its ill-deserved obscurity, recover the multiracial origins of American popular culture, and reconstruct the porous and generative social world of free Black and poor white people in the tumultuous years before the Civil War. Challenge dancing, I argue, was more than an occasional leisure activity for the urban masses. It was a recognized sport, a form of remunerative labor, and a means of upward mobility for the truly talented, despite the disadvantages of their race, class, gender, or generation. Its popularity among the working classes made Diamond and Juba marketable theatrical attractions recruited by P. T. Barnum and other stage and circus impresarios. Challenge dancing was also a betting sport that shared much in common with boxing, including its unsavory reputation, vulgar spectators, and scrappy practitioners. Diamond and Juba's rivalry and successes as challenge dancers can tell us much about social relations in this era, about shifting structures of opportunity, and about the role of physical talent in determining individual destinies.

Dancing challenges on and off the stage offer a new prism through which to view the central tensions of mid-nineteenth-century America. Though largely forgotten now, challenge dancing was an everyday form of entertainment and personal expression. Countless men, women, and children met in jig-dancing contests for pleasure and profit in taverns, theaters, circuses, and market squares throughout the United States and Canada. With roots in both Ireland and Africa, challenge dancing flourished in the ethnically mixed neighborhoods of port cities along the Eastern Seaboard and thriving river cities to the west. While set largely in the Northeast, this is a story of people in motion across North America and the United Kingdom who created not only a new common dance practice but also a new space of cultural contest, display, betting, and even (at times) racial cross-identification as white dancers sustained alliances with African Americans and Black dancers claimed Irish heritage to garner status.

A main theme of this book is the prevalence of interracial cultural exchange in the antebellum era. Challenge dancing was a creolized form of jig dancing, produced by pervasive Black-Irish social interaction, that became an aesthetic language shared by poor, marginalized, and oppressed people. Jigs were lively partner and solo step dances with British and European origins. However, in the United States, people interchanged the terms "jig dancing" and "Negro dancing" when denoting a style of dance derived from the jigs, reels, and hornpipes of Irish "set dancing" and the rhythmic footwork, hip play, and upper body movements of African dance practices.[7] Performed to alternating tunes during a set, these "Negro jigs" invited challenges and competitions between couples and solo dancers, often called "break-downs" by contemporaries. The winner of a dancing match was the person ("the best dancer" or "sometimes the archest wag") who held out the longest and performed the greatest variety of steps, which encouraged borrowing not only from rival jig dancers but also from other dance genres.[8] These shared skills became the tools of the dancing trade.

The demographic profile of challenge dancers, as I've been able to determine, opens up a second important theme: children's and women's little-noted participation in the sport and in the creation of American popular culture more generally. While competitive jig dancing was a prevalent working-class social practice, the number of professional challenge dancers was never large (I have identified forty males and eleven females working in the 1840s and 1850s), and their ranks were dominated by boys and young men between eight and twenty-five years old, of whom at least one in four were African American. Girls and women challenge danced too. When Charles Dickens saw Juba dancing a breakdown in a Five Points tavern in New York City in 1842, his opponent was a young mulatto woman. Why has no one noted that before? Female jig dancers did compete in public in the 1840s, but their scanty and often sexist depiction in contemporary sources (most were dismissed as prostitutes) has led modern scholars to replicate these biases and underestimate women's contributions to American dance.

Diamond and Juba command attention as two of the first theatrical and athletic celebrities in the United States. They attained stardom by performing, separately and together, across the nation (though never in the South for Juba) and abroad. Diamond's tours took him into Canada, and Juba performed in England, Scotland, and Ireland. Both men were lionized in the press and widely imitated or impersonated—their names on a bill sold tickets, even when lesser dancers blacked up and tried to replicate their routines. Many other jig dancers issued and accepted challenges, but it was Diamond and Juba who transformed jig dancing from a hybrid, plebeian, communal activity into a lucrative commercial spectacle.

These two performers were bound together by the challenge dancing on which they built their reputations. Although of different races, they matured as dancers in the same environment, performed the same steps, worked for many of the same employers, and enhanced each other's careers as partners and competitors before they went their separate ways. They also shared one other biographical trait: early death. Juba died at about age thirty in 1854, and Diamond followed him shortly at age thirty-four in 1857. Their stories ended there, but not their legacy, which lives on in the mélange of competitive dancers and dance practices interacting across the globe today.

This book follows these two talents from their earliest days as street and tavern dancers to the pinnacles of their success in glittering pleasure gardens and legitimate theaters. It describes their childhood in New York City's Sixth Ward, their indentured servitude as young stage performers, and their expanding but still incomplete liberty as top-billed celebrities. It explains how a poor immigrant boy and a free Black youth gained money and fame in a society steeped in anti-Irish and proslavery sentiment with the help of newspaper editor George B. Wooldridge, impresario P. T. Barnum, and novelist Charles Dickens. It situates their divergent paths—from Juba's self-exile in England to Diamond's choice of opponents—in America's deepening racial and class antagonisms. It also charts the waning of their careers and the decline of challenge dancing as an interracial sport in the 1850s, when popular culture was reformed to serve a middle-class market and politicized by debates over slavery's expansion.

Neither Diamond nor Juba left behind personal papers. Consequently, important aspects of their lives remain shrouded in mystery, more the subject of speculation than certainty. Gaps in the historical record include Juba's birthdate and marriage year and Diamond's court-martial in the Mexican War. I have been forced to glean their political views and family backgrounds from accounts by their contemporaries. Few of their utterances have survived. Nevertheless, fifteen years of archival research in the United States, England, Ireland, and Scotland have netted an abundance of sources that have enabled me to reconstruct their lives and the diverse social and cultural environments through which they moved. These sources include theatrical material such as playbills, posters, sheet music, librettos, scripts, scrapbooks, letters, memoirs, theater annals, and minstrelsy chronicles. Another often-untapped primary source is the physical steps and gestures of the dancers. As a historian and a dancer, I have tried to get at those by dancing the dances described in the literary and visual record (albeit not at the level of my subjects) and working with scholars and performers who specialize in contemporary and historical Irish and African dance and music practices.

The journalistic record is also rich. In addition to the flash press, respectable daily and weekly newspapers advertised and reported on challenge dances and dancers, transforming them into celebrities whose onstage and offstage antics commanded attention. Encyclopedic city guides, market books, and travelogues, including Charles Dickens's famous *American Notes*, contribute to this cultural work. I've also discovered relevant material in boxing manuals, sports annuals, folklore collections, and the narratives of once enslaved people. These are supplemented by official documents such as police reports, census data, and military records and by visual sources such as engravings, genre paintings, and daguerreotypes. I use these documents to create scenes that invoke the time and places in which Diamond and Juba danced and to bring to life some of the characters and people they encountered.

Valuable as these historical sources are, they are all shot through with racist characterizations and sexist stereotypes. These can be difficult or uncomfortable to read and should never be taken at face value. They remind us that American society was built on systemic inequality even as it touted every citizen's ability to rise out of the station into which he or she had been born. But such sources also tell us that Americans stranded on the bottom rungs were resisting oppression in myriad ways, such as white and Black people dancing together, women dancing with as much physical prowess as men, and people accepting Black dance as quintessentially American. To get at those things, all of which were crucial to the success of challenge dancers such as Diamond and Juba, I have had to look for and try to understand the contradictions in the sources, to read against the grain of history.[9]

Juba is known to scholars today as one of the few African Americans who shared the stage with whites in the 1840s. He is the subject of several important scholarly essays and makes appearances in many works on minstrelsy and the origins of American dance. He is also a character in three novels.[10] Diamond has been less studied. He, too, surfaces in works on minstrelsy and American tap dancing, but as an Irish American who often performed in blackface, Diamond is regarded by most scholars as an early appropriator of Black culture. Juba is the innovator in these works and Diamond the imitator. My research challenges that accounting.

This book highlights what I see as the central paradox of Diamond and Juba's story and of America's racial history. Challenge dancing turned these two opponents into collaborators who together created what Diamond aptly characterized as a "purely American" art form. In much the same way, chattel slavery and the freedom struggle made Black and white people into cocreators of this imperfect union and cogenerators of the incredible cultural energy that followed. This energy, which continues to surge up from its streets, its youth, and its past, radiated from Diamond's and Juba's dancing. To know their story is to better understand America's.

Diamond and Juba contributes to four seemingly unconnected areas of nineteenth-century social history: childhood, labor, sport, and minstrelsy. The age at which Diamond and Juba launched their careers cannot be attributed simply to their youthful precociousness. The "structural forces" of commercial capitalism, early industrialization, democratic politics, antislavery agitation, and the proliferation of cheap newspapers also played a part. In the second quarter of the nineteenth century, displaced farmers, desperate immigrants, and fugitive slaves converged on waterfront cities throughout the country, creating populations dominated by youths under twenty. Theaters, garden saloons, circuses, and other entertainment venues sprang up to serve this audience, and child performers found ready acceptance in these various worksites.

Like most challenge dancers, Diamond and Juba started dancing for tips and prizes as young children and mounted the stage as employees in their early teens. Dancing may have seemed like child's play to middle-class audiences, but the children they were watching knew it was work. Young dancers experienced the division of labor like other workers and claimed their liberty when they could.[11] Their status as child workers affected the content and reception of Diamond's and Juba's dancing. They had to perform what their managers wanted and discover what their audiences liked. Following popular convention, both dancers performed in "wench" costumes and wore blackface makeup. While adults who cross-dressed were rarely taken seriously, the androgynous countenances of juvenile dancers made their cross-dressed performances more believable and enjoyable. Conversely, a young performer's repertoire and expressive freedom expanded when he or she portrayed another gender or race.[12]

Young female dancers added to the form and content of challenge dancing in oblique ways. Not only were they the partners and opponents of young male dancers honing their skills in social settings, they provided a source of new material in professional settings. Juba incorporated the toe-stepping pirouettes of European danseuses into his champion dances, and Diamond's first matches on the stage were travesties of contests between ballerinas.

The competition and speculation that fueled America's market economy in the mid-nineteenth century impacted diverse cultural practices, of which challenge dancing was one. Contests of skill, strength, speed, and endurance provided sociability and recreation, and betting permeated the nation.[13] Entertainers of every stripe advertised their performances as grand trials of skill. To drum up a crowd, jig dancers exchanged challenges in the popular press and took on the trappings of the prizefighting ring. In both sports, contestants engaged in "bouts," "toed the mark," and demonstrated their "Science" for wages, wagers, and belts. The correlation with boxing gave jig dancers prestige outside the theater.[14]

The gamblers and boxers present at Diamond and Juba's matches helped transform challenge dancing from a working-class game into a manly sport and jig dancers into athletes. Unfortunately, that conversion entailed the exclusion of female champions. Traditionally, everyone in lower-class communities took part in the competitive dancing. But as workingmen fought to gain status in a society dominated by middle-class values, they accepted the notion that males belonged to the public sphere of competition and females to the private sphere of cooperation. White, Black, and immigrant men might still get together to exhibit their moves in the heat and sweat immediacy of a tavern dancing match, but by the 1860s there was no place left for women.

Both Diamond and Juba danced onstage in blackface costumes. They also worked for minstrel companies—bands of mostly white singer-musicians who performed harmonic renditions of "Negro songs" interspersed with caricatures of Black people's language and culture. Scholars in diverse fields have demonstrated the damaging effects of the racist stereotypes perpetuated by blackface minstrelsy in the nineteenth century and beyond. Showy, false, insulting, and often violently dehumanizing, blackface performance was a manifestation of a white audience's desire for cultural and racial superiority. But the message sent by blackface and its effect on performers and audiences were neither simple nor transhistorical.[15]

Challenge dancing clearly intersected with and was ultimately co-opted by blackface minstrelsy, but the two activities should not be conflated. The origins of competitive jig dancing in racially mixed communities distinguished it from other forms of blackface entertainment. White middle-class audiences usually viewed competitions between minstrel dancers as hilarious parodies of Black people's social customs, but the working-class audiences who packed the pit and gallery of playhouses, amphitheaters, and saloons judged the dancing on its own terms. As amateur dancers themselves, these patrons expected contestants to be highly skilled and well matched. And they were rarely disappointed. The ability, artistry, and stamina of challenge dancers set them apart from other minstrel performers.

Irish American challenge dancers wore blackface onstage because it transformed their jigs, reels, and hornpipes into American dances.[16] It also hid the dancer's identity from the audience, a fact that played out differently in our two dancers' careers. Stage names and blackface costumes made it possible for Black dancers to perform in white venues and, in Juba's case, generate international renown. (Lane danced as Juba, Master Rattler, Master Diamond, and Boz's Juba but never under his surname.) They also made it possible for Lane and a slew of other dancers to impersonate Diamond and benefit from his fame.

Diamond and Juba maintained independent careers by exploiting the popularity of blackface minstrelsy. But rather than letting minstrelsy define them, challenge dancers piloted the minstrelsy trade (for a time). Minstrel musicians depended on champion dancers to draw them a crowd, enabling stars such as Diamond and Juba to remain autonomous and demand high salaries.

Diamond and Juba is a labor history of the art of challenge dancing. In reconstructing the working lives of these two extraordinary jig dancers, I have sought to write cultural history "from the bottom up." Although the managers, entrepreneurs, and owners who helped shape the nineteenth-century entertainment world are necessarily treated, my emphasis throughout is on the dancers themselves: their needs and aspirations, victories and defeats. The chapters that follow narrate the story of Diamond's and Juba's rise and fall as challenge dancers in order to resurrect the structure of opportunity on which they built their careers. Every art form acquires its meaning and value from the conditions of its production and reception. Critical recognition and financial success depend not just on individual talent or genius but on prevailing social, economic, political, and cultural ideas, institutions, and events. The history of challenge dancing reveals that structure and in so doing disrupts many of the unconscious assumptions that shape our understanding of Black-Irish relations, child labor, commercial entertainment, the popular press, sports, minstrelsy, masculinity, and celebrity. Told together, Diamond's and Juba's life stories recapture more fully the experiences of the remarkable though often obscure men, women, and children who aspired to develop their creative abilities, express their deepest selves, and earn their livings doing so.

PART I

RISING FROM THE STREETS

1

OUT OF THE MIX

In 1839 Phineas T. Barnum, a twenty-eight-year-old paste and blacking merchant, stepped out of his shop at No. 101½ Bowery Street in New York City and headed toward the waterfront. He walked with long strides, scanning all that was around him with keen eyes. A phenomenon of respectability, he wore a knee-length coat over a velvet waistcoat, with a golden watch fob looped from his buttonhole to the timepiece in his pocket. His receding curly hair was parted on the side, and fashionable muttonchop whiskers framed his wide, pockmarked face. He was scouting for the main chance, something that would bring him fame and wealth.

Before entering the wholesale business, Barnum had clerked for a grocery, opened a retail fruit and confectionery store, kept a porterhouse, edited newspapers, and done an equestrian circus's accounting. He'd also dabbled in the "amusement business," successfully exhibiting a few individual acts and a small troupe of performers. He liked that business best. The whole range of amusements, "from the highest to the lowest," is merchantable, he wrote in his autobiography. The "love of amusement" is "an insatiate want of human nature." "The old word 'trade' as it applies to buying cheap and selling at a profit, is as manifest here as it is in [any] dealings," which left him always on the prowl for talent to exploit.[1]

The opportunity Barnum spotted that spring presented itself in the curious form of little boys dancing lively competitive jigs known as "breakdowns." The first boy he chose was Irish American. He called him Master Diamond. When that boy ran away a year later, Barnum hired an African American boy. He called him Master Rattler. These dancing boys were lucky to be noticed by a man who could turn their antics into a paying proposition. But they would develop their own ideas about who deserved to profit from the fame and wealth they generated.

Barnum never specified where he met Diamond, whom he described as "really a genius in the dancing line." One contemporary claimed that Barnum "accidentally discovered" Diamond about the wharves of New York. And since his business was only a few blocks from the East River, that information is likely correct. Barnum said he entered into a contract with Diamond's father, put an agent in charge of the lad, and called public attention to his extraordinary merits, "though I did not then appear in the transaction." Through this management, insinuated Barnum, Diamond "became justly celebrated as the best negro-dancer and representative of Ethiopian 'break-downs' in the land."[2]

Irish and African American boys could be found dancing jigs in two places in 1839: inside a tavern dance-house or outside in the streets and market squares. One contemporary said that Diamond "was seen and noticed in private by many, but it was left for Mr. Barnum to bring the youthful dancer to public notice." Another writer gave Juba similar origins: "Having been seen by many people in private, he became a sort of pet in the city, and by this means was introduced on the stage."[3] By "in private" the writers meant that these boys had danced for friends and neighbors at parties or balls. In the country, dances were held in kitchens and barns or outside. In cities, working-class people held their "private" dances in semipublic places, such as a tavern's barroom or rented room upstairs.

* * *

Diamond and Juba emerged from a place where people came together to dance recreationally and competitively, and their successes rested on this rich interaction. The concentration of people in antebellum cities and the nation's growing market economy fostered an entertainment industry. New York City was alive with commerce in the 1830s. Working docks, market streets, manufactories, and businesses lined lower Manhattan's waterfront districts (fig. 1.1). Merchant vessels and trading ships, brigs and clippers, steam-powered ferries, fishing boats, and tugs came and went at every hour of the day laden with goods and people. Countryside migrants and immigrants from Ireland, England, Germany (called Dutch), Italy, China, and the West Indies mingled with sailors and boat hands from everywhere else across the world.

The Irish who came to New York City in the early nineteenth century settled in the poorest neighborhoods, where the highest population of African Americans lived. By 1830 these two populations were close to equal, with approximately eighteen thousand alien Irish and fourteen thousand native-born Black inhabitants. Both populations grew after 1827, when the British government repealed all restrictions on emigration and nearly four hundred thousand Irish immigrated to Canada and the United States and when enslaved Blacks in New York State were officially emancipated, if not always liberated.[4]

Legal emancipation and manumission (the voluntary freeing of enslaved people) sharpened the apprehension and enmity many Northern whites felt for Black Americans, but the working classes of both races often accepted each

FIGURE 1.1. Children could be found challenge dancing at New York's public markets, situated on the Hudson and East Rivers a block in from the city's numerous ferry docks, packet ship ladings, and fishing boat slips. *Cities of New-York and Brooklyn, &c. &c. By W. Williams, Entered, according to Act of Congress, in the year 1847 by W. Williams in the Clerks Office of the District Court of the Southern District of New York.*

other as neighbors and friends more readily than did their "social betters."[5] In these unsegregated neighborhoods, poor white and Black people rubbed shoulders in the streets, drank and danced in the same public houses, rented rooms in the same buildings, and even intermarried. Their shared locality and social mingling supported the cultural borrowing that made challenge dancing common to all.[6]

The Tavern

The streets outside Barnum's warehouse bustled with workers, shoppers, and strollers in the early evening. Cartmen encouraging mules to "get along" overtook omnibus horsecars stopping for homebound passengers. Clanging tools in workrooms behind storefronts gave way to the jangle of cooking pans drifting up from basement taverns. Barnum would have investigated these public houses, perhaps taking some supper, a meat pie or oyster stew, or imbibing an alcoholic beverage as he surveyed the scene. Some places were populated by Black customers, others by white, and still others by men, women, and children of every color who came to eat, drink, and socialize.

Challenge dancing often took place in these working-class taverns. When the fiddler, who might be Black or might be Irish, rose from his chair and held his violin in the air, the dancing couples swiftly formed two lines on the floor—"black and white, white and black, all hug-em-snug together."[7] The tune was struck and the dancers commenced, rollicking through a jig or reel, prancing forward and back, taking hands to chassé down the center, linking elbows to swing about, then pulling apart for a moment of competition, each partner adding moves to accentuate his or her style.

Sometimes in among the adults there figured a bantam-sized Irish boy who knew his steps: jigs, reels, and hornpipes, double shuffles and pigeon wings. (Combinations of these steps were known as "negro dancing," although they merged dance traditions from regions of Ireland as well as Africa.) At the end of the set, such a boy was often challenged by a teenaged girl who strode to the middle of the floor to face him. She might have been a skilled dancer recently arrived from the old country with pale skin and red cheeks or a favored local dancer with deep brown skin and serious eyes who intended to out-step him. Usually a crowd gathered round, loyalties were divided, bets were struck. As the fiddler pulled his bow across the strings, the competitors met eyes and launched into the dance. According to Irish and American accounts, the footwork was always lively when the boys faced the girls, who lifted their skirts slightly to show off the quickness of their feet. When the fiddler changed tunes, the dancers changed places, moving slowly at first, then commencing a new step, "which threw the preceding one quite into the shade." Sweat, whoops, and "hurroos" followed them round the room, the temperature rising with each exuberant move. Then without interruption, doors were lifted off their hinges and slipped under the dancers' feet, "which now beat an accompaniment to the music, as if a couple of expert drummers had suddenly joined the orchestra." If the girl tired out but the boy was unflagging, another girl ran forward to take her place, while the bantam kept on dancing, jumping, cutting, bending, spinning, and hopping. The winner was the dancer left standing when the musician hit the final note. At that point, cheers of mirth and triumph erupted, money changed hands, the boy paid the fiddler, and the winner bought drinks all round.[8] Perhaps it was then, in such a place, that Barnum, the speculator, introduced himself to John Diamond and his father.

Irish and African American children grew up going to public houses. Sites of exchange and leisure, taverns were the loci of social life for urban working-class families. They provided a place where poor people could engage in communal forms of entertainment—from eating, drinking, and talking to card playing, music making, and dancing—depending on their size. Advertisements indicate that most licensed taverns served some sort of "viands and relishes"—meat pies, oysters, eggs, beefsteaks, Welsh rarebit (grilled cheese)—along with one or more alcoholic beverages—porter, beer, stout, claret, or cider, either imported or made by the proprietor. Home-brewed alcoholic beverages were also sold in unlicensed bars in front parlors, basements, and second-floor rooms. Sometimes called "Irish groggeries," these establishments closely resembled shebeens (unlicensed home- or kitchen-based liquor sellers) in nineteenth-century Ireland. Mostly run by women, groggeries were patronized at any time, day or night, by families and neighbors who came there to drink and socialize or carry away "pails of beer" (fig. 1.2).[9]

Many taverns kept some open floorspace for set dancing (what Americans today call square dancing or contra dancing). Others had a second room where dances took place. Some taverns provided tables and chairs; others pushed benches up against the walls. A few featured a makeshift stage used by musicians who played

FIGURE 1.2. Diamond and Juba grew up in a neighborhood where grog shops and "low" taverns were often run by women and characterized by easy conviviality among a mixed clientele. Junius Henri Browne, *Low Groggery,* from *The Great Metropolis: A Mirror of New York* (American Publishing Company, 1869), 659.

for the dancers or anyone else who came to share a talent in exchange for a drink or a plate of food or, as one barkeeper noted, "for free gratis for nothin', just for fun of the thing." No admission was charged on "free and easy" nights, when the customers provided the entertainment. But tavern keepers who hired a dance band or fiddler sometimes charged a ten-cent entry fee, which included a three-cent glass of whiskey.[10]

Hundreds of licensed and unlicensed alcohol-selling establishments could be found scattered between Broadway and the East River in nineteenth-century New York City. Most were attached to the proprietor's home or a related business—corner grocery, theater, eating saloon, boardinghouse, brothel. In 1839 Orange Street alone held more than a dozen taverns run by immigrants and native-borns. An Irish husband and wife ran a liquor and grocery business at 17 Orange Street, and an African American couple shared the keeping of a tavern ballroom on the corner of Anthony and Orange Streets. John Roache (race unknown) kept a tavern at 23 Orange Street with rooms front and back for what one newspaper called his "promiscuous company."[11]

Before the Civil War, writers used the term "promiscuous" to describe public meetings that brought together white and Black men and women. They used words with vaguely sexual connotations when referring to abolitionists who were not behaving appropriately according to white middle-class standards. Similarly, publicans who entertained both sexes, any race, and all ages were said to keep "disorderly houses." The term "disorderly," meaning "contrary to rules or established institutions" (to the "order" that maintained the status quo), became a euphemism for brothel, used in court or by officials to justify raids, arrests, and closures of lower-class establishments. Some brothels did hold dances, and some taverns did have rooms where assignations took place. But, generally, the mixed company at neighborhood taverns reflected the mixed communities they served.

The easy exchange between Black and Irish families in lower-class taverns is unmistakable in an 1840 *Evening Tattler* account of a police raid on a New York "gambling house." In this case, the title "gambling house" provided validation for the violent intrusion of the new professional police force (empowered by the rising industrial elite to make arrests wherever they saw fit) into a working-class business.[12] Sharing an evening of drink and leisure activities were about twenty men, women, and children "of all sizes and colors." The place seemed well run, for directing the attention of the crowd was "a master of ceremonies, an out-and-out darkey." Entertaining themselves "free and easy" style were "a little black rascal of twelve years, assisted by two little white ones of eleven or under," sitting at a table "roaring a love song," while "a knot" of juvenile "amalgamationists" in a corner of the room applauded the exertions of a tiny Black dancer "who was jumping 'Jim Crow.'" When the police burst in, the patrons protected each other: Chairs, tables, "glasses and tumblers went crash, crash, crash, in all directions—and to crown the whole, two feminine blocks of ebony and a little Irish woman set up a pullaloo that was equal to the keen of a Munster funeral."[13] While clearly crafted to amuse readers and fuel the middle-class dread of miscegenation, the article's depiction of lower-class mayhem offered readers a glimpse at the goings-on in an integrated establishment, a place where boys like Diamond and Juba might have gone to dance with girls and other boys, perfected their steps, and practiced their trade.

To Market

Taverns were not the only places children could be found challenge dancing in 1839. They also danced in the streets. City markets served as informal schools for professional challenge dancers. They brought together youths and adults who engaged in competitive jig dancing for money and prizes. These competitions presaged the challenge dancing introduced to the stage by Diamond and Juba's generation.

At Catherine Market, a few blocks from Barnum's Water Street office, African American dancers gathered to compete on most Sunday mornings. A young male dancer carrying a large bunch of eels would challenge another carrying the same to a jigging match, the winner of three trials to take both bunches. They appointed judges, gave another dancer one eel each to beat "juber" for them, took off their coats, and commenced the sport. Across the square, a couple of girls engaged in a similar dancing contest, a young boy beating time for them. If the banter of the male opponents got nasty, the girl champion who "had just finished dancing, and won the eels," stepped in to separate them. The next trial usually took place between two of the younger boys, who "put in some mighty big licks" while their daddies sang and beat for them, passing on the family business.[14]

The writers who recorded such scenes were bemused by these confident youngsters. They also noted how their dancing entertained the shoppers and drew in customers, how it put cash in their pockets and food in their mouths. Barnum may have introduced himself to the winning dancer out there in the street after witnessing such a contest. Or he may have simply eyed the coins and prizes and stored the scene in his memory for future reference. Jig dancing created an excitement that Barnum knew he could sell.

If they were anything like other children their age, the lads Barnum hired spent a lot of time down by the wharves. By the 1830s every waterfront city from New Orleans to Toronto boasted several dockside markets—vibrant, cosmopolitan centers of commerce, labor, sociability, and recreation. Philadelphia had six; New York had fourteen (fig. 1.3). Most were located one block in from the water.

FIGURE 1.3. The diverse crowd, boardwalks, and proximity to the Camden Ferry made this Philadelphia fish market on the Delaware River a good spot for dancing contests. In this depiction, women carry baskets of seafood and chase thieving dogs, while men negotiate fish carts and carry heavy bushels of mollusks, young sailors walk arm-in-arm, a Black woman lectures a relaxed-looking Black man, and a white man smoking a cheroot waylays a neatly dressed white woman holding a fish. Frank Leslie, sc, *Representation of the Philadelphia Fish Market,* from *Gleason's Pictorial Drawing Room Companion,* ca. 1852, Library Company of Philadelphia Print Department.

The rivers on both sides of Manhattan were lined with market houses. Fulton Market on the East River comprised a long and low open structure, plastered and whitewashed, with round stone pillars supporting arched roofs that covered double ranges of stalls on three sides. It opened onto a paved square with a water pump at each end and a separate shelter in the center for unlicensed country vendors around which a plethora of hucksters displayed the sum of their provisions in carts, pots, barrels, and baskets. Ferry houses bookended Fulton Market, the ferries transporting both sellers and buyers from Brooklyn.

East River markets supplied New Yorkers with produce, goods, and entertainments from Long Island. Hudson River markets served ferry passengers coming from New Jersey and provided a place for "north river country" people to sell their produce and wares to the whole south and west population of the city.[15] At one market the vendors displayed "several stands of smoked eels, with heads and skins on, smoked halibut, tripe, pigs' feet, plates of boiled lobsters, crab, and other delicacies of that stamp"; an Irish woman sitting on the ground and cradling her green and ripe fruit blocked the door of a dry goods store; and an old man meandering through the crowd sold raw oysters from a large basket, opening the mollusks with a stout clasp knife for buyers who ate them, fat and intensely salty, out of the shell.[16]

Children labored and peddled at city markets. At Fulton Market the apprenticed boys hung carcasses in back of the licensed butchers' front-facing stalls, while the children of vegetable vendors stocked cellars under the inside eaves, and fishermen's boys pushed wooden carts filled with "the 'week's catch' of clams, mussels, eels, lobsters, shrimps, [and] small sand-porgies" up the nearby slip, "the smacks arriving hourly from the fishing grounds, a few miles out in the Atlantic Ocean, and near Sandy Hook."[17] Those boys always made a considerable noise and bluster in the sale of their stock—"the refuse pieces of stale halibut, weakfish, [and] bunches of herring." Boys and girls also figured among the hawkers, competing with the seagulls' restless cries, their distinctive voices ringing out in the crisp morning air: "radishes, radishes," "soap-fat, soap-fat," "Milluk! Milluk! Milluk-ho!" Or they circulated and scavenged in small gangs, overturning carts and making off with the bruised fruit, taunting, racing, and "pitching into each other." Other children earned pennies and food by running errands for the retailers, holding horses, flogging newspapers, chasing hats, or demonstrating some remarkable talent, one of which was dancing jigs and breakdowns.[18]

Barnum might have spotted his boys dancing in several likely spots: on a pier where the wooden planks had a good timbre, in the open square next to their parents' display, or on a walkway fronting the family business. On Buffalo's steamboat wharves, one boy who was "precocious as a jig dancer" and another who "beat time with his hands expertly" on his thighs displayed their peculiar talent outside the tavern of the latter boy's mother, attracting admiring crowds that "strew[ed] small coin around the feet of the dancer." An eleven-year-old Philadelphia boy debuted his jig-dancing show in his father's slaughterhouse: "admission 6¼ cents, with the privilege of looking at the cattle." Our boys' East River location might have been the clearing beside the fish market in front of the ship chandlery, where sailors came to buy provisions, passengers waited for the ferry, and jig dancers, historically, gathered to compete.[19]

Public "Negro Dancing"

City markets were "public" venues where jig dancers turned their talents into employment. Nineteenth-century market chronicler Thomas De Voe claimed that around 1800, when the market house on Catherine Street was built, "public 'negro dancing'" was introduced to New York City.[20] Slaves from nearby towns and farms who came to Bear, Slip, Fly, and Catherine Markets to sell their meager harvest were ever ready "by their 'negro sayings or doings' to make a few shillings more. So they would be hired by some joking butcher or individual to engage in a jig or break-down, as that was one of their pastimes at home on the barn-floor." Market dancing was most common on Sundays and other holidays when African Americans congregated "with their trifles to sell, and their friends to meet or visit." Dancing on the street for small change, also called busking, was an old British and European custom. These public performances became more lucrative when vendors hired street dancers to provide entertainment that would attract customers to their stalls. "The large amount collected in this way [by those that could and would dance] after a time produced some excellent 'dancers,'" one butcher told De Voe. "In fact, it raised a sort of strife for the highest honors, i.e., the most cheering and the most collected in the 'hat.'"[21]

Markets were neutral ground where dancers from different communities met to compete. On New York's Hudson River side, free Black people from the city danced for eels at the old Hay Market, and enslaved Black people from New Jersey (which adopted gradual abolition in 1804 but did not pass an act outlawing slavery until 1846) met at Bear Market to "sometimes engage in a break-down." According to another of De Voe's interviewees, these dancers "were not so early accomplished as their Long Island friends." However, competition improved their skills. On days with a late tide, "the Jersey negroes [who] had disposed of their masters' produce ... would 'shin it' for the Catharine Market to enter the lists with the Long Islanders, and in the end, an equal division of the proceeds took place." Their successes then "brought our city negroes down there," recalled a partisan Manhattanite, "who, after a time, even exceeded them both, and if money was not to be had 'they would dance for a bunch of eels or fish.'"[22] These contests attracted the attention of children recently arrived from Ireland not because the contests were so unusual but because they seemed so familiar.

John Diamond's family emigrated from Ireland in the 1830s. His father was probably John Diamond, an Irish laborer who arrived in New York in 1835 with his wife, Elizabeth, and six children to support, including a seven-year-old son named John. Or he may have been Nicholas Dimond, who kept a tavern on New Street between 1835 and 1841 and who began spelling his name Diamond in 1839.[23] "The boy's father is in the city," Barnum wrote a theater manager in 1840, "but being a foreigner & therefore not so competent to attend to engagements, he has given me power of attorney for the same."[24]

William Henry Lane was the child of Margaret Reed, a freeborn Black woman originally from New Jersey whose employments went unrecorded. His stepfather, Zachary Reed, was a dancer, barber, and oyster cellar proprietor in New York's Five Points district. Lane learned much of his art from an African American "jig and reel dancer of extra-ordinary skill" named "Uncle Jim" Lowe and from his stepfather.[25] Like their dances, the surnames of Lane, Lowe, and Reed reveal the blending of Irish and African cultures. Enslaved people mostly took their names from their former "owners," who were often their relatives through nonconsensual sex. Emancipated slaves were free to take new names or claim the names, ethnic identities, and cultural practices of their white ancestry. Consensual alliances between Black men and Irish women were not uncommon in early America's lower-class districts, and the three dancers' surnames may have been the product of those.[26] But even if Lane's, Lowe's, and Reed's surnames were a residue of slavery, their retention suggests that some African Americans valued their Irish heritage.

To an Irish immigrant, dancing for eels would have looked a lot like cake dancing. Sketches of Ireland written between 1682 and 1850 describe adjudicated jig-dancing contests called "cakes" for the prize awarded the winner (as in "she takes the cake"). In many rural regions, it was customary among the poor, whose usual fare was "potatoes and milk," to spare "some few halfpence" from the household purse to dance for a cake made of oatmeal and sugar. Cake dances were held in an open area or at a crossroads next to an alehouse on Sundays and other holidays from work. Young and old of both sexes from miles around came to enjoy "the pleasures of the cake," which might include "dancing, courting, coshering [chatting], whiskey-drinking, card-playing, fighting, and sometimes a little ribbonism [antilandlord agitation]" (fig. 1.4). The alewife, whose trade was enhanced by the festivities, often provided the cake, but the dancers paid the piper (a penny a jig). The cake was won by the dancing couple who held out the longest or by the best dancer or "the archest wag," who presented it to "his favourite *cailín*" to cut up and divide among all the company.[27]

FIGURE 1.4. In Ireland, cake dances were held at a crossroads next to an alehouse and attended by young and old of both sexes. The alewife, whose trade was enhanced by the festivities, often provided the prize cake, but the dancers paid the musician a penny a jig. This 1870s depiction of a local pattern, or saint's day festival, captures the generational breadth of cake dance attendees, including a Black Irishman and his wife, who are closely watching the dancers' feet. Dancing for eels was the urban American equivalent of cake dancing. M.F., "The State of Ireland; Making the Best of It," *Illustrated London News*, Dec. 6, 1879, 536–537.

24 · RISING FROM THE STREETS

While different in style and steps, competitive mixed-age and mixed-gender dance was also traditional in many West African communities. In the Senegal and Gambia regions, dancers and musicians met in an area cleared for dancing and formed a ring inside of which a man or woman danced until challenged by another dancer, who eventually took over, was challenged in turn, and so on for hours on end.[28] These dancers and their descendants melded their competitive dance traditions with Irish traditions in North America (fig. 1.5). On Southern plantations, slaves carried on the practice of jig dancing for a cake made of cornmeal and cabbage long after their Irish American counterparts gave it up. They also turned African-style competitions, such as striding along on a narrow plank, into "Cake-Walks" to entertain the master and mistress, who sometimes provided the cake.[29]

In Northern cities, African American families would "save up their odd change thro' the week, and then on Sundays proceed to the market" to dance for eels or fish. City people with no access to garden produce or wild fish and game were happy to dance for eels, popular fare among country people in England and the United States. Performers of every ilk worked for food. At the Pantheon, a tavern on Houston Street, white professionals received "a frying of eels in compensation" for their songs and dances, one patron recalled, as that was "the habitual recompense at that time in the places of this class in New York." Long Island's

"The Sabbath among Slaves."

FIGURE 1.5. Enslaved people in the American South maintained and combined British and African forms of amusement. Here they are drinking and getting drunk (universal), playing the gourd banjo and patting juba (African American), jig dancing (Irish), hurling (Scottish), and wrestling (African). "The Sabbath among Slaves," in *Narrative of the Life and Adventures of Henry Bibb, an American Slave, Written by Himself* (New York, 1850), 22.

numerous inlets were rich breeding grounds for eels and oysters, making both inexpensive in the early nineteenth century. In fact, out west in the 1830s "Eels" was the nickname for all Yankees, Black and white.[30]

These prizes made challenge dancing more than a male recreation. Irish and African American wives and mothers who saved up household cash to make the cake or buy the eels sponsored these dancing contests. In Philadelphia markets, the stakes were catfish, placed in a basket if skinned and in a tub if not, "and as fast as either party won, [they] were carried off by the wenches and sold, and the proceeds divided."[31] This division of labor and divvying up the prizes figured into the trade economy of lower-class families.

Observant children noticed that successful market dancers had mastered both Irish and African dance practices. All the participants in "the regular 'shake-down'" at Catherine Market had to confine their dance steps to a board or shingle five to six feet long and of large width. They worked "several together in parties," each bringing his favorite shingle as part of his stock-in-trade. "Their music or time was usually given by one of their party . . . beating their hands on the sides of their legs and the noise of the heel."[32] Dancing on a board was an Irish custom. Dancing to the beat of the hands and heel was an African custom.

In rural Ireland, "sometimes a door was taken off its hinges and laid down on the middle of the floor, and there the performer exhibited his strength and agility," reported a nineteenth-century folklorist. "The great effort was to exhibit all varieties of steps and dances, without once quitting the prostrate door on which the exhibitor took his stand," explained another Irish writer in 1854: "the jumps, the 'cuttings' in the air, the bends, the dives, the wrigglings, the hops."[33] This practice was widespread and respected in country parishes. Even hedge-school dancing masters taught their students how to compete on an unhinged door* (fig. 1.6). The technique of patting the body to create music was transported to America from the African kingdom of Kongo in the form of a thigh-slapping dance called "juba" or "patting juba" in the vernacular of the American South, borrowed from the KiKongo words *zúba* and *nzúba,* meaning to strike a blow with, knock, hit, thrust, and (in dialect) dance.[34] This melodic drumming practice (later called "ham-bone") traveled upriver with enslaved and free people, lending an African rhythmic pulse to Northern dances.

The multiracial crews of merchant ships and British emigrants headed to the New World circulated the custom of dancing on a circumscribed wooden platform. They danced on boat decks, cart boards, tabletops, cellar doors, wooden ballasts, and the lids of hogshead barrels, surfaces recommended for their particular

---

* Hedge schools were small informal schools in Anglican-dominated Ireland that secretly and illegally provided education to children from Catholic and dissenting Protestant families.

FIGURE 1.6. The Irish practice of dancing on a board (or a door taken off its hinges) was adopted by African American market dancers. The dancer had to exhibit all varieties of steps and dances without leaving the prostrate door. Here, the Irish dancing master encourages his student to aggressively beat the floor ("welt the flure") and step lively ("foot about"). "Bravo Dick! welt the flure!! foot about!!!," from *The Hedge School,* designed and etched by W. H. Brooke, ARHA, Dublin (Wm. Curry Jr. and Company, March 1830).

spring, acoustic qualities, or small size.[35] Dancers exhibited their skill with and without shoes. A "Cape Cod" boy, for example, "dance[d] the true fisherman's jig, barefooted, knocking with his heels, and slapping the decks with his bare feet, in time with the music."[36] Not all jig dancers competed on shingles, but at Catherine Market, where the majority came from ethnically mixed communities on Long Island, they did. So, too, did young Diamond, who was advertised in 1840 as "the very beau ideal* of a little Long Island darkie."[37]

The Long Island Mix

The eclectic nature of America's dancing culture was illustrated in a newspaper description of a ball at Raynor's, a popular retreat in Williamsburg, Long Island, in 1833. At eight o'clock, three Black fiddlers sawed away at "set dances—flat foot

---

* "Beau ideal" meant both ideal beauty and an embodiment of the highest excellence.

reels—Virginian pidgeon wings and Kitefoot shuffles," winding up the whole "with a Long Island Waltz." Raynor had hired three musicians that night both to provide volume and to spell each other, since balls lasted from four to six hours. At nine o'clock refreshments were served, and at ten a "Spanish Mock minute" was tried. At eleven the dancers performed Rail Road* exercises, and by twelve the girls were "laying down in fine *style*—not on the floor, but dancing, the real old fashioned eel dance, their partners some asleep, others stowed away."[38]

Whether the dancers were Black, white, or both is not specified, but the set dancing was clearly an American hodgepodge, mixing regional and ethnic steps and styles. "Flat foot reels" featured traveling steps performed with the heels close to the ground in the style developed by agricultural slaves. The next tune called for bounding leaps, or "pidgeon wings," where the legs beat together on one side with knees bent (in the "Virginian" style) rather than extended (in the ballet manner). The third set introduced the twisting foot shuffles developed by enslaved African and Native Americans on the Aronoco River in Virginia, named "Kitefoot" after a type of tobacco cultivated there. Shuffles were common to the dances of the Irish, Africans, and Native Americans (fig. 1.7). The set dancing ended with a waltz—a fashionable couple dance enjoyed by polite society in Europe—adapted to a local tune. Then, after a break for food and drink, the company mimicked the stately minuet as danced by South Americans, supposedly, in boots and spurs.

At the end of the night came the challenge dance, or "breakdown." Having outlasted their male partners, now sleeping under the tables, the female dancers competed with each other, laying down their footwork in fine style. The writer called this competition "a good old fashioned eel dance." Despite the unmistakable sexual connotation when the term was applied to women, in the 1830s "eel dance" was a synonym for competitive breakdowns danced by males or females, no matter the prize.

The dancing at places like Raynor's was enriched by the assortment of people who lived and worked on Long Island. Since the seventeenth century, indentured servants who were Irish, European, and Native American worked the island's farms and plantations alongside enslaved Black people from Africa, the Caribbean, South America, and the Southern states. Whaling and fishing ports on the coasts also brought these inhabitants into long-standing contact with seamen from around the globe. When Long Islanders crossed the East River in skiffs and ferries to exchange goods, gossip, and amusements with their New York neighbors, they added to everyone's economic, social, and dancing activities.

---

* The dancers reproduced the sounds made by a train with their feet.

FIGURE 1.7. Long Islanders danced Kitefoot shuffles because immigrants and Natives swapped dance and music practices throughout North America, as indicated by this set dance performed by Métis dancers and fiddlers (the descendants of Indigenous women who married French and Scottish fur traders) in what became the Dakota Territory in 1861. Métis dance, Devil's Lake, Dakota Territory, ca. 1870, drawn by Corporal Louis Voelkerer, Company A, Thirty-First US Infantry. Minnesota Historical Society.

Dancing Masters

The older prizewinners at city markets served as role models for young aspiring jig dancers. From them, children learned the tricks and demeanor of the trade, not only what steps to dance but also what equipment to bring, what to charge, what to wear, and how to carry themselves. "After a great number of trials and a deal of sweating," the boys dancing at Catherine Market made way for the local champion, who appeared "with a shingle under his arm for the purpose of showing all those his science, who might feel so disposed for the sum of three cents." He called himself Caesar, noted a regular spectator, was always on hand on a Sunday morning, "and has never been known to lose a bunch of eels—generally winning enough to last him thro' the week."[39] What Caesar and other dancers did at city markets was very like what Irish dancing masters did at patterns (patron saint's day fairs). He demonstrated his skill in a place where lots of people would see him. He charged dancers who wanted to learn his method, or "science," a small fee. And he competed with champion dancers from other regions for prizes.

In Ireland, the country dancing master was poor because his patrons were poor. He taught for very little money, supplementing his income by passing the hat after "performing on an unhinged door or 'welting the flure' in the village alehouse" or facing the music at a dance party held for his benefit toward the end of his term.[40] Although itinerant, dancing masters kept to their own districts and respected the territories of others. Nevertheless, casual meetings at fairs or sporting events sometimes led to challenges. Then the two masters would "dance it out" in public trials* of skill "to the joy and edification of the spectators, frequently, without any eventual decision."[41]

Master dancers identified themselves regionally by their appearance and dancing style. Long Islanders tied their hair "up in a cue [sic], with dried eel-skin" (from a harvest or win). New Jersey contenders were "known by their suppleness and plaited forelocks tied up with tea-lead."† The association of mode of dress and dancing prowess had African and Irish roots. Dancing masters in African communities identified their status through body adornment, drawing from their environment whatever finery it offered them—animal skins, feathers, shells, pigments, with which they made their costumes and colored their bodies. The Irish dancing master advertised his station with a "castor or Caroline hat" above and "pumps and stockings" below, while his pupils polished their shoes and converged on markets and fairs in the shabby vests, wide cravats, or other raiment identified with their local gang or faction.[42]

Attitude and swagger supplemented this attire. The respect shown expert jig dancers in lower-class communities encouraged bragging and teasing, which often led to fighting among male participants. In Ireland, "*brag* dancers" at taverns and fairs called out step dancers from rival districts. It was "not unusual for crack-dancers from opposite parishes, or from distant parts of the same parish, to meet and dance against each other for the victory," noted Irish writer William Carleton in 1833. "But as the judges in those cases consist of the respective friends or factions of the champions, . . . many a battle is fought in consequence of such challenges." In North America, enslaved and free Black people witnessed these competitions and battles firsthand. In fact, the African American word "shindig" for dance came from the shin-kicking brawl or "shindy" that often ended an Irish ball.[43]

Spirited displays in some West African dances singled out the best dancers among the young men, who often became leaders of their peers in other social

---

* If the circuits of two dancing masters bordered a particular townland, they sometimes vied for it by dancing a trial. The one who demonstrated better agility and fitness and the greatest number of steps won the competition, and that townland became part of his territory.
† The metal strip used to tie up bags of tea.

and political contexts. These dances also gave dancers a chance to show off for the opposite sex. Poking fun in a dance could be done respectfully, or it could be harsh or vulgar depending on the context. Boasting about one's skill was expected of dancers, but if a dancer could not back up his claims, it could lead to humiliation, followed by aggression or even violence.[44]

The boy dancers who scuffled at Catherine Market engaged in this kind of fighting for honor. But the dancer with the most self-assurance was the girl champion who intervened. Former house slave Sylvia Dubois, who learned to jig as a child at weekly frolics held at one or another master's house in Great Bend, Pennsylvania, was equally confident. Her favorite steps were "the eleven times, the twelve times, and the thirteen times. . . . These were the steps my grandfather, Harry Compton, used to like, and all other good dancers," she explained in an 1883 interview. The names of the steps signaled the quickness and intricacy of the footwork. "Why, when I was young, I'd cross my feet ninety-nine times in a minute and never miss the time, strike heel or toe with equal ease, and go through the figures as nimble as a witch." Dubois's prize step, a rapid crossing of one foot over the other called "cutting" or "cover the buckle," figured prominently as a demonstration of agility in Irish step-dancing competitions.[45]

These boys and girls exhibited attitude along with their steps because for Irish and Black people, jig dancing was always more than a social and economic activity. It embodied two overlapping histories of survival and resistance. Colonized simultaneously by the English and the Catholic Church, Irish people danced to create and maintain an identity in terms of locality and ethnicity.[46] On the one hand, the Catholic Church hierarchy condemned dancing due to the heavy drinking and brawling that usually accompanied it, while the English considered such activities "natural" to an "uncivilized" people like the Irish. On the other hand, the British colonial elite valued dancing as a primary means of socialization. Young people who could dance well moved with confidence within British society, or, in the case of a talented step dancer from the lower classes, with pride.[47] This contradiction gave dancing a political significance in the eyes of the Irish peasantry and lent a kind of outlaw mystique to itinerant dancing masters and their scholars. Irish dancers who mastered the intricacies of jigs, reels, and hornpipes showed that they had control over their minds and bodies, thereby proving to their colonizers that they were civilized, says dance scholar Catherine Foley, "only in an Irish way."[48]

African Americans took pride in their dancing due to a different set of contradictions. Stripped of individuality and family ties by the violence of chattel slavery, enslaved and free Black people danced to express and maintain an identity that was distinctive and communal. However, many African Americans joined the Protestant Church, which discouraged and eventually condemned dancing as a stimulant of the passions. Dancing was also considered a "natural" talent of Black people, associated with their "uncivilized" African origins. To prove that they were civilized, many African Americans gave up dancing altogether. Others turned their dances into a Christian activity. But dancing gave some individuals a means to improve their lives economically, which in a capitalist society is considered the pathway to socialization. When Black dancers attracted the attention of paying spectators with their extravagant jigs, reels, and hornpipes, they too proved that they were civilized, only in an American way.

Raised in traditions where how you danced announced your community, young Irish and African American dancers emulated each other and all the other good dancers around them. That was how Diamond and Juba became champion jig dancers, masters of a dance form that belonged to a working-class subculture, mixed in race and gender, popular if not dominant, and undeniably North American.

It is unlikely that either youngster was surprised when a gentleman who had watched him dance for several days and pronounced him a little genius took aside his father or mother for a private discussion. The parents of children who excelled in jig and breakdown dancing brought them to public places to show them off, solicit tips, and secure engagements. Irish American Richard Carroll began jig dancing for hire at parties at age five, and Luke Cavanaugh performed "Negro figures" in low taverns at age seven. William Henry Lane danced at the balls of Black laborers at age eight, and thirteen-year-old Diamond was entertaining people long before Barnum "discovered" him.[49] An agreement whereby Barnum arranged their sons' engagements for a percentage of the takings would have benefited any of those boys' families.[50]

Barnum never said where he negotiated with Diamond's or Juba's parents. He might have met them in a tavern or market square, at their workplace, or in his Water Street office. Wherever the deal went down, it was not an unusual event, just a life-transformative one for the boys involved. For with that handshake, Barnum plucked them out of the society that made them challenge dancers, set them down among people they didn't know, and asked them to do things they'd never done before.

2

HUMBUG'S APPRENTICE

John Diamond made his stage debut on April 1, 1839, in New York's stately, four-columned National Theatre at the corner of Leonard and Church Streets. The National had begun life in 1833 as the Italian Opera House and now, under the management of William Mitchell, was one of the city's leading venues. New York's former mayor Philip Hone called it "the prettiest theatre in the United States."[1] Diamond entered from a back alley opposite the African Methodist Episcopal church, with his polished pumps clutched under his arm. Backstages were notoriously dark and grubby, the air rank with the odor of sweat and unwashed costumes, the side wings illuminated only by oil lamps set in niches in the walls. Diamond might have heard the whistles of the stagehands adjusting the ropes and backdrops up in the flies as he pulled off his half-boots and put on his dancing shoes; then he probably moved to the wings, where he could see the actors rehearsing through the side panels and, as young dancers are wont to do, tattooed a little melody on the floor to warm up.[2]

The auditorium was dim in the daytime. The large chandelier that lighted the house and stage hung from the carved ornamental ceiling snuffed and cold. The only interior light originated from dusty windows behind the balcony seats, illuminating the plank board benches in the pit and transforming the unlit footlights lining the stage into tiny shadowy gravestones.

Diamond's job that evening was to dance an interlude during the "new Drama entitled NICK OF THE WOODS," derived from a celebrated novel of that name. From the wings, he probably saw the actor Edmond S. Conner render the role of "Nathan Slaughter, *alias* Wandering Nathan, *alias* Nick of the Woods," a devout Quaker who turns into a raving Indian killer after encountering a family of wounded pioneers. As the curtain fell on this carnage, the little dancer would have entered downstage center, "with his face well blackened, and a woolly wig," and danced a lively jig, entirely unrelated to the play, as a light diversion during the scene change.[3] With that act, John Diamond became "Master Diamond, the celebrated Ethiopian dancer," and a dance created by Black-Irish mixing became commercial entertainment.

During his first year indentured to Barnum, Diamond turned himself into a professional by doing whatever he was told to do. He danced in theaters and circuses, took a stage name, wore blackface character costumes, tried to sing and act, imitated girls, faced off with rival dancers, and traveled across town and up and down the coast. Some of these practices were entirely new to him, others more familiar. In either case, Diamond's experience provides a new perspective on antebellum entertainment. To the young jig dancer, theaters and circuses represented workplaces as well as sites of amusement. Dancing was physical labor performed by children who competed with each other and with adults for work. It was also a language whose meaning was contingent on who was dancing and who was watching. As Barnum's "apprentice," Diamond was inducted into America's theatrical world, learned its traditions and quirks, and quickly moved from a novice filler-in to a star performer.

Theaters

Entr'actes like Diamond's were a mainstay of antebellum theater. Every theater offered from two to four plays a night and one or more short entertainments between the plays. The simplest programs began with a drama, melodrama, or operatic ballet and concluded with a light comedy, farce, or burletta. Dividing them were entr'actes that ranged from singing, dancing, musical instrument playing, and storytelling, to circus acts such as juggling, acrobatics, and horse handling, to mechanical specialties such as puppeteering and moving panoramic views on painted canvas. Plays were also "irrelevantly" interwoven with "turns" or interludes with no connection to the narrative.[4] Such was the case when Diamond performed "an Ethiopian dance" during a scene change for *Nick of the Woods* on Monday, April 1, 1839. On Tuesday he also danced between *Nick* and a farce entitled *Turning the Tables*. And on Wednesday, for the "Benefit of the Fire Department Fund," the theatrical greenhorn was paired with circus singer-banjoist John Washington Smith.[5]

Entr'acte work was peripatetic. The second week in April, Barnum moved Diamond to the less elegant but popular Franklin Theatre on Chatham Street for a two-week engagement. Adjoined on one side by the Tradesmen's Bank, the Franklin was a long, narrow building that seated "uncomfortably" about six hundred persons.[6] The theater's twenty-nine-year-old manager, William

Dinneford, known for his long locks and hooked nose, practiced "go-a-head for novelty."[7] In addition to his stock company, he featured circus acts, "Negro" delineators (white actors, dancers, and musicians who performed in blackface), and child performers such as little "Miss [Mary Ann] Gannon," a ten-year-old comic actor, dancer, and singer of Irish parentage. Master Diamond danced "his Medley Dance and Double Shuffle, accompanied on violin by the 'Green Mountain Boy,'" at the Franklin, which announced his benefit and last night on April 20.[8]

Benefits and last nights were regular events with customary anticipations on the early stage. Benefits attracted audiences expecting to see the beneficiary's "favorite" acts, and "last nights" brought in people who had not yet seen a performer or company or who wanted to see them one last time. All the talent at a theater received one benefit per season, as did the manager, doorkeepers, prompters, police force, orchestra conductor, and so on. On that night, the person whose benefit it was received a prenegotiated percentage of the profits from the ticket receipts. Theater managers also held benefits for people distressed by calamity or needy in other ways, such as cities suffering from disease epidemics, managers whose theaters had burned down, widows of actors, and fire companies requiring equipment. Despite sharing the proceeds with the beneficiary, theater managers profited financially from benefit nights if ticket sales were high and enhanced their reputations for benevolence if low.

Theater and circus performers depended on benefit nights to bolster salaries kept low by seasonal contracts and irregular work. They also "donated" their names and services to other people's benefits as a form of mutual aid. In 1843 ballerina Emma Ince's contract gave a theater's managers permission to use her name "for such Benefits (within the time named) as they shall choose to announce."[9] Performers who agreed to stay on after their own last night to perform at other people's benefits asked the management not to advertise that fact, for if it is "known that another performance is to take place (and it always is known, whatever precautions may be taken to prevent it)," complained actor John Buckstone in 1841, it "*will* injure the previous night."[10] Announcements of reengagements also appeared after a performer's "last night."

Unlike actors hired for the season, entr'acte performers who were engaged for a week or fortnight (two weeks) often took a benefit at the end of each stint. When Barnum hired out his dancer, each sixth night presented an opportunity to increase attendance and revenue if advertised as Diamond's "last night" (as it would be if he was not reengaged). "His terms for a week would be $6 per night for five first nights," Barnum wrote a prospective client in January 1840, "and 1/3 gross Receipts on the sixth night." For the second week he asked for "$5 pr night for five nights 1/4 gross on the sixth."[11] Master Diamond advertised his last night and benefit after one week at the Franklin, then stayed on another week dancing at the benefits of others.

Barnum introduced Diamond to the New York stage at an auspicious time. During the 1830s, several theaters were built in low-rent areas not far from the waterfront, where they served as nuclei for clusters of eating houses and gambling shops.[12] The Park Theatre in lower Manhattan (built circa 1802) had been America's closest equivalent to London's Drury Lane Theatre. In England, "legitimate" playhouses were licensed by law, and their productions were regulated by the lord chamberlain. In America, no national laws regulated theater productions, and municipal statutes seldom did more than establish licensing fees, control overcrowding, or provide for fire safety.[13] Americans applied the term "legitimate" to theaters "licensed by fashion" (meaning patronized by people with the means to display currently in vogue dress and behavior) that focused on "pure drama and the highest performances in the histrionic art."[14] But the popularity of the Old Park waned in the late 1830s as public taste shifted. Some critics blamed this vitiated taste on American democracy. "The Bowery Theatre had introduced 'sensational' acting," reasoned contemporary historian Benson Lossing, "and was attracting the multitude of theatre-goers."[15] The people wanted entertainments to express their common (called "vulgar" at the time) interests rather than elevated ideas and attitudes.[16] Others blamed the shift on the Panic of 1837, which caused a cloud to hang over theaters that "no 'Star' could successfully shine through."[17]

Creative theater managers such as Dinneford cut through the gloom by studding their programs with more humor and variety. Mixed repertories broadened the range of patrons who identified with their theaters. They also lowered admission prices, thereby extending downward in class and age the makeup of their audiences.[18] These spectators were as interested in seeing Diamond dance as in watching the plays.

Diamond entered an entertainment world captivated by child performers. He was thirteen years old in 1839. During the 1820s and 1830s, rural and foreign migrants flooded seaboard and riverine cities seeking employment in industrial markets and lowering the median age to under twenty. In those same years, the number and critical acceptance of child entertainers peaked on the American stage.[19] Antebellum audiences loved to watch precocious children perform. Their clever feet and lithe bodies were Young America in the flesh, proof that the nation's egalitarian institutions could produce genius. To tap this market, Barnum lowered Diamond's age to "only 12" in 1839 and "only 13" in 1840, "and yet unequalled in the World!!!"[20] Expertise at so young an age enhanced the brilliance of his dancing.

Master Diamond's stage name broadcast his youth. The title "Master," reserved for male children, signposted both Diamond's expertise and his dependency on

FIGURE 2.1. On a typical theater stage, Master Diamond danced in front of the proscenium arch and wings, lit by footlights and the house chandelier, with a canvas backdrop as scenery. "Whitlock's Collection of Ethiopian Melodies. As sung with Great Applause by William Whitlock at the Principal Theatres in the United States, 'De New York Gals,'" 1846, Sheet Music—Negro Minstrels. Courtesy of American Antiquarian Society.

parents or guardians. Girl dancers were titled Miss or Mlle. When a boy dancer came of age, he was identified by his first and last names together or as Mr. or when plural as Messrs. Girl dancers who had come of age added their given names to their stage names as well, but many continued to call themselves Miss So-and-So even after marrying, because young single women attracted larger audiences than old married ones. Diamond's height was also milked for its marketing effect. No one ever described Diamond's looks, and no daguerreotype of him exists, but his stature (he never did grow tall) was often remarked upon. He was "little Diamond," "the very beau ideal of a little Long Island darkie," and "little *Jim along Josey*."[21] His size was emphasized to remind audiences that he was just a boy. "This little fellow is improving wonderfully," noted the *New York Herald*, "and will make a mighty big noise before he is much older."[22]

The theater setting enhanced this impression. Master Diamond danced in front of the proscenium arch, lit by the footlights and house chandelier. Behind him a scene painted on a canvas backcloth was lowered from the fly loft by a system of ropes and pulleys (fig. 2.1). Realistic lighting effects were not needed or desired, as soft or dim lighting added to the backdrop's effect, especially when fronted by three-dimensional stage props. A little darkness added to the verisimilitude of the actors' makeup and camouflaged any shabbiness in the scenery or costumes. The almost equally lighted auditorium also encouraged audience participation in the performances. Not until the 1850s did gas lighting make it possible to dim the house lights and light the stage more directly, altering the perception and relationship of the audience to the action onstage.[23]

Costumes

Barnum provided Diamond with costumes customarily worn by character dancers. They included a seaman's jacket and scarf for hornpipes, a Scottish kilt for the Highland fling, and a Harlequin's outfit for Ethiopian dances. Individual performers were usually responsible for purchasing and maintaining their own costumes, but managers provided outfits for children and pageants that included the entire cast. Performers or their managers contracted costumes from artisanal shops.[24] In New York, A. J. Allen, costumer, and John Silvers, tailor, took orders at 1 Mulberry Street, ran a "Dramatic Agency" above their shop, and kept a warehouse "for the purpose of making to order at the shortest notice every description of Costume either for the Stage, the Amphitheatre, or the Ball Room."[25]

Costumes conveyed information about a performer's skills. To signal that his was a dancing and not a singing or speaking role, newspapers depicted Master Diamond in a modified Harlequin's outfit (fig. 2.2). The Harlequin was a mute theatrical character, often a lighthearted, nimble, and astute servant, who dressed in a black domino mask and diamond-patterned suit, recognized by contemporaries as an abstraction of a beggar's patched attire ("rags and ribbands"). Because he was mute and concealed his face, the Harlequin had to express himself through body movements. Diamond's blackened face, cross-hatched breeches, and striped stockings invoked that comedic character, but he also wore the white blouse and black pumps of the professional hornpipe dancer.

Other prints capture Diamond in costumes identified with Black rural and urban characters. On the cover of *Whitlock's Collection of Ethiopian Melodies*, he dances in front of a country idyll backdrop, suggesting he is performing a "Virginny breakdown" (fig. 2.1). He is portrayed in blackface wearing a wide-brimmed hat, blousy white shirt, and short striped pants held up by suspenders. Only his dancing pumps depart from the rustic scene. His banjo-playing accompanist sports colorful mismatched diamond-patterned trousers and checkered vest. Another print shows Diamond in the long woolen underwear and knee-high Hessian boots of a Black deckhand or waterfront worker.[26] In a third, he is dressed like the working-class youths in his audience, a tough of the period,

FIGURE 2.2. Master Diamond's "Negro jig" dancer costume (workingman's blouse, diamond-patterned trousers, and blackened face) was an American version of the "rags and ribbons" worn by the masked commedia dell'arte Harlequin figure. "GRAND CONCERT AND COMICAL ENTERTAINMENT," *Cabinet* (Schenectady County, NY), Sept. 8, 1840, 3; *Mr. J. Durang in Character of Harlequin. Animation Scene. In five positions,* a watercolor by John Durang (1768–1822). The York County Heritage Trust, PA.

street urchin, or newsboy. Here he dons a slouch hat, well-worn trousers and coat, white checked shirt (worn roguishly open at the chest), seaman's flowing necktie, and fireman's heavy boots with red socks rolled over the tops (fig. 2.3). Theatrical prints are somewhat unreliable sources. Often, after an engraving of a performer was designed and cut, the plate or woodblock became part of a publisher's stock, available for anyone to use. However, the variety and rarity of these prints suggest they depicted Diamond doing particular dances.

Blackface

These costumes initiated Diamond into a theatrical convention wherein white performers impersonated various kinds of Black people. Actors blacked-up to play high-born Moors, such as Shakespeare's Othello, and low-born servants, slaves, and laborers. Traditionally, these lower-class characters transgressed their social bounds by putting one over on their betters. Dozens of plays featured slaves who were wiser than their masters or sooty-faced bootblacks who mocked the

FIGURE 2.3. One of John Diamond's costumes was the typical ragtag attire worn by newsboys and other poor kids working city streets or dancing on the docks. *Master John Diamond*, hand-colored print, in character, MS Thr 1848, box 2, Houghton Library, Harvard University.

absurdity of moralistic admonitions to cleanliness. This bottom-on-top humor resonated in the Age of Jackson (1828–1848), when the extension of political rights to white men without property encouraged the working classes to assert their rising status in social and cultural ways.

Theater that spoke directly to the shared experience of working people often did so in a Black idiom. Nevertheless, blackface performance emerged from and reinforced the racist notion that all "coloreds" were inferior to all whites. Its humor depended on that underlying message. Blackface thereby normalized white supremacy and racial slavery. That message was always present when blackface was worn; but when Diamond danced, other messages came to the fore. As social scientist James C. Scott notes, art that flows upward from below can never be thoroughly controlled by those in power. In 1841 an abolitionist at a theater exhibiting blackface acts was shocked to see "hundreds" of colored people in attendance, "among whom were many very respectable looking persons."[27] He assumed that these spectators were too ignorant to recognize that blackface was a weapon of social containment. But what he could not see was that in theaters open to Black and white people, the stage was also a platform for the display of alternative cultural identities.

Jig dancing was a physical utterance, a form of communication whose meanings and implications depended as much on who was speaking and who was receiving the message as on the costume worn by the dancer.[28] This is the nature of entertainment. Many people in his audiences saw Diamond's blackface costumes as acknowledgments of the hybrid origins of his dances, as the bringing of lower-class amusements onto the legitimate stage. Blackface transformed a cultural relationship into a commercial entertainment made "socially acceptable" by its implied racism. It also placated those in his audiences for whom a blacked-up performer impersonating Black dancers was perfectly respectable but a white boy *emulating* them was not.

Types of "Negro Dancing"

We can see this phenomenon at work when we look at Diamond's blackface costumes as part of the theatrical tradition of character dancing. When theaters announced that Master Diamond would perform an "Ethiopian dance," they placed his act among the "characteristic" ethnic dances regularly inserted into theater programs. These dances were thought to express the innate character of particular ethnic or national groups, such as the Andalusian cachucha, Moorish Alhambra, Polish cracovienne, and Scottish/Highland fling (fig. 2.4). They were not identical replicas of their originals; they were shaped to sell to a particular market. The National Theatre called Diamond's dancing "Ethiopian" to indicate its suitability for middle-class audiences.

FIGURE 2.4. Diamond's "Ethiopian dance" figured among the "characteristic" dances regularly performed on the stage. Here, Austrian ballerina Fanny Elssler performs the Polish cracovienne. These dances were thought to express the innate character of particular ethnic or national groups. *Fanny Ellsler* [sic] *dancing the cracovienne,* [1839], by C. G. Jerome Robbins Dance Division, New York Public Library. New York Public Library Digital Collections.

The title "Ethiopian dance" did not identify Diamond's dance as "African." It signified that he combined European and African dance practices.[29] To his contemporaries, Ethiopia represented the enlightened community of Christianized Black Africans described in Psalm 68, verse 31: "Ethiopia shall soon stretch forth her hands unto God." African American observer James Thomas clarified the distinction between Ethiopian and African dances in his nineteenth-century memoirs. "All the country over," he said, "where there were any blacks," everyone was dancing American creations such as "'Rubin Rede,' Juba, and 'Jumping Jim Crow.'" But he judged "Juber and Partner," two dances he saw performed "on the congo green in New Orleans," African imports, "modified slightly," since he never saw a white man dance those dances.[30] Master Diamond's "Ethiopian dance" belonged to Thomas's first category.

Diamond also performed "characteristic" dances associated with common operatic groups such as clowns, hunters, peasants, or sailors. The sailor's hornpipe, distinguished by costumes and gestures found in the racially and ethnically mixed maritime world, was a mainstay of playhouse and circus programs, enjoyed equally by middle-class patrons (whose etiquette training included genteel hornpipes) and seamen on leave (who flocked to dockside shows*).[31] Hornpipes were largely percussive dances performed by males and females in hard shoes to a slow $\frac{2}{4}$ measure, which allowed for complex steps that alternated hopping and skipping movements with the beating out of rhythms by the feet.[32] Professional dancers called hornpipes "walk-arounds," as traditionally the dancer "'circumnavigated' the floor twice, in opposite directions," before launching his or her exhibition "with arms crossed, or poised, or whirled."[33]

Hornpipe dancers were judged by the number of different steps they could devise and execute perfectly on each foot. Philadelphia dancer John Durang choreographed a twenty-two-step hornpipe in 1789 for his blackface role, the Carib native Friday, in the pantomime *Robinson Crusoe, or Harlequin Friday*. Borrowing moves from international character dances and local jigs, Durang's hornpipe combined French glissades with African American "heel and toe haul backs," forward running on the heels, Irish cut-the-buckles, numerous shuffles, Scotch step backs, "whirligigs," and pigeon wings ("executed in part by jumping up and striking the legs together").[34] Diamond's "Camp Town Hornpipe" incorporated similar steps.

Any dance performed in blackface fell under the general category of "Negro dancing." Diamond's generation applied that name to two types of stage dancing. What Americans called "jigs" represented one type of "Negro dancing"; what they called "grotesque" or "novelty" dances represented another. The word "grotesque" referred to dancing with no perceivable rules. These dances might be based on African American dance practices or European dances or just made up. They featured comically exaggerated or repulsively ugly movements or gyrations that did not seem to stem from extensive training. Many of these dances did require practice and skill, of course; but their purpose was to add humor to an act, not

---

* The theater season coincided with the cold weather when ships were docked. Hence, some sailors and dockhands who were experienced with rigging systems and canvas sails found work as stagehands. Their tradition of whistling signals on ships and docks to raise and lower sails and cranes may also be the origins of that cueing custom backstage.

to call attention to the dancer's expertise. The most famous example of this style of "Negro dancing" was "Jump Jim Crow" as performed by blackface actor T. D. Rice in 1832. "Rice's appearance was much in his favor," recalled a contemporary. "Over six feet tall, he could tell a good story[,] Sing a good song and do [a] little dancing but no jigs. . . . [H]e was looked upon as a novelty."[35] Rice "sang verses and danced a few grotesque steps between them. Of course this would come under the heading of Negro dancing," added another chronicler. "Master Diamond and Juba, the colored boy, also danced but their efforts were in the form of jigs," he explained. "Later these jigs were danced under the titles of 'Champion Jig,' 'Rattlesnake Jig,' 'Smoke House Jig,' 'Grape Vine Twist' and 'Virginny Breakdowns.'"[36] Diamond and Juba's "Negro dancing" encompassed the jigs, reels, and hornpipes of British and European step dancers, the creolized breakdowns of African American market dancers, and the hybrid figures of the set dancers at taverns like Raynor's. These steps might be serious or humorous, but they always highlighted the elevated skill and creativity of the dancer.

Blackface dancing was also referred to as "nigger" dancing. In September 1839 Boston's National Theatre would call Master Diamond the "best little nigger that we have ever had."[37] That description had an undeniably derisive valence while surreptitiously alerting audiences that this boy's jig dancing derived from racial mixing. Before 1808 the N-word was simply a synonym for slave, a recognizable (albeit degraded) class of Black involuntary laborer. But as soon as Northern slaves began to be freed by gradual emancipation, whites transferred the term, along with the negative connotations of enslavement (dependence, ignorance, and immorality), to all people of color, making it a powerful anti-Black verbal assault. "Nigger" also served as a descriptor and epithet for white people who interacted socially and culturally with Black people.[38]

Extravaganzas

The descriptive titles of Diamond's early jigs—medley dance, double shuffle, Negro hornpipe, and "Camp Town Hornpipe"—reflected their origins and nature. Such names indicated that the dances would be performed to tunes without words. When attached to a song with lyrics, "Negro" dancing served as the culmination of a song-and-dance act called an "extravaganza." Extravaganzas usually consisted of a popular ballad in Black English dialect combined with some comic business and culminating in an astonishing "terpsichorean" refrain.* They might be performed by a single person if he could sing, play the banjo or fiddle, and dance at the same time or by a duo (a singer-musician and dancer) or trio (fig. 2.5).

---

* Terpsichore (the art of dance) is one of the nine Greek Muses. Terpsichorean derives from *terpsis* (delight), *terpein* (to enjoy), and *choros* (dances).

FIGURE 2.5. A solo extravaganza performer might sing and dance while playing a musical instrument. In a circus ring he performed on an acoustical wooden platform, raised by slats to enhance the sound of his tapping feet. *Jenny Get Your Hoe Cake Done, The Celebrated Banjo Song, as sung with great Applause at the Broadway Circus, By J. W. Sweeny* (Firth and Hall, No. 1 Franklin Square, ca. 1839). Courtesy of American Antiquarian Society.

Master Diamond mostly performed extravaganzas with a singer-musician, as singing was not one of his strong points.

Diamond danced two extravaganzas at the Franklin Theatre—"Sich a Getting' up Stair, and Jim along Josey." The tune to "Jim along Josey" came from the sea shanty "Haul Away Joe," a work song sung by Atlantic sailors pulling ropes in British and African coastal regions and slaves rowing canoes and poling flatboats on interior waterways.[39] In America "to josey" meant to go, to hasten on. The refrain "Hey get a-long, get a-long Josey / Hey get a-long Jim a-long Joe!" echoed the call of Black cartmen or canal boatmen urging a mule or donkey to "get along" or "jog along."[40] Free and unfree workers in Diamond's audiences recognized and enjoyed the song's references.

The extravaganza of "Jim along Josey" had transatlantic origins. Among the mock "Proceedings of Learned Societies" in English caricaturist and illustrator George Cruikshank's *Comic Almanack for 1836* was "an inquiry into the probable author of 'Jim along Josey.'"[41] British comic singer Edmund "Ned" R. Harper introduced a stage version of the song in his 1838 drama *The Free Nigger of New York*.⁴² Diamond danced it the next year, and by 1840 so many Americans had performed it, the *Baltimore Sun* claimed that "Jim along Josey" had "absolutely driven Jim Crow out of fashion."⁴³

Master Diamond expanded his repertory of "Negro" character dances when he moved to Washington, DC's National Theatre in June 1839. According to one early blackface delineator, "There were as many distinct dialects and mannerisms among the 'Darkies of the South' as among the '[Natives] of the North.' The Kentuckian differed as much from the Virginian as the Alabamian did from the South Carolinian. Or the 'field hand' from the 'genteel house servant.'" It was "the proper and distinct rendition of such differences," he claimed, "that made such a success of the white man's imitation of the Negro."⁴⁴ Diamond's upbringing and skills of imitation enabled him to render those differences in dances described by enthused Washingtonians as "the greatest display of heel and toe genius ever witnessed in this city."⁴⁵

John Diamond's first season as Barnum's apprentice ended on June 27. To avoid the heat, many theaters closed in July and August, "the dullest months of the year for business," and reopened in late August or September. A financial recession made business particularly slack in the summer of 1839.⁴⁶ The young dancer may have returned to his parents for part of that time, but that does not mean he stopped working. At the very least, he choreographed and rehearsed the dances he would perform for Barnum the next season up in New England, where he played his first female role.

The Black Bayadere

From mid-September through November 1839, Diamond danced at William Pelby's National Theatre in Boston for four consecutive two-week engagements. On most nights, he performed his "celebrated" dances between the drama and the farce as usual. But on October 18, his benefit night, he danced the entr'acte *and* starred in the concluding entertainment, "LA BAYADERE IN OLE KENTUCK! Or . . . .The Maid of Guinea," a one-act "Travestie of the 'Maid of Cashmere.'"⁴⁷ A concocted burletta that twisted a famous ballet into a comment on current events, *La Bayadere in Ole Kentuck!* was written and directed by J. Hudson Kirby, a young Londoner who had recently arrived in America.⁴⁸ Kirby, who first appeared on the American stage in 1837, wore a variety of theatrical hats during his short career (he died in 1848)—actor, writer, director, stage manager. His strong melodious voice and bombastic style made him "the favorite of the newsboys"*

---

* The designation "newsboy" encompassed newspaper sellers and other child hucksters and workers.

who filled the shilling seats in theater pits and galleries to see his dying scenes, giving rise to the saying: "Wake me up when Kirby dies."[49] He also knew how to combine genres to their liking.

The playbill for Diamond's benefit night production, a long, narrow page afflicted with every possible variation of capital letter, included a hyperbolic description of the burletta (fig. 2.6). At first glance, passersby might have taken Diamond's act for a simple blackface parody of the French operatic ballet *La bayadère amoureuse* (1830), performed in the United States under the title *La Bayadere; or, The Maid of Cashmere*. But if they stopped to read the playbill's summary of scenes, songs, and dances, shrewd readers would have noticed that the plot, although structured around the ballet's storyline, was a rendering of a legal case currently unfolding in a Hartford, Connecticut, courthouse.

The success of Diamond's "Travestie of the 'Maid of Cashmere'" depended on a "shared public culture."[50] Everything about his *Bayadere*—from the setting, characters, and tension to the music, dancing, and resolution—was a reference to something else. A travesty is a cross-dressed representation or something disguised, often in a ridiculous way.* It is used to poke fun at current tastes, call attention to absurd situations, and discuss controversial topics. To travesty does not mean to simplify. Master Diamond's part alone was a multilayered disguising—an enslaved South Indian transmogrified into an African captive, a white person performing in blackface, an American boy posing as an Italian woman, a jig dancer filling a ballet dancer's role.

The original opéra ballet of *La bayadère amoureuse, ou, Le dieu et la bayadère*, with music by Daniel Auber and libretto by Eugène Scribe, tells the story of an enslaved temple dancer (*bayadère*) and the god Brahma, who has assumed mortality and must endure life's evils, including death, unless he finds a young woman who perfectly and purely loves him.[51] Brahma, now called the Unknown, wanders about Cashmire (today's Kashmir), where he sees the bayadère Zelica (Zoloe in the original French version) dancing for the Grand Vizier. Zelica, who is unfamiliar with the local language, must make her sorrows and joys known through movement. Both the Vizier and Brahma fall desperately in love with Zelica, who rejects the Vizier for the Unknown. Brahma decides to test her love by calling for a trial dance between Zelica and her sister, Fatima, and declaring Fatima the winner, despite Zelica's superior skill. Although hurt and jealous, Zelica hides the Unknown when the Vizier's soldiers arrive to arrest him. The thwarted guards seize Zelica and prepare to burn her alive. The purity of her love having restored the Unknown to his divine state, Brahma rises from the smoke and carries Zelica into the heavenly clouds.

---

* The English word "travesty" comes from the French *travesti* (disguise) and the Italian *travestire*, which combines *trans* (across) and *vestire* (to clothe).

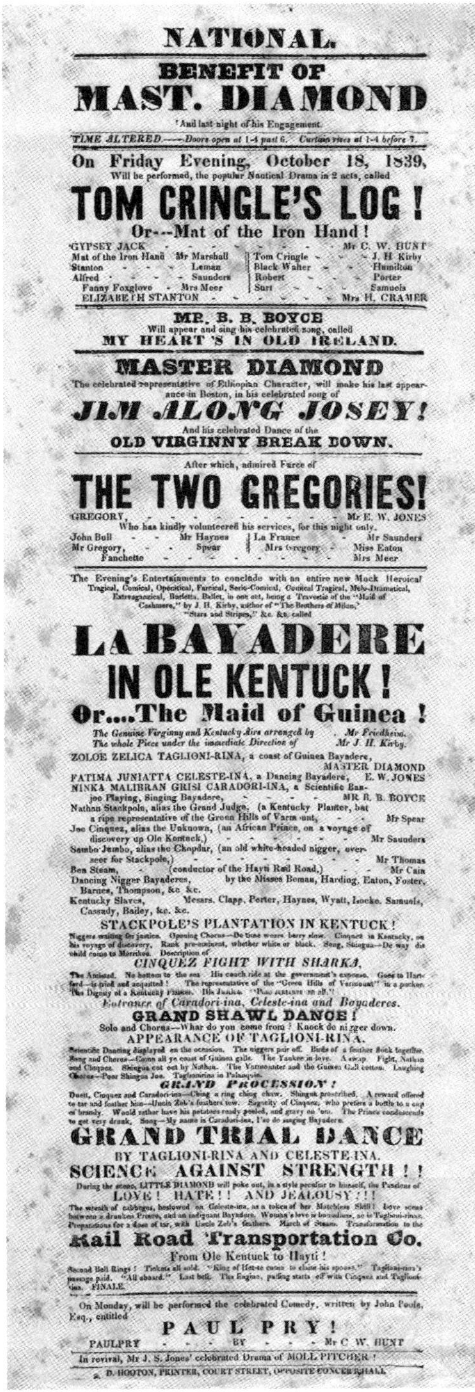

NATIONAL.

BENEFIT OF

MAST. DIAMOND

And last night of his Engagement.

TIME ALTERED.——Doors open at 1-4 past 6. Curtain rises at 1-4 before 7.

On Friday Evening, October 18, 1839,

Will be performed, the popular Nautical Drama in 2 acts, called

TOM CRINGLE'S LOG!

Or---Mat of the Iron Hand!

GYPSEY JACK - - - - - - - - Mr C. W. HUNT
Mat of the Iron Hand Mr Marshall | Tom Cringle - - - J. H Kirby
Stanton - - - - Leman | Black Walter - - Hamilton
Alfred - - - - - Saunders | Robert - - - Porter
Fanny Foxglove - Mrs Meer | Surt - - - Samuels
ELIZABETH STANTON - - - - - - - Mrs H. CRAMER

MR. B. B. BOYCE

Will appear and sing his celebrated song, called

MY HEART 'S IN OLD IRELAND.

MASTER DIAMOND

The celebrated representative of Ethiopian Character, will make his last appearance in Boston, in his celebrated song of

JIM ALONG JOSEY!

And his celebrated Dance of the

OLD VIRGINNY BREAK DOWN.

After which, admired Farce of

THE TWO GREGORIES!

GREGORY, - - - - - - - - - - Mr E. W. JONES
Who has kindly volunteered his services, for this night only.
John Bull - - Mr Haynes | La France - Mr Saunders
Mr Gregory, - - Spear | Mrs Gregory - Miss Eaton
Fanchette - - - - - - - - - Mrs Meer

The Evening's Entertainments to conclude with an entire new Mock Heroical Tragical, Comical, Operatical, Farcical, Serio-Comical, Comical Tragical, Melo-Dramatical, Extravaganzical, Burletta, Ballet, in one act, being a Travestie of the "Maid of Cashmere," by J. H. Kirby, author of "The Brothers of Milan," "Stars and Stripes," &c. &c. called

LA BAYADERE

IN OLE KENTUCK!

Or....The Maid of Guinea!

The Genuine Virginny and Kentucky Airs arranged by . Mr Friedheim.
The whole Piece under the immediate Direction of Mr J. H. Kirby.

ZOLOE ZELICA TAGLIONI-RINA, a coast of Guinea Bayadere, MASTER DIAMOND
FATIMA JUNIATTA CELESTE-INA, a Dancing Bayadere, E. W. JONES
NINKA MALIBRAN GRISI CARADORI-INA, a Scientific Banjoe Playing, Singing Bayadere, - - - - - MR B. B. BOYCE
Nathan Stackpole, alias the Grand Judge, (a Kentucky Planter, but a ripe representative of the Green Hills of Varm-unt, - - Mr Spear
Joe Cinquez, alias the Unknown, (an African Prince, on a voyage of discovery up Ole Kentuck,) - - - - - - - Mr Saunders
Sambo Jumbo, alias the Chopdar, (an old white-headed nigger, overseer for Stackpole,) - - - - - - - - - Mr Thomas
Ben Steam, - (conductor of the Hayti Rail Road,) - - - Mr Cain
Dancing Nigger Bayaderes, by the Misses Beman, Harding, Eaton, Foster, Barnes, Thompson, &c &c.
Kentucky Slaves, Messrs. Clapp, Perter, Haynes, Wyatt, Locke, Samuels, Cassady, Bailey, &c. &c.

STACKPOLE'S PLANTATION IN KENTUCK!

Niggers waiting for justice. Opening Chorus—De time wears berry slow. Cinquez in Kentucky, on his voyage of discovery. Rank pre-eminent, whether white or black. Song, Shingua—De way dis child come to Merrikee. Description of

CINQUEZ FIGHT WITH SHARKA.

The Amistad. No bottom to the sea. His coach ride at the government's expense. Goes to Hartford—is tried and acquitted! The representative of the "Green Hills of Varmount" in a pucker. The Dignity of a Kentucky Planter. His Justice.

Entrance of Caradori-ina, Celeste-ina and Bayaderes.

GRAND SHAWL DANCE!

Solo and Chorus—Whar do you come from? Knock de nigger down.

APPEARANCE OF TAGLIONI-RINA.

Scientific Dancing displayed on the occasion. The niggers pair off. Birds of a feather flock together. Song and Chorus—Come all ye coast of Guinea gals. The Yankee in love. A swap. Fight, Nathan and Cinquez. Shingua cut out by Nathan. The Varmounter and the Guinea Gall cotton. Laughing Chorus—Poor Shingua Joe. Taglioni-rina in Palanquin.

GRAND PROCESSION!

Duett, Cinquez and Caradori-ina—Ching a ring ching chaw. Shingua proscribed. A reward offered to tar and feather him—Uncle Zeb's feathers tew. Sagacity of Cinquez, who prefers a bottle to a cup of brandy. Would rather have his potatoes ready peeled, and gravy on 'em. The Prince condescends to get very drunk. Song—My name is Caradori-ina, I'se de singing Bayadere.

GRAND TRIAL DANCE

BY TAGLIONI-RINA AND CELESTE-INA.

SCIENCE AGAINST STRENGTH!!

During the scene, LITTLE DIAMOND will poke out, in a style peculiar to himself, the Passions of

LOVE! HATE!! AND JEALOUSY!!!

The wreath of cabbages, bestowed on Celeste-ina, as a token of her Matchless Skill! Love scene between a drunken Prince, and an indignant Bayadere. Woman's love is boundless, so is Taglioni-rina's. Preparations for a dose of tar, with Uncle Zeb's feathers. March of Steam. Transformation to the

Rail Road Transportation Co.

From Ole Kentuck to Hayti!

Second Bell Rings! Tickets all sold. "King of Het-te come to claim his spouse." Taglioni-rina's passage paid. "All aboard." Last bell. The Engine, puffing starts off with Cinquez and Taglioni-rina. FINALE.

On Monday, will be performed the celebrated Comedy, written by John Poole, Esq., entitled

PAUL PRY!

PAULPRY - - - - BY - - - - Mr C. W. HUNT

In revival, Mr J. S. Jones' celebrated Drama of MOLL PITCHER!

D. HOOTON, PRINTER, COURT STREET, OPPOSITE CONCERT HALL.

FIGURE 2.6. Performed by Master Diamond in Boston in 1839, *La Bayadere in Ole Kentuck!* amalgamated the stories and characters from the popular operatic ballet *La Bayadere; or, The Maid of Cashmere* and the case of the *Amistad* uprising currently being tried in a Hartford, Connecticut, courtroom. "National. Benefit of Mast. Diamond," playbill, Oct. 18, 1839, MS Thr 1848, box 10, Houghton Library, Harvard University.

Antislavery Travesty

Kirby turned Auber's two-act ballet into a one-act travesty by ripping content from the newspaper headlines. On August 29, the *Long-Island Star* reported that a Spanish schooner named the *Amistad* had been captured a few days earlier while anchored off the coast of Montauk, New York. The vessel was transporting a cargo of men who had been kidnapped in Africa and illegally sold as slaves in Havana, Cuba.[52] (The international slave trade was outlawed in 1808.) According to the *New London Gazette*, the ship was on its way to Haiti when the Africans rose up, cut the throats of the captain and crew, and took possession of the vessel. They spared two passengers to navigate the boat back to Africa, but, having no navigation skills themselves, they did not realize they had been kept close to the North American coast. The *Amistad* was discovered by a US brig, seized, and transported to Connecticut (where slavery was, technically, still legal), where the Africans were imprisoned. A trial ensued regarding the status of the Africans as enslaved property or as free people, which became an abolitionist cause.

The *Amistad* case captivated Northerners. Thousands of curious people, a few with a genuine commitment to antislavery, visited the New Haven jail and Hartford courtroom in September to gawk at the Africans. Some journalists and artists mocked the proceedings; others rendered the leaders of the revolt sympathetically.[53] The "master spirit" behind the revolt was a man called Cinques (he pronounced his name Shinequau), noted the *Gazette*. "His countenance, for a native African, is unusually intelligent, evincing uncommon decision and coolness, with a composure characteristic of true courage, and nothing to mark him as a malicious man."[54] Three days after the Africans were incarcerated, *The Black Schooner or the Pirate Slaver Armistad!* [sic], a "Nautical Melo-drama, in 2 acts" opened at New York's Bowery Theater for one week. The play's central characters were Zemba Cingues and Inez, an invented damsel in distress who may have given Kirby the idea of combining the ballet and the news story.[55]

Joe Cinquez was Brahma in Kirby's play, and the *Amistad* Africans were female bayadères from the "coast of Guinea." Master Diamond danced the part of "ZOLOE ZELICA TAGLIONI-RINA." Italian ballerina Marie Taglioni was the most famous dancer in the Western world in 1839. An innovator who was known for blending physical power with ethereal refinement, she rose to the top by feminizing the male bravura style (an appropriate model for a boy dancing as a girl).[56] Taglioni introduced *La bayadère amoureuse* to Paris in 1830 and London in 1831, after which her fame spread with newspaper accounts of her European successes.[57] She never danced in the United States, but in July 1839, three months before Diamond arrived in Boston, her brother Paul and sister-in-law Anna (Madame Taglioni) had danced at Pelby's National Theatre.[58] Another male dancer

FIGURE 2.7. Diamond's character Taglioni-rina and her rival, Celeste-ina, in *La Bayadere in Ole Kentuck!* copied and mocked the stage convention wherein female dancers cross-dressed to perform nonspeaking male roles. Popular in America, the Parisian dancer-actor Céline Céleste was known for playing male characters such as "Hamet (a dumb Arab Boy)," who spoke only through dance. *MADlle CELESTE as The Wild Arab Boy* (J. P. Hall, 1834), Jerome Robbins Dance Division, The New York Public Library. New York Public Library Digital Collections.

played Zelica's sister and dancing rival "FATIMA JUNIATTA CELESTE-INA." Parisian dancer and actress Céline Céleste, Taglioni's keenest competition for *La bayadère amoureuse*'s starring role, was touring the United States for a second time in 1839. Known for dancing male roles with panache, M'lle Céleste had aroused such enthusiasm five years earlier that her fans carried her through the streets on their shoulders. It was also rumored that President Andrew Jackson, an ardent admirer, adopted her as a citizen of the Union (fig. 2.7). In September, Céleste had followed *The Black Schooner* onto the Bowery stage, another possible prompt for Kirby.[59]

The role of Taglioni-rina introduced Diamond to the ballet version of challenge dancing. After 1830 *La Bayadere*'s grand trial dance became the vehicle for introducing a new danseuse (female ballet dancer) to the stage, often by pitting the novice against the current luminary.[60] Enterprising American ballerinas quickly excerpted and turned that scene into an entr'acte. The young Philadelphia danseuse Mary Ann Lee danced *La Bayadere* trials against almost every teenaged ballerina on the American stage, and others followed suit (fig. 2.8).[61] In May 1839 she faced Emma Ince in Philadelphia for the benefit of Kensington's Globe Fire Engine Company, and in June she vied with Julia Turnbull at New York's Bowery

FIGURE 2.8. Young American danseuses such as Miss Mary Ann Lee converted the grand trial dance from the operatic ballet *La bayadère* into a separate entr'acte, paving the way for trial dances onstage between young male jig dancers. *Mary Ann Lee as 'Fatima'* [winning the laurel wreath], in *"The Maid of Cashmere,"* from a lithograph by Duval after a drawing by Ancora. Library of Congress.

Theatre. Miss Ince likewise took the lead role, challenging her peers and winning the sobriquet "La Petite Taglioni."[62] This cohort of girl ballet dancers paved the way for the stage challenges of boy jig dancers such as Diamond.

During the grand trial dance between Taglioni-rina and Celeste-ina, "LITTLE DIAMOND poke[d] out, in a style peculiar to himself, the Passions of LOVE! HATE!! AND JEALOUSY!!!" in dumb show. The playbill described the match as "Science Against Strength" (a phrase derived from boxing matches in which one pugilist relies on trained moves and the other on brute force).[63] Nevertheless, the drunken Cinquez bestows the prize on Taglioni-rina's rival. Still, her love is boundless. When Stackpole's* men arrive to arrest the African Prince, she hides him in her cellar and prepares to take "a dose of tar, with Uncle Zeb's feathers" in his place.

Kirby concluded his travesty as did Auber with Brahma saving the bayadère. But rather than ascending into heaven, Cinquez and Taglioni-rina catch the

---

* Kirby's Grand Vizier character was a plantation owner called Nathan Stackpole who shared peculiarities with the judge presiding over the *Amistad* case.

underground railroad to the Black republic of Haiti: "March of Steam. Transformation to the RAIL ROAD TRANSPORTATION CO. From Ole Kentuck to Hayti! Second bell Rings! Tickets all sold. 'King of Het-te come to claim his spouse.' Taglioni-rina's passage paid. 'All aboard.' Last bell. The Engine, pulling starts off with Cinquez and Taglioni-rina. FINALE." Diamond delivered his finale in "locomotive" steps, sliding or dragging his feet along the (possibly sanded) floor to make slow chugging noises, then speeding up and adding taps to the chugs (like the clicking of metal wheels crossing the joints in the tracks), and tearing along at top speed (trains could do twenty-five miles per hour at that time) until he disappeared into the wings.

Dancing *La Bayadere* educated Diamond. It showed him that theater audiences were smart, that girl dancers were his theatrical rivals, that slavery was causing problems in the North, and that some people danced themselves out of bondage. When we look back and see a performance in blackface, we think we know what it meant. But unpacked, Diamond's *Bayadere* reveals the confusing array of ideas and events people at the time were attempting to make sense of.[64] The sense that Barnum made of the play was more limited. He turned the "Black Bayadere" into a lucrative addition to Diamond's repertory, pulled out and offered as an "opposition act" whenever a famous European ballerina was in town.

* * *

While Diamond danced in Boston, Barnum tried to book him at mid-Atlantic theaters, where he knew some managers from earlier days. When he didn't hear back, he hired Diamond out to an equestrian circus that was wintering in New York City. Placing Diamond in a circus was not Barnum's first choice, but it had its benefits. Circuses stationed in large cities drew large crowds. Master Diamond won "great renown" at the circus that winter, attracting the attention of theater proprietors and extravaganza musicians.[65] He also joined a cohort of child performers who gratified their audiences and grumbled about the adults who handled them.

Broadway Circus

Two months before Diamond joined the show, workers had erected wooden walls and a canvas roof on a vacant lot between Broom and Spring Streets and posted playbills at inns and livery stables announcing "BROADWAY CIRCUS.—Messrs. Welsh, Bartlett & Co.—THIS EVENING" in the Grand National Equestrian Arena at 509 Broadway.[66] The weather was exceptionally cold, making the streets dangerously icy. The tent was sturdy and tolerably warm inside. Local sail makers and wagon builders had been consulted, so it was a tight ship. Several braziers had also been purchased, but those were for the spectators.[67] Circus players felt warm enough during their acts, but they froze while waiting to enter the ring or changing costumes in a separate tent or costume wagon parked nearby.

The evening's performance on January 20, 1840, commenced at 7:00 p.m. Master Diamond would kick off the second part of the show at 10:00. "On opening in New York that winter, and during the whole of our stay," recalled bareback rider John H. Glenroy, "we used to give about three hours ring show and about one and a half hours stage show every evening" (fig. 2.9).[68] Diamond probably surveyed the scene as he waited his turn. Inside the tent was a single forty-foot ring surrounded by a low wooden fence with a gate through which the horses entered and exited. Ring and riders were lighted from above by hundreds of candles on a rigged-up chandelier made of boards nailed together in a triangle shape around the center pole and hoisted above the action by a pulley. On one side, the workers had assembled stair-like rising benches of bleached wooden planks (hence the term "bleachers") that could seat up to a thousand people. These were the "box" seats, which carried a premium price of fifty cents a person. Few youths of Diamond's class sat there. Working lads and lasses bought the twenty-five-cent "pit" tickets and stood, squatted, or sat in chairs directly behind the ring fence, wherever they could squeeze in.[69] The seats and standing room overflowed with people that night, and those who could not get in were milling about outside. The circus had been in town since November, and Master Diamond was the only new act on the bill.[70] Perhaps they had come to see him.

If he watched the ring show, Diamond would have seen Mr. Cadwallader and Miss Wells "making love" as Cupid and Zephyr on horseback; the "positionist" and his three fearless children executing acrobatic feats; "Mr. Mulligan vaulting over

FIGURE 2.9. Welch's Broadway Circus, where Barnum placed fourteen-year-old Master Diamond in January 1840, featured horseback, strength, and tumbling acts performed by adults and children, including bareback rider Master John Glenroy, an eleven-year-old apprentice with four years' experience who performed aerial somersaults off the back of a horse. "Welch, Mann, and Delevan's *Superior, Splendid, and unequaled* National Circus," *Cumberland Valley Sentinel* (Chambersburg, PA), Aug. 25, 1845, 3.

a squadron of mounted cavalry, through a number of balloons"; Master Glenroy crouching on the flanks of his galloping Arabian before flinging his body upward in a backward somersault; "the flying Highlander" skipping across a slack rope; and Mr. Garvey, the American Hercules, lifting an immense weight.[71]

When, finally, it was his turn, "young Diamond" probably trotted to the center of the ring, where the circus hands had set down a wooden pallet raised by slats, followed by Mr. Sweeney carrying both fiddle and banjo.[72] Both performers wore mismatched diamonds and stripes, had greased and darkened their faces, and had covered their hair with wigs of tight brown curls. Sweeney may have stood alongside the board as he placed his fiddle under his chin and struck up a lively hornpipe. Diamond immediately circled the tiny stage in both directions, then jumped on it with a clack and set to in a whirlwind of "UNHEARD-OF, OUT-LANDISH and INIMITABLE LICKS."[73] "Licks" is what streetwise connoisseurs called the original phrases composed by jig dancers. Diamond's licks might have combined "regular double shuffles" (three beats made by a step and two strokes with the ball of the opposite foot moving out and back), "locomotive" steps, "rattling" (rapid-fire toe and heel taps), heel running (a humorous opposite to ballet toe dancing), ankle breaks (bending at the ankle from side to side), and asymmetrical twists and turns ("as supple and elastic as a piece of whale bone").[74]

With every change of tune, Diamond would have jumped off the board, walked around some more, jumped back up, and commenced again. The *Herald* compared his flying feet to the "scarpering" of Samuel Swartwout, the "Collector of Customs for the Port of New York" accused of embezzling a million dollars and fleeing to England.[75] American advertising was full of exaggeration at the time, but Diamond's large audiences, encores, and reengagements suggest that his dancing "fit the bill." When his shoes finally hit the dirt and he took his bow, a roar must have swept around the arena, for according to the next day's *Evening Post*, "Master Diamond was called out and compelled to repeat his negro dances five or six times."[76]

Two circuses settled into New York City for the winter of 1839–1840: Welch, Bartlett & Company, managed by longtime circus proprietor Rufus Welch, and June, Titus, Angevine & Company, managed by the horse rider Henry Rockwell, who set up inside the Bowery Amphitheatre (formerly the Zoological Institute at 37 Bowery).* Dozens of circuses were tramping through the nation, providing cheap entertainment to city and country audiences. Equestrian circuses might be large or small; some came with animal menageries. They set up in public gardens, city commons, militia grounds, empty lots, and open fields or worked in

---

* The term "amphitheater" referred to any structure with rows of seats that were stacked one above another on both sides or around an open space.

theaters, museums, village halls, or saloons fitted up for their performances. The Northern traveling season lasted around eight months, from April until November. In winter, circus companies disbanded, journeyed south to warmer climes, or took up winter stands in large cities, where local talent expanded their rosters and circus employees found other work.

The ring shows of equestrian circuses included horse-team handling, bareback trick riding, horseback dramas, infant riders, and floor and aerial acrobatics—balancing, juggling, tumbling, contortions, slack rope and trapeze stunts, vaulting, and weightlifting. Their stage shows included music, dancing, clowning, and acting. That winter Welch bolstered his show with eight "Negro" singers, musicians, and dancers. Rockwell did the same. These extravaganza performers served the same function as "clowns to the ring," giving the horses, riders, and acrobats time to rest or change costumes between acts. Or they provided the stage show that closed the program.

Several "Negro" delineators moved between the Broadway and Bowery circuses that season, doing their own renditions of "Jim along Josey" and watching Diamond's progress.[77] His success inspired a few musicians to take on their own boy. John Washington Smith introduced "his pupil" Master (Thomas) Coleman to the Bowery Amphitheater in January, and after Diamond left the Broadway Circus in February, Joel Sweeney brought "his colored pupil" into the ring.[78] Sweeney's apprentice was likely Black, since the popular press reserved the adjective "colored" for African American performers, and according to another musician, Sweeney had learned his singing and dancing technique from the "plantation and cornfield negroes" with whom he socialized.[79] These children were not replicas of Master Diamond. Each had his own style and steps. But to please their audiences they often danced the "Camp Town Hornpipe," Diamond's signature step. Most of them also learned their master's trade: banjo playing.

Labor Arrangements

Diamond encountered all sorts of child performers at the circus. Boys and girls sang, danced, acted, and played musical instruments, rode galloping horses, clowned around, made human pyramids, and tumbled on rugs and ropes. Most of them were born into families of entertainers. Others were apprenticed to adult performers or managers as small children and grew up in the business. And some began as stagehands—grooms, lamp trimmers, prop minders, drivers, ring builders, and assistants—who watched and learned, trying out and devising stunts to audition when ready. Diamond joined Welch's circus as P. T. Barnum's "pupil," a synonym for apprentice in the entertainment business.[80] Traditional apprenticeships were in decline by 1840, but Irish and African American parents still bound their children to tradesmen or merchants for years of service. Public officials and guardians of the poor also routinely signed orphans, half-orphans, and runaways into contracts. When Diamond's father granted Barnum power of attorney over his son's engagements, he relinquished his control over the boy. In practice, this manager-talent relationship resembled halfway apprenticeships in other industries. Children were still bound to unrelated adults, but those adults were no longer required to train them.[81] They provided young talent with work in exchange for lodging and a pittance to live on and lawfully commanded their profits until they reached maturity. This arrangement benefited street and tavern dancers, whose incomes were intermittent at best. But it caused resentment in youngsters who made large sums for their masters. Master Glenroy, whose father apprenticed him to circus equestrian George Cadwallader at "seven years four months old," later complained: "I never received the sum of Fifty Dollars from the whole of my earnings, [Cadwallader] appropriating all to himself."[82] Barnum probably made a similar arrangement with Diamond's father.

Diamond did not learn the dancing trade from Barnum, but he did learn about the entertainment business. Successful managers were not experts in the field of every performer they handled. Rather, they had the perspicacity to hire a good act when they saw it.[83] Barnum was not a dancing master, he was a speculator, someone who figured out ways to make money from other people's talents. He found venues, negotiated contracts, and developed strategies to draw in the public. He wrote Diamond's ad copy, provided his costumes, hired musicians, and commissioned scripts. Barnum may have asked Diamond to change things he didn't like or add a new move or character to his repertory, but he expected the dancer to choreograph his own dances.

* * *

Barnum fully expected Diamond's circus exposure to generate more theater work. And he was not disappointed. The day after Diamond's successful circus debut, Barnum forwarded newspaper clippings in a letter to a theater manager in Philadelphia, requesting an engagement. "There certainly is no mistake but with the *varieties* which can be given by Master Diamond and his *Masterly* and *unequalled* dancing," wrote Barnum. "He is beyond all doubt the best negro dancer in America = his singing is quite middling but his dancing is absolutely beyond all calculation *astonishing* . . . [*and*] he is *good* in the *Highland Fling* and *Sailors Hornpipe* for both of which he has the proper *costumes*. . . . So much for the *boy*, . . . Now do you want him a week or two?"[84] That manager did want him, but before Barnum received his reply, Diamond had caught the eye of the Chatham Theatre's new managers, who staged his first dancing match in New York.

3

TRIALS OF SKILL AND SERVITUDE

The New Chatham Theatre was crammed from pit to dome at 10:00 p.m. on Thursday, February 13, 1840. Asserting their expanding rights, New York's sturdier white males—sailors, shopmen, clerks, carpenters, mechanics, "and other people of that kidney"—had paid twenty-five cents to squeeze onto the pit benches next to their mates, shoving the poor fellows sitting at the ends onto the floor. Others stood behind the seats, a protective arm around their "gals" and an elbow ready for anyone who got too close. In the first-tier boxes, gloved young ladies rested on the seats while their gentlemen escorts, having paid fifty cents for the privilege, leaned on balcony ledges or perched with dangling legs on coats draped over the balustrade. Above them in the gallery, for the recently reduced price of twelve and a half cents, African Americans of all classes—cooks and servers, oyster-house proprietors, dockworkers, seamen, and deckhands—sat with the more "delicate" white patrons, who dared not risk the pit. Old men and a good number of women, mostly roughly clad but of decent looks, a few "profligate and abandoned" looking, mothers with their families, and one or two with a babe in arms, shared the benches with packs of dusky-faced children on their own—newsboys, butcher boys, chimney sweeps, and the like.[1]

Amid the crowd stood a reporter from the *Spirit of the Times*. The weekly's editor, William T. Porter, usually stuck to turf and field sports, but he must have thought a trial of skill danced onstage for a substantial wager was worth covering. For nearly a week, New York's penny papers had sparred in their coverage of Master Diamond's coming event. On Saturday, February 8, the *Morning Herald* announced that "the rival negro dancers, Diamond and Pelham, [would] give several of their characteristic dances for a wager of $500" at the Chatham that night for Mrs. Gibbs's benefit.[2] That same day, the *Evening Post* published a retraction under John Diamond's signature:

WHEREAS, some person . . . has caused it to be announced by the editors of various morning papers, [that] my challenge had been accepted, and that I was to dance this evening, on a wager of FIVE HUNDRED DOLLARS, . . . this [is] not a fact. . . . [A]lthough Mr Pelham, as well as others, has talked of putting up the money, he has not dared to do so, and should he or any other person accept my challenge, due notice of that fact will be given to the public.

☞ My money now lies at the North American Hotel, waiting for a customer.[3]

No one stepped forward immediately, giving audiences time to go and see the two dancers separately. Three days later, after a flutter of anticipation had built up, the *Herald* related the "fact" that a match between Diamond and Pelham would take place on Thursday night.[4]

The New Chatham Theatre had opened in February with "a powerful company" in a "light, musical, and intellectual order of performances." Master Diamond joined the force as entr'acte variety. The first week he danced his "celebrated Camptown Hornpipe" and "tallest kind of Virginia breakdowns and Long Island double-shuffles." Then another Broadway Circus dancer was added to the program: twenty-five-year-old Richard Ward Pelham. Diamond challenged Pelham to put up his money that same day.[5]

Everyone issued challenges in midcentury America. The speculation and "get ahead" spirit that fueled the nation's expanding market economy instigated competition in almost every realm. Rural and urban inhabitants turned their work into games, holding ploughing matches, yarn-spinning marathons, and newspaper-folding competitions. Duelers published challenges to defend their honor and politicians to call out their opponents on particular issues. Other challenges were simply marketing ploys. The manufacturers of a remedy for "female complaints" advertised their product with a $500 challenge.[6] Entertainers of every ilk made challenges to advertise their talents, publicize their shows, drum up business, and rescue their reputations.

Diamond and Pelham's match received an enthusiastic follow-up report in the *Spirit of the Times:* "On Thursday last, a match for $500 a side (we wish they may get it!) came off between the rival negro dancers, Diamond and Pelham. The house was so crowded at 10 o'clock, that a friend of ours could not obtain sight of the stage. Master Diamond is said to have 'flaxed out' young Pelham, who claims to be 'de mos science nigga!' The tunes 'chawed up' on the occasion, were 'Juba'—'For I'm gwine to the Alabarme'—'Go way, nigga'—'Jimmy, is yer hoe-cake done!'—'Shinbone Alley,' etc., etc."[7]

This brief account communicated much information to the journal's readers. The late start (10:00 p.m.) and packed house indicated that spectators had come to the Chatham from other theaters and dance-houses just for the match. The style of the dancing, as well as the length and structure of the contest, was conveyed in the long list of tunes. Descriptions such as "chawed up" and "flaxed out" evoked the dancing's physicality and the audience's verdict.* The high stakes had promised a top-notch competition, which everyone agreed it was. However, the reporter's caveat "we wish they may get it!" implied that the award had not been presented onstage as advertised.

Diamond's Chatham Theatre match was the first staged challenge dance he performed under Barnum's management. To market his dancer, Barnum threw out the broadest of nets, drawing on every lucrative theater custom, borrowing from other popular entertainments, and stealing advertising ideas. Trials of skill and dancing matches became a pivotal tactic in this campaign. With the help of the popular press, Barnum took that working-class pastime, revised it slightly, and sold it back to "the people" as a commercial spectacle.[8]

To the dancer and his audiences, however, a staged dancing match represented more than a show. It validated their tastes and expertise. Dancing challenges, even faked ones, changed Diamond, often in ways his manager did not welcome and could not control. They connected him to his public, made him friends, and added to his self-importance. The more he danced, the more he comprehended what he wanted to do.

Dancers in the House

Diamond's challenge delivered a boon to the Chatham's owners. Opened in September 1839, the New Chatham Theatre had lost money during its four months in operation. Charles R. Thorne and Thomas Flynn and their wives were comedic actors used to pleasing diverse audiences, so in January, Thorne bought out Flynn's stake and made him stage manager, after which Flynn led the theater to profit by conforming to "the public taste."[9]

Chatham Square was a muddy crossroads lined with wooden sidewalks in February (fig. 3.1). Its storefronts, darkened by canvas awnings, had not been bustling. Nevertheless, the theater boasted "a full and very respectable audience" for the first performance of *Romeo and Juliet* "travestied," after which "Young Diamond astonished the gallery with his double shuffle genius," noted the *Herald*, which also announced his upcoming match.[10] Flynn knew his business: Diamond's dancing was a real pit and gallery magnet.

Filling the New Chatham Theatre was no easy feat. The building's front encompassed 143–149 Chatham Street, and its auditorium was twice the size of the

---

* The term "flaxed out" came from cloth production: the beating of flax plants on the ground to break open the stalks and expose the linen fibers. The preparation of flax for spinning and weaving required rippling (marking or scoring), retting (soaking), grassing (bleaching), breaking, flaying, flogging, and scutching (beating), words also associated with pugilism.

FIGURE 3.1. New Yorkers braved rain, mud, and darkness to attend Master Diamond's dancing match against circus performer Richard W. Pelham at 10:00 p.m. on February 13, 1840, in the New Chatham Theatre. *Chatham Square, New York,* [ca. 1853–1855], daguerreotype, Gilman Collection, gift of the Howard Gilman Foundation, 2005. The Metropolitan Museum of Art, New York.

Franklin's. The pit alone seated seven hundred, with as many as fourteen hundred ticket holders packing the benches for benefits and last-night performances.[11]

Whether they specialized in dramatic or comedic fare, most antebellum theaters admitted anyone who could pay for a ticket. Some theaters sat the various classes in separate parts of the auditorium; others set aside box seats for their more "aristocratic" patrons and mixed the other classes in the rest of the house. The ground-floor pit (called the orchestra today), entered through a basement-level door beside the main entrance, contained long benches rather than fixed individual seats, with standing room on the parquet (wooden floor) at the back. The balconies, reached through the main doors or a side entrance, held benches constructed with backs and divided into "boxes" by boards on each side for comfort and class segregation. In the topmost balcony or "gallery," the benches were simply tiered one above the other. The raised stage gave everyone (except those stuck behind a pillar) a good view (fig. 3.2).[12]

The mostly young men in the pit were an entertainment in themselves, asserting their new political rights by vociferously announcing their opinions, crowding

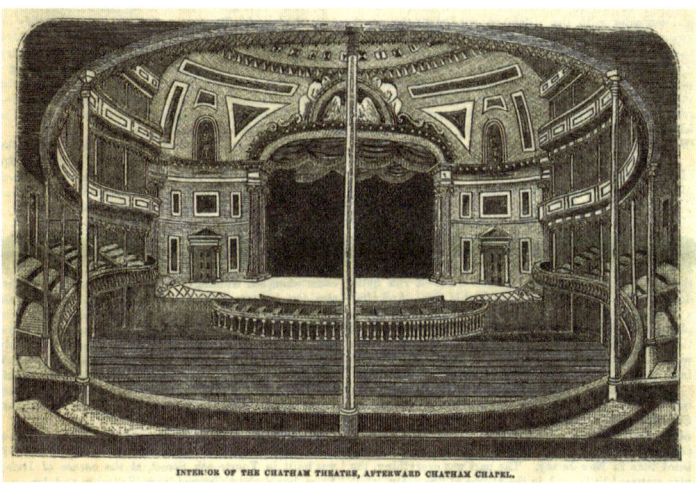

FIGURE 3.2. Almost anyone who could afford to pay attended the theater, but the various classes often sat in separate parts of the house. Sturdier males sat on benches in the pit (the area called the orchestra today). Wealthier spectators sat in the more expensive first and second balconies, where the benches were divided into "boxes" for comfort and segregation. The lower classes occupied the topmost balcony or gallery. *Interior of the Chatham Theater, Afterward Chatham Chapel, New York. From an Original Drawing by A. J. Davis,* H. A. Thomas, Lith., 743 Broadway, New York.

stages, bawling for encores, hissing villains or any actor who caused displeasure, commenting loudly on persons in the boxes, whistling, singing, stamping, applauding uproariously, and scuffling. "Boys in their teens were proud when they grew able to cope with [this] billowing turmoil," according to old-timers.[13]

The attendance of women increased with the number of theaters. To attract middle-class women, some managers devoted their front seats "exclusively to the LADIES" and reduced prices so that working women whose wages were above poverty level could purchase gallery tickets. Others accommodated prostitutes, who attended solo and in groups to solicit clients, by designating an area in the balconies as their province.[14]

The ages of theatergoers also plummeted in the 1840s. Children sat with parents or guardians in every section of the house, but there were no laws or customs keeping minors from entering theaters alone. "Boys of six, eight, ten, and twelve years would get together twelvepence to buy a ticket for the Chatham pit," recalled a New York chief of police a few decades later. Likewise, the Olympic Theatre's pit, once reserved for mature men, overflowed "with newsboys and butcher boys from Fulton Market" on Saturday nights.[15]

Most theaters reserved a place for African American ticket holders. Usually they were sent to the uppermost balcony, although some theaters offered "Colored Boxes" for middle-class patrons, and others allotted the parquet behind the pit to white and Black working-class spectators, sometimes divided by a cordon rope, sometimes not.¹⁶ In slave states, free and enslaved Black people often sat together. When Master Diamond danced in New Orleans and Mobile in 1841, "Free colored People" and "Colored Servants" with "a pass from their owners" were seated on the right-hand side of the theaters' third tier. One Philadelphia theater turned its third tier into a "colored gallery" during the post-1837 recession, but even before that time theatrical companies counted on the patronage of Black theatergoers. "A great proportion of our audience consists of persons of this caste," one manager complained in 1833 after the District of Columbia placed a curfew on African Americans out after nine o'clock, "and they are consequently deterred from giving us that support that they would otherwise do."¹⁷

Flynn agreed to stage Master Diamond's challenge to lure in this democratized audience. "There will be a great anxiety" to witness this "eccentric exhibition," anticipated the *Morning Herald* on February 13. "Those who expect to see this match danced had better apply early or they may meet with disappointment," added the *Post*.¹⁸ These warnings seem to have worked, since the respectable audience that came to the Chatham on Wednesday to see Shakespeare travestied proved a handful compared to the multitude that showed up on Thursday night for Diamond and Pelham's dancing match.

The men, women, and children who packed Diamond's audiences brought their own understanding of jig dancing to the theater. That was why dancing matches worked as moneymakers. They were recognizable, something audience members could assess for themselves. Their appeal stemmed in part from "imaginary participation based on past experience of real practice."¹⁹ Most working people enjoyed the match because they too jig danced competitively. They were not naïve; their experience as spectators and participants gave them the confidence and competence to judge for themselves which dancer was more accomplished and deserved to win. Their acceptance of a staged match as a real competition reveals how working-class audiences and middle-class managers drove the developing cultural economy together.

The list of tunes in the *Spirit of the Times* validated this competency. Those titles communicated rhythms, steps, and styles and informed readers that each competitor had danced for as long as he could (in set-dancing style) while the musician moved from one tune to the next. Urban writer George Foster of the *New-York Daily Tribune* observed this shared knowledge in action at an integrated tavern in Philadelphia in 1848. When the Black fiddler "strikes up 'Cooney in de holler,'" he noted, "the company immediately 'cavorts to places,'" and the dance proceeds in tolerable order for a few minutes. Then the excitement grows, "the dancers contorting their bodies and accelerating their movements" and the fiddler calling out the figures in an effort to be heard.²⁰ Most of the spectators at Diamond's dancing match knew the tunes the reporter listed, the steps that accompanied them, and the thrill of competition. They came to see which dancer, Diamond or Pelham, could take *their* culture to the limit.

The Wager

The young workers who swamped urban theaters viewed every jig, reel, and hornpipe danced on the stage as a kind of challenge. They came to see dancers reputedly better than their local heroes and expected them to prove it.[21] Outstanding dancers responded by inserting difficult and novel steps into their acts: dancing hornpipes in fetters (an act derived from the prison scene in *The Beggar's Opera*), cutting comic parodies of each other, performing "double" and "triple hornpipes" (dancers executing the same steps in perfect synch), and competing in trials of skill. Hornpipe dancers were the first to stage competitions. To attract audiences to his benefit in January 1840, nautical hornpipe dancer James O'Connell published a card in the *Baltimore Sun* informing the public that after playing "a piece dramatized from his LIFE AND ADVENTURES," he would compete with Mr. Riaan (Ryan) "in a MATCH DANCE" (fig. 3.3). In September he danced a trial of skill with James Sanford for Sanford's benefit at Chatham Theatre.[22]

A trial of skill drew a bigger audience than a solo performance, and a wager, which turned a trial of skill into a match, increased that audience even more. Wagers informed the public that the contestants were willing to take a risk to prove their prowess. Spectators gambled at dancing matches too. "Jig dancin' was thought to be a big thing, as it was," explained one aficionado. People bet on "favorite jig-dancers, just as they [did] on favorite horses or walkers."[23] Ads for the Diamond-Pelham match announced that judges would "award the stake to the successful competitor on the stage, and in the presence of the audience" to add credence to the match. Competitions that included wagers demanded a victor be named. Spectators expected or at least wished (like the *Spirit of the Times* reporter) that the dancers, who were working people like themselves, would benefit from the $500 stakes. But the follow-up report only stated that Diamond was "said to have 'flaxed-out'" Pelham, thereby informing readers that the promised adjudicators had not materialized. Letting the audience decide the winner of a dancing match was common practice at the time, but failing to present the money onstage as advertised was a red flag. Nevertheless, the Diamond-Pelham match became the benchmark for future contests.

Diamond and Pelham's match did not fall on either dancer's benefit night. Rather, it began a series of performances designed by Barnum to squeeze as much money out of Diamond's engagement as possible. Diamond danced at the Chatham for another week, during which time he performed in a blackface "divertissement" with Pelham and "Mr. and Mrs. Bennie" for Mrs. Bennie's benefit. His own benefit on February 19 was announced with an "Edict" in the *Morning Herald*: "Know ye that I, Master JOHN DIAMOND, . . . vouchsafe . . . to come the grand double shuffle and breakdown, to the delight of all white folks and the terror of Long Island niggers. . . . I will even condescend to personate a WHITE character, in contrast with

FIGURE 3.3. Diamond was not the first male dancer to compete onstage. To increase ticket sales on his benefit night, Dublin-born dancer-raconteur James F. O'Connell added a trial of skill or match dance to his acts. O'Connell (a.k.a. "the tattooed man of 'the Cannibal Islands'") claimed he was shipwrecked on the Caroline Islands, was captured and tattooed by local natives, and escaped death by dancing hornpipes for his captors. "He displays much agility in his heels—a tattooed diploma on his arms—Irish wit in his head—a rich brogue on his tongue—and relates his wonderful yarns in good nautical style," wrote the admiring *Cleveland Herald & Gazette,* July 7, 1837, 2. From *The Life and Adventures of James F. O'Connell, the Tattooed Man* (W. Applegate, Printer, 1845), 31.

Mr. Lee, . . . who has come on from New Orleans for the especial purpose of coming to time in DINAH CROW," a popular blackface female character. That night, Diamond sparred again with Pelham, "not to decide a wager, but to submit it to the audience, which of the two can come it the strongest in the smoke house dance, Virginia break down, Long Island double-shuffle, or the Camptown hornpipe."[24] This successful triune of dancing match, Black and white benefit-night extravaganza, and nonwagered trial of skill proved so successful that Barnum repeated it wherever he could find a local opponent for his dancer.

* * *

Diamond's second dancing match bailed out the manager of Philadelphia's Walnut Street Theatre. English comedic actor Francis Courtney Wemyss had settled in Philadelphia in 1822; organized his own company, which was split equally between men and women; and leased the theater at 829–833 Walnut Street. During Andrew Jackson's presidency, a period of intense nationalism, Wemyss turned the Walnut Street Theatre into a performance of Americanness. He decorated the auditorium with patriotic paintings and medallions and commissioned a giant wooden eagle—eighteen feet wide and six feet high, clutching a ribbon that read Walnut Street in its talons—to be placed at the top of the proscenium arch in honor of Washington's birthday in 1835. Charles Durang, son of Philadelphia dancer John Durang, recalled the scene that day: "From the shop in Kensington, where it was carved, to the Walnut Street Theatre, it was carried in a large wagon drawn by six horses, preceded by a band of music, with a large 'star-spangled banner' flying over it, with about a thousand persons of all ages and conditions following."[25] Wemyss filled the playhouse with native talent, from the artists and mechanics who created his scenic backdrops and ingenious stage mechanisms to the writers and performers of the plays. His policy was to debut a new show every Saturday night, a strategy that usually ensured one full house a week but kept his company incessantly rehearsing.[26]

Nevertheless, the Walnut Street / American Theatre (the names were used interchangeably) was suffering in 1840 due to ticket price increases (demanded by stockholders to discourage rowdy patrons), which lowered attendance; melodramatic spectaculars, which raised costs; and a nationwide recession. In late January, Wemyss was allowed to restore the original ticket prices (boxes, fifty cents; pit, twenty-five cents), but it was too late. "On the 3 of February, I announced a return to the good old prices, and a new piece," he later wrote, but "all would not do." Even with beautiful scenery and costumes, the play failed, "the first night yielding only 277 dollars." Wemyss blamed the failure on his pit customers, who "were too justly offended to forgive the past, and left me to extricate myself"—a difficult prospect, as pit receipts accounted for almost half his nightly income.[27] This situation convinced Wemyss to engage Master Diamond.

Barnum's Philadelphia campaign began almost immediately. On February 27, two nights after checking into Harbach's Hotel, Diamond danced to an almost empty house at the Walnut, returning on the 29th to join Miss Lee, Master Reed, and other volunteer dancers at Mrs. Sefton's benefit. That same day, a card published under James Sanford's signature appeared in the *Public Ledger:* "CHALLENGE ACCEPTED!! MASTER DIAMOND having challenged any Man or Boy in America, in the sum of $200 to $500, for a trial of skill at *Negro Dancing,* in all its varieties, I have accepted the Challenge, and put up $250 against the same amount staked by Master Diamond." Sanford also laid down his terms: "The match, which will consist of a variety of BREAKDOWNS, JIGS, REELS, &c, will come off at the *Walnut St. Theatre,* on MONDAY EVENING next. Judges will be chosen and sworn, and give their verdict from the Stage."[28] Barnum had arranged another match.

* * *

The scene outside Walnut Street Theatre on March 2, 1840, was anything but orderly (fig. 3.4). Unable to get in, a boisterous crowd blocked the wide sidewalk and spilled onto the cobblestones down Walnut Street and around the corner on Ninth. It probably included knots of tough-looking youths making bets and predictions under the overhanging lamps or leaning against a wall near the front steps, intent on begging "checks" or tickets from people departing early. The overflowing house, the first in months, did not just benefit the theater's manager. A little fruit stand under an awning at the end of the building would also have done a brisk business that night. Shouting and laughing probably wafted from the licensed taverns across the road, and a colored oysterman in coat, cravat, and apron may have parked his barrow at the curb, ready to pry open the purchases of young couples taking the air after the play, their white faces lit by the glow of his candle lamp. The auditorium was already crammed with twice the number of bodies to seats, but no one seemed willing to leave the vicinity. The stage was set for a showdown. The upstart Master Diamond was squaring off with twenty-six-year-old James Sanford, Philadelphia's favorite son.[29]

For a week prior to Diamond's arrival, Sanford, a singer of "Negro" melodies and a dancer, had filled the entr'actes at Walnut Street, priming the stage for the competition to come. He was no stranger to Barnum, who had hired Sanford in 1836 to perform with his one-wagon circus.[30] The extravaganzist had felt no allegiance to his employer, however, and left after a fortnight at Camden, South Carolina, where Barnum also lost one of his musicians, "a Scotchman named Cochran, who was arrested for advising the negro barber who was shaving him to run away to the Free States or to Canada."[31]* In the winter of 1839–1840,

---

* Barnum claimed he donned blackface to fill the vacancy and was mistaken for an African American, implying that his performance was superior to that of his deserters.

FIGURE 3.4. Diamond danced his second theater match against Mr. James Sanford at Philadelphia's Walnut Street / American Theatre in 1840. On the right-hand side of the main entrance the artist has depicted two men descending to a cellar-level door where the pit patrons entered the theater. *Theatre, Walnut Street, Philadelphia,* 1831, etching, Historic American Buildings Survey, Philadelphia, Pennsylvania. Library of Congress Prints and Photographs Division, Washington, DC.

Sanford was performing with banjoist Joel Sweeney at Broadway Circus in New York City, where he probably witnessed Diamond and Pelham's dancing match.[32]

The results of the Diamond-Sanford match appeared in the *Philadelphia Public Ledger* on March 4, two days after the event, in an advertisement for Master Diamond's benefit. "The judges decided that Sanford was the best singer," it said, "but Diamond gave the greatest variety of steps, and therefore won the wager." This split decision, meant to appease Sanford's Philadelphia admirers, would have been unsurprising if the challenge had been between extravaganza performers. After all, Diamond's singing was, in Barnum's words, "quite middling."[33] But this was a dancing match, which explains the "Acknowledgement" under Diamond's signature in the next column: "The judges having decided that I gave the greatest variety of steps, (and the bet having been upon negro DANCING in all its varieties,) Mr. Sandford very honorably gave up the wager to me."[34] It is doubtful that Diamond penned that missive, since an apprenticed dancer would not have received the wager. Its purpose was rather to publicize his benefit.

Gag Bills

The goings-on at the Walnut Street Theatre drew the attention of the Philadelphia-based *Alexander's Weekly Messenger,* which sarcastically praised Wemyss for replacing "legitimate drama" with "the more refined and intellectual amusement of Negro dancing" to up his receipts. "On Monday evening a regular gag bill was issued, stating that a wager would be decided—$500 a side . . . as to which was the best Negro dancer. Who won we have not been informed, but we hear the house was literally crammed—no doubt the only thing that was required."[35] The *Messenger* was certainly correct about that result: "To see Master Diamond and Sanford," recorded Wemyss, "[my pit patrons] honour[ed] me with their presence, to the amount of seven hundred and four tickets, in a house of 740 dollars."[36] The match brought in almost three times as much as the theater had made on its best night for several months.

Barnum did not admit at the time that the wagers he advertised were fakes. However, thirty years later he compared Diamond's matches to a juggling competition Barnum had staged in 1835. To attract customers when the snow was deep and "houses were slim," he added a challenge to the playbill of a juggler he was managing, snaring another juggler, who took the challenge seriously. Barnum privately arranged the whole "business." He paid the opponent $30 to perform the contest (in lieu of the wager of $1,000), contracted with the theater for one-third of the receipts if the contest brought in $400, and announced "a great trial of skill" on posters and through the press.[37]

The *Messenger*'s critic sensed the same business at the Walnut, but he did not deny that a trial of skill had been danced on March 2. What he referred to as a "gag" was the wager. He doubted that either dancer would see that $500, the same suspicion voiced in *Spirit of the Times* about the Diamond-Pelham stakes. Barnum never felt any qualms about presenting "gag bills," he wrote, because "the public appears disposed to be amused even while they are conscious of being deceived." To Barnum, fake wagers were simply part of a business arrangement that put money in his purse.[38] When the house sold out, such arrangements also strengthened his business and personal connections to theater managers and owners. But he didn't fully understand what dancing matches meant to Diamond's audiences.

Wemyss attributed Diamond and Sanford's success to Barnum, who "knows better than any body how to gull the public." But plebeian credulity cannot account for the excitement generated by the match. Promoters are never shy about giving themselves credit for their performers' achievements. Both showmen recognized Diamond's dancing abilities, but neither man felt the need to interrogate the mechanisms of Diamond's popular appeal. Diamond's audiences were not amused while "conscious of being deceived" because they were not deceived. No one questioned whether a trial had been danced, because both dancers were that good. What the press balked at was the fake stakes. Wagers mattered, because everyone knew an apprentice's wages were minuscule at best. Barnum only deceived himself if he thought Diamond and his audience accepted that arrangement, as the dancer's subsequent moves would demonstrate.

68 · RISING FROM THE STREETS

Companionable Rivals

What Diamond gained from his match with Sanford turned out to be more personal than financial. As they rehearsed and performed, the two dancers got to know each other. Despite the ten-year gap in their ages, Sanford became Diamond's friend and ally (fig. 3.5). He also turned Philadelphia into a kind of hometown for the young dancer and a safe place to assess his situation. The veteran dancer had loads of "friends" (what we call fans) in the region, people who bought him drinks at local saloons and returned again and again to see his acts. Prominent among them were "soap-locks" and "minute men," the "regulars" of independent fire engine and hose companies who came to theaters to applaud the "Fireman's Song" and the "Fireman's Trumpet Hornpipe."

Firefighters also became Diamond's loyal supporters. Local and autonomous, hose companies in Northeastern cities reflected the neighborhoods that supplied their rosters. Among the young men who ran with the engines were native-born or ethnic whites and a few African Americans. Unruly, competitive, and proud, firefighters raced through the streets pulling their water pumps for sport and tussled in front of burning buildings to claim the honor of serving the public.[39]

FIGURE 3.5. "With never a hair on his head out of place," James Sanford (Master Diamond's Philadelphia opponent) belonged to the set of rowdy fellows known as "soap-locks." They soaped their hair to give it a sleek appearance, sported a curled lock at each temple, and lounged about the markets, engine houses, and wharves ready to engage in a row. Detail from "Songs of the Virginia Serenaders," Sheet Music—Negro Minstrels. Courtesy of the American Antiquarian Society. Detail from Nicolino Calyo, *The Soap locks,* ca. 1840, gift of the Estate of Paul Mellon, BA 1929, LHDH 1967, Yale University Art Gallery.

They sported ritualized regalia— red button-down shirts, braces, rolled-over socks, and black laced boots. These new "friends" appreciated Diamond's skill and derring-do, and he acknowledged their loyalty in return through style, costume, and repertoire. On March 9 Diamond danced a grand trial of skill with Sanford and "Mr. Hoffman, a Native Fireman."[40] No wager was announced. Pitting a local firefighter against Diamond after a play called *The Philadelphia Fireman* was enough to increase attendance. Their patronage may also have inspired Diamond to add "Durell, a Fireman" to his character dances later that year.

Must Keep Moving Somewhere

Between March and June 1840, Barnum staged Diamond's triumvirate up and down the Eastern Seaboard, hired twenty-six-year-old fiddler and banjoist William M. Whitlock to tour with Diamond, and adjusted his prices to fit his dancer's growing fame.[41] In a letter to Wemyss, Barnum increased the percentage he expected to receive to "1/2 clear" for Diamond's fifth night benefit and one-third for Whitlock's seventh night benefit if they took in less than $250, or one-third for Diamond's and one-fourth for Whitlock's if less than $175. "I name those low amounts for fear of *wet* nights," he explained, clearly anticipating better receipts. "I expect a *Trial of Skill* can also be got up—I have a good *dancer* ready = Terms on that night 1/2 clear if over $300 1/3d if less," but he expected that "there will be $800 or $900 that night." Barnum said nothing about increasing Diamond's cut. He may have given him a bonus for dancing a match, but Barnum and the theater's manager divided the receipts. If the weather "is fair we will get *crowded houses,*" Barnum assured Wemyss. "You know I can effect this if I have a few days to do it in and I will do it." Times were hard, Barnum's wife was pregnant, and Diamond was Barnum's cash cow. "Please answer me immediately," he begged his friend. "If you say *no* I must try the Holiday St. [in Baltimore] or else go to Albany &c. + wait for you   Must keep moving somewhere."[42]

Being a professional dancer, Diamond quickly discovered, entailed one journey after another. In 1840 he danced one night to two-week stretches in New York City, Brooklyn, Albany, Washington, DC, Baltimore, Philadelphia, New Haven, Norwich and Hartford, Connecticut, Providence, Rhode Island, and Boston. He got to those cities in a variety of conveyances. The trip from New York to Philadelphia could be made by ship or inland via some combination of ferry, coach, steamboat, and railroad. In the 1830s, new roads and stagecoach lines (coaches drawn by relays of fresh horses, or "stages," spaced out every forty miles) spread across the Northeastern states. Passenger cars on trains were a less common means of travel. Railway tracks slowly increased from 13 miles in 1830 to about 2,808 miles in 1840 to 9,021 in 1850, but they only connected short distances, since railroad companies used tracks of different gauges. In 1846 the trip between Washington and New York still involved five train changes and one ferry ride.

Steam-powered locomotives were also noisy and dirty, with iron wheels grating and squealing against the rails and showers of ash and cinders from wood-burning engines blowing in through the glassless windows.[43]

Diamond's dancing helped usher in what came to be known as variety theater. In May he and Whitlock joined Mr. W. H. Williams, a comic singer, actor, and storyteller "from the London Theaters," in a "Grand Musical and Comical Olio" at Union Hall in Hartford, Connecticut.[44] The word "olio" (from the Spanish *olla podrida*) meant a miscellany of acts. He also worked again for William Dinneford, who had renamed the Franklin the New Theatre of Mirth and Variety, and William Mitchell, who had been set adrift when the National Theatre burned down in September 1839 but who now managed the Olympic, a small, neatly fitted-up theater on Broadway between Howard and Grand that he called the "house of farce, burlesque, and burlesque ballet opera."[45]

Priced to court the democratic classes, a seat at the Franklin cost "37½ cents, the highest, and 12½, the lowest," recalled a patron in 1848, and "for the same sums one could get excellent seats" at the Olympic, where the price of admission was "50 cents to the first tier, 25 cents to the second and third, and 12½ cents to the pit."[46] "Luckily, the Franklin is well ventilated, and the audience can 'keep cool,'" declared an ad for Diamond's benefit on June 1, which featured two farces, *The Lottery Ticket* and *Paddy O'Rafferty*, and Master Diamond in two new pieces "written expressly" for his genius.[47]

Both of Diamond's acts, for which Barnum said he paid "seven hundred dollars," were burlesques of known events, plays, and actor-dancers. One was "a Ballet Divertisement, entitled Jim Crow and all his Family!" which gave the diminutive dancer a chance to trade on and outshine blackface actor T. D. Rice's famous "Jim Crow" character.[48] In *Negro Plantation*, Diamond played Bob Springheel, a dancing parody of Spring-Heeled Jack, a dark and mysterious cloaked figure who pounced on predominantly female wayfarers in the English countryside. That foreign reference was not lost on Diamond's viewers. In 1838 the *Times* of London had published an anonymous letter describing the attacker as "fleet-footed and, according to rumor, almost superhumanly agile," after which his alleged exploits were circulated internationally in "penny dreadfuls" and low stage dramas.[49]

The other new act was *Manager's Son, Or—The Five Disappointments*, which burlesqued *The Manager's Daughter*, a currently popular afterpiece starring Miss Davenport, the "infant prodigy." Born into an English acting family in 1829, Jean Margaret Davenport began playing "difficult and most arduous parts" at age seven. In 1836 she was cast as the tomboy Little Pickle in the *Spoiled Child* and, after one season, graduated to full-fledged adult roles such as Shylock in *The Merchant of Venice*. *The Manager's Daughter* toured New York, Philadelphia, Boston, and Washington in 1838 and America's Western cities in 1839, where Davenport also played King Richard in Shakespeare's *Richard III*.[50] In publicity and puffs (promotional reviews), she was praised for expressing an emotional depth that belied her years, particularly rage, grief, and despair.[51]

Crossing lines of gender, race, or age gave child performers a chance to demonstrate the breadth of their talents. The androgynous features of girls and boys helped their audiences take their cross-dressed characters more seriously.[52] In fact, young "wench-dancers" (blacked-up boys in female costumes) complained that men often mistook them for girls and waited at stage doors insisting on marrying or purchasing them.[53] Cross-dressed children had an effect on viewers that was different from that of cross-dressed adults. Middle-class audiences thought of children as unselfconscious and sincere performers who made no distinction between performance and play (hence the term "playacting"). They became the make-believe character or person they enacted. This assumption made it easier for audiences to suspend disbelief. Even professional critics took for granted the genuineness of Davenport's emotional depth and Diamond's "Negro dancing," if not the sincerity of the adults who promoted them.[54]

Described as a "protean farce," *The Manager's Daughter* (1837) was a rewrite that had been commissioned for Davenport of the 1827 English farce *Strolling Country Actors; or, The Manager's Son*. Jean played Margaret, the manager's daughter, and her father, Thomas D. Davenport, played Mr. Davenport, Manager of the Theatre Royal. The word "protean" (from the Greek sea god Proteus) was used when an actor assumed a number of characters in one play as evidence of his or her versatility. During this fifteen-minute caper, the "Young Phenomenon" performed five characters in rapid fire. "The assortment of parts ostensibly 'interpreted' by the marvel," carped one critic, were Hector Earsplitter, a growing Yankee; Effie Heatherbloom, a Scottish lassie; Fergus O'Botherwell, an Irish bogtrotter; Paul, the Minstrel Boy from *la grande nation* (France); Sapinella Thespis, an actress of first-rate genius; and, finally, Miss Jean Margaret Davenport as herself, "a young lady nine years of age" (fig. 3.6).[55] These characters showed off Davenport's skill at impersonation in speech, song, and dance. (She danced "Jim Crow" and the "Spanish Fandango" as Hector and a "Scotch dance" as Effie.)

In *The Manager's Son*, Diamond played John or Jack Dumpy, the manager's son, a local actor filled the manager's role, and Davenport's five "interpretations" became "The Five Disappointments": "Sawney Mc Taelight, Simon Suckegg, Durell, a Fireman, Paddy Falreedy, and Mad'lle Pirouette."[56]* These ethnic character roles gave Diamond the opportunity to exhibit his skill at dancing the Highland fling, the "Fools Dance," the "Fireman's Trumpet Hornpipe," and an Irish jig. He also challenged Europe's four most famous ballerinas: "DIAMOND as the *French*

---

* Simon Suckegg (from Simple Simon), who swaps his wife for a duck egg in folktales, replaced Davenport's Yankee character Hector, and Mad'lle Pirouette replaced Davenport's French character Paul, the Minstrel Boy.

FIGURE 3.6. Thomas D. Davenport's management of his daughter Jean Margaret's early career set a precedent for P. T. Barnum's management of Diamond. The inspiration for Master Diamond's "new piece entitled MANAGER'S SON Or—The Five Disappointments" was Miss Davenport's "protean farce" *The Manager's Daughter*. Diamond danced parodies of the seven female and male characters played by Davenport, one of which was herself. *MISS DAVENPORT of the THEATRE ROYAL HAYMARKET, only 10 Years of age. As the SEVEN CHARACTERS in the MANAGER'S DAUGHTER, performed by her with extraordinary success,* by Pierce James Eagan, hand-colored etching, ca. 1840, Macdonnell Collection. National Portrait Gallery, London.

Danseuse, in which he will utterly extinguish Taglioni, Augusta and Celeste, and throw the admired FANNY ELSSLER Totally, entirely, and forever in the shade."[57] And like Davenport, for his grand finale Diamond played himself: "*DIAMOND* in the *Negro Camptown Hornpipe, Ole Wirginny Breakdown, Smoke-House Dance, and Five Miles out of Town Dance.*" Managers such as Barnum learned what worked from actors such as the Davenports, and dancers such as Diamond learned some tricks as well. Imitating oneself after imitating one's rivals would become a favorite device of champion jig dancers.

Casting Diamond in *The Manager's Son* was only one of the ways that Barnum imitated Thomas Davenport's managing style. T.D. was P.T.'s role model. He was also, reputedly, the model for Vincent Crummels, the theater company manager in Charles Dickens's *Nicholas Nickleby,* published serially in England and pirated in the United States between 1838 and 1839. A skilled manipulator, Davenport supposedly stationed men in different parts of the house to call for Jean between the acts and at the end of the play, "until the audience, not being acquainted with the trick of the trade, imagine her acting must be something extraordinary."[58] In 1838, when she was nine years old, Jean performed a monologue called "Child of Nature! Or, Sketches from the Life of and by Miss Davenport," which illustrated the course of her career up to that point. How interesting her two years of experience might have been only her audiences knew, as no written copy has survived.[59] Never a man to miss a trick, on March 1, the day after Diamond's match with Sanford, Barnum published "MEMOIR of the 'Phenonomy'—MASTER DIAMOND, the unrivalled 'negro dancer,' with a correct *Likeness* of him in his celebrated dance, 'the Wirginy Breakdown'" in Philadelphia's *Daily Evening Mail*. Again, no copy has survived. Theater critic T. Allston Brown later commented that, "having an eye to business, [Barnum] conceived the idea (i.e. gag) to write a life of Master Diamond. A greater amount of nonsense is seldom if ever put together—*but it took!* Barnum reaped a harvest."[60] What Brown failed to mention is that Barnum stole the idea from Davenport, whom the "master of humbug" expected to surpass with his own "Young Phenomenon."

These new acts increased Diamond's time onstage and in rehearsal, but not his salary. His offstage movements also intensified. Barnum booked Diamond at Boston's National Theatre on June 3, which meant he had to depart the morning after his June 1 benefit. The trip from New York City to Boston took at least a day and a half, no matter how you got there. The cheapest route entailed taking a steamboat to Providence (twenty-three hours), where stagecoaches waited to carry you the remaining fifty miles to Boston. That trip took from five to ten hours, depending on weather, toll houses, gates, and stops to change horses. Diamond and Whitlock's trip probably took closer to ten, since it had rained the night before, and drivers sometimes asked the passengers to get down and walk when the horses' hooves fought for purchase on steep and muddy hills. Boys Diamond's age usually rode on top, in imminent hazard of being jerked off as the coach lurched behind the jangling team. But if it was particularly wet and cold, he may have ridden inside, where it reeked of mildew, the dirty straw covering the floorboards, and that wet-sheep aroma emanating from sodden woolens.

If all went well, our travelers would arrive in Boston in time to check into their hotel, take some repast, and make their way to the theater. Along that route, they would have passed a great many playbills slapped onto brick walls and wooden fences announcing Master Diamond's acts in enormous letters and everything else in very small ones.

Diamond's two-week stay at the National Theatre followed the usual routine. He performed all of his new dances and plays and on June 5 challenged "any man in the United States to compete with him in Negro Dancing" for $500: "NOW

NIGGERS TOE DE MARK. And the juvenile will prove that he is the *KING OF DIAMONDS.*"[61] "Toe the mark" was a boxing phrase that referred to a line scratched in the dirt to divide the ring. At the beginning of each round, the fighters were required to put their toes up against the line—to come up to scratch or to the mark—to prove they were fit enough for the bout.[62] That familiar challenge targeted Boston's racially integrated sporting community, as did the shout-out to "any man" able to match the $500 wager. John Smith's pupil Master Coleman, touted as Diamond's equal by some of the Northern papers, was in Boston with Welch, Bartlett and Company's circus that week.[63] But no one seems to have stepped forward.

Disgruntled Apprentice

After Boston, Barnum sent Diamond and Whitlock to Washington, DC, for one week, then up to Philadelphia to perform at M'Arann's Garden. They opened on June 22, Miss Emma Ince's benefit night, in a program billed as "the greatest combination of talent that has ever yet appeared for twenty-five cents." The performance in the garden's sunken open-air amphitheater began at eight o'clock with "a grand concert." Emma and Fanny Ince danced "the most beautiful steps and figures" at nine, followed by an array of vocal and other acts, including Master Diamond and Mr. Whitlock at ten, and finally a fireworks demonstration of the eruption of Mount Vesuvius.[64]

Diamond and Whitlock were to perform at M'Arann's Garden "for five nights only, previous to their going to Canada." But the dancer had other plans. After the show on Saturday, June 27, Diamond met his friends James Sanford and Dick Carlisle outside the gate at M'Arann's Garden, where they were approached by "the delegates of his master." Assuming that Diamond was running away, Barnum's men grabbed hold of him, and "quite a rumpus ensued." Everyone pushed and shoved and pulled Diamond this way and that, so that "between them the lad was in a fair way of being torn to pieces," reported the *Public Ledger*. The scuffle continued all the way to Chestnut and Seventh Streets, where, to avoid being taken by Barnum's men, the dancer "placed himself under the protection of the watchman."[65]

Diamond probably regarded "Captain Stewart of the watch" as his ally. Ordinarily, city watchmen did not break up fights. Most of them were laborers moonlighting for extra cash and not part of a professional police force. Only a small number of men had full-time employment as police or watch officers. Stationed at sentry posts every few blocks, the watchmen's job was to look out for fires and discourage robberies and other petty crimes by their presence.[66]

Captain Stewart took Diamond into custody until the courthouse opened on Monday morning. According to the *Ledger,* the "celebrated Lilliputian imitator of negro dancing" was difficult to see amid "a vast and many colored array" of disheartened "spirits" standing in the dock. Twenty-seven cases of drunk and disorderly conduct were "disposed of" before Diamond pleaded his case to the recorder. "[He] has not been very well treated by the person to whom he is indentured, a Mr. Barnum, of New York," noted the reporter, and would like to end ties with his master. "The master appeared both personally and by his counsel, Samuel H. Perkins, Esq.," added the *Ledger,* "and Col. James Page appeared for the boy and his friends."[67]

After hearing Page's statement on the matter, "the Recorder dismissed the boy, as not having jurisdiction" to plead his case, then immediately arrested Diamond as an "absconding apprentice" on a warrant issued by Alderman Joel Cook. Sanford and Carlisle were also arrested "for attempting to seduce Master Diamond from his legal protector and guardian." New York's *Evening Post* claimed that to ensure their appearance on Tuesday afternoon at two o'clock, a bail of $5,000 each was set, "in default of which, they must remain in prison till the sitting of the Court in November next. Diamond in the mean time remains in Philadelphia a few days, awaiting the settlement of a legal point."[68]

The class and ethnic background of the counsel for Diamond's trial may have helped the dancer. Barnum's lawyer, Samuel H. Perkins, was a Scottish Presbyterian and member of the St. Andrew's Society of Philadelphia. Diamond's counsel, Colonel Page, was a member of the State Fencibles, a local militia company of mainly Irish and Scottish descent. Page also defended Sanford and Carlyle, who were charged with beginning the ruckus. Alderman Joel Cook, who represented Philadelphia's Thirteenth Ward, was a grocer by trade. The legal point they were to decide was whether or not Diamond was bound to Barnum while in Pennsylvania. On Thursday, July 9, Alderman Cook dropped the case against Sanford and Carlisle. He then discharged Diamond, reported the Philadelphia papers, the grounds being that "the indentures by which Barnum claimed him were not binding in this State" and because Barnum's prosecutors did not appear.[69]

Temporarily free, Diamond stayed in Philadelphia, kicking up his heels with Sanford in a double "Camp Town Hornpipe" and "Grape Vine Twist" at the Walnut Street Theater.[70] Meanwhile, up in New York, Barnum sought advice on how to get him back. Until then, he would need to find a dancer capable of filling Diamond's shoes at his new venue: Vauxhall Gardens. The dancer Barnum hired was Juba.

4

MASTER RATTLER

In June 1840 P. T. Barnum rented the saloon at Vauxhall Gardens in New York from Bradford Jones, a caterer known for his punches and ice creams. Jones's headliner at that time was Miss S. G. Shore, the Albino Lady, "a Natural Curiosity, unprecedented in America," who sang airs accompanied by the Tyrolean Brothers. They performed three nights and then the saloon went dark, reopening on June 25 under Barnum's management. The pleasure garden met Barnum's entrepreneurial aspiration to find a respectable venue that appealed to a popular audience. With the leasing of the saloon, Barnum took on the role of "public man." No longer would he keep his name out of the transaction. He was now "director of amusements," with the entertainments entirely under his control. He called his program "CONCERT AND DANCES!" and envisioned Master Diamond as its star. But in mid-July, the independence-seeking dancer was still in Philadelphia, so Barnum returned to the market district and dance-houses to search for a replacement. The dancer he found was a ten-year-old African American named William Henry Lane.[1]

Dancing on the Edge of Town

Situated between Fourth and Sixth Streets, Vauxhall Gardens was only a mile uptown from Lane's neighborhood in the teeming Sixth Ward, yet it seemed a world away. Horse-drawn omnibuses traveled up and down Broadway, but they did not always allow Black people on board. Some African Americans rode up to Lafayette Place on the outside platforms of the Harlem Railroad cars, rain or shine, paying full price for the privilege. It all depended on the whim of the conductor. Lane and his mother likely caught a ride with an accommodating stage or cart driver on the Bowery or, like most working people, they just walked (fig. 4.1).[2]

FIGURE 4.1. All professional dancers lived peripatetic lives in the 1840s, but free African American dancers faced more obstacles in Northern cities. Because many drivers of horse-drawn streetcars or omnibuses on Broadway in New York did not allow Blacks onboard, Master Rattler either walked uptown to work at Vauxhall Gardens or caught a ride with an accommodating stage driver or cartman on the Bowery. *Old Storehouses Cor. of Pearl & Chatham St. 1861*, Miriam and Ira D. Wallach Division of Art, Prints and Photographs: Print Collection. New York Public Library.

As Lane headed uptown, his surroundings opened out from dusty lanes flanked by dilapidated buildings into wide crosshatched streets lined with fine houses. Here pedestrians paraded in multicolored dress—ladies with parasols and fluttering ribbons, young gentlemen with their collars turned down, Irish laborers in blousy work smocks, Black coachmen in double-tailed coats, and barefooted newsboys with blooming cravats.[3]

The cellars and parlors Lane had danced in so far were mainly patronized by African Americans. This new place, Vauxhall Gardens, attracted whites. The Bowery-facing buildings fronted gardens where people went to promenade. If you stood across the street, you could see the tops of the trees behind the wooden fence surrounding the grounds. That fence had made the place exclusive twenty years ago. Now even soap locks and servant girls went there to strut around, sample the shows, and dance under the sky, trying on their American freedom.

The saloon's manager had given Lane a trial run at the benefits of an English singer, American dancer, and "Italian" puppeteer, then slotted him into the regular program. This "array of talent defies all competition!!" claimed the saloon's ads.

The boy was touted as a prodigy (always a good draw) on the bills and identified as the "rival of Master Diamond" (another good draw), but he actually filled a vacancy left by "the charming dancer" Miss Mary Ann Lee, who had moved over to one of the theaters.[4]

The performers Lane worked with surely knew he was Black, but it's not clear how many in the audience could tell. Jig dancers blacked-up and used stage names, and the saloon was dimly lit. Racial ambiguity provided Lane a safeguard against white audiences who might be angered by his superior performance. Dancing in a cellar tavern was less remunerative than dancing at Vauxhall Gardens, but it was safer.

A white employer such as Barnum had little problem proposing terms that surpassed those offered to most African American children. Steady work and pay, even if low, looked pretty good to street or tavern dancers working for tips. It also stood in stark contrast to the exploitation experienced by enslaved dancers forced to perform for no income at all. Lane and his parents would have accepted Barnum's offer because it provided better money and greater autonomy than other forms of labor open to him.

Few details about Lane's early life remain beyond the general circumstances that might have impelled him to work for Barnum. Lane belonged to a free Black urban workforce that relied on networks of family, neighbors, and friends for survival. The employments open to adult Northerners dwindled after emancipation. In the early 1800s, New York census takers recorded Black men working as artisans, carpenters, barbers, masons, shoemakers, coachmen, and at other skilled trades. (Black women's trades and employments were not yet recorded.)[5] But after 1827, white competition and assumptions about African Americans' "place" compelled the majority of men and women into occupations with little chance for advancement—day laborers, servants, and similar menial manual jobs. Physical labor rarely paid well, while service work ranged from the lowest-paid household and boardinghouse domestics to better-remunerated coffeehouse waiters and bartenders to the highest-paid hotel and ship stewards.[6]

Dancers and dancing teachers might have been counted as skilled laborers or as service workers, since their work was physical and carried out in homes or tavern dance-houses. But they also fit professional and entrepreneurial categories. The number of free Black people engaged in upper-end professional artistic, educational, clerical, and scientific occupations was even more limited by racist attitudes than in the artisanal trades, as well as by closed educational institutions. Few middle-class whites hired Black physicians, midwives, teachers, ministers, or clerks, which meant that most professionals dispensed their services on a fee basis to the most economically deprived portion of the urban population. Musicians accounted for almost one-quarter of Black professionals in cities outside of slave states, and master dancers who worked alongside them may have shared their professional status (fig. 4.2).⁷ A few who were hired by both white and Black patrons, such as the famous Philadelphia band leader Francis "Frank" Johnson, did relatively well economically.

The success of Black entrepreneurs also depended largely on an African American clientele. The larger and more diverse the Black population in a city, the

FIGURE 4.2. Professional musician, composer, and band leader Francis Johnson amassed many elite white patrons. Ann Rush, daughter-in-law of patriot doctor Benjamin Rush, inscribed the flyleaf of her music composition book with the phrase "Presented to Mrs. A. Rush by Frank Johnson, a Black musician of our Balls and Parties, in 1820," suggesting that Johnson gave music lessons as well. "Francis Johnson" (1792–1844), watercolor, Joseph Muller collection of music and other portraits. New York Public Library.

greater the number who engaged in activities classifiable as entrepreneurial or mercantile. Both men and women ran dry goods stores, taverns, boardinghouses, restaurants, brothels, and even a few pleasure gardens and theaters. Black dancers worked for these establishments as professionals but were also small-scale entrepreneurs themselves. Every city's mercantile class included such marginal self-employed operators as clothes washers; seamstresses; cart drivers; scavengers; peddlers of coffee, food, and small wares; and street performers.[8] The boys and girls who danced for eels, coins, and catfish fell into this category.

Child labor was integral to the survival of most free Black families. Parents with irregular low-paying employment depended on their children to provide much-needed additional funds. Black children worked in the most dangerous urban occupations, such as chimney sweep and street trader, which entailed hawking newspapers, shining shoes, and performing acrobatics, music, and dance in public places. Even very young children earned pennies fetching and carrying, delivering messages, and helping out in other ways. Many children between the ages of ten and fifteen did not even live with their families, whose survival depended on finding them paid indentures or unpaid boarding situations.[9] But that was not the case for Lane. Barnum may have managed Lane's dancing career in the summers of 1840 and 1841, but he did not indenture the boy. His mother, Margaret Reed, and stepfather, Zachary Reed, probably relied on their employed son's contribution to the family income.

Most African American dancers depended on jobs provided by Black employers and only occasionally crossed over into white venues. Like other entertainment occupations, jig dancing was intermittent work, and the number of people who claimed it as a full-time occupation was never large. About thirty white and ten Black men and boys show up in advertisements between 1840 and 1860, while travelogues and stories suggest that a much larger number worked in unadvertised places. The earnings of young dancers fluctuated, depending on the occupational category they were put into by the person paying them. A Black freelance dancer such as Lane might have earned more than a white indentured dancer of the same age such as Diamond. However, it is doubtful that Barnum paid any of his employees well, as profit was his primary goal.[10]

The actual number of African Americans who worked as professional dancers is hidden from historical view. They belonged to a shadow economy that figured into the formal economy and labor market but was rarely recorded in public records.[11] Dancing was not a job listed in censuses, nor were many types of children's work counted. Black-run venues almost never advertised, and white proprietors rarely broadcast the race of their performers. People kept on the bottom rung of the social ladder, whether successful or barely scraping by, risked verbal and physical assault and arrest for real or trumped-up crimes at any time. Northern

Black people with visible jobs were also vulnerable to slave catchers, who had no qualms about kidnapping free people and selling them down south. In this treacherous geography, blacking up provided Black dancers with an ambivalent disguise. Early blackface characters, from "dusky" South American Jacardos to "sooty" Ethiopian Sals, reflected the diasporic roots of America's Black population while at the same time covering up the many shades of African American experience.

Pleasure Gardens

New York's Vauxhall Gardens might seem an unlikely place for Lane's introduction to the stage. The first pleasure gardens in America, established in the late eighteenth century, sought to combine European gentility and sophistication with American ingenuity and republican principles. Several early proprietors called their gardens "Vauxhall" after London's Vauxhall Gardens. New York's Vauxhall took its design from London's eponymous resort as well. Its grounds, encompassing all of Lafayette Place (from Fourth to Eighth Streets between the Bowery and Broadway), were entered on Bowery Street through the saloon (a large and lavish barroom) or the circus (a round or oblong building containing an arena surrounded by tiered seats) (fig. 4.3).[12] The extensive plot of land was "tastefully laid out in garden walks, shaded by a fine growth of forest trees," like a grand country estate. The "pleasant and airy" saloon theater was cleverly designed with walls that opened on both sides, offering cross-ventilation on hot nights, and according to Vauxhall's ads, there would be "no postponement on account of the weather, as the Saloon can be closed at a moment's notice." On pleasant evenings, auditors passed from the saloon to the garden during intermission, "where a brass band made metallic the night air," partook in refreshments "of every variety and of the best quality," and walked on winding paths through "a beautiful grove interspersed with blooming plants and luxuriant shrubbery."[13]

Originally located outside the city limits yet close enough to be accessible, pleasure gardens offered urban dwellers an escape from the noise, dirt, and sweltering heat of summer and a cool and spacious alternative to more distant waterside resorts. However, by 1840 America's rapidly growing cities had engulfed most pleasure gardens, making city center gardens more common than the rural variety.[14] M'Arann's Garden in Philadelphia, from which Diamond absconded in June 1840, was established as a botanical garden in 1823 and relaunched as a city pleasure garden in 1839.[15]

At 408 Bowery, Vauxhall Gardens was well within New York City's boundaries in 1840 yet quite a ways uptown. This distance inconvenienced patrons on foot, but it also gave the venue some cachet. "Stages and Cars pass the Garden and

FIGURE 4.3. Lane danced for Barnum in the saloon theater at New York's Vauxhall Gardens under the stage name Master Rattler. Pleasure gardens were city gardens that also served as entertainment venues. Vauxhall's saloon theater had slatted windows that opened on both sides, offering cross-ventilation on hot nights and easy closing when it rained. On pleasant nights, saloon patrons entered the garden during intermission to walk on winding paths, buy refreshments, and enjoy a brass band. Anonymous, *Vauxhall Gardens and Theatre, and Cook's Circus, Bowery, New York, 1835*. Prints (visual works) of New York City Theatres, TCS 54, Harvard Theatre Collection, Houghton Library, Harvard University.

will be in waiting at the close of the Performances," Barnum informed his public. Other pleasure gardens advertised their proximity to public conveyances as well, thereby assuring would-be patrons of their modishness and accessibility.[16]

We can imagine Diamond dancing at one of these places, but Lane? Initially, racial segregation was not a given at pleasure gardens. In the early 1800s, anyone who could pay for a ticket was admitted so long as they were decently dressed, and even those who could not pay were admitted to the gardens when no entertainments were scheduled. In a few years, proprietors began requiring everyone to purchase a ticket for two shillings (twenty-five cents) before entering, redeemable for refreshments up to that amount.

A handful of short-lived resorts catering exclusively to African Americans opened in the 1820s when the main pleasure gardens stopped admitting them.[17] Cities in free states with relatively large Black populations attracted other free people and escaped slaves, creating economically diverse and socially stratified communities that provided work and audiences for African American performers. To satisfy a desire shared by New York's fashionable free Black public in 1821, former ship steward William Alexander Brown launched the African Grove in the back garden of his house on Thomas Street (behind the city hospital), just outside the Sixth Ward. Brown charged twenty-five cents admission, gladly paid by other Black society folk looking for a pleasant place to congregate.[18] His patrons strolled through the gardens showing off their fashion and liberty, consuming ice cream and ice punch, listening to vocal and instrumental music, and enjoying the fireworks. "These evening entertainments were not dry affairs," recalled actor Ira Aldridge. "Brandy and gin-toddies, wine-negus, porter and strong ale, with cakes and meats, enabled the audience to gratify several senses and appetites at the same time." To this sensory mix, James Hewlett, "a very fine singer" and thespian, added dramatic readings (fig. 4.4).[19] Brown's success proved that a class of African Americans interested in genteel and intellectual amusements existed in New York.

Other pleasure gardens catering to Black New Yorkers sprang up in subsequent summers. In 1829 the lessee of Military Garden (at the corner of Broadway and Prince Street) changed its name to Haytian Retreat and opened it up to African Americans. These businesses did not go unnoticed by the white public. In a published response to some disapproving person, Military Garden's owner said that he had taken no part in converting his property into "a retreat for colored people."[20] Brown's African Grove also faced opposition. According to one version of the story, local watchmen shut down Brown's garden in September 1821 after his neighbors complained about the noise of his evening serenades. Brown shifted his efforts indoors and opened a theater for African American productions, a timely and possibly planned move that coincided with the end of the summer when most gardens closed and theaters reopened.[21]

Despite efforts to pass them off as elite provinces, pleasure gardens had become decidedly popular venues by 1840. New York's Vauxhall Gardens was "a healthy romping place, [and] as the price of admission was nominal and the charges for refreshments moderate, on fine afternoons and holidays it was crowded with women and children."[22] Americans shared a general belief in social equality for whites, but when traditional class boundaries eroded, a tension developed between notions of egalitarianism and appropriate behavior. The sight of working-class urbanites romping around in their Sunday clothes disturbed the middle-class managers of some pleasure gardens, who resorted to codes of conduct or brought in police to inhibit unruly or inappropriate behavior, vandalism (such as trampling the plants), and pickpocketing. These constraints worked less well than the dividing line of price. Niblo's Garden charged "discriminating" patrons fifty cents to enter its Promenade Saloon. Other places charged a shilling or as little as six and a half cents, inviting in a broader clientele. Under Barnum's proprietorship, entering and rambling around Vauxhall Gardens was free, but admission to the saloon cost twenty-five cents, making it "a favorite resort for the democratic masses."[23]

FIGURE 4.4. In the 1820s New York's Black community was diverse enough to support pleasure gardens and a theater. African American actor James Hewlett gave dramatic readings in both. Here he imitates British Shakespearean Edmund Kean's portrayal of Richard III. "Mr. Hewlett as Richard the third in imitation of Mr. Kean. 'Off with his head so much for Buckingham. I am myself alone.'" TCS 44, Harvard Theatre Collection, Houghton Library, Harvard University.

For many patrons, a pleasure garden's foremost attraction was that it allowed them to be seen and to see others promenading along the paths and byways. For others, it was the shows. Variety bills germinated in pleasure gardens, where amusements ranged from orchestral and band concerts to a jumble of adult and child acts to spectacles such as balloon launches, illuminations, and the firing of signal cannons.[24] At New York's Vauxhall, Lane joined a "combination and succession" of novelty and variety that included singers of "sentimental, comic and negro Songs," dancers, a teller of "droll stories," and a puppeteer. Dancing predominated—"young ladies" performed ballet and "fancy" dances, Mr. and Mrs. Bennie presented "characteristic and splendid" duets, Mr. Brookes imitated danseuses, C. L. Schlim danced Highland flings, and J. L. Garretts and others danced hornpipes. Professor Grobe, "presiding at the piano forte," accompanied them all.[25]

Barnum added Lane to the program on July 18, 1840. He introduced him fictitiously as "the little 'Wirginny Nigger,' only 12 years old, who can out dance the nation, and come some 'Heel and Toe Breakdowns,' that are a caution to all darkies, and no mistake!" On July 20 Lane danced the "Ole Virginny Breakdown" under the provocative stage name "Master Rattler the Rival of Master Diamond." And for his own benefit on July 24, he upped his status to "MASTER RATTLER the successful rival of Master Diamond."[26]

Lane's stage name divulged the dancer's talent but not his family background. It told the public that he was young (Master) and loose-footed (Rattler). In dance, "rattling" referred to a percussive step in which the heel and toe made a quick succession of short, hard sounds.[27] Lane would later call himself Juba, the name of an African American dance probably derived from the Haitian *giouba(e)*, a general term for sacred and secular stepping dances, or from the Ki-Kongo words *zúba* and *nzúba*, meaning "to strike, cudgel, batter" and "dance of the chief (with women)."[28] More significant than these stage names to identifying his race, however, was the fact that Lane's surname never appeared in advertisements, suggesting he or his employers wanted to hide his identity.

Despite the disguising of his name, it is clear that this dancer was Lane. At Vauxhall he danced a variety of "unapproachable" "Negro" jigs, including "A New Medley Breakdown" and "Heel and Toe Dance." He capered through the "Five Mile out of Town Dance" and the "Ole Wirginny Breakdown." And he sang and danced "Negro extravaganzas."[29] But he didn't dance white character dances such as the Irish jig or Highland fling. Rattler may have been adept at those dances as well, but he couldn't dance them, because he was dark-skinned. If a Black dancer performed white character dances, the audience would have perceived them as "Negro" jigs.

Barnum had worked with Black performers before Lane. In 1835 he made quite a good living exhibiting Joyce Heth, an aged raconteur who posed as the enslaved nurse of George Washington. Most African Americans working in white-run pleasure gardens were employed as waiters or gardeners, but individual actors and musicians did appear on evening programs as well. James Hewlett performed songs and monologues at Brooklyn's Military Gardens, resorts in Saratoga Springs, and Albany's Vauxhall in 1825 and 1826.[30] A Black performer's race might be integral to his professional persona, but announcing it in advertisements could attract unwanted public scrutiny. For Barnum, the problem was not that Lane was African American. Barnum hid Lane's name and race so that he could use him as he needed in the future.

Rattler's designation as Diamond's rival signaled to patrons that Vauxhall was open to a little punting. In late July J. L. Garretts, a.k.a. the "Dutchess County Plough Boy," challenged Henry Manning, a local dancing master, to "a trial of skill" in the sailor's hornpipe. "Having observed a remarkable modest 'challenge' in yesterday's Herald, signed Henry Manning, in which he talks about 'Braggers,'" wrote Garretts in a letter to the *Herald* on July 24, " . . . and, believing the challenge was intended for me, although I never made such a boast as he pretends, I stand ready to meet him . . . at any time and place he will name, for the sum of $100. The money is now waiting at the Bar of Vauxhall Gardens, and he can cover it as soon as he dare, or 'draw in his horns.'"[31] Barnum hosted the challenge. The trial was held in the Vauxhall Gardens saloon on July 27 amid a riot of "Hornpipes Dances &c."[32] Manning apparently lost, as he did not appear at Vauxhall Gardens again that summer.

Diamond Returns

Lane danced as Master Rattler at the saloon for two weeks before Barnum was able to retrieve John Diamond. Diamond had challenged his indenture after hearing that his father, who had given Barnum power of attorney over his son, had died, and because Diamond was underage, Barnum had to negotiate a new arrangement with whoever became his guardian. The "Person and Property Guardianship" form filled out by a surrogate of the county of New York on July 29, 1840, had two parts (fig. 4.5). The top half was a petition appeal made by "John Dimond [sic]," an orphan under age eighteen, to have "Joseph W. Harrison, a printer in New York," appointed his guardian and protector of his inherited property and legal rights. While the contract uses the spelling Dimond, the signature, which does not look like it was written by a child, reads "John Diamond." Diamond had no property or estate "to his knowledge or belief." His only inheritance of value was his legs and his talent for dancing, which are the subject of the bottom half of the document, prepared by the commissioner of deeds. In that part a third party (Barnum), acting like an investment broker, contracted with the guardian (Harrison) to invest that property (Diamond), promising a return of $100 a year plus $12 a month. Who chose Harrison to be Diamond's guardian is unclear, but his role was to act in the boy's best interests and make the best bargain he could for him. The contract also bound Diamond to Barnum for three years, with no language stating whether it could be broken or renegotiated once Diamond learned how much money his dancing brought in by way of ticket receipts.[33]

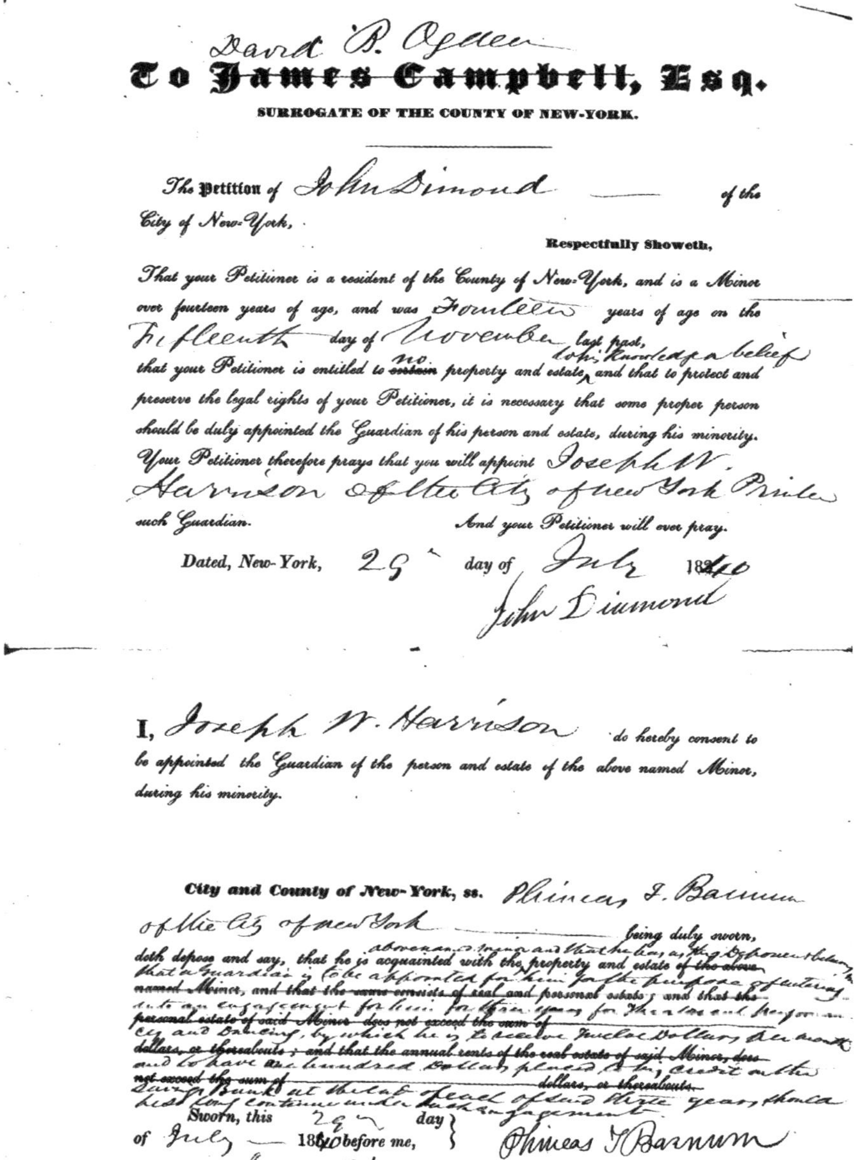

David R. Ogden
To ~~James Campbell~~, Esq.
SURROGATE OF THE COUNTY OF NEW-YORK.

The Petition of John Dimond of the City of New-York,

Respectfully Showeth,

That your Petitioner is a resident of the County of New-York, and is a Minor over fourteen years of age, and was Fourteen years of age on the Fifteenth day of November last past, that your Petitioner is entitled to ~~certain~~ no property and estate, to his knowledge & belief and that to protect and preserve the legal rights of your Petitioner, it is necessary that some proper person should be duly appointed the Guardian of his person and estate, during his minority. Your Petitioner therefore prays that you will appoint Joseph W. Harrison of the City of New York Printer such Guardian.

And your Petitioner will ever pray.

Dated, New-York, 29th day of July 1840

John Diamond

I, Joseph W. Harrison do hereby consent to be appointed the Guardian of the person and estate of the above named Minor, during his minority.

City and County of New-York, ss. Phineas T. Barnum of the City of New York being duly sworn, doth depose and say, that he is acquainted with the ~~property and estate of the above named Minor, and that the same consists of real and personal estate; and that the personal estate of said Minor does not exceed the sum of dollars, or thereabouts; and that the annual rents of the real estate of said Minor, does not exceed the sum of dollars, or thereabouts.~~ abovenamed minor and that he has, as the deponent believes that a Guardian is to be appointed for him for the purpose of entering into an engagement for him for three years for theatrical performances and Dancing, by which he is to receive Twelve Dollars per month and to have one hundred Dollars placed to his credit in the Savings Bank at the end of said three years should he so long continue under such engagement.

Sworn, this 29th day of July 1840 before me,

Phineas T. Barnum

Isaac Fitz
Commr of Deeds

FIGURE 4.5. After Diamond's father died, Barnum legally bound the dancer to himself for three years. Diamond was left no property or estate. His only inheritance of value was his legs and talent for dancing. That property is the subject of the bottom half of this petition. "John Dimond," File# 1840-0001, (Article 17) Person and Property Guardianship Petition, Municipal Archives of New York City.

Barnum held on to Master Rattler after reclaiming Master Diamond as a kind of insurance in case his recalcitrant dancer scarpered again. He also announced that Diamond would only appear for a very limited period "previous to his departure" for London and Europe.[34] That forewarning did portend a journey for Diamond, but not overseas. Like similar notices of pending engagements in foreign parts, its purpose was to induce attendance and, in this case, add legitimacy to an American art form. It also, like Lane's retention, covered the contingency of another Diamond desertion.

The two youths may already have known each other, having grown up in the same neighborhood. But it was their simultaneous employment at Vauxhall that made them partners and rivals in the field of professional jig dancing. "There will be rare sport and a perfect jam at these delightful gardens tonight," declared the *Herald* when Diamond opened at Vauxhall on July 29.[35] Masters Rattler and Diamond did not dance a match at the gardens. Newspaper programs reveal that Diamond danced in the first half of the show and Rattler danced in the second, giving Barnum liberty to employ Diamond elsewhere after nine o'clock and encouraging audiences to stay for both parts.

Barnum billed his new show "Stupendous Attraction" and varied the lineup every night. The performance commenced at eight o'clock with Professor Grobe at the piano. In Part I Dan Gardner sang "Dinah Crow" in women's clothes, presented Master Gardner, "the Wonderful Prodigy, only 5 years of age," in a hornpipe, and did "Gymnastic Feats" with his son. (Dan Gardner's entire family were all-round circus performers.) Master Diamond danced a fireman's hornpipe and an Irish jig. Master Booth told a Yankee story. Miss Clementine danced a "Favorite Hornpipe." Master Diamond laid down his "Five Mile out of town Dance" and "Ole Wirginny Breakdown." And to end the half, Whitlock sang a "Negro Song" and paired with Diamond in a "Banjo Extravaganzical Breakdown." In Part II Mr. Gardner did "Grecian Exercises on the wire volante" and sang a comic song. Mr. Garretts danced a Highland fling. Mr. Brooks imitated three famous danseuses in his "Grand Dwarf Dance." Miss Clementine and Mr. Gardner danced a "Grand Cavatina" duet. And the show concluded with Master Rattler's "Negro Extravaganzas and Breakdowns," accompanied by Whitlock.[36]

Because no rivalry was played up between Rattler and Diamond, Diamond simply took over as featured artist. From July 29 until August 6, his name was printed at the top of Vauxhall's ads in capital letters, and Master Rattler's name was printed lower down in lowercase type. The catchphrase "unrivalled, unequalled and unapproachable . . . Dancer and Delineator of Negro Character" also stressed Diamond's primacy.[37] However, the dances listed in the programs make it clear that Rattler's and Diamond's dancing was pretty near indistinguishable, rendering the two dancers interchangeable. Every other night, when Rattler disappeared from Vauxhall's bills, two Diamonds could be found on New York stages. On those nights, someone billed as "the real Simon Pure" Master Diamond filled Rattler's place in the second part of Vauxhall's program, while another Master Diamond appeared at Chatham Theatre.[38] In other words, when Diamond was dancing at the Chatham, Lane danced as Master Diamond at Vauxhall. This switch did not go unnoticed by everyone in the audience. "Black diamonds, which used to be a term metaphorical, applied to Schuylkill and Virginia coals, has now become a phrase of real import," noted the *New York Evening Tattler*. "The black diamond of the finest water is one now at Vauxhall Gardens—one Master Diamond, usually *white*, but who can be black upon occasion."[39]

Stage names and blackface enabled white and Black dancers of comparable skill, age, and size to impersonate each other. But to do so they had to cork up. The mutability of race in this particular situation did not diminish its power to circumscribe a Black dancer's career.[40] Both Diamond and Lane could pose as Master Diamond, who was Vauxhall's primary ticket seller, but Lane's repertory was limited by his race. At his August 5 benefit, John Diamond danced the sailor's hornpipe "in white character" and five dances "in Negro character," all jigs that required no singing. The next night, Lane danced his "celebrated Negro breakdowns" as Master Rattler, but he did not perform any "white character" dances. After that, Rattler went missing from the bills entirely, while Master Diamond danced simultaneously at Vauxhall and the Chatham.[41] The popularity of jig dancing had increased the number of venues in which a young Black dancer might earn a living, but he could only do so through dances identified as Black.

Diamond's Teacher

In mid-August, changes in Vauxhall's program signaled Barnum's imminent departure. "MISS KEAN, the accomplished Vocalist, from the Southern Theatres" and Mrs. Miller, who sang the "Negro song, Clar de Kitchen," were brought in the week of August 12. The next week a new concluding act was added: a comic ballet performed by Mr. Davis, Miss Clementine (Vauxhall's resident danseuse), and another actor.[42] Black South American thespian Louis Davis varied his line of business (very like that of his white contemporary J. H. Kirby), choreographing, dancing, writing, and acting. At Vauxhall he played mulatto characters such as Jacardo in his own rendition of *L'amour Or, Wine No Poison* with Miss Clementine and Dusty Bob (an English dustman) opposite white circus performer Dan Gardner's African Sal in a *Comic Pas de Deux, from Tom and Jerry*.[43] Davis was never advertised as "late of" some theater, suggesting he worked primarily for circuses, which hired more Black performers than did theaters in the North. His employment at Vauxhall gave Lane a Black colleague to work with and an adult to travel with when he performed shows out of town that September.

As usual, Vauxhall Gardens' late August advertisements made the venture appear a great success. But Barnum, who was losing money, had already decided to abandon it. He held his own benefit on August 24 and had Master Diamond dance at another benefit the next night.[44] Then Barnum relinquished the establishment and removed John Diamond to Philadelphia.

When James W. Bancker, Albany-based circus equestrian, manager, and agent, took over Vauxhall on August 29, 1840, his first action was to announce the return of Master Rattler. "He intends challenging Diamond or any other negro dancer, to dance with him for $500," the *Herald* apprised its readers. "We should like to see the trial between him and Diamond."[45] Bancker had entered the entertainment business in 1824 and comanaged Vauxhall Gardens in 1839.[46] Under his renewed control, Vauxhall's exterior aesthetics continued to attract New York's rising middle classes, while the saloon catered to more plebeian tastes. The dancing was lively, the singing was comic, the ballets were satirical, and the alcohol flowed. Entry into the gardens was still free, and saloon tickets cost twenty-five cents, and Bancker kept the thirty-minute intermission between the vaudevilles for promenading and refreshments. But he added living statues, infant recitations, and more gymnastic feats to the programs. He also rehired Davis, whom he described as very clever "in getting up Ballets and pantomimes." And he gave Master Rattler top billing in capital letters, after which Lane added Diamond's "Camp Town Hornpipe" to his repertory and dubbed himself "the young darkie Rattler, teacher of Diamond, whose Breakdowns can't be beat."[47]

II

CHAMPIONS OF THE WORLD

5

NORTH AND SOUTH

While John Diamond and William Lane were trading turns in the saloon at Vauxhall Gardens, a ballerina performing downtown pulled Master Diamond into the political fray. Sometime after midnight on August 15, 1840, a mob "assembled in front of the American Hotel, in Broadway." Some two hundred people were there to serenade visiting Austrian danseuse Fanny Elssler, and another four or five thousand had come to prevent the serenade. The serenaders—German amateur musicians who had gathered to perform for their countrywoman—were outnumbered twenty to one by the preventers, who at half past one o'clock began driving the musicians from the street, knocking down music stands, smashing instruments, and beating the fallen (fig. 5.1). "The whole affair was disgraceful," reported the *New Era*, "and the getter of it up retired from the field extremely mortified." Then, in a moment of partisan field reporting, that same Locofoco newspaper added: "It is intended, from what we could gather in the crowd, to get up a grand serenade next week in honour of Master Diamond, who evinces more agility of limb than Fanny ever was capable. All we have to say is, to 'tell Chapman to crow.' The Whigs were surely defeated this morning." With that kicker, the writer cast into sharp relief the political nature of dancers and dancing styles.[1]

Twenty-nine-year-old Fanny Elssler had debuted at New York's Park Theatre on May 14 to rave reviews (see fig. 2.4). The daughter of a musician's copyist and valet, Elssler began training for the ballet as a child, gained experience dancing in Vienna, then traveled to Naples, Berlin, London, and Paris, winning international fame and the attention of royalty. Praised for her verve, excellent technique, and sensuality in the cachucha and other character dances, Elssler enjoyed unprecedented success in the United States.[2] For two years, her fans had clamored for tickets, cried during her performances, and purchased Elssler-brand champagne, bread, and cigars. However, within a week of her New York premiere, the press

94 · CHAMPIONS OF THE WORLD

FIGURE 5.1. In August 1840 New York nativists attacked German musicians serenading the Austrian ballerina Fanny Elssler in front of the American Hotel (you can see her in the far left window of the building). Partisan Locofoco newspapers covering the riot pulled dancers into the political fray by aligning Elssler and her German serenaders with the Whigs and Diamond and the antiserenaders with the Democrats. In this cartoon, lithographer, publisher, and caricaturist H. R. Robinson offers a Whig perspective on the event. *Fanny Ellsler's* [sic] *last serenade or the soap-locks disgraceful attack upon the Germans,* printed and published by H. R. Robinson, New York, 1840. Library of Congress.

questioned whether she deserved praise or censure for her "pirouettes and pigeon wings," costumes of "*modest* nakedness," and astronomical fees.[3]

By contrasting Diamond with Elssler, the *New Era* recognized the partisan politics that fueled the "riot and outrage" in front of the American Hotel. Intense political fragmentation characterized the 1830s. An opposition party had formed during the presidency of Democrat Andrew Jackson (1829–1837). Its members called themselves Whigs, the name of England's antimonarchist party, and dubbed Jackson "King Andrew" in response to his unprecedented executive actions. The Democrats derided the Whig Party in return for its devotion to the wealthy via its support for federally funded internal improvements, banks, higher education, and protection for manufacturers. The Democrats prevailed in two elections by increasing white male suffrage and appealing to the interests of native-born and immigrant workingmen. Learning from their losses, the Whigs used similar tactics in the 1840 presidential campaign to unify a coalition of smaller parties behind their candidate, aging Indian Wars veteran William Henry Harrison.

In the *New Era* article, Elssler and her serenaders represented the Whigs, Diamond and the antiserenaders the Democrats. The phrase "tell Chapman to crow" came from a letter written by a Democratic editor in Indianapolis who, despite news that votes were turning to Harrison, advised a colleague to "Crow, Chapman, Crow. We have much to crow over," in other words, to brag that the Democrats were winning and thereby bolster their campaign. After Harrison won the election, the phrase quickly became a political byword for prematurely announcing victory and "Crow, Chapman, Crow" a favorite Whig rallying cry.[4] Reclaiming the Chapman quote from the Whigs, the *New Era* pronounced the riot a victory for the Democrats—or the sorts of Americans who preferred Diamond's native talent over Elssler's foreign airs.

The article's appearance in a Locofoco newspaper also aligned Diamond's dancing with nativist politics. Like the 1840 presidential campaign, the Elssler ruckus took place during an economic depression that undermined the Democrats' power. During the 1830s, two radical factions had emerged within the Democratic Party: a secret society nicknamed the Know-Nothings that was anti-Catholic, anti-Irish, xenophobic, and populist and progressive in its stance on issues of labor rights, government spending, and opposition to slavery; and the Equal Rights Party, nicknamed Locofoco (after the brand of matches used to relight the hall after mainstream Democrats doused the gaslights to end the radicals' first nominating meeting), made up primarily of workingmen and reformers waging war on monopoly and legal privilege. More anticorporate than anti-immigrant, Locofocos formed a party to protest the skyrocketing prices of "Bread, Meat, Rent, and Fuel" and oppose legislation that forced native-born workers to "compete in every way with immense numbers of foreign poor."[5] In Locofoco terms, Diamond's "Negro jigs" belonged to native born workers, and Elssler's imported cachuchas belonged to workers' capitalist exploiters.

Nativism frequently sparked riots and disruptions at antebellum theaters.[6] And the adulation of female dancers inevitably brought out a coalition of finger-waggers. Nevertheless, the *New Era's* approval of the antiserenaders caused a flurry of responses. The *Morning Chronicle,* a British American newspaper, castigated the rioters for their undemocratic behavior toward "inoffensive German citizens,"[7] while the *New-York American,* a Know-Nothing paper, took the opportunity to criticize President Van Buren's immigration policy and New York City authorities' failure to send out watchmen or police to quell the violence. That paper insisted that the riot was the inevitable outcome of misguided Democratic legislation and an inflammatory speech published by "the vagabond *George W. Dixon*" impugning the ballerina's virtue and calling for an old-fashioned "Cherivarie."* Dixon, editor of the *Polyanthus,* was also a well-known buffo singer and "Negro" dancer.[8]

The scene under Elssler's window demonstrated that divisions in American society had politicized dance. What Diamond thought about the use of his name and image is hard to imagine. Was he flattered by this rowdy Democratic embrace or indifferent to politics? And what about Lane, who also danced "Negro jigs" as Master Diamond? Did he think about the irony of the situation, knowing that a Black dancer could not have been serenaded by anyone without causing a riot?

Diamond received his "grand serenade" ten days later, but not in New York. "Fanny Elssler it appears is not the only dancer that has enthusiastic admirers," reported the Philadelphia *Public Ledger*. "On Wednesday night [August 25], a number of the friends of Master Diamond, the 'negro dancer,' made a public demonstration by serenading him at his boarding house. He jumped from bed at the first note of the music, and his heels incontinently struck into the smokehouse dance with variations."[9] Diamond probably arrived in town late that night, flopped onto the boardinghouse mattress, and propped his bootheels on the bedstead. Outside, the intermittent rumble of coach wheels on cobbles mingled with the thin whisper of a familiar tune, just discernible in the distance, that grew louder and more disordered until it reached his building. Then up he bounded to join the charivari. The *Ledger* mentions no party participation, just Diamond's inexpensive lodgings (a far cry from Elssler's big hotel) and enthusiastic response to the serenade, both of which aligned him with working-class politics.

The Camp Town Dancer

The dancer's deeds endeared Diamond to Philadelphians, and he felt comfortable among them. They watched him compete with Sanford in March and followed his court case in June. Since the early 1800s, migrations of rural African Americans and immigrant Irish Catholics had created a city with more economic than racial divisions. These newcomers settled in densely populated alleys and courtyards on the edges of town. By 1840 the majority of free Black and Irish residences were clustered in the districts of Moyamensing and Southwark on Philadelphia's southern border, considered "a second Five Points" by contemporaries familiar with New York's notorious slum, although Black households remained in the Northern Liberties and scattered throughout the city.[10] Francis Courtney Wemyss's American Theatre sat between these districts at Ninth and Walnut Streets.

Diamond expressed his affinity for this community in his signature step, the "Camp Town Hornpipe." Unlike the title "Wirginny Breakdown," which evoked

---

* A charivari was a noisy, discordant serenade performed by a group of people to celebrate a wedding or chastise a reprobate husband, wife, or public official.

a plantation setting, "Camp Town Hornpipe" conjured up a city space. A camp town was a racially diverse city suburb that began as a soldiers' camp during the Revolutionary War. Philadelphia's camp town was situated along the Delaware River in the Northern Liberties, a rough and lively district where ship carpenters from Kensington fought with butchers from Spring Garden on Saturday nights and New Jersey slaves danced against Philadelphia freemen on Sunday mornings. The district's southern border was Callowhill Street (named after William Penn's second wife, Hannah Callowhill), a wide east–west road with seven market houses and numerous fish stalls down the middle and along one side where African Americans competed for catfish in jig-dancing matches.[11]

Contact and familiarity did not mean continuous ethnic harmony. The rising aspirations and upward mobility of Black and immigrant Philadelphians riled up white workers whose own livelihoods were threatened.[12] Forced to accept low wages in highly capitalized enterprises, apprentices and journeymen could no longer look forward to one day owning their own shops. Animosity increased when native-born whites had to compete with Irish and Black workers seeking the same jobs.[13] In 1828 local artisans attacked a group of Irish weavers at a Kensington tavern, and in 1834 and 1835 jobless white workers, complaining that Black workers could find employment when they could not, rioted in African American neighborhoods. However, most of the rioters passed by lower-class areas in order to reach middle-class neighborhoods where Black churches, Masonic halls, and other symbols of economic and social success were concentrated.[14]

In 1840 working-class Philadelphians confronted their oppressors more directly. While Diamond was dancing at the Walnut Street Theatre in March, residents in Kensington and the Northern Liberties reacted against a judicial tribunal that gave a private railroad company permission to lay rails along the street on which they lived and owned property.[15] Stories about men, women, and children carefully replacing cobblestones torn up by railroad workers ran in the *Ledger* alongside Master Diamond's announcements. When he absconded from M'Arann's Garden in June, they were tearing up rails and burning buildings. The debate was still raging in August, when Diamond was serenaded.[16] That serenade may not have been grand, but it was telling. One month later, the *Philadelphia Inquirer*, a paper devoted to maintaining "the rights and liberties of the people" as against the abuse and "usurpation of power," described Diamond as "the Philadelphia negro dancer," claiming him as the city's own.[17]

On the Road

Diamond set out from Philadelphia with a little troupe got up by Barnum in early September. His fellow performers were Yankee character actor Charles Jenkins, Signor Marriotte and his Fantoccini (marionettes), and a fiddler. They headed to upstate New York; took a typical circus route that included Schenectady, Auburn, Troy, and Albany; then followed the Erie Canal to Buffalo.[18] In predominantly Irish Troy, Barnum picked up another jig dancer to pose as Diamond's opponent when needed. Francis Lynch was fourteen years old when his widower father indentured him to Barnum, who called him an "orphan vagabond," a label Lynch resented.[19]

The company's fiddler was most likely Black, as neither Barnum nor the papers that praised his playing gave him a name. Violins were more common than banjos as dance accompaniment in 1840,* and Black fiddlers were favored musicians at country and city dances (fig. 5.2). Playing for dancers was a fiddler's bread and butter. White and Black folk, North and South, hired free and enslaved African Americans to play for dancers in private and public venues. Black fiddlers also advertised themselves as "masters" of music and dance.[20]

Black fiddlers were kept in demand by a good musician's ability to intensify the pleasures of dancing. The old axioms "face the music," "penny a jig," and "pay the piper" reflected that relationship. The fiddler or piper in Ireland expected the dancers to pay him at the end of each set. Musicians and dancers in America maintained that tradition. In the upstairs ballroom of a hotel in Philadelphia's Southwark district, a reporter for the *New-York Daily Tribune* observed this musician-dancer synergy in action. At the climax of the dance, "the black fiddler increases the momentum of his elbow and . . . the dancers, now wild with excitement, leap frantically about [until "at length" the dance concludes]. As soon as the parties recover, the fiddler makes his appearance among them and receives from each gentleman a tip as his proportion of the ceremony of 'facing the music,' and the floor is cleared for a new set."[21] On the road with Barnum, Diamond and Lynch honed their steps to the tunes of the Black fiddler, who revised his own style to fit their Black-Irish jigs.

Barnum's agent and advertiser John Hallett preceded the troupe, making venue arrangements and posting small handbills that included a blank place for the date and place of the performance. Newspaper advertisements, which cost one dollar for a one-inch column in metropolitan areas and less in rural parts, supplemented these posters.[22] Smaller troupes ran ads as close as possible to their arrival. Bigger companies placed notices ten days in advance listing all the dates and places of upcoming performances in the region.

Diamond and his companions "endured the privations, vexations, and uncertainties" of itinerancy.[23] Small companies usually stopped for a day or two at smaller towns in between bigger cities, appearing in village halls, hotel dining rooms, and tavern ball or concert rooms. Such rooms were generally thirty by fifty feet, with a six-foot makeshift stage at one end and chairs or benches set out on the floor.[24] At Schenectady, Barnum rented Union Hall for one night, advertised

---

* Although the same instrument, it was often said that violins sing and fiddles dance.

FIGURE 5.2. The white artist William Sydney Mount captured the respect enjoyed by Black fiddlers in his Long Island community in his painting *Right and Left,* which depicts a young and well-dressed local musician with a jaunty demeanor. William Sidney Mount, *Right and Left,* 1850, oil on canvas, 30 × 25 inches. Courtesy of Long Island Museum.

with a woodcut of Diamond, and reserved front seats for ladies. At Auburn, the troupe played Chendell's Concert Room for two nights. And in Buffalo, they provided entr'acte entertainment at the Eagle Street Theatre for two weeks.[25] Traveling troupes often turned back after reaching Buffalo, although competition in Northeastern cities made moving on the right option for some.[26] In October,

Barnum's little band of performers crossed Lake Erie to play Toronto, Canada, then headed southwest to Delany's Saloon in Springfield, Illinois, where Diamond showed up local fiddle dancers; Detroit's National Theater; and, at the end of November, Chicago's Saloon Building Hall.[27] At that point, Marriotte and his Fantoccini headed back east. Without the puppets, the load lightened considerably: just a banjo, a violin, and a few costumes. The company reached St. Louis in early December, then thinned out again when Jenkins and Lynch snuck away together. Disappearing talent was nothing new to Barnum, who simply boarded a steamer with Diamond and the fiddler (the only two who really mattered) and headed down the Mississippi River, stopping to perform in Vicksburg and send word ahead of Master Diamond's imminent arrival to New Orleans.[28]

Meanwhile, back in St. Louis, Jenkins and Lynch approached the manager of a theater they hoped to rent. He described them in a letter to the theater's owner as an "'all-fired' relator of Yankee Stories" and a dancer "who wishes to *show up* Master Diamond."[29]

Precarious Relationships

As uncertain as life was for Diamond in Barnum's company, Black entertainers such as Lane and Louis Davis encountered more precarious situations. On September 12, 1840, the steamboat *De Witt Clinton* paddled down the Hudson leaving two razor-edge wakes of foam on the river's dark skin. On board were Master Rattler and Louis Davis, returning to New York City after an Albany engagement. They disembarked in the brackish morning air, said their goodbyes, and set out for their separate homes. Two days later, Davis was taken into custody. A deckhand from the *De Witt Clinton* had reported to the police magistrate that "a South American negro, named Louis Davis" had stolen a parcel that a stranger in Albany had entrusted him, the deckhand, to deliver "to one of the City Banks." Taking the white deckhand at his word, Justice Ephraim Stevens ordered Davis's arrest. Two local officers soon returned from the Bowery with Davis in tow; the parcel was not recovered. "The negro was, however, committed in default of bail," reported the *New York Herald* in an article headlined "Somewhat Suspicious."[30] The title suggested that the *Herald's* court reporter considered the deckhand suspiciously well informed about who had stolen a parcel *he* had been charged with delivering. Also suspicious was the imprisonment of Davis when no evidence had been found.

The *New York Daily Express*, which also reported Davis's arrest, identified him as "Lewis Davis 'alias Master Juber, a gentleman ob color'" who is "at present engaged in travelling through the states, dancing negro extravaganzas, breakdowns, &c."[31] That description did not just provide readers with a stage name and occupation for Davis; it also gave the *Express* a pretext for ridicule. The title "Master Juber" classified Davis as a young jig dancer (or juba dancer), while the description "gentleman ob color" indicated he was an adult with African heritage. The contradictory pairing of the respectable title "gentleman" with the dialect pronunciation "ob color" was a common comic device. It suggests the *Express* reporter had some difficulty fitting this educated "South American negro" into his notion of a Black dancer.

While it was not unusual for "travelling" performers, white or Black, to be accused of theft and held in default of bail, coming before Justice Ephraim Stevens boded ill for Davis. Stevens was notorious for perpetrating illegalities while serving as police magistrate and justice for the Court of General Sessions in New York's Eighth Ward. For example, in 1842 he was charged with issuing an unlawful arrest warrant and secretly transporting New York resident Edward Saxton, a supposed fugitive slave, to a Maryland jail without a trial.[32] These activities directly violated a bill passed by New York State's Whig-dominated legislature and signed into law in 1840 by Governor William Seward guaranteeing a trial by jury to persons accused of being fugitive slaves. Known as personal liberty laws, such bills strengthened the legal tools available to abolitionists seeking to protect the rights of African Americans throughout the state.[33] Stevens was also accused of discharging prisoners from the penitentiary on Blackwell's Island and bringing them to New York to vote Locofoco in the spring elections.[34]

Fortunately, Davis was released from custody before he could be spirited away. James W. Bancker may have provided bail or surety for his release. Relationships between white employers and Black performers were not exceptional. They were also not always effective protection. What was amazing was that African American performers who were confronted with defamation, prejudice, and arrest practiced their trades at all. Northerners whose work was public-facing confronted those perils on a daily basis. Even worse, they risked being kidnapped into slavery. The anonymity offered by New York City's large African American community attracted many runaway slaves, whose presence exposed all Black people to unwarranted seizure. Free Northerners were commonly arrested and "hurried into slavery," defying habeas corpus procedure. Bancker, whose base of operation was Albany, may have booked Davis and Lane's upriver engagement, or Davis arranged it as the boy's dancing partner and protector. Either way, Master Rattler had been named in the report of Davis's arrest, making him liable to be set up as well.

Davis resumed his place in Vauxhall's concluding ballet on September 14.[35] While he was away, Dan Gardner had taken his place opposite Miss Clementine, suggesting Davis's absence was expected. He had still been slated for a comic dance in Part I of the program, but his inclusion did not guarantee his presence. Circus managers such as Bancker were used to finding someone to fill in for performers who were out of commission due to an injury, a conflicting engagement, or desertion. The public rarely missed them so long as someone in the company performed the act, dance, or feat advertised on the bill.[36] The itinerancy of theatrical and circus companies made these sorts of exchanges less apparent, just as a garden saloon's dim light made it possible to replace one jig dancer with another.

Louis Davis drops out of the public record the third week in September. It's hard to know why. He might have been released until his trial and, despite the lack of evidence, gone to jail anyway. But that outcome would have been recorded by the press, as it was in 1837 when "James Hewlett, the negro tragedian," was arrested for stealing a watch and sent to prison for two years (then mercilessly jeered at for marrying a white woman he met there).[37] More likely, Davis shifted over to an unadvertised Black-run venue or found some other way to scrape by. He might have left town with a circus. Or maybe, because he'd been targeted, he moved to another city, passed for Spanish, and became someone else.

William Lane's whereabouts, while sporadic, are somewhat easier to follow. He danced "Rail Road Hornpipe" and "A New Medley Breakdown" under the name Master Rattler at Bancker's benefit on September 23, Vauxhall's last performance of the season. Then he too drops out of the public record, temporarily. Perhaps shaken by Davis's sudden reversal of fortune, Lane and his parents decided it was best that he dance closer to home in places where he was known. He probably worked in New York's Five Points district, adding to the family purse and polishing his skills, because he resurfaced the following summer, working again for Barnum, as Vauxhall's lead dancer.

New Orleans Levee, 1841

Diamond, Barnum, and the fiddler arrived in New Orleans by steamboat on January 2, 1841. A city of commerce, opportunity, and oppression, New Orleans would have offered Diamond a confusion of new sights and sounds (fig. 5.3). Steamers and sailing ships lined the levee as far as one could see. Passengers threaded their way through barrels of sugar and molasses, bales of cotton, cartloads of pumpkins, and sacks of grain rolled and carted and stacked into a maze of merchandise higher than the hat on your head. Stevedores shouted and sang in French and Spanish and a strange-sounding English, winched bales onto the decks of outbound ships, and relieved holds of crates of liquor and fine china from Europe and England and barrels of silks and calico from China and the Northern states. Amid these doings, small clutches of white men stood talking, relaxed, hands in pockets. Colored women in patterned headscarves sat beside baskets of fruit, or loaves of bread and cakes under fringed napkins. Black men and boys in brimmed straw hats prodded recalcitrant mules, lounged atop grain sacks, or sat dangling their legs; others gathered in wide passages bareheaded and in stocking caps, lifting knees, throwing up arms, clicking heels, or leaning forward, patting thighs, looking on, calling out, nodding, nudging, pointing. Dancing.

NORTH AND SOUTH · 103

FIGURE 5.3. Work and dance took place on the New Orleans levee, where Diamond paid African American locals to teach him their steps. *The New Orleans Levee in the late 1850's* in Herbert Asbury, *Sucker's Progress: An Informal History of Gambling in America from the Colonies to Canfield* (Dodd, Mead, 1938), 198.

Straight ahead lay St. Louis Cathedral and the Cabildo, bordered by gardens, courtyards, and boardwalks, where light-skinned girls skipped rope, their long, dark plaits bouncing on their backs; kneeling boys played at marbles, jabbering away in French; dark-skinned girls in calico shifts traded fancy breakdown steps; and Dutch nurses sat in groups beside their little charges.[38] In the streets beyond, sharp smells—cooking spices, boiling fat, tobacco smoke—exuded from shuttered doors, while music—guitar chords, voices, laughter—wafted down from wrought-iron balconies. Above that area lay the "slave-pens." Due to various colonizations, 1840s New Orleans had a racially diverse population with peculiar hierarchies often based on skin color. At slave auctions, lighter-skinned mulattoes were displayed in fancy dress outside market houses, while deeply colored field workers—scarred men, weary women, and children far younger than Diamond—waited in walled-in yards to be prodded and sold to the highest bidder.[39]

After 1812, steamboat travel opened up the Mississippi Valley to North–South trade, transforming New Orleans into a major regional and international port and riverfront cities into significant stands and winter quarters for circus companies. With its large population, New Orleans also became a favorite destination for touring international celebrities, creating great competition among theater owners.

Barnum's party put up at a boardinghouse on St. Charles Street, convenient to New Orleans's impressive English-language theaters and the Camp Street circus building, described by one prospective renter as a makeshift amphitheater inside a stable. As Barnum's charge, Diamond would have encountered Southerners like and unlike people up north. White and Black servant girls bickered in the hotel kitchen where he stayed. Colored men carried wardrobes between the dressing rooms at the theaters where he danced. Sturdily built, sparrow-throated, and agile-limbed children and adults waited beside him behind the curtains. And Creole women rested gloved hands on the forearms of bearded white men in the box seats at his shows.[40] What he saw of or thought about the enslavement of African Americans is unknown. But he did sneak back to the levee to dance with the workers.

During his sojourn in New Orleans, Diamond became increasingly aware of the value of his skills and the way Barnum was exploiting him. The three-year contract Barnum had drawn up and John Diamond had signed in July 1840 specified that the fourteen-year-old was "to receive Twelve Dollars per month and to have one hundred Dollars placed to his credit on the Savings Bank at the end of each said three years, should he so long continue under such an engagement."[41] No codicil was added regarding the profits accrued from ticket sales, benefit nights, or dancing matches. Barnum negotiated to split those with each theater's manager and paid Diamond his regular salary.

Barnum claimed in his memoirs that before reaching New Orleans, his touring troupe had earned nothing beyond "current expenses" (publicity, travel costs, and about two dollars a day room and board per person) and the small remittances he sent home. "Profits were yet in the dim future." When he couldn't pay his hotel bill at the end of the first week, Mrs. Gillies, his widowed landlady, sent him notice to "pay or quit." He promised that if she waited until Diamond's first benefit, funds would surely come in. "The worthy landlady" had a low opinion of showmen, however, and demanded his pocket watch as security.[42] That left Diamond's contract as Barnum's only asset.

The day after he arrived, city newspapers informed the public that Master Diamond was at the St. Charles Hotel and "will probably be engaged by some of our managers." But Barnum did not wait to hear from them. Instead, he took Diamond to the office of Noah Ludlow, comanager with Solomon "Sol" Smith of the New American Theatre. These two actor-managers also operated theaters in St. Louis, Vicksburg, and Natchez. "Mr. Barnum waited on us with his boy," recalled Ludlow, "a lad of about sixteen years of age, whom he called 'Master

Dimond'" (Ludlow and Smith preferred the Irish spelling). He "proposed that we should engage him to dance for a few nights between the plays and farces, saying, as an inducement, that he would draw a gallery audience for us, and would not be displeasing to other portions of the house." As Barnum's price was modest ("yes, reader, *modest*," wrote Ludlow, "he was not the 'great showman' then"), "we engaged the boy for five or six nights, without ever seeing him dance, and the result was what Mr. Barnum said it would be." Diamond's "exhibitions of suppleness" delighted the audience. "He could twist his feet and legs, while dancing, into more fantastic forms than I ever witnessed before or since."[43] As he was only trying out, Diamond did not appear in the New American's advertisements the first week of January. However, his subsequent relations with members of the cast confirm that he danced there then.

New Orleans theaters packed their programs with circus people. Soon after opening the New American, Ludlow and Smith pulled up the pit floorboards, remodeled the auditorium into an equestrian ring, and introduced a stud of horses and riders in a successful effort to increase ticket sales. Their great feature when Diamond arrived was Jimmy Robinson, apprentice and adopted son of John Robinson, the theater's equestrian manager. To add allure to Jimmy's act, Smith changed his name to Juan Hernandez. "He was a wonderful child, not over eight years of age," recalled Smith, and he "could execute the most difficult and dangerous equestrian feats, besides singing comic songs and acting children's parts on the stage." He also demonstrated gymnastic "posturing" and danced the sailor's hornpipe.[44]

The second week in January, the New American expanded its equestrian show even further. In December, Jeremiah P. Fogg and Samuel P. Stickney's circus had "raised its canvas in the lower *faubourg*, the inhabitants of which were mostly French and very fond of equestrian performances." So Ludlow and Smith invited Fogg and Stickney to join Robinson's circus at their theater, more to prevent the former from drawing away customers than because they expected to gain from the arrangement.[45] On "the Eighth of January," a holiday commemorating General Andrew Jackson's 1815 rout of the British from New Orleans, the New American added the horse spectacle Timour the Tartar and Miss Johnson in a "Broadsword Hornpipe" to their evening program and announced a matinee performance aimed at children. Not to be outdone, the more prestigious St. Charles Theatre began its program that same week with the child-friendly "spectacle of 'Aladdin, or the Wonderful Lamp,'" and announced the engagement of Master Diamond.[46]

Barnum's goal for Diamond had always been the St. Charles Theatre, New Orleans's "'temple' of the legitimate," managed by comedic actor James Henry Caldwell.[47] Like Ludlow and Smith, Caldwell operated numerous theaters in the South. He came to New Orleans in 1820, managed the French theater for three years, then built the first American Theatre on Camp Street in the city's outskirts, helping establish New Orleans's "American section." Caldwell also lit his theater with gas, laying the foundation for the large fortune he would accumulate from gas lighting companies. In the 1830s he expanded his theater operations to Natchez, Mobile, Huntsville, Nashville, St. Louis, Louisville, and Cincinnati, thereby creating a Southern theatrical circuit that enabled him to employ a stock company year-round. This circuit helped him entice star performers to the South. He built the mammoth St. Charles Theatre, which seated up to five thousand, in 1835 and the New Theatre in Mobile in 1840, routing Ludlow and Smith, who retreated to New Orleans and challenged Caldwell's dominance by opening the New American.[48]

Diamond moved to the St. Charles Theatre on January 10, 1841. Having achieved his goal, Barnum did not waste any time. He advertised Diamond as "(only 13 years of age) . . . and the best Negro dancer in the world!!" and then set the ball rolling: "Master Diamond hereby challenges any person in America to a trial of skill at negro dancing, in all its varieties, for the sum of $200 to $1000." For five nights, Diamond danced a "Naval Hornpipe in character" between the first two plays and "a greater variety of heel-and-toe eccentricities than there are changes in a kaleidoscope" as the second entr'acte. "He cuts pigeon-wings with variations, aggravations, illustrations and alterations," reported the *Daily Picayune*. "He seems to be a sort of combination of quick silver and India-rubber. . . . He cuts fantastic contortions with a grace positively superlative."[49] The newspaper also praised the unnamed fiddler: "The individual who accompanies Master Diamond upon the stage and who executes upon the violin, or, to speak in the classical language of our colored population, 'plays de fiddle,' certainly deserves much credit. He looks and walks the character to the life, and some of his touches are of the genuine 'hoe down,' 'corn-field' order."[50] Barnum most likely authored these witty reviews. Nevertheless, they captured qualities in Diamond's dancing noticed by theater critics, newspaper editors, and rival managers in the audience.

While in New Orleans, Diamond took every opportunity to interact with the locals. "He could daily be found on wharves, freely distributing his 'pic's.' among the darkeys," reported the *New York Sporting Whip* two years later, and "nightly did he give proofs of his knowledge of levee nigger."[51] Through that monetary exchange, his picayunes (six-and-a-quarter–cent coins) for their steps, Diamond acknowledged the value of the Black dancers' skills, expanded his own repertoire, and provoked a strong performer-audience identification. He captured and complicated the steps and habits of African Americans "with the greatest fidelity," noted the *Picayune,* making his style "peculiarly his own," added the *Whip.* That was how he filled the gallery seats from Boston to New Orleans and why he would annoy some critics.[52] He brought Black people's dancing to the white Southern stage, thereby elevating its status.

Barnum announced Diamond's benefit "and positively his Last Performance" at the St. Charles Theatre on January 15. He called the bill "War in Texas!!!," a provocative reference to battles then raging between the Republic of Texas and Mexican forces in the town of San Patricio. But the program had nothing to do with the war. Diamond performed five different acts: "the *Black Bayadere Dance a la FANNY ELSSLER!* . . . which *pre*-haps will lay Fanny Elssler forever in de shade"; "Rival Caesars," "a humorous Sketch" with Mr. C. "Mick" Saunders, on loan from the New American; the "Highland Fling, in character"; "his Extravaganza of 'Ginger Blue'"; and "a variety of *Break Downs*."[53]

This program addressed all three sections of the audience. "The Black Bayadere Dance" and the Highland fling were for the boxes and balconies. Elssler was touring the nation's principal cities but had yet to come to the Crescent City, making her name quite the draw. Even before he arrived, Barnum had tapped her fame by sending word to the papers that Diamond would appear in New Orleans previous to his departure for Havana.[54] Barnum never intended to take Diamond to Cuba. Rather, he wanted people to connect his protégé to the great ballerina, who was due to visit Havana on her way to New Orleans that winter.

The "Rival Caesars" skit and "Ginger Blue" extravaganza were for the mostly male pit patrons, as both conflated dancing and fighting and demonstrated masculine sexual bravado.[55]

Diamond's breakdowns were for the gallery. They demonstrated his peculiar style for the people he socialized with during the day.

This combination of highbrow-lowbrow comedy was highly successful. The previous week, when the St. Charles drew regular houses, Barnum had charged around six dollars per appearance for the dancer and fiddler together, making his weekly income in New Orleans around thirty dollars. But he negotiated for more on January 15 if the receipts reached $250. "That night I received nearly $500 as my half-share of Diamond's benefit," Barnum boasted some years later, "Mr. Manager Caldwell, of the St. Charles Theatre, retaining the other half, as per agreement."[56]

As usual, Diamond returned the night following his benefit. "The tide continued to flow," recalled a delighted Barnum, "for I received $50" that night. He also announced in the *Picayune* that Diamond's challenge had been accepted by "a person of this city" willing to wager $250 that "he can best him in the 'breakdown' line." But as Barnum had yet to find a dancer to make that "person" flesh and blood, he hedged his bet. The match might not come off right away, he added, owing to Diamond's engagements elsewhere, "although he is 'bound' to be on hand before the 10th of February, or forfeit the amount."[57] The term "bound" encased in quotation marks signified that Diamond belonged to Barnum and the St. Charles Theatre. Nevertheless, on January 18, while his contract holder scrambled to find him an opponent, Diamond danced on his own hook at the New American Theatre for Mick Sanders's benefit.[58]

The next morning, the *Picayune* declared that "A GRAND MATCH DANCE!! For a wager of Five Hundred Dollars" would come off that night. "Some daring young genius aspires to win the bet offered by little Diamond, and there is to be a grand tilting match of heels and toes, too."[59] Sol Smith, who attended the event to find out what the New American's competition was up to, described what he saw in his diary: "At the St Charles, a Yankee Humbugger named Barnum got up a pretender *bet* of $250—on the dancing—negro dancing!! of Master Dimond & a 'Mr. Mercer' of Kentucky (as the bills had it) . . . a supernumerary came out with Diamond & shuffled out, squatted, turned & twisted in imitation of the youthful hero—a tall person came forward & announced that Master Diamond had won the wager & thus ended the humbug!"[60] Smith was appalled by the success of such a brazen fabrication. "Humbug! Humbug!! Humbug!!," he wrote a few days later. "Nothing but humbug has been running in my head ever since that Dimond affair at the Saint Charles—the 'trial of Skill' in black Dancing." Still, he told Ludlow, Diamond "will be the attraction against us."[61] Barnum had received $479 as his share of the ticket receipts after the match.[62]

Smith was not the only Southern critic of Barnum's "humbug" contest. A wave of editorials hit the press after the St. Charles match, pondering the effect that Diamond's "'*leg*-itimate' triumphs over the '*le*-gitimate' drama" would have on American theater. Some critics were angry that a "little Flibbertigibbet" like Diamond could more than rival established actors and dancers such as "Forrest, Booth, Marble, Hill, Celeste and Elssler" at the box office and in the hearts of the public. "If a sterling play and farce will draw $300 to the St. Charles, and a negro dancer will draw $1500, which bill is the manager likely to offer?" asked the French and Spanish language *Omnibus*. The *Vicksburg Daily Whig* was dismayed that "on the night that [Irish comedic actor] Tyrone Power played for the benefit of the orphans at the American theatre, . . . there was hardly audience enough to clear expenses; while this Ethiopian dancer drew to the St. Charles the largest house of the season!" Others worried that Diamond's act had insulted regular audience members. "For, though the 'match dance' did bring $1500 to the house the other night our impression is that it has kept out quite as large an amount since."[63]

No one blamed the dancer for the humbug. "We are saying nothing . . . against little Diamond," declared the *Picayune* on January 26. "He is a smart boy, and capable of amusing us, but the gag dance was positively an outrage upon all taste." Even "true lovers of the legitimate" acknowledged themselves "pleased with the negro extravagance of Master Diamond." One critic wondered aloud why mirroring "the *dark* countenance of Nature" was considered any different from mirroring white ethnicities: "Is not Diamond as good a picture of a little descendant of Africa as Powers is of an Irishman, Ranger of a Frenchman, Marble of a Yankee?" If "using the name of Diamond in their connection" lowers their status, he asked, why is he "playing upon the same stage with them?"[64] The answer to that question, according to the *Mobile Register,* was that Diamond mirrored his source too well: "'He dances as much like a nigger as possible,'" another editor quoted the *Register* as saying. Then added, "at the 'risk of public indignation,'" that he avers "'such Jim Crow exhibitions are neither useful nor ornamental'" (fig. 5.4).⁶⁵ Diamond's expertise in "black Dancing" was both worrisome and attractive.

After his financial triumph, Barnum arranged a little tour for Diamond. "Engagements at Vicksburg and Jackson did not result so favorably," he later reported, "but on our return to New-Orleans we again succeeded admirably—also subsequently in Mobile."⁶⁶ In Vicksburg the playgoers were disappointed when the dancer did not arrive on time. Barnum had booked steamboat tickets for Wednesday morning but then decided to take the *Sultana* on Sunday instead. Rainstorms had drenched the region since early January, and it rained again on the day they were set to travel upriver. But it wasn't the weather so much as the other passengers that caused the delay. Barnum wanted to avoid riding on the same boat as a group of equestrians from Fogg and Stickney's company. He believed they had been interfering with his dancer. Diamond stayed two weeks at

FIGURE 5.4. To draw an audience to the New Theatre in Mobile, Alabama, this playbill depicted Master Diamond stepping forward on his heel to mock ballerina Fanny Elssler's toe-dancing and challenging "any other *white* person" to a wagered trial of skill in "Negro Dancing." New Theatre playbill, Mobile, Alabama, Feb. 22, 1841, MS Thr 1848, box 10 (Diamond, Master), Houghton Library, Harvard University.

Vicksburg, where a "young Buckeye from Cincinnati" accepted his "Challenge" in the *Tri-Weekly Sentinel* to compete "for two hundred dollars" on February 6. "Another humbugging match dance came off a few nights since at Vicksburg," someone complained to the *Picayune*, "between Master Diamond and some fellow probably employed for the purpose."[67] The critic was almost certainly Sol Smith, who had himself rented the Vicksburg Theatre and booked Barnum and Diamond. He probably lost money when they arrived late.

The Consequences of Humbug

Barnum responded to these disparaging comments in "A Card" to the *Picayune* leveled at his primary detractor. Despite rumors, he declared, Master Diamond would not be appearing at the New American Theatre. "It is certainly true that Mr. Sol Smith made an engagement with Master Diamond for the Vicksburg Theatre, from which place he has just returned with the most triumph and success. He therefore wishes to remind his numerous friends that it is at the *St. Charles* he hopes to see them again." Making the most of the bad publicity, Barnum then issued an even more extravagant challenge: "In answer to certain croakings respecting gag match dances, Master Diamond gives notice that he has deposited $1000 at the Box office of the St. Charles Theatre, which sum he will bet against $500 that he can beat any person in the world. . . . These anti-gag gentlemen can now have a chance at a match after their own fashion, as soon as they desire it."[68]

Diamond responded in his own way to the bickering. He danced that St. Charles challenge, sailed with Barnum to Mobile, and on February 23 danced another match at Caldwell's New Theatre. Then he headed to a bank, overdrew the money Barnum owed him by ninety-five dollars, and went looking for the district where white, Black, and circus people congregated to drink, dance, gamble, and carouse.[69] Either fifteen-year-old Diamond was out on a lark, or all the talk about money and humbug had given him the idea that he could do better working for someone else.

Although Barnum would not own up to it, Diamond was aware that the matches were shams.[70] Barnum's deceptions had not enriched the dancer. Even worse, they threatened his reputation. Barnum liked to say that he dreamed up these contests, but he did not bring something new to the stage. He repackaged a lower-class cultural practice to sell to an outsider audience. Diamond, who had no choice but to dance whatever his master liked, may not have minded humbug matches at first. After all, they gave thousands of people a chance to judge his dancing for themselves. But the pretend stakes and shoddy opponents he endured in the South alienated the dancer from his peers. Customarily, the winner at Irish dancing matches bought "all the company" present a glass of whiskey, "he who 'took the sway' having to maintain the dignity of his position by lavish spending, instead of being both socially and financially a winner."[71] But when the wager was fake and his manager pocketed the receipts, the underpaid dancer simply did not have enough cash to treat his friends and fans. Diamond's sense of "fair play" would also have kept him from padding his meager wages by taking side bets on a match he knew was counterfeit. What was missing from Barnum's challenges was a chance for Diamond to make his name on his own terms.

Barnum, who had some idea where his wayward protégé had gone, wrote a letter to "Fogg & Stickney, Ludlow & Smith and all others whom this may concern" threatening to sue. He began it with the same sort of warning placed in Southern papers by the owners of stolen or runaway slaves. "Gentlemen," he wrote, "whereas Master Diamond is lawfully under an unfulfilled contract bound to me by his Guardian, and whereas said Diamond has absconded from my employ, this is to caution you against employing or in any manner harboring him on penalty of the law, as I am determined to pursue the legal course which is in my power, against any person or persons who shall attempt to deprive me of my legal rights." He also charged Diamond with stealing money and spending it "in Brothels and other haunts of Dissipation & vice" and threatened to publish full details of the dancer's character and conduct if anyone else hired him.[72]

When Diamond showed up in New Orleans a week later, broke and contrite, Barnum believed he had triumphed. "Master Diamond has at last come to his senses and has *voluntarily* returned to me," he wrote to Smith in a letter offering the New American "a little dancing" on "*unusually* low terms" as an "offset to the 'divine Fanny,'" who was due to debut at the St. Charles. "On each night, if you wish, he will dance the 'Black Bayadere' *á la Elssler,* also all his other dances, and play a little *burletta* which in Mobile took first-rate and was pronounced *the best thing he does.*" Barnum knew that someone at the New American Theatre had attempted to "seduce" Diamond from his employ, he told Smith. "However, should we engage, nothing should be spared on my part to ensure a successful engagement to the management."[73] Diamond did not make the same promise. He bided his time, planning his next escape.

Fanny Elssler's imminent arrival to New Orleans was not just on Barnum's mind. That February, the managers of the city's prominent theaters had learned that the ballerina would charge $1,000 per night to exhibit her acclaimed ballet dances and $250 per week for her supporting dancers, Madame Arraline and Monsieur Sylvain. Caldwell of the St. Charles, who tried to negotiate, eventually accepted her terms. In an artfully managed publicity campaign, he then announced that during Elssler's stay, boxes and parquet seats had to be purchased a day in advance, and single seats had to be purchased the morning of the performance at the box office. Boxes, which seated up to twelve, began at sixty dollars. Single seats, if you could get them, went for four or five dollars each.[74] Even so, hundreds of people could not get into the St. Charles on Elssler's first night, prompting other theaters to figure out ways to siphon off the Elssler-mania overflow.

Diamond was only one of several candidates for the job. In February, Ludlow had hired Mrs. Fitzwilliam, a young London actress who approached him with a play called *Foreign Airs and Native Graces* that was well suited to rival the St. Charles. "In the performance of this play Mrs. F represented several characters, among them a French danseuse, and as this character she gave imitations of Fanny Elssler in her different dances, and not bad resemblances either," admitted Ludlow, "a little extravagant, perhaps, but far from contemptible." Cheeky Mrs. Fitzwilliam (née Fanny Elizabeth Copeland) became the New American's "bright particular" star, cramming the house without the aid of the horses, Smith wrote to a friend, "throwing from 900 to 1000 people into fits (of laughter), and causing them to forget the hard times, short crops, and every thing else of a disagreeable nature."[75] When the "divine" Fanny finally arrived in New Orleans on March 6, 1841, Ludlow and Smith timed Fitzwilliam's play to begin just as Elssler's performance at the St. Charles was ending so that those people who could not get in and those who had just seen Elssler dance could come to the American to watch their "Fanny" imitate the great danseuse.

John Diamond did not dance à la Elssler that March. Nor did he stick around New Orleans. "After extorting large sums of money from me," grumbled Barnum, "he finally absconded." With no idea where "his boy" had gone this time, Barnum boarded a steamboat on March 12 and headed back up the Mississippi and Ohio Rivers to Pittsburgh, where he found Charles Jenkins, who had abandoned him in St. Louis, exhibiting Frank Lynch as Master Diamond. Barnum reacted by publishing an ironical review in a local paper; Jenkins sued him for libel; Barnum sued Jenkins for stealing "Master Diamond's name and reputation"; and both spent time in jail. "Each having had his turn at this amusement," declared Barnum, "we adjourned our controversy to New York where I beat him."[76] What he meant by that and didn't tell his readers was that by the time Jenkins and Lynch returned to New York in June, Barnum was exhibiting his own Diamond impersonators. John Diamond may have deserted Barnum down south, but "Master Diamond" kept on dancing for him up north.

Barnum had been on target when he accused the managers of the New American Theatre of having designs on his dancer. But it wasn't Smith and Ludlow who ended up luring Diamond away. Four days after Barnum left New Orleans, Ludlow's son-in-law Matthew Field wrote to his wife, Cornelia, that "Fogg & Stickney have got Diamond with them up the river, and no doubt they are flourishing likewise."[77]

After eight months on the road, Barnum returned to New York City without John Diamond. Tired of the itinerant life, he leased the saloon at Vauxhall Gardens again in August 1841 and hired his brother-in-law John Hallett to manage it under Barnum's direction.[78] Admission to the gardens was still free and to the saloon twenty-five cents, "children with their guardians half price." The program contained its usual mélange of male and female singers, dancers, storytellers, and "protean" actors, with the occasional puppeteer or gymnast thrown in. Regularly featured were ballet pantomimes, Irish ballads and comic duets, Scottish dances, "Ethiopian" and African American songs, sailor's hornpipes, and one-act plays. Many of these same acts could be seen at other city varieties that summer, including Scudder's American Museum on Broadway and Arcadian Gardens on Bleecker Street.[79] What set Vauxhall apart was its new Master Diamond and the introduction of dancing matches to the program.

   From August 21 to September 23, William Henry Lane danced and competed at the saloon under the stage names Master Diamond, Master J C Diamond, and (possibly) Mr. Consent. The stolen stage name afforded the Black dancer concealment and attention at the same time.

Dark Transactions at Vauxhall

On September 19, 1841, the *Sunday Flash* published a letter denouncing the "Double Refined Humbug" that had been drawing crowds to Vauxhall Gardens for the last few weeks. The first deception, wrote the correspondent, who used the moniker Mammy Daddy, was that the saloon's managers "have procured a fellow to dance negro extravaganzas, who not possessing any personal merit, has wisely assumed the name of one who does, (we refer to the celebrated Master Diamond)." The second was that to more effectually "gall those who are weak enough to be humbugged by them, they get up mock challenges, and thus manage to give a collateral interest to that, which would otherwise be the most dull affair in the world." As an example, he called attention to the appearance in last Monday's *Sun* of "a mock challenge from one, the Butcher Boy, to a dancing master of the name of Schlim, for Fifty Dollars. Mr. Schlim, being of course 'all set,' replies the next day with an acceptance, and a pleasant request that the Butcher Boy oil his joints forthwith. Comment upon this wretched farce is unnecessary."[80]

   A second communication, providing "still further insight into these *dark* transactions," was published in the *Sunday Flash* a week later. The writer, Rapsay Darby, who styled himself "fully acquainted with all the particulars of the matter," verified that Vauxhall's Diamond was indeed a fake. Far from "being the true Master Diamond, whose name he assumes, he is no more or less than a veritable negro," declared the writer, "and the same negro, too, who was brought out the last season under the name of 'Rattler,' by no less a person than the notorious Barnham [sic], . . . whose protégé the lad now is. . . . The boy is fifteen or sixteen years of age; his name is 'Juba;' and, to do him justice, he is a very *fair* dancer. He is of harmless and inoffensive disposition, and is not, I sincerely believe, aware of the meanness and audacity of the swindler to which he is at present a party."

That this young dancer had taken Master Diamond as his alias was not the trouble here. No one in this exchange was called by his actual name. Even the editors of the paper were addressed as Messrs. Scorpion, Startle, and Sly. Far more damning, according to Darby, was the inauthentic portrayal of the actual sport: "As to the wagers which the bills daily blazon forth, they are like the rest of the business—all a cheat. Not one dollar is ever bet or staked, and the pretended judges who aid in the farce, are more *blowers,* who are compensated for their share of the performance by a little ticket, which is enstamped with the cabalistic inscription, of 'Good for three cents at the bar.'"[81]

The fact that the two letters appeared in the *Sunday Flash* tells us something about their intent. The *Flash* was one of a surprising number of weekly journals published in the early 1840s that uncovered and brazenly published a captivating composite of titillating humor, gossip, and opinion about the goings-on at brothels, theaters, and illegal sports events. In mockingly scandalizing stories and columns, the flash press extolled the exploits of young republicans out to enjoy their American liberty and exposed the hypocrisies of seemingly respectable citizen scoundrels. Under the guise of shock and ridicule, they also provided solid information about the people, places, and pursuits they derided, such as the fashions worn by prostitutes, the public balls of African Americans, and the locations of cock and dog fights.

Daddy and Darby's letters likewise informed the people by indicting rogues. Everyone was fair game in a periodical saturated with sexual, racial, and class satire, but the best targets were always people who wielded some social, economic, or political power. (They were also the most likely to pursue libel suits, which may explain the epistolary format of the critique.) In exposing Vauxhall's fake Diamond and challenges, Mammy Daddy meant to censure the managers, not the dancers, for cheating the audience. Similarly, Rapsay Darby held off identifying Juba's name and race until after the season had ended, the content and timing of his letter calculated to offer readers as much detail as possible about the dancer while excoriating his employer.

The dancer's race was not what made Vauxhall's humbug contemptible, it simply made the managers' wickedness more palpable. In a postscript to Darby's letter, the editors of the *Flash* accused Barnum of sacrificing Juba on the altar of his own "infernal avarice." Barnum's first and worst sin had been his exhibition of Joice Heth years earlier. This African American woman claimed to be the 161-year-old nurse of

George Washington. Heth demonstrated considerable theatrical talents, spinning tales about "dear little George" and her life as a slave, singing hymns, answering questions, telling jokes (fig. 5.5). Barnum advertised her as "The Greatest Natural and National Curiosity in the World" and after her death invited the public to a postmortem examination (to which he charged admission) to determine her real age.[82] "Not satisfied with making your bread and butter out of a church-yard ghoul, whose soul you have helped to damn by making her a party to your unprincipled practices," charged the three *Sunday Flash* editors, "you have laid your remorseless hand upon one of her own descendants." Black people, whether old and female or young and dependent, were easy pickings for an unprincipled capitalist. Juba was entangled in a swindle not of his making. He was not to blame.

Or was he? Darby's insistence that Juba was unaware of his employer's machinations may also have been calculated. A dancer who worked for the same employer two years in a row was no innocent. Black performers were constantly exploited, to be sure. But they also understood what it took to succeed in a white man's world.

FIGURE 5.5. At a time when the American Revolution was fading from contemporary memory, African American performer Joyce Heth devised an exhibition in which she told tales and jokes, sang songs, and answered questions in the guise of George Washington's ancient slave nurse. Heth, like Lane, had worked for Barnum, who was good at spotting and exploiting marketable African American acts. P. T. Barnum, *The Life of P. T. Barnum Written by Himself* (1855), 158.

By dancing under the alias Master Diamond, Lane (or Juba) followed what became a typical career path. To succeed as a jig dancer on the American stage required not just talent but also a willingness to engage in the deceptions of the age. Lane's multiple performance names reflected the economic and social realities of his trade. As markets for goods and services increased in the 1830s and 1840s, people left the land and flooded the cities. New York's population grew by hundreds of thousands. Engulfed by this vast sea of faces, names were changeable and identities fluid. Untethered individuals bundled themselves into communities based on their manner of dress and deportment, the entertainments they chose, the newspapers they read. They posed as whom they wanted to be and worried about imposters in their midst.[83] Vauxhall's jig dancers joined in this confidence game, ensnaring customers with stage names and dancing competitions that simultaneously verified their authenticity and concealed their identities. Dancing as Diamond, Lane—a Black dancer posing as a white dancer disguised as a Black dancer—twisted the twine even further. He made a living and a name both by taking the white boy's place and by getting found out.

The idea that people were duped by Vauxhall's fake Master Diamond seems remote. Lane/Juba first appeared at the saloon in late August 1841 billed as "Master J C Diamond" (also spelled Dimond); he was joined by "Master F Diamond, late of the Chatham" on August 26. Billed as the "rival darkies," Master J C Diamond and Master F Diamond danced separately during the show (just as John Diamond and Master Rattler had done the year before), then each performed a medley of dances back-to-back as the conclusion of the program. A week later, just in case anyone thought they were the same dancer, Vauxhall's managers pitted the "TWO DIAMONDS!" against each other in a grand trial dance, proclaiming, "This will be the closest Match ever witnessed."[84] The next day, Master F Diamond moved to Scudder's American Museum and Lane stayed at Vauxhall, adding to the variety in ingenious ways as "Master Diamond, King of Darkies," who danced "a most Outlandish Breakdown, sitting on a Chair."[85]

Lane used Diamond's name purposefully. Competitive jig dancers were not averse to promoting themselves through association with the famous dancer. Lane's Master Rattler advertised himself as "Diamond's teacher," a Master Rawston billed himself as "the rival of Master Diamond," and a Master Jackson called himself "the successful rival of Master Diamond."[86] Whether those claims were true didn't really matter. Each dancer used Diamond's name in his ad to "hook his wagon to a star," as the old rhyme said. And with John Diamond safely out of town, emulation became impersonation. At least four Master Diamonds appeared on Northern stages in 1841. Other Diamonds emerged in 1842, including Master Hawk Diamond, who danced at Peale's New York Museum and Picture Gallery.[87] Few people blamed young dancers for impersonating the star to secure employment. Most were given the name by the adults they worked for anyway.

Frank Kent, who also danced as Master F. Diamond, "did not wish to go by any name save his own," explained the *Whip*, "but they under whose guardianship he has been have invariably forced it upon him, and thus it was no sin of his."[88]

Lane was not the only African American to pass himself off as "the true Master Diamond" either. The people who went to Vauxhall to watch two Master Diamonds dance a match were probably not surprised to find a blacked-up white dancer pitted against a blacked-up Black dancer, which is what they got. Another showman, R. W. Lindsay, claimed in court that in 1840 he had "got a negro boy, which he called 'Master Diamond,'" a perfect prodigy in dancing and singing, and "posted up flaming hand-bills through the country" announcing the dates of his performances. Meanwhile, Barnum got himself "a smart white boy," blacked him up, and went "along Lindsay's route a few days in advance, exhibiting the 'genuine' Master Diamond, thus reaping the fruits of Lindsay's labors, without any expense for advertising."[89] The American Museum designated its Diamond "a white boy" to distinguish him from the Black dancers in the Diamond field. When John Diamond danced at the New Theatre in Mobile in February 1841 the bill specified that he delineated "the Ethiopian character superior to any other *white* person."[90] Managers would not have called attention to the race of their white dancers unless Black dancers were on the stage.

These Black dancers help clear up some of the confusion caused by a biographical sketch of John Diamond written in 1873 by the editor of the *New York Clipper*: "Juba's success was the means of bringing out another darkey named Johnny Diamond, who hung out around the old Fly Market of this city. Diamond was first brought into public notice by the enterprising P. T. Barnum, at Vauxhall Garden, about 1840, when he was 17 years of age." The author identifies Juba as Black and Diamond as Barnum's protégé, which are both correct. So why does he identify Johnny Diamond as African American? Rather than a mistaken turnabout, this dark-skinned market dancer may have been one of the Black Master Diamonds performing in the 1840s. One chronicler of minstrelsy claimed there were "two 'Jubas' and three 'Master Diamonds'" working at that time. That estimate seems low if all the variations are included.[91]

A few savvy newspaper editors spotted these duplicates. In August 1841 Boston's *Daily Atlas* reported that "a Master Diamond" was among the attractions at New York's Chatham Theatre, adding the qualifying "a" because according to the papers on the writer's desk, Master Diamond was also dancing at Vauxhall Gardens and Scudder's American Museum.[92] Other editors noticed it too, thanks to the newspaper exchange system. In the Postage Act of 1792, Congress subsidized the distribution of newspapers by mail at low rates and allowed printers and editors to exchange newspapers among themselves for free.[93] This exchange system became the main source of content for most newspapers. It also got news to remote places and made local events national. The reprinting of news was not always immediate. For example, the *New York Tattler's* disclosure in August 1840 that Vauxhall's Diamond was occasionally Black was not reprinted in the *New Orleans Picayune* until January 1841, when John Diamond was in that city.

Mock Challenges

Grand dancing matches and trials of skill became as regular as clockwork at Vauxhall saloon. Most of these matches began as a challenge or challenge acceptance published as a letter or paid advertisement in the penny papers. The first challenge—the manager's offer of fifty dollars "to any person who could successfully compete with Master Diamond at negro dancing"—was accepted on September 1, 1841, by "Master Miles, a butcher boy, well known as a regular break-down dancer." "Judges have been chosen to decide upon the merits of these rival darkies," said Vauxhall's ad, "and a most laughable and exciting scene may be expected."[94] Diamond was declared the winner on the saloon's stage. Over the next few days, Lane danced the "Camp Town Hornpipe," "Ole Wurginny Breakdown," "Black Bayadere Dance," "Smoke House Dance," and "Five-Mile-out-of-Town Dance" and performed his benefit and last night as Master J C Diamond. These performances annoyed James Rees, editor of the *Dramatic Mirror and Literary Companion,* who advised Vauxhall's proprietors "to withdraw such a humbug as *this* Master Diamond" and "give us the real Simon Pure, or none."[95] They did not heed his advice.

Lane was reengaged the following week and another "Grand Match Dance! for $50!" was set for September 6 between Lane's Mast J C Diamond and Master Miles, now called the Catherine Market Roarer, with one element altered. "The dancer who receives the greatest applause from the audience, receives the $50," the *Post* apprised its readers, "in consequence of the dissatisfaction of Master Miles with the verdict of the Judges at the late trial of skill."[96] The objection, whether genuine or a ploy, was common enough at dancing matches to keep the excitement going. It identified young Joe Miles as a proud competitor willing to duke it out with whoever came along, which he did the following night. However, rather than facing "the unapproachable Diamond" again on September 7, Miles danced a grand trial dance with no stakes attached against Golark, the Washington Market Screamer. And Lane's Master Diamond danced a trial against Mr. J. Green, the Fireman, on September 10.[97]

These dancing matches must have gone over well, because the next week Barnum launched a challenge dance campaign. On Monday the Butcher Boy's challenge to Schlim, the dancing master, was published in the *New York Sun.* On Wednesday, Vauxhall's ad reported that Mr. Green, "a Fireman of this city," had challenged Schlim "to meet him in three distinct Dances, for the sum of Fifty Dollars," and that the challenge had been accepted, the money put up, judges chosen, and the contest set to take place in the saloon that night, with the decision "delivered from the Stage." The next night, Green, the fireman, Miles, the Catherine Market Screamer, and Mr. P Keenan, the Fulton Market Roarer, danced a grand trial of skill for twenty-five dollars. And on Friday, for the benefit of Old Phil (another performer who never used his surname and may well have been African American), billed as the Tompkins Market Roarer, and Master Miles, now the Catherine Market Rattler, danced a grand match dance with a Mr. Consent, the Long Island Screamer, for twenty dollars. That same night, Master Keenan and Mr. Green danced an exhibition match, and "the great match dance for $200 between Master Diamond and the North River boatman" was held. The *Flash* published Mammy Daddy's letter "Double Refined Humbug" that Sunday.

Vauxhall's blaring advertisements were more than a list of blustering humbugs. They called out to a newspaper readership that would have understood the references. The raucous names and grandiose challenges invoked familiar stage personas and mimicked the cacophonous cries of butcher boys, newsboys, firefighters, screamers (a person remarkable for speed or impact), roarers (a boasting, aggressive, swaggering character along the lines of Davy Crockett), and boatmen (à la Mike Fink, King of the Keelboaters) competing in urban spaces. The dancers portrayed white and Black characters they might have been in real life, offering theatrical reenactments of a contemporary pastime they might have engaged in—challenge dancing.[98] Their stage names help us see what the people sitting at the tables expected to see.

Dancing was an ephemeral activity often only preserved in advertisements, which makes the origins of this era of newspaper advertising a significant part of this story. Dozens of publications advertised, criticized, and distributed information about theatrical entertainments in the 1830s and 1840s. Vauxhall bought ad space in established major dailies such as the *Post* that covered commercial and political news and in "penny papers" such as the *Sun* and *Herald* that combined hard news with sensational, crime, and human interest stories related in a strong editorial voice. Founded in the 1830s by journeyman printers turned editors, the penny papers tapped a previously untapped growing urban market—street-smart and literate working-class people hungry for inexpensive literature that addressed their needs and interests. Unlike their "blanket sheet" predecessors, which sold for six cents per copy by subscription, the smaller format penny papers sold for one cent each on the street or delivered, and subsidized publication costs by selling advertising slots.[99] The major dailies quickly adopted this economic model. Editors vied vigorously to be the first with the news, dispatching hundreds of children to hawk their editions and cry out their headlines. And advertisements, including a regular Amusements column, became an expected, sales-generating, and often entertaining newspaper feature.

Sporting male weeklies such as the *Flash* and the *Whip* cost six cents and carried no hard news but in other ways resembled the penny press model. They were aggressively marketed on advertising placards and thrust into people's faces by newsboys "at all the landings, ferries, and other places of resort."[100] Their tone and features betokened a "man-about-town" readership, many of them want-to-be street-smart clerks and "gay fellows" with time and income to burn, but they attracted a wider readership, including many enthusiastic working-class women. They advertised drinking and oyster saloons, eating and coffee houses, and public halls available to rent, as well as midwives, surgeons, and medicinal cordials for male and female complaints. Although published in New York City, the flash papers were marketed and read in towns and cities throughout New York State and up and down the Eastern Seaboard, from Toronto to New Orleans.[101]

Vauxhall Gardens reached the democratic masses through all these paper types. The major dailies carried its advertisements and a quiet word or two about the show, the penny papers printed the ads and the dancers' challenges, and the flash press described and critiqued the whole affair.

Anxious to benefit from the attention stirred up by Mammy Daddy's letter, Barnum reengaged Lane to dance as Master Diamond, arranged several more dancing matches, and, to keep people in the gardens buying refreshments, withheld the presentation of the judges' verdict until after the intermission. With a little finagling, even negative press might be turned to one's advantage. "[I] had much rather be roundly abused than not to be noticed at all," testified Barnum time and again. "The cry of 'humbug'" never harmed him. It "added to the notoriety which I so much wanted."[102]

Becoming Juba

Employment at New York's Vauxhall Gardens saloon gave Lane more than money. He also collected material he would use to build his career. The final week of the season, September 20–24, he shared top billing with Miss Mary Ann Gannon, who performed all the characters in one-act plays, sang solos and duets, and danced a variety of steps and styles (fig. 5.6). The two performers, boy and girl, balanced each other's acts. She danced the "Cracovienne Dance"; he danced the "Black Bayadere Dance."[103] She cut up in a comic duet; he danced a breakdown with a chair. He won applause in trials of skill; she won praise for miscellaneous talents. They learned from each other. Ballet was still a novelty in 1840s America, unburdened by expectations of decorum. La Petite Cerito and Master Henry, the infant wonders, "only 4 years old!," delighted and astounded because they were so small. Mary Ann Gannon and Mary Ann Lee were popular because they were eclectic and fearless in their abilities. They trained their bodies to move like

FIGURE 5.6. Actor-dancer-singer Mary Ann Gannon and Lane/Juba, now dancing under the stage name Master Diamond, learned from each other while sharing the stage at New York's Vauxhall Gardens saloon in 1841. *Miss M. A. Gannon, The dramatic wonder, 12 yrs. of age, at the Boston Museum. As Little Pickle, in the sketch of the "Spoiled child"* (Thayer and Company, Lith. [1843]). Courtesy of the American Antiquarian Society. *"Miss M. A. Gannon"* as Josephine in *"the Actress of All Work,"* drawing by Augustus Toedtberg, box 3, miscellaneous portraits collection, MS Thr 158.1, Houghton Library, Harvard University.

their European rivals. They studied the boys' feet and stole their hornpipes. They traversed the stage in funny little steps and breathtaking leaps. They sang and acted in men's clothes. They showed Lane what lower-caste performers had to do to succeed professionally.

Vauxhall provided Lane with a professional stepping stone. The last performance of the season was Friday, September 24. Rapsay Darby's letter revealing the race and preferred stage name of Vauxhall's Master Diamond appeared two days later in the *Sunday Flash*. Without being obvious, it told Lane's admirers and anyone else interested in seeing a Black dancer as good as John Diamond that they should look for the dancer named Juba. Lane/Juba could not have asked for better publicity.

6

UNDER CANVAS

At the end of his life, James Thomas could still remember Diamond coming to Nashville with the circus fifty years earlier. "Among the pleasures [we] used to enjoy, I believe none surpassed the old time Circus," he wrote in an unpublished autobiography. "From the time the circus bills were posted, the town was deeply interested." When the caravan of horses and brightly painted wagons passed, every boy tried to see how close he could get. "If he got a chance, he would put his hand on the Pony. He would lay around and see the tent put up and figure on getting in Early to hear the first tune and see the grand entry." Every boy liked to kneel behind the circular fence, Thomas recalled, as "near to the horses heels as the ring would allow. In that place he could see all that passed," smell the sweat radiating from the horses' rumps as they cantered round the ring, taste the dust coloring the shafts of light angling in from the canvas flaps, feel the thump of the tumblers' weight as they landed feet over hands on carpets thrown over the dirt, and hear the hammering and sanding of the dancer's shoes on the wooden plank next to the center pole.[1]

Thomas was a fourteen-year-old mixed-race apprentice barber earning twelve dollars a month when Diamond arrived in 1841. His African American mother, Sally Thomas, the proprietor of a small clothes-cleaning business, had purchased his freedom when he was six years old, but under Tennessee law he remained "in bondage" as long as he resided in the state. His father, John Catron, a white judge who served as associate justice of the United States Supreme Court after 1837, did nothing for his son. Young Thomas hired himself out as an apprentice to Frank Parrish, also enslaved, whose barbershop in the public square served influential people of both races.* In 1846 Thomas opened his own highly successful barbershop

---

* Although Tennessee laws forbade the hiring of a slave's time from the slave himself, James Thomas, Sally Thomas, Frank Parrish, and many other enslaved people in David-

FIGURE 6.1. James Thomas was a fourteen-year-old barber's apprentice in Nashville when he saw John Diamond dance with a circus. Although Tennessee laws forbade the hiring of an enslaved person's time from himself or herself, Thomas, his mother, and other Davidson County slaves not only hired out their own time, they established small businesses and accumulated small amounts of property. Eyre Crowe, *A Barber's Shop in Richmond, Virginia*, from the *Illustrated London News*, Mar. 9, 1861.

in the house where he was born, near the city banks, the Davidson County courthouse, and the Tennessee capitol (fig. 6.1). In 1851 he petitioned successfully for his freedom and for immunity to stay in Nashville, where he secured a nest egg before moving to St. Louis, Missouri, and investing in real estate.[2]

As he aged, Thomas wrote down those aspects of his life he thought other people might find interesting.[3] Seeing Diamond dance made it into those pages. "About 1842, John Diamond came with a circus. Toward the close of the performance a platform was brought out and Diamond, came in black, asked the Master in the band to play 'Camptown Hornpipe' or some other dance. He would walk around the board, then jump on it, and dance in a manner as though he would pick it up with his feet, jump-off, again walk around, and say something nigger like and dance again. The people thought that the best part of the show."[4] In this brief recollection, Thomas presented not only a rare glimpse of Diamond's dancing

---

son County not only hired out their own time but also established small businesses and accumulated small amounts of property. These entrepreneurs circumvented the laws through the acquiescence of both slaveholding and nonslaveholding whites.

act but also an indication of his appeal across the color line and the significant ways circuses circulated cultural practices while entertaining the populace.

From June to November 1841, John Diamond traversed the western edges of the South with an equestrian circus company, an experience that would influence the course of his career. By choosing circus work over Barnum's management, the dancer allied himself with the era's most far-reaching and influential form of commercial entertainment. Traveling circuses made Diamond a household name in Black and white rural and urban communities across the country. They modified his dancing style as he tried to please "the people" in each region by capturing and augmenting their steps and style. Six months on the road also affected Diamond's character. It tested his stamina and brought out his belligerent side. Itinerant work was difficult, and circus people—rough or gentle, married or single, white or Black, child or adult—were perceived as outsiders who were either idolized or expelled for the pleasures they tendered.

Diamond's Departure

Diamond's interest in working for equestrian circuses resulted in multiple offers and a swelled head that impacted the fortunes of his handlers. Back in January 1841, Sol Smith had lamented to Noah Ludlow, his partner at the New American Theatre, "We have stuck our feet in it in engaging Fogg & Stickney." Smith had come to realize that two circus companies in one theater brought in more headaches than profits.[5] In February he moved Fogg and Stickney's circus to the Camp Street arena and asked Diamond's friend Mick Sanders to act as manager, keeping John P. Robinson's company at the New American. But when the tumblers were forced to perform "without a carpet! F. & S. not having any, and we being obliged to use ours at the theater," he decided to pack Sanders's contingent off to Mobile, where, as it turned out, "Dimond, (the inimitable!)" was dancing at Caldwell's New Theatre.[6] It was after Sanders arrived that Diamond withdrew his pay from Barnum's account and went missing for a week.

Smith had planned to show Fogg and Stickney's company in New Orleans for the first two weeks of March but soon became "decidedly in favor of lightening expenses one way or the other." The winter circus enterprise was flagging, a problem exacerbated by continual rain and deepening mud.[7] Competition was also mounting. Two menageries (caravans of exotic animals) had settled into an arena near the St. Charles Theatre. Smith figured that financing a trip back to Mobile or up the Mississippi River to Natchez and Vicksburg would be less expensive than keeping the circus in New Orleans. Besides, if they did not send Fogg and Stickney's party back to those cities while they were still under contract, "*they will go on their own after*—and thus injure us in our visit with the *American* com[pan]y afterwards."[8] Duly sent to Mobile, Fogg and Stickney pitched a tent in the "Public

Square" from March 11 until April 15. Before they left New Orleans, however, an equestrian contingent broke off and headed to Vicksburg, where Ludlow's son-in-law Matt Field espied Diamond with them.

Aware now that he had the power to work where he pleased, Diamond deserted Fogg and Stickney's renegade contingent after a fortnight, returned to New Orleans, and "volunteered" for Master Hernandez's benefit at the New American on April 7, 1841, the same night Fanny Elssler took her benefit at the St. Charles Theatre. He stayed the week, dancing between the plays and circus acts, assisting at John Robinson's benefit, and taking his own benefit on April 10, for which he received (at last) a percentage of the receipts. Then he changed employers again. The next week, Fogg and Stickney's circus paraded back into New Orleans, set up a tent under their own auspices at the St. Charles arena, announced that they had engaged Master Diamond, and opened to a good house.[9] These actions abrogated their contract with Ludlow and Smith, which stipulated that Fogg and Stickney perform under the aegis of the American Theatre in certain cities for one year. Smith decided not to interfere personally and instead went to court to gain an injunction.[10] Since January, he reckoned, he and Ludlow had paid Fogg and Stickney $8,200 while continually suffering losses from dwindling receipts and the expense of keeping those "infernal piebald horses!"

Master Diamond added another incentive for the injuntion. Ludlow, who was managing the theater in St. Louis that spring, advised Smith to try to engage Diamond before he left New Orleans, which Smith agreed to do, "tho I don't think he can be depended on at all, unless we can contrive to keep a portion of his pay in hand as security," he replied in a letter written Sunday morning, May 2. "He continues to play with F.&S.—had a benefit last night—Nelson says $120 (about)—probably 60 or 70." "The talk is now that F.&S. go direct to St. Louis in a day or two! . . . They are a d——d slippery sett, altogether, those Equestrians—I don't know whom to trust." At 10:00 p.m. Smith added a postscript to his letter:

> I see the tent of Fogg & Stickney is struck—and they are off for St. Louis in the boat which carries this package!!! I can't get the contract out of the court to-day but will send it immediately. . . . They will no doubt play hell with our business in St. Louis for awhile. . . . I am sick—sick of dealing with rogues—and I think if we can get rid of all Equestrians (after a while) we had better. If you can see Diamond the instant he arrives, I think you can get him on some terms. I would try, if I were in your place. It might be done through [Mick] Sanders.[11]

Ludlow did get Diamond. Fogg and Stickney's stand under canvas in St. Louis overlapped with the appearance of Robinson's equestrians at the St. Louis Theatre, which Ludlow had had altered in the "Amphitheatrical way."[12] Transporting the American Theater's circus to St. Louis was expensive, lamented Smith. "The Platte was to carry the baggage free because of the large number of passages engaged and now only a few are going by that boat."[13] But Ludlow made the expense worthwhile. Master Diamond moved from Fogg and Stickney's tent to the St. Louis amphitheater at the end of May. Unfortunately, or to their "eternal credit" as Smith later put it, the St. Louis public was not interested in seeing horses perform inside a theater. After only a fortnight, he recalled, "it was found expedient to send off Robinson and his troupe, 'horse, foot, and dragoons,' on a traveling expedition."[14] "Little Dimond" stayed just as long as the horses did.[15]

John Diamond never reminisced in print about why he moved between circus companies and venues or how it felt to be approached by several employers at the same time. However, other circus people's memoirs can offer some insight into his actions. Hugh Lindsay, who aspired to be a circus clown, began his career in 1823 handing "poppets" to the puppeteer as a stagehand for Myers and Mestayer's circus in Philadelphia. When finally put into the clown character, "I made a splendid hit, and got rounds of applause from the audience," he later wrote. "Oh, then I was made! I felt big, I assure you, reader. I was called the best clown about the building. I conceited then I was some 'pumpkins.' I then wanted my salary raised, and it was granted." After that Lindsay was approached by the manager of a different circus, who wanted "the best clown he had ever seen . . . but we could not agree about the salary, for he never was guilty of paying high wages to anybody. I went off with another company."[16]

Since 1839 Diamond had been called "Unrivalled," "Unequalled," "the Best in the World," heady words for an adolescent boy to hear. It is probable that by late 1841 he too considered himself "some 'pumpkins.'"

The Circus Ship

John Diamond set off on a tour of the western South "exclusively attached" to John Robinson's equestrians (now called the American Circus). The American Circus left St. Louis in early June, took their first stand in Louisville, Kentucky, then in July caught the riverboat to Cincinnati. Steamboat service up and down the Mississippi and Ohio Rivers was not cheap. The fare from Louisville to Cincinnati cost $3 per person or around $100 for the troupe. That fare could be paid for by one average house, which Smith reckoned at $160, if things went well. But he also had to pay $200 freightage to transport the horses and luggage by mail boat.[17] Diamond and the equestrians traveled by riverboat at the beginning and end of their journey and overland by wagon caravan in between.

The American Circus did good business in Louisville and Cincinnati, both of which were burgeoning cities in the 1840s with populations of 21,210 and 46,338, respectively (a 103 percent increase for Louisville and 150 percent for Cincinnati since 1830). Every night the canvas "was uncomfortably crowded," reported Smith's Cincinnati relatives, who wondered why the circus only stayed a fortnight.

When Smith arrived in Cincinnati on July 25, he learned that it had been his agent J. P. Bailey's decision to pull out prematurely and also that Bailey had failed to pay a $550 bank draft. "I intended to stay until next Friday," Smith complained to Ludlow, "but I have determined to . . . follow up the company till I find it, and see what the d——d they are about. I am in hopes Baily has paid Robinson his note—yet I scarcely believe Robinson would ask for it."[18] In Cincinnati, Robinson had purchased (against Smith and Ludlow's account) "a first-rate music car, which cost $140," two horses, and a pony, and he had hired three wagons (drawn by twelve horses) to transport the tents and other luggage.[19]

Following trade routes across the nation, itinerant circuses resembled eighteenth-century commercial fishing and whaling ships. The American Circus's proprietors, Ludlow and Smith, were the ship's owners. The ringmaster, agents, and advertisers were the captain and officers. On the road, John P. Robinson managed the American Circus's ring show, James P. Bailey acted as treasurer, and V. M. W. Letton was advertiser, "and an excellent one he is," Smith wrote Ludlow. "Every thing is arranged, properly—license procured—bills put up—business made—lot hired, &c- and no time is lost. He advertises to play twice in each town—(3 oclock & night) and then on to the next in the same way." Most likely, Letton also arranged the printing of the music sheets sold at the performances. The circus performers and stagehands were the ship's crew members and deckhands, one major difference being that circuses included female performers and hands (often, but not always, wives and daughters) (fig. 6.2).[20] Besides the horses, the American Circus included twelve riders and acrobats, one clown, several musicians, a dancer, and probably a dozen other people who worked as hostlers, drivers, workmen, seamstresses, laundresses, and cooks. Circus people may have seemed a slippery set to Smith, but he counted on them to do business with local merchants and printers, negotiate with licensing and law enforcement, build the performance venue, and please the public.[21]

It took Smith two days to overtake the circus at Millersburgh, Kentucky, where he found "a great carelessness" and a dancer on strike. Smith arrived at 4:00 p.m. on July 27 after the troupe had begun performing the matinee show to a sixty-dollar house. "The first thing I heard of (from Baily) was the agreeable fact that J Eversell & Master Dimond had had a fight in the dressing Room & neither of them would appear on that occasion." Smith immediately "enquired into the affair" and determined that it was not worth writing about; "they both performed at night," he wrote Ludlow the next day, "house $30" (120 paying customers). That dismal number suggested that Diamond's absence from the three o'clock show had disappointed the audience and kept people away.

No one recorded the cause of the fight between the dancer and the rider. It may have been induced by rivalry, boasting, harassment, or simply the stresses of itinerant life, which for a teenaged boy alternated between exhilarating praise,

Little Alice, the Child Rider, waiting at the tavern for the baggage to leave.

FIGURE 6.2. Although they did not appear as regularly in advertisements as boy stars like Diamond did, girls and women worked as performers and hands for itinerant circuses. *Little Alice, the Child Rider, waiting at the tavern for the baggage to leave,* from *The Old Clown's History; in Three Periods. Introducing Graphic Sketches of Show Life in its Multifarious Phases. On the Route, Under the Canvas, in the Hotels, and at the Roadside caravansaries with Characteristics of Distinguished Showmen. Embellished with numerous engravings,* by John Tryon (Torrey Brothers, Printers, 1872), 78.

boredom, and toil. Writing in 1912, theater historian T. Allston Brown assumed that Barnum had dumped Diamond in New Orleans (rather than the other way around) because "the dancer was an uncontrollable and vicious youth."[22] Was Diamond uncontrollable, or did he want control? Was he naturally difficult or simply responding to his environment?

Although dancing was a pleasurable entertainment, for Diamond it was also a form of physical labor. Jig dancing was strenuous and demanding, and the stamina of circus performers had to match the appetite of their audiences.[23] A circus program lasted up to four hours, and if there was a matinee, the program was performed twice a day. Circus troupes with small rosters had to fill the same number of hours, which meant the performers might be expected to stay in the ring for as long as thirty minutes.[24] Diamond's act lasted at least that long or longer depending on the number of encores he gave. Circus employment also entailed what must have felt like an interminable amount of downtime. Diamond only performed once toward the end of each show, requiring him to wait his turn in the dressing-room tent during the other acts. Plenty of time and opportunity to get into a muss with a colleague.

Smith suspected that a bigger problem lay behind the low receipts at the second show. That evening, he found "the back entrance entirely unguarded—and lots of people doing nothing. I placed one of the waggoners [sic] there, after seeing [a]bout 15 walk in (all of whom I gently *walked out*)," he reported to Ludlow on July 28.

> We have committed a most egregious blunder in sending the company off without one of us along. It is my firm belief we should have $2000 more in pocket at this time if we had had a pair of our eyes on them. I do not say where the blame is. . . . There is no authority here. . . . I found Robinson finds fault with Baily, & Baily with him—So they go on in rather a queer way. . . . Robinson swears at them & Baily papers everything over, getting along as easy as he can. I believe he does his best, but *that* is bad enough for us. I do believe he is honest—but he plays cards.[25]

Fighting and swearing were commonplace among circus men. And every town had temptations for sporting people, who gambled on "the races, cock fights, and everything else, including Faro & cards."[26] Robinson and Bailey's foibles had affected their ship's discipline and productivity. Still, the proprietors relied on their performers, managers, and hands to keep the enterprise afloat.

The next morning Smith rode with the circus to Paris, Kentucky, where he had a long talk with Bailey and Letton. The three men settled on a route that would take in all the towns surrounding Lexington (twenty miles below Paris), then down through southern Kentucky, and back up to Louisville in four weeks' time. There, they would meet again to make fresh plans. Their choices were to continue the circus on through Tennessee, send it back south by boat, or sell the concern to Robinson, "giving him time on the purchase money, over and above what we owe him."[27]

Smith may have persuaded Diamond back into the circus ring by invoking his contract. Traveling circuses also resembled fishing vessels in their employment system. Circus owners were responsible for their employees' food and housing along the route and only paid salaries if there was a surplus over these daily expenses. Most contracts also included a "holdback" provision that gave the proprietor the right to keep 50 percent of an employee's salary until the end of the season and then only pay that person if he or she was still with the company. This system helped circus proprietors keep their employees from looking for a better deal elsewhere. Like ship owners, circus owners had to contend with mutineers, strikers, and deserters who quit once they were paid up.[28] Every stand, like every port, gave circus workers a chance to defect. Smith and Ludlow must have held back most of Diamond's pay ("as security"), for despite his reputation for undependability, he stuck with the American Circus for the rest of the year. Or he may have liked working for Robinson.

As ringmaster and lead rider, John P. Robinson set the tone for the trip. He supervised Diamond inside the ring and offered an example of manly working-class independence. Robinson had worked his way up in the business. His father, a Scotsman, fought with the British in the Revolutionary War, remained in America, and opened blacksmith shops in Albany and Utica, New York. Not wanting to follow that trade, young John ran away to New Bedford, Massachusetts, to join a whaling ship's crew. But the rough life he witnessed and a storm that returned the ship to port convinced the boy to desert. Back in New Bedford, Robinson found work in a livery barn and the following spring applied for a job as hostler for a small traveling show. He stayed with that show for a year and then moved to another circus, where he performed menial jobs for four years, all the while learning to ride, breaking in baggage draft horses for the ring, and working up a sensational four-horse act (fig. 6.3). His career as a showman began in 1818, when a noted two-horse rider canceled his engagement with Henry Rockwell's circus. With youthful audacity, the fifteen-year-old offered himself to Rockwell, the equestrian manager, as a substitute for the missing rider, exhibited the act amid skeptical laughter from the circus "bosses," and was hired for five dollars a week.

Robinson became well known in the circus business for his riding ability, powerful physique, and foul mouth.[29] He acquired his first company by sneaking up on a gang of mutineers who had hijacked a circus and convincing them at gunpoint

FIGURE 6.3. Circus equestrian and ringmaster John P. Robinson, known for his horse handling and sensational four-horse act, supervised Diamond in the ring and offered him an example of manly bravado during the summer of 1841. Newspaper engraving of Black equestrian Joseph Hillier performing a typical four-horse maneuver in which the rider straddles two cantering horses while other horses pass between his legs. *The Squib,* July 30, 1842. Courtesy of Steve Ward.

to return it to the owners. For this action, he was given an interest in the company for a nominal fee. He was not a tightfisted employer, but he protected the money he made and expected his performers to earn theirs. As an example of Robinson's temperament, his son Gil offered this story: Noticing a bugle player trill a few notes and then stop during his first rehearsal, Robinson blurted out: "Why don't you go on and play?" "I can't," responded the musician. "I've got thirty bars rest." "Rest nothing," bellowed Robinson. "I hired you to play and you're going to play or quit. You can rest all you want after the show."[30] Robinson's rough management seems to have suited Diamond's developing character.

A Wretched Long Journey

The American Circus played in and around Lexington until the end of July, tramped and rattled through southern Kentucky for four weeks of one-day stands in August, and headed back to Louisville in September. That summer Diamond traveled nine hundred miles on winding, bumpy dirt roads, most likely in a wagon cramped with other nonequestrian performers (fig. 6.4). Few city boys knew how to ride. The journey between stands was often quite long. Up north a slow-moving summer

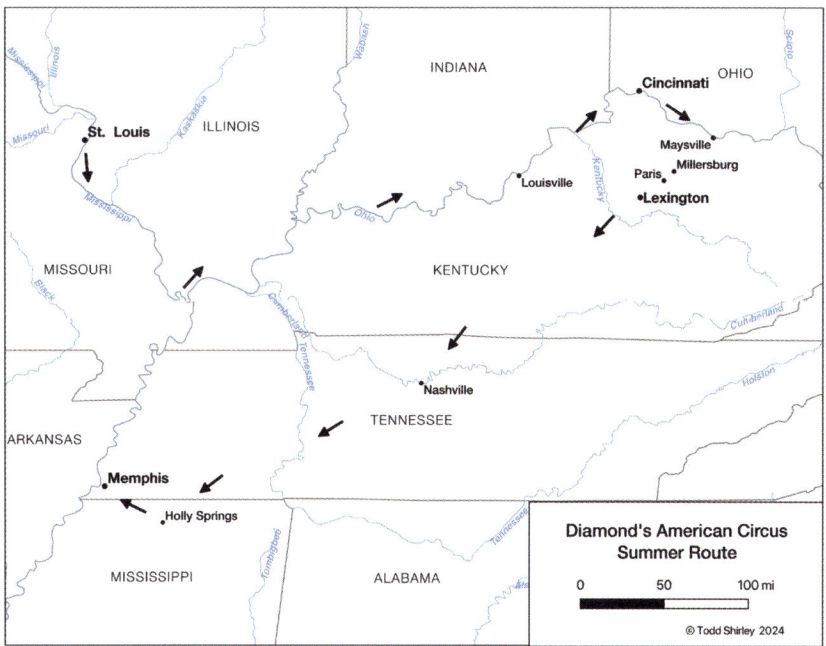

FIGURE 6.4. Diamond traveled nine hundred miles with the American Circus (John Robinson's equestrians) from late July to November 1841. Map courtesy of Todd Shirley, ©2024.

caravan of wagons, people, horses, and baggage might cover the ten or fifteen miles from one village to the next in a morning, whereas out west it sometimes took four or more days to travel the one hundred or more hot and dusty miles between towns and cities.[31] Antebellum roads came in every variety and changed with the weather. In the Northeast, dirt roads used for carrying freight were often well packed and tended, but in the South, they were just as likely to be swampy or nonexistent. In rain, muddy roads became quagmires that trapped the wheels of the wagons, and streams became dangerous rivers to be forded. When Barnum took a small circus into the West in 1837, his jig dancer drowned crossing the Kentucky River in Frankfort, where the bridges continually washed out.[32]

No matter how popular you were, there was little glamour in traveling with a circus in 1841. Circus caravans often set out in the wee hours of the morning to make the trip by early light. The nights could be "as dark as a coal hole," as well as stormy with rain and wind or thunder and lightning.[33] Traveling on such nights, the wagoners easily lost their way and had to send someone ahead as scout to mark the turns with a stick or fence rail at any crossroads. Rest was infrequent and sleep often interrupted.[34] If there was no roadside house, the company camped beside the road, the drivers burning smudge fires over a tract of land to ward off mosquitoes, then spreading the canvas sidewalls out on the ground for everyone to sleep under.[35] When the skies were clear and the air balmy, the journeys were recalled as bearable if not enjoyable. But when the rain fell, making the roadways impassable, or when frosty air stiffened the limbs, traveling with a circus was nothing but discomfort.

After Louisville, Diamond and the American Circus trekked 175 miles south to Tennessee. James Thomas and the other boys may have been waiting out on the road the day they pulled into Nashville and set up at a lot on College Street. "We were always met and escorted into town by all the boys, five or six miles from the show grounds," recalled a musician with L. B. Lent's circus. The youngest boys, awakened by the gray streaks of early dawn, were the first ones out to see the circus roll in. Older boys arrived by seven or eight o'clock, and by nine o'clock "a few grey hairs" were sprinkled among the waiting crowd.[36] Exhausted after nights with little rest and dressed in clothes they had slept in for days, circus folk often looked the wretched nomads that they frequently were, a grouchy and sorry lot.[37] But to boys like Thomas their arrival seemed a grand parade.

Weeks before a circus landed, its advertiser appeared to post bills and rent a half-acre of land just outside town or a vacant lot in town "Behind the Court House," "Near the jail," or "On the Commons." When the caravan neared the designated location, the performers camped with their wagons for the night, and the slower-moving baggage wagons continued on ahead. As soon as they arrived, the workmen unloaded the boards, canvas, and center pole, drove the stakes, and pitched the tent, sledgehammers ringing and white shirts glowing in the dim light of dawn.[38] The ring bed might be dirt or grass or covered in sawdust to shield the horses, riders, and audience from dust or mud, and the bleachers were built on one side or all the way round. When the work was done the hands and drivers breakfasted at a hotel contracted by the advertiser and waited for the performing animals and people to arrive.

Itinerant circuses set up tents as a practical shield against the cold, wind, rain, or hot sun and to keep nonpaying spectators from seeing the show. When daylight filtered in through the canvas or a makeshift candelabra illumined the ring, it also set the space apart from everyday life. The dim lighting inside circus tents softened the performers' stage makeup and disguised any wear and tear in the costumes. Blown-out candles caused tiresome delays on stormy nights, but they also added to the excitement.[39]

For the spectators, circus day was a day of leisure, its entertainments a cheap, greatly anticipated diversion. In rural areas, the tent and grounds also served as a meeting place like a post office, church, or harvest dance. Matinees were added to evening performances so that families coming from far-distant farms could attend and get home again the same day. Showman Robert White remembered the young men coming in their best shirts and trousers and the young women wearing frocks adorned with ribbons and lace: "If they were courting, the girls rode horseback behind their swains; if they came in the family wagon, the girls hoped to find a ride home behind some youthful admirer."[40] But for most people, the main excitement was inside the tent. With only a single ring, the tent made everyone in the audience feel close to the action.[41] They were also close to each other, standing up or seated on hard, narrow boards, cramped together for hours on end, an experience a reporter for *The Tennessean* called "the longest day they live."[42]

What "the people" encountered when the American Circus opened in Nashville on September 28 was their own skills and holiday activities carried "to a pitch they had not leisure to attain," notes theater scholar J. S. Bratton, "but which they would directly and by experience be able to judge and appreciate."[43] They saw Robinson elevating the plowman's team handling to an enviable art with his effortless control of four galloping horses; six-year-old Master Hernandez spending more "of his time in the *air*" than on his horse's back; a clown creating hubbub as hands rolled a carpet onto the dirt and placed a pallet in the center; a slack rope artist outdoing with a backward flip the joiner's dangerous journey across a narrow beam; a juggler perilously spinning the housewife's carefully stacked china plates atop six dowels; and, finally, "the best part of the show," the diminutive Master Diamond cutting their favorite dances into fabulously intricate designs.

Thomas, who played the fiddle, may have remembered Diamond calling for the "Camp Town Hornpipe" because the score had been sold in the tent. Circuses were purveyors of new and traditional music. During performances, boys often passed to and fro through the crowd selling things to eat or drink and, sometimes, printed song sheets of the tunes that accompanied the acts, such as the piano music for "Camp Town Hornpipe, as danced by Master Dimond" (fig. 6.5).[44] Music added to

Figure 6.5. "Camp Town Hornpipe" was John Diamond's most popular dance. The proprietors of the American Circus, both of whom spelled his name Dimond, probably commissioned this sheet music to sell as a souvenir during Diamond's performances. *Camp Town Hornpipe as danced by Master Dimond* (William Hall and Son, n.d.). Courtesy of the American Antiquarian Society.

the flair and ambience of the show. The first time Diamond came to Nashville, he danced to a circus band, recalled Thomas. "When he came again, he had a fiddler in back to sit on the ring along the side [of] the board."[45] As a large concern, Fogg and Stickney's circus traveled with a band of ten musicians. Robinson engaged six musicians when the financial condition of his show "warranted the 'extravagance,'" recalled his son Gil. And when it did not, "there was music, to be sure," but it was furnished by a lone musician, often Robinson himself, "who sat with his back against the center pole and played the violin."[46]

Cuts and Splurges

In October the circus journeyed 210 miles south by land from Nashville to Holly Springs, Mississippi, where Master Diamond and Master Hernandez dominated all the advertisements and reviews.[47] The circus "had along Master *Diamond*, the great dancer," noted the editor of the *Holly Springs Gazette* on November 4, and "well he can *shine*—but he is mighty *black*. The way he *cut* swells, *cut* capers, *cut shines*, *cut* dashes, *cut* a figure, and splurges—*Oh! De-lordy!* But the mischief of it was, he was a wretched long time a '*cutting* out.'" While clearly impressed with Diamond's skill, the writer was somewhat baffled by the popularity of Diamond's "mighty *black*" cuts (dancing steps) and splurges (boisterous, extravagant displays) and the length of his set. The writer was also surprised by the size and makeup of the audience. "We never saw such a crowd, crowded into such a place before, in *this* town," he remarked after the American Circus had been showing for a week. On one side of the tent were seated "all the starry host of beauty's select, and on the other side a black, angry (no *laughing*) cloud of *niggers*. All 'went on as merry as a marriage ball.'"[48] White women and Black people (the italicized N-word suggesting they were slaves) were packed together under canvas, taking equal pleasure in watching a white boy dance "Negro jigs." The *Gazette* editor did not know whether to approve or disapprove. Why *did* "the people," to use Thomas's words, like Diamond's mighty Black, mighty long performance?

The reaction of Southern audiences to Diamond's act suggests he altered his dances while traveling with the circus. One of the pleasures of circus life was dancing with the locals. On the road, evening performances ended about nine or ten o'clock, after which a frolic with the "lads and lasses" might commence and last all night long. Some dances were held especially for the performers, and when the dancing ended the circus boys "had a chance to accompany girls home," if they didn't have to go off early to reach the next stand. In larger towns, circus men and boys might go to a tavern, dance-house, or brothel where a ball was already in session.[49] Diamond took his cues from the local dancers he met outside of work, whose mixture of white and Black dance practices varied from place to place.

Around Nashville, people learned the art of dancing from a free "colored man" named Jordan McGowan who ran a music and dancing school when James Thomas was a boy. Rachel Gains, who had been enslaved in Davidson County, said that about "eve'y two weeks de Marster would sen' for Jordan McGowan who wuz de leader ob a string music ban.' Dey would get dere Friday nite early end de slaves would dance in de grape house* dat nite an all day Saturday up ter midnite."[50] McGowan instructed many of Nashville's "leading people" in dancing etiquette. He also taught dancing to their servants and house slaves,† who introduced him in turn to "new steps of their own with new names of some comical sound at which they were adept."[51]

In Kentucky a different dance tradition developed. "We danced some of the dances the white folks danced, the minuette, the reels, and other dances common in those days," ex-slave Robert Ball Anderson recalled of his early life in Green County, "but we liked better the dances of our own particular race." These were "individual dances, consisting of shuffling of the feet, and swinging of the arms and shoulders in a peculiar rhythm of time [which] developed into what is known today as the Double Shuffle, Heel and Toe, Buck and Wing, Juba, etc." People proficient at such dances "could play a tune with their feet, dancing largely to an inward music, a music that was felt, but not heard."[52] The routes Diamond followed that summer, the mixed audiences attending his shows, and the dance names (such as buck-and-wing) shared by Black and blackface performers suggest that swaps were made when the circus came to town. Diamond's act probably changed as he passed through Mississippi, Tennessee, Kentucky, and Ohio, delighting spectators and winning friends with steps and moves that matched the inner music of the people in any given location.

The success of circuses depended on the patronage of all sorts of ordinary people. General admission to the American Circus in Nashville was fifty cents, children and servants (or slaves) half price. In rural areas it may have been less. As a barber's apprentice with a monthly salary, Thomas was able to pay for his own ticket, but not everyone could afford the cost of entry to the circus tent. Children in rural areas found ways to earn the money—picking blackberries, collecting eggs and churning rolls of yellow butter to sell, or "cutting 'jimpson weeds' around the old church in the public square."[53]

Circuses admitted or barred Black people depending on local customs. But advertisements from the early 1840s almost always included seating arrangements

---

* Wine was made from Catawba grapes grown in Ohio and Kentucky.

† "The young people had all learned to waltz a little," recalled James Thomas, so when they saw pictures representing a dance called "la Polka," they set out to learn that dance too. "The servants of cultured people soon caught the Polka from what they saw. With the aid of their young mistress they were soon able to open the eyes of those less fortunate."

for African Americans. Occasionally, white and Black people attended separate performances, such as when a large plantation owner bought out a show for his workers. In most areas, however, people were simply partitioned into different sections by ropes. A circus in Charlotte, North Carolina, announced that "the pit is entirely enclosed for blacks"; one in Providence, Rhode Island, advertised "separate seats for colored"; at a circus in New York City places were "set apart for colored persons"; and in Holly Springs the American Circus directed white and Black people to different sides of the tent.[54]

Dancing and Fighting

As a member of an itinerant circus, John Diamond encountered moral and social prejudice. People voiced their opinions about circuses from the bleachers, newspapers, and pulpit. Church people "would raise a cry against us when we came around," recalled showman Robert White. "But then, you know, there were always others who weren't so particular, so that wherever we drove our stakes we were pretty sure to have a good house."[55] Protestant polemicists construed the circus as a wicked and frivolous waste of time and money. Some negative responses stemmed from the circus's integration of white and Black audiences. But most complaints centered around one of the circus's most appealing aspects: its display of bodies, particularly scantily clad ladies and bare-chested men doing acrobatic stunts. The *Gazette* editor, taken aback by the spectacle of young white women savoring the movements of a taut youth dancing in a Black way, expressed both kinds of objections.

People also condemned circuses for the unruly persons they attracted. On circus day, gangs of young men high on liquor or just plain fired up by the excitement congregated near the exhibition site, making "dust-ups" or street fights (and the occasional full-fledged riot) a regular feature.[56] Horse races, election days, agricultural fairs, Fourth of July celebrations, and other public gatherings also drew crowds of leisure takers, food and drink vendors, pickpockets, loafers, rabble-rousers, and gamblers (fig. 6.6). Circus detractors saw little difference between the disorderly mob swarming the pavilion and the workers inside. When Robinson's company arrived in Holly Springs on October 28, 1841, the fall races had already filled the streets with "an everlasting ratling of hacks—gallopping of horses—hooping of bad boys—cursing and swearing of drunken men," complained the *Gazette*. "To-night we look for the circus belonging, *so they say*,—to the American Theatre, New Orleans, and it is to bring along Master Diamond, the dancer who we expect will *cut up* some rare splurges here. Well, it would all do very nice if it were not for the money it takes, and the *sin* it leaves."[57]

In certain regions, circus people were welcomed like returning friends by merchants, hotel managers, and tavern keepers, who stood to make a sizeable profit

FIGURE 6.6. Circuses, horse races, election days, agricultural fairs, Fourth of July celebrations, and other public amusements drew crowds of old and young, Black and white, male and female leisure takers, food and drink vendors, gamblers, pickpockets, loafers, and rabble rousers. W. S. Hedges, *A Race Meeting at Jacksonville,* Alabama, 1841. Birmingham Museum of Art.

during their stay. Respectable "ladies and gentlemen" visited the hotels where the performers were staying to eat and socialize with them, and locals sponsored dances to which all the circus workers were invited. But as the number of troupes multiplied, they lost that trust. Bareback rider John Glenroy remembered staying at a hotel in New Hampshire where the manager "took from our bed rooms the bed clothes, water pitcher, etc. and in fact everything moveable except the beds even taking the mattresses and leaving us the rope bottoms of the beds to lie on." Also, "he would not allow us to eat at the same table with his other guests, saying that showmen were no company for gentlemen."[58]

Circus people's ballyhoo, daring display, and vulgar language offended some people, to be sure. But the incivility of locals could outshine the coarseness of the showmen and women. For every town where boys like Thomas came out determined to pat the ponies, there was another where youths gathered on the hillsides to pelt the wagons with sticks and rocks. Worst of all were local rowdies who came out bent on disrupting the show and "whipping the actors." Certain counties were known for harboring ruffians who insulted the performers, interrupted their acts, and picked fights with the circus men. If they couldn't get in twice on a single ticket or were ejected for smoking in the tent, they "stormed the castle" (cutting a slit in the canvas after the show began and creeping in without paying), threatened to demolish the wagons and "kill the d——d showmen," or lounged around outside waiting for the orderly part of the audience to leave before commencing "their hellish treatment."⁵⁹ Circus performers were suspicious outsiders who faced vilification and risked violence at every stop.

The response of itinerant circus people to their detractors reflected their liminal social position. Antebellum showmen liked to tell stories about pulling pranks on their "enemies," who were invariably outliers like themselves—superstitious Black people and old cynical white women. In one such story, John Robinson ran through an African Methodist Episcopal congregation during a service wearing a red suit and devil's horns after hearing that the preacher had condemned his circus. In another, a circus man secretly sprayed an African American audience with blackened water because an old man among them was denouncing the show as the devil's work. The tellers of these tales did not see their actions as motivated by racial antipathy. They were targeting people who targeted them. But their choice of Black victims shows that circus men knew where they stood on the social ladder and at whom people in their position could laugh with impunity. On the other hand, their perambulations gave circus people the liberty to choose their friends. In another story, a showman boasted about defending a Black man who tried to protect the circus. After a performance in Lewistown, Pennsylvania, the orderly portion of the audience retired as requested, he recalled,

> but some twenty rowdies, Juniata river rangers,* held back, and said they would go just when it suited them. The landlord's black hostler told them they had better go out of the canvas as requested, as the showman wanted to lock up the animals. They told the black man it was none of his business, and then they knocked him down and beat him. Mr. Pursel and myself interfered in behalf of the poor hostler. We lent a hand and knocked down a half dozen of them; the rest backed out. Then they all left, swearing vengeance at the show folks.⁶⁰

What Diamond learned from the circus men around him was disrespect for people who denounced you and loyalty to those who defended you.

Robinson's reputation and tall stature may have kept rowdies itching for a fight away from the American Circus, or it may have attracted them to it. Most bareback riders, tumblers, dancers, and musicians had a slighter build. Circus folk who heard in advance that ruffians were on their way either packed up and left or prepared to give them "the hot end of the poker" by sending the women back to the hotel, arming themselves with animal whips, and enlisting powerful men who were known fighters to stand by them. "For myself, I never was a quarrelsome or fighting man, and did not like to fight if I could avoid it," Hugh Lindsay admitted. "But sometimes I had to fight in self-defense."⁶¹

---

* The rangers were a group of armed men who roamed around the Junita River, a tributary of the Susquehanna River in central Pennsylvania.

Diamond proved himself a dancer and a fighter. After Holly Springs, the American Circus caravanned forty miles north to Memphis for a two-week stand in November, then boarded a riverboat and headed back to New Orleans and the American Theater, where Diamond danced between the acts the week of November 22.[62] He also danced after the show ended. Late-night dancing and drinking could lead to fighting, according to tales told by circus performers. In one story, a drunken sword-swallower insulted a young woman at a dance in New Jersey, and the young men of the town vowed to flog him. A fellow performer interfered and put him to bed, then stayed up himself dancing with the girls until daylight. In another, a handsome circus performer at a dance in Georgia stood talking to a young woman when "a villain" came in with a bowie knife and carved his face into gashes.[63] Such attacks led to the development of a "rallying signal among circus men when in trouble." According to John Glenroy, a circus performer "went with some of the rest of the company to a dance house, and there got into some trouble and was knocked to the ground with a slung shot.*" When he hit the floor, "he shouted out 'Hey Rube' to one of the other members of the company, and every member of the circus who was in the hall immediately went to his assistance."[64]

In New Orleans, Diamond might have chosen to attend a dance in the French Quarter, where subscription dress and masquerade balls (open to the public) took place at hotel and theater ballrooms almost every evening, gentlemen $1.50 or $2.00 and ladies gratis. The Washington and American Ball Room reserved Tuesdays and Fridays for "Quarteroon women." Or he might have gone to a ball at a tavern or brothel. Trouble began when Mr. James Barron, a resident of New Orleans, verbally insulted Diamond at a dance on November 25. That insult was not recorded in the papers, but considering that Barron was a native Southerner and Diamond a stroppy Northern circus dancer, it is not hard to imagine. Subsequent accounts of the incident called the insult "fancied" rather than actual, but the little dancer took it seriously enough to draw a penknife and stab Barron three times.[65]

Diamond was thrown into jail for the night and then released, or so it seems. The next week, his name was listed among the entertainments being offered at the American, although Master Hernandez danced the sailor's hornpipe as the entr'acte on November 26. In the meantime, Barron filed an affidavit against John Diamond for wounding him "with intent to kill." The *Daily Picayune* announced Master Diamond's benefit and last appearance on December 2. The editor did not mention Diamond's pending arraignment, but he did comment on his dancing: "This boy's abilities are certainly of a very remarkable and amusing character, although we should like them better any where else but on the regular stage." Diamond had turned sixteen in August. He was arraigned on December 3 by

---

* A piece of metal or stone (shot) fastened to a strap or thong and used as a weapon.

FIGURE 6.7. "Calaboose" was the familiar name given to the jail cells behind the Cabildo, or city hall, in New Orleans, where the municipal recorder sent Diamond and other "suspicious persons" to serve a thirty-day sentence. *Lafitte Cell in the Courtyard of the Cabildo*, 1950. New Orleans Historical Society.

Paul Bertus, recorder of the First Municipality, and sent to the "calaboose" to await trial at "Criminal Court" (fig. 6.7).⁶⁶

In the Calaboose

Diamond's arrest for what the *True Flash* called "cutting queer shines" in the Crescent City, quickly became national news. On November 30 the *Albany Evening Journal* reported that Master Diamond, "well known as an enactor of negro characters," had been committed to jail in New Orleans for stabbing Barron.⁶⁷ The *Philadelphia Ledger* ran the story on December 2, the *Connecticut Courant*, *Dramatic Mirror*, and *True Flash* on December 4, the *Albany Argus* and *Hudson River Chronicle* on December 7, and so on up and down the route Diamond had covered with Barnum the previous year (including Sing Sing, New York; Hartford, Connecticut; and Coldwater, Michigan). These notices in "Last Night's Mails" columns kept John Diamond in the public eye. As did the *Picayune*'s response to the *Boston Post*'s denial of the arrest, which exposed the dancer's impersonators up north.⁶⁸*

---

* On December 15 the *Daily Picayune* reprinted the *Boston Transcript*'s report that Master Diamond had been jailed for the stabbing and the *Boston Post*'s rejoinder: "We rather think this will be news to Master Diamond. He concluded an engagement at Harrington's Museum in this city last Saturday." To which the *Picayune* editor retorted: "The sum and substance of the business is, friend Post, your Master Diamond has hooked the name of the Master Diamond in our calaboose."

Diamond spent a month languishing in jail. The "intent to kill" charge does not seem to have held up in court, however, probably because the weapon he wielded was a penknife, an extremely small blade used to sharpen quills, peel and cut fruit, or stab pieces of meat out of a communal stew pot at the dinner table. According to press coverage, Diamond had acquired the attributes of an outlaw—inconstant, uncontrollable, dangerous. But none of that checked his career. The *Dramatic Mirror, and Literary Companion*, which jested on December 4 that Master Diamond had walked "out of his profession and into the stabbing business," casually informed its readers on December 25 that he had "been liberated from prison in New Orleans" and "resumed his avocations."[69]

For six months in 1841, John Diamond navigated the vagaries of circus itinerancy, spreading his name and notoriety across the West and South. By the end of his tour, he had become so famous that sporting people christened their racehorses and prize bulls after him, and newspapers used his dancing as a metaphor for the state of the economy: "There were more failures this week than mail failures," noted the *Picayune* on January 8, 1842, "more break-downs than those of Master Diamond."[70] Diamond experienced a different performing context riding with the circus. It liberated the recalcitrant teenager from adult control and introduced him to wage labor and management. It unleashed his inclination to do battle with those who slighted him and also to stand by his friends.

* * *

Diamond joined Jim Sanford at the St. Charles Theatre in New Orleans on December 29. They worked as a team. At Sanford's benefit on January 2, 1842, they performed a variety of acts and local dances, "the Corn Shucking Jig—Grey Eagle Waggoner—Black Rose—Fashion—and a Week in the Country," accompanied by the "Ole Wirginny Paganini, Mr. Winn," on the fiddle. That program included a new gender-bending piece called "BLUE JACKETS! Or, How to Man a Navy" with an all-female six-member cast and concluded with "MASQUERADE! Or, The Negro Doorkeeper" with Sanford as the doorkeeper and Diamond as Elssler.[71]

At Diamond's benefit on January 4, Mrs. Richardson opened in Dion Boucicault's comedy *London Assurance*, and "Master Diamond and Mr. Sanford" presented "a great trial of skill," during which some "'extra licks'" were thrown in to "astonish the admirers of *pedalology*. Such a bill," declared the *Picayune*, "coupled with the fact that it is also Master Diamond's last appearance, should cause his friends to muster in strong force."[72] They called the act "GRAND MATCH DANCE" but did not announce a wager. Diamond would save those matches for a different audience and opponent.

7

A SENSATION IN PRINT

In the spring of 1842, Juba captured the attention of a visiting British writer who would catapult him to international fame. Thirty-year-old Charles Dickens and his wife, Catherine, arrived in New York City by steamer on February 14 after a month visiting Boston and New Haven. The harbor they entered was overrun with newsboys hollering mastheads and headlines from skiffs bobbing on the water below or clambering on deck to prod passengers with their cache of penny dailies and weekly journals, including the very periodicals that pirated Dickens's stories. The famous author had come to accept laurels for his books *Oliver Twist, Nicholas Nickleby,* and *The Old Curiosity Shop,* visit sites of interest, gather material for his fiction and nonfiction writing, and broach the unpopular subject of an international copyright law. During their stay in the metropolis, the Dickenses were "feted, danced, dinnered, journalized, [and] speeched" at "the homes of the *elite* of the city" and honored with a great ball in Tammany Hall.[1] But Dickens did not seem amused, and his American hosts, already annoyed by the author's lectures on copyright, soon became resentful. "It was in New York that it was first suspected that Charles Dickens would not be likely to approve American slavery," wrote G. W. Putnam, who served as Dickens's secretary during his four-month tour of the States, "and the newspapers began extensively to exhibit that unfriendly feeling toward him which afterward became so violent and even malignant."[2]

Tired of hobnobbing with New York's well-to-dos, Dickens spent his last day in the city on a walking tour. With a party of acquaintances, including an alderman and a few journalist hangers-on, he set out from the Carlton House Hotel and headed up Broadway under an unseasonably hot late afternoon sun on Friday, March 4. Broadway's shining pavement stones, plethora of omnibuses, "many-colored crowd," and "the great blocks of clean ice being carried into shops and bar-rooms" to cool "the pine-apples and water-melons profusely displayed for sale" struck Dickens favorably. The group took in Wall Street, then crossed back over Broadway and entered the Bowery, another long main thoroughfare where the stores were poorer and passengers on horse-drawn streetcars less gay.[3]

Up the road stood the party's first stop, the city's house of detention, a menacing Egyptian-style edifice called the Tombs. The English judicial system, which Dickens abhorred, seemed almost civilized compared to the treatment he saw there. He described the building as long, narrow, and lofty, with four galleries of cells one above the other. "Those at the bottom are unwholesome, surely?" Dickens asked the man with keys, who was showing him around. "Why, we *do* only put coloured people in 'em," the guard assured him. "That's the truth."[4]

The thoroughfare was "dotted with bright jets of gas" by the time Dickens emerged from the prison and joined William H. Stephens and A. M. C. Smith, "two heads of the police," who would serve as escorts for the night. A neighborhood watchman, Stephens knew the area's businesses and residents, and they knew him. He was the same officer who had fetched dancer-actor Louis Davis from the Bowery and taken him to Justice Steven's court in September 1840. Following his guides, Dickens entered the quarter of New York's Sixth Ward known as the Five Points (after an intersection where five streets met), "which, in respect of filth and wretchedness," he later wrote, "may be safely backed against Seven Dials," the slums of St. Giles parish in 1840s London (fig. 7.1). Here, too, were "lanes and alleys, paved with mud knee-deep," underground chambers where people came to "dance and game," and "ruined houses, open to the street, whence, through wide gaps in the walls, other ruins loom upon the eye."[5]

Stephens led the author down an alley and up a rickety flight of pitch-dark stairs, where "a negro lad, startled from his sleep by the officer's voice—he knows it well," noted Dickens, lit a candle and showed them a number of miserable rooms with "great mounds of dusky rags upon the ground" that stirred and arose and revealed themselves to be "heaps of negro women waking from their sleep: their white teeth chattering, and their bright eyes glistening and winking on all sides with surprise and fear, like the countless repetition of one astonished African face in some strange mirror." A moment later, Stephens plunged down some stairs and opened a door, inviting them into a surprisingly pleasant cellar dance-house—"the assembly-room of the Five-Point fashionables." "Heyday! the landlady of Almack's thrives!" exclaimed Dickens, who was greeted by "a buxom fat mulatto woman, with sparkling eyes," her head "daintily ornamented with a handkerchief of many colors." He also noticed the finery of the landlord, who ushered him in—a smart blue ship steward's jacket, a gleaming watch-guard chain round his neck, a thick gold ring upon his little finger. "How glad he is to see us! What will we please to call for? A dance? It shall be done directly, sir: 'a regular break-down.'"[6]

A SENSATION IN PRINT · 145

THE FIVE POINTS IN 1859
Crossing of Baxter (late Orange) Park (late Cross) & Worth (late Anthony) Sts.

FIGURE 7.1. African and Irish Americans rubbed shoulders on a daily basis in New York's Five Points district, where Dickens saw Juba dance. In this image a Black woman and an Irish woman with a Black child in tow buy fish from two white male fishmongers. *The Five Points in 1859: Crossing of Baxter (late Orange) Park (late Cross) & Worth (late Anthony) Sts.* "For D. T. Valentine's Manual, 1860."

As soon as the dance was called for, a corpulent Black fiddler and tambourine player stamped on a small raised "orchestra" and struck up a jaunty measure. Six couples immediately took the floor, "marshaled by a lively young negro, who is the wit of the assembly, and the greatest dancer known. He never leaves off making queer faces, and is the delight of all the rest, who grin from ear to ear incessantly. Among the dancers are two young mulatto girls, with large, black, drooping eyes, and head-gear after the fashion of the hostess, who are as shy, or feign to be, as though they never danced before." And then the dancing commenced.

"Every gentleman sets as long as he likes to the opposite lady, and the opposite lady to him," observed Dickens, "and all are so long about it that the sport begins to languish, when suddenly the lively hero dashes in to the rescue."

> Single shuffle, double shuffle, cut and cross-cut; snapping his fingers, rolling his eyes, turning in his knees, presenting the backs of his legs in front, spinning about on his toes and heels like nothing but the man's fingers on the tambourine; dancing with two left legs, two right legs, two wooden legs, two wire legs, two spring legs—all sorts of legs and no legs—what is this to him? And in what walk of life,

or dance of life, does man ever get such stimulating applause as thunders about him, when, having danced his partner off her feet, and himself too, he finishes by leaping gloriously on the bar-counter, and calling for something to drink, with the chuckle of a million of counterfeit Jim Crows, in one inimitable sound![7]

Dickens's "lively hero" was the dancer recently identified in the *Sunday Flash* as Juba. The quotation comes from a travelogue Dickens kept during his journey through the United States, published in October 1842 under the title *American Notes for General Circulation*. The publication of *American Notes* caused a great stir in the United States. Not only did it record Dickens's reflections on what he saw as the deleterious effects of democracy on the nation's white citizens, it also incorporated African Americans into the American narrative. Dickens's visit to a Black-run tavern in Five Points generated a flurry of press coverage that spring. But it was his positive description of Juba's dancing that most offended the English author's American fans. That description also redirected the dancer's career.

Dickens's powerful image of Juba's dance has been cited as evidence for the Black foundations of American tap, the African and Afro-Caribbean heritage of American dance, the melting pot of Five Points, the authenticity of Juba's dancing compared to other elements of minstrelsy, and Dickens's significance to Juba's career (fig. 7.2).[8] However, certain aspects of the scene have been consistently overlooked. Dickens's position as a foreigner and fiction writer opened up possibilities for a different kind of spectatorship. He cut through prejudices and wrote down details his contemporaries rarely noticed or considered worthy of notice. His English references, the class distinctions he saw in the Black community, and the female dancers in that passage illuminate the world in which Juba danced. They also demonstrate how sometimes it takes a novelist and an outsider to invoke the notion that a different perspective of reality is attainable.[9] Dickens's impact on Juba's career demonstrates the important role the press played in establishing challenge dancers as celebrities and jig dancing as a sport. The week after Dickens departed, New York's penny and flash papers began printing articles recounting his Five Points tour. These stories included scenes that would appear in *American Notes* six months later, but their depictions did not match the Englishman's. These American "insiders" described the same dancing and women Dickens would describe, but their accounts were steeped in racism and sexism. Most significantly, no one singled out Juba for praise until after *American Notes* arrived.

Almack's Mystique

The dynamism of Dickens's Five Points descriptions came from the contrasts he set up between the familiar and the unexpected. He distilled the places he visited and the poverty and achievement he witnessed into two contrasting composites— a dilapidated tenement square and a lively cellar dance-house—filtered through

FIGURE 7.2. Dickens called the cellar tavern he visited in New York in 1842 Almack's. This 1870s illustration from his *American Notes* depicts male and female dancers performing the breakdown at the end of a Black-Irish set dance. *When Suddenly the Lively Hero Dashes to the Rescue,* from *American Notes and Pictures from Italy by Charles Dickens,* illustrated by A. B. Frost and Gordon Thomson (D. Appleton and Company, 1878), 44.

an English lens. He saw Englishness in the most unlikely places. Nearly every house along Anthony Street was a "low tavern," he wrote, decorated with "coloured prints of Washington, and Queen Victoria of England, and the American Eagle."[10]

Dickens's contemporaries understood his English references. In keeping with a naming practice popular in the United States, he called his dance-house Almack's, wittily and advisedly, to evoke a scene of affluence and propriety. Almack's was the name of fashionable assembly rooms in London's upscale West End that had been established by William Almack in 1762 as a private men's club. In the 1770s Almack's function broadened when "powerful women of influence" banded together to organize large exclusive balls there. Entrance to Almack's ballroom required acceptance by the women's committee, payment of a subscription fee, a card of admission, and proper dress and address.[11] By calling his hostess the "landlady of Almack's," Dickens identified the proprietors of New York's Almack's as the upper crust of African American society. To further the connection, he singled out two young dark-eyed mulatto women in colorful headscarves who feigned shyness as though they'd never danced before (when, clearly, they knew what they were about), echoing the fashionable young white women at London balls.

It is impossible to verify the exact venue Dickens described in *American Notes*, since none of the Americans who accompanied him mentioned seeing Juba dance. In and around the Five Points, "Almack's" served as a nickname for any place where large numbers of "cultured" people collected to dance.[12] On March 6 the *New York Herald* reported that Dickens's party had "entered nearly all the dens in the vicinity of the Points, and the dance houses in Anthony and Church streets, including Pete Williams' saloon and Almacks." Among those "dens" was John Frazer's corner porterhouse at 52 Walker Street, also called "Almack's in Orange street." According to the *Whip and Satirist of New-York and Brooklyn*, Frazer only admitted "genteel negroes," about a hundred of whom were assembled the night Dickens stopped in. The master of ceremonies, possibly Frazer himself, was "a gentleman of color" who called to the fiddler for "de Boz Quadrille."[13] Dickens also went to Tom Read's cellar ballroom in the rear of No. 25 Howard Street, "known among the blacks and 'kidneys' [flashy-type youths] as Almacks."[14] Dickens probably saw Juba dance in one of those dance-houses. Someone later claimed that he saw him at Pete Williams's saloon, which is possible, although the press separated Williams's place from Almack's in their accounts.[15]

By choosing the name Almack's, Dickens alluded to another English reference Americans would have picked up on: sportswriter Pierce Egan's popular *Life in London or, the Day and Night Scenes of Jerry Hawthorn, Esq., and his elegant friend Corinthian Tom, accompanied by Bob Logic, the Oxonian, in their rambles and sprees through the Metropolis.** Published serially from 1821 to 1828, *Life in London* follows the fictional characters Jerry, Tom, and Bob into the worlds Egan inhabited as a boxing reporter and man-about-town. Pirated versions of Egan's book were exported to America in 1822, along with William Thomas Moncrieff's stage adaptation, *Tom and Jerry, or Life in London*. Other plays featuring Egan's characters appeared and ran continuously on American stages for several decades, popularizing the sporting man's "flash" lingo used by the book's narrator and characters. In fact, a version of *Tom and Jerry* was playing at the Chatham Theatre the week Dickens arrived in New York.

Much of Egan's trademark vocabulary had passed into American vernacular by the 1840s. "Kidneys," for example, was an Americanization of Egan's "kidwys" and "kiddiesses." In one installment of *Life in London,* Tom, Jerry, and Logic are taken by a gentleman friend to a tavern dance-house in London's East End called ALL-MAX, "a good pun and full of *spirit*," notes Logic, "max" having replaced "gin" as genteel slang for liquor. Run by a landlady and her husband, the small room is packed with a motley crew of regular customers: "Lascars [sailors from

---

* The protagonists' names referenced their social status: a Corinthian was a wealthy amateur sportsman, an Oxonian was someone who attended Oxford University, and Hawthorn was a topographic name for a country gentleman who lived behind a hawthorn hedge.

FIGURE 7.3. England had its flash equivalents to Almack's in Five Points. Here, the mixed-race "sons & daughters of nature," including Dusty Bob and African Sal (Mrs. Dusty Bob), are "footing the *double shuffle* against each other" at All-Max in London's East End. Pierce Egan, *Life in London, or The Day and Night Scenes of Jerry Hawthorne, Esq. and his Elegant Friend Corinthian Tom in their Rambles and Sprees through the Metropolis*, illustrated by George and Isaac Robert Cruikshank (Sherwood, Neely and Jones, 1821), 286.

India], blacks, jack tars, coal-heavers, dustmen, women of colour, old and young, and a sprinkling of the remnants of once fine girls, &c. were all *jigging* together," said the narrator, "provided the *teaser of the catgut* was not *bilked* of his *duce* [provided the fiddle player got paid]."* That mixture of humanity was illustrated by the brothers Isaac and George Cruikshank in the book's 1821 edition. "Lowest 'Life in London'" depicts All-Max's customers and workers, including the four slumming men-about-town, the corpulent landlady, a black waitress, a number of laboring men, and two prostitutes, one white and one Black, sitting on Logic's knees. At the front of the scene sits an old white woman holding a Black baby that is reaching out to a white man and Black woman facing off in a jig, suggesting the mixed-race couple are its parents (fig. 7.3).

American journalists highlighted racial integration in the venues Dickens visited, as if it was an American phenomenon. "As much of London low life, as he has seen," claimed the *Herald*, "this visit was entirely original, as most of the places they entered were the resort of blacks and whites, mulattoes and mustees,† mixed together like whortleberries and cream."[16] Considering Egan's popularity in America, this statement seems strikingly disingenuous. The Black population in England was

---

* To bilk is a technical term from cribbage, meaning to spoil an adversary's score.
† Offspring of a white person and a person who is one-quarter Black.

small compared to that in the United States, but that number had been enlarged by loyalist exiles from the American colonies after 1783 and people freed by Britain's 1834 Slavery Abolition Act. Racial mixing was common in England's lower-class and maritime districts, and interracial marriage, although limited by social custom, helped blend the Black population into the general public within a few generations. Conversely, in America antimiscegenation laws made it illegal for white and Black to marry, thereby maintaining "the proper racial and moral order." The large number and class diversity of America's Black population were probably more interesting to Dickens than simple racial mixing.

To establish Almack's as a respectable establishment and dispel the assumption that the women present were prostitutes, Dickens portrayed everyone inside, apart from his own entourage, as colored.[17] In contrast, the American press peopled its Black-run dance-houses with Black, yellow (mixed-race), and white women to signal their vulgar and dissolute character. "The way some of the darkies 'broke down' and 'heeled and toed' at Almacks and Pete Williams's saloon was a caution to all pine floors," declared the *Herald*, "and the perfume that rose from the combined motley mass was almost thick enough to be cut into slices. . . . The 'lion' of the night [Dickens] was the observed of all observers, and the yellow girls closed round him and the good looking Alderman, as though they wished to examine into all particulars."[18] The "corporeal smells and animal passions" being repudiated by the rising middle classes permeated American descriptions of integrated gatherings, creating expectations in the pleasure-seeking white men who infiltrated the Five Points and normalizing the abusive treatment of white women who deigned to interact with Black people.[19]

Dickens despised America's "licentious press."[20] In "Boz at Five Points," the *Whip* slanderously identified "Frank McCabe, in Anthony street," honored with the party's first visit, as "a white man who keeps a house of entertainment and prostitution for negroes of both genders." The *Whip* writer also placed the apartment Dickens visited with Officer Stephens upstairs at McCabe's, where, he claimed, "four negresses were discovered without so much as a fig-leaf, far less a rag to cover their nakedness, lying on the bare floor, intermixed with four or five dogs, who were doing their best to keep them warm, and one buck negro."[21] Business directories at the time listed Francis McCabe as the keeper of a tavern at 146 Anthony Street. Some grocers and saloonkeepers in lower-class districts did rent out rooms for trysting, but the *Whip*'s description was simply an eroticization of the destitute poor for white men's entertainment. Where Dickens found the abject poverty and fear caused by slavery and racism, American journalists imagined wanton Black women.

The Almack's in *American Notes* was probably Tom Read's place, which was broken up by the police a month later. Counted as "one of the lions of the city," Read's ballroom attracted New York's Black elite, especially "the head cooks and waiters of our first families," reported the *New York Aurora*, "and many of our young men about town used to drop in by way of curiosity." At midnight on April 19, 1842, the city's "indefatigables [police] entered with ruthless hands this temple of Terpsichore [dance], and carried off all the negro ladies and their beaux to the silent gloom of the tombs."[22] The author of the *Aurora* article, most likely its editor, Thomas Nichols, did not specify a cause for the arrest or why the dancers were "one and all, brought before the sitting magistrate, compelled to disclose their names, occupations, and whereabouts, and then to find bail each and every one in the sum of $100." Instead, he mocked the clothes and deportment of Read's relatively affluent Black clientele, who arrived "most elaborately dressed" in satin and velvet to dance "gallopades, quadrilles, and mazurkas," suggesting that the police were called in to warn them away from putting on airs.[23] These were not respectable people being wronged by the police, he reassured his readers, for "towards night the negro belles would of course get a little elevated, and then Jump Jim Crow and Jim Along Josey were the tunes called for." Unlike the *Aurora*, the *Herald* did not bother to ascertain the class of the dancers. It simply reported that Read's place was raided at midnight, and twenty-four "black, white, and speckled danseuse [female dancers] landed in the Egyptian saloon," as if everyone knew that women who integrated dance-houses were committing a crime.[24]

Danced off Her Feet

The "regular breakdown" Dickens saw at Almack's was familiar to the English author, who had seen set dancing before. Only Juba's style of movement was new. In the 1840s "breakdown" referred to both the "riotous dance" at the end of an Irish ball and "a dance in the peculiar style of the negroes."[25] Contemporary Irish author William Carleton described a breakdown he'd seen in County Tyrone, Ireland, twenty years earlier. After selecting "his own sweetheart" and assuming a station on the floor so that "both should face the fiddler," the male dancer commenced quietly and gradually began "to move more sprightly." Then just as the set seemed about to fizzle out, "up he bounds in a fling or a caper—crack go the fingers—cut and treble go the feet, heel and toe, right and left. Then he flings the right heel up to the ham, up again the left, the whole face in a furnace-heat of ecstatic delight" (fig. 7.4).[26] What Dickens saw in Five Points was an uninhibited melding of Irish and African American dance. Juba punctuated the cuts, trebles, and flings of an Irish breakdown with African turned-in knees, toe and heel spins, and orbiting eyes.

The dance of Dickens's "lively hero" was familiar in one other way. Juba was not performing solo. He and his "sweetheart" were competing. He won applause by dancing "his partner off her feet." With that detail, Dickens acknowledged that the woman dancing opposite Juba was also engaged in serious competition. The scene he recorded was not created by men alone. The first proprietor to greet

FIGURE 7.4. Dickens's description of Juba's dancing resembled contemporary accounts of Irish dancing. "Up he bounds in a fling or a caper—crack go the fingers—cut and treble go the feet," wrote William Carleton in 1840 about the champion dancer he saw showing off at the end of a set dance in County Tyrone, Ireland. Detail from unidentified artist, *Dance of Peasantry on the Lawn at Carton* [House, Maynooth, Kildare, Ireland], from the *Illustrated London News*, Aug. 18, 1849, 125.

him was the landlady. Dickens judged that the pretty, well-mannered girls were actually skilled dancers, and Juba's female partner was also his opponent. Dickens could see that these women were not just decorating the room. They actively participated in the economic, social, and cultural life of the times.

So who was the lively young heroine dancing with Juba that night? Only once was she identified, and that was in a send-up of *American Notes* put on by several white blackface performers who knew Juba from Vauxhall Gardens. They called Dickens's hero Black Bill (for William Lane) and named his partner "Black Bet (the 'mulatto girl, with large, black, drooping eyes')."[27] Her actual name is, unsurprisingly, lost to posterity. But she must have been an extraordinarily good dancer and very sure of herself to face "the greatest dancer known." Equally deft and courageous was a mulatto girl in Ned Buntline's 1847 "real life story" *Mysteries and Miseries of New York*, who demanded respect for her dancing skills. When notorious nativist Bill Lord commanded the prettiest "yaller gals" in a cellar dance-house to match his boys in a set, wrote Buntline, an ugly, ragged, "mud-colored" girl countered: "Purty is as purty does, sah! Dem's my senterments." "So they're mine, too," conceded Lord, who found her a partner.[28] Female jig dancers shared a self-assured competitiveness with their male peers and were admired for it.

Juba may have chosen his opponent, or she chose him. No jig dancer who frequented tavern dance-houses was surprised to see women challenging men. In Ireland, it was traditional for a young female to initiate the competition. Toward the end of the evening, recalled Irish American writer R. Shelton Mackenzie, a "joyous, light-hearted damsel would suddenly start up, while the music was playing, and, placing herself before the dancing-master, . . . silently challenge him to dance with her. . . . Then, challenger and challenged would commence an Irish jig—a dance so violent that . . . the very recollection of it makes me feel as if the barometer was some two hundred in the shade."[29] Superior dancing prowess and stamina, not gender, ruled the dancing arena.

Nineteenth-century writers routinely labeled intrepid female dancers "viragos" (manly women or female warriors), "trulls" (prostitutes), or "strumpets" (promiscuous women). Prescriptive literature masked as description insisted that a man expressed "his joy of dancing through vigorous and agile movements" and a woman expressed hers through a "delicate vivacity . . . equally gentle and animated."[30] But not all female dancers fit the prescription: "Instead of dancing with the native modesty so peculiar to our countrywomen," Carleton saw one girl dancing "with the unseemly movements of a tipsy virago, or a trull in Donnybrook." While not saying she was a prostitute, Carleton associated her competitive spirit with masculine sexual liberty. However, he cautioned his readers not to take such bold exuberance as "a specimen of what Irish-women are"; it was simply the young competitor's enthusiastic response to the encouragement of her peers: "Whoo! Judy, that's the girl; handle your feet, avourneen; that's it, acushla! stand to me! Hurroo for our side of the house!"[31]

Every working-class woman enjoying herself in public risked being branded a prostitute in antebellum America. Socially peripheral yet symbolically central, prostitutes provided a stark opposition to the emerging ideal of middle-class womanhood—the virtuous "angel in the house." The prostitute's centrality pushed to the periphery the thousands of working women plying other trades—boardinghouse managers and shopkeepers, cleaners, cooks, laundresses, seamstresses, milliners, delivery girls, street sweepers, peddlers, waitresses, and mill workers—so near and copious that they became invisible. Many of these women and girls labored for wages so small that a short time without work could reduce them to absolute distress. For some, sexual bartering served as a temporary solution to immediate difficulties. For others, it became a permanent profession. There were also those who turned to prostitution because they shunned dependency and other symbols of middle-class respectability.[32] However, for most lower-class women, "prostitute" might better be thought of as a traditional form of

FIGURE 7.5. Working-class women and men went to drinking places to find skilled dancing partners. That this woman wore shoes made specifically for dancing indicates that she took her jigging seriously. "The Sailors' Boarding-House," from Thomas B. Gunn, *The Physiology of New York Boarding-houses* (1857), 280.

remunerative labor than as an identity. Or if that is what a woman was when she engaged in sexual bartering, why not give her a different identity when she engaged in another activity?

Prostitutes were not the only women who jig danced in antebellum America, but it is possible that they were the only working-class women willing to dance with men from outside their community. White middle-class males who encountered young women dancing in taverns depicted them in harsh terms. Journalist George Foster admired the white "b'hoys" who integrated dance-houses but not the white girls, whom he called even more "horribly disgusting" than the "negresses, of various shades and colors."[33] "The male dancers are all sailors" (meaning all ethnicities), Thomas B. Gunn wrote about balls at seamen's boardinghouses, "their partners being coarse, fat, vulgar-looking young women, whose bloated features indicate confirmed habits of drunkenness" (fig. 7.5).[34] Of course, the dancers did not see themselves in this way. Their views were better expressed by the woman's dancing shoes in the picture that accompanied Gunn's description, which indicated that she took her jigging seriously. Working-class men and women went to tavern dance-houses and sailors' boardinghouses to find other dancers who knew the steps—the only feature that really mattered.

The association of dancing with prostitution helps explain the dearth of women in histories of American dance. A few brave young women did take their champion dances to the stage. In January 1842, for example, Miss Rosley demonstrated her "science of heel and toe" at the Arcadian Circus on Bleeker Street. But even professional dancers had to endure accusations of immorality. "Park Benjamin of the New World, calls Fanny Ellsler [sic] 'a common prostitute,' which is as gross a libel as was ever printed," noted the *Flash,* "but he escapes, because, forsooth, he is a respectable man and an accomplished gentleman. This should not be. There is no evidence whatever before the American public that Fanny has ever swerved from virtue. If she is a prostitute at all, she is not a common, but an uncommon one." And now, "under pretense of refuting the calumny, [Thomas Nichols] repeats and circulates it," complained the *Flash* while indulging in the same practice.[35]

Nance and Suse

In June 1842 the flash papers ran a story about a dancing match between two young white women on Boston's Long Wharf. The match gained press attention because the opponents, Nance Holmes and Suse Bryant, were well-known brothel prostitutes. They were also well-known jig dancers. This story documents the existence of female same-sex dancing matches. It also provides a splendid blow-by-blow account of a typical 1840s challenge dance. Allusions to the dancers' sex work permeate the story, yet underlying its provocative and degrading commentary on the dancers' sweat, brassiness, and alcohol consumption is an undeniable appreciation for the young women's skill, artistry, and athletic prowess.

It all started the previous month when two American ballerinas, "the pretty Miss Mary Ann Lee and Miss [Julia] Turnbull," entered Boston's theatrical arena "as Gladiators" to "battle for the wreath that should crown the victor, as queen of the American Dance." (Lee was dancing at the Tremont Theatre and Turnbull at the Olympic Saloon.) According to the *Whip and Satirist,* this rivalry heightened the competition in brothel parlors, "nightly converted into ball rooms, where each [woman] strives to outvie the other in the dance." The newspaper claimed that Nance Holmes (called Ann in this story) and Suse Bryant had recently exchanged blows in a three-round "Plug Muss" (fistfight) on the Boston Common, and now they were entering the fray as dancers to determine who had "the most grace and activity."[36] The "bargain" between Holmes and Bryant was published in the *Whip and Satirist* on June 11, and "full particulars, together with an engraving of this affair," appeared in the *Libertine* on June 15 (fig. 7.6).

The *Libertine*'s account of the match begins with the opponents arriving to Long Wharf in "a crowd of females," who took over the public space. "They were rival parties, arm in arm," he noted, "all giggling and talking as fast as woman can."[37] Brothel prostitutes participated in a distinctive female subculture that set them apart but did not entirely exclude them from general working-class

FIGURE 7.6. Women challenge danced too, and there were recognized champions among them. Unfortunately, the popular press only paid attention to those known as prostitutes. *Sketches of Characters—No. 27. GRAND TRIAL DANCE between NANCE HOLMES AND SUSE BRYANT, ON LONG WHARF, BOSTON,* from the *Whip and Satirist,* June 25, 1842, 1. Courtesy of the American Antiquarian Society.

culture.[38] Male dancers also arrived in gangs to their matches. Working-class youths often gathered in single-sex groups for entertainment and protection in the 1840s. At this match, Holmes represented the English tribe of dancers and Bryant the Irish.

To prepare a competition space, the women began by sweeping the wharf, a seemingly female activity. However, sweeping and brooms also appear in descriptions of males dancing. "Their day's work was over," Irish author Charles Kickham wrote of two young men in Tipperary, and "Barney began at once to practice his steps on the well-swept floor."[39] Barney and Tom were training with an itinerant dancing master who expected the floor to be swept before the lesson. Stepping or hopping over a broom (brush) laid on the floor also featured in Irish dances, a practice adopted by African Americans.

The out-of-doors competition drew a large mixed-race crowd of women, men, and children. The dancing was accompanied by "the violin of a half white negro barber" hired for the occasion, while another "man of the sable-hue" handed round programs. In the first part of the contest each dancer performed solo, and in the second part they danced together. Two "gentlemen" were selected as judges, and the spectators bet among themselves. "The first dance on the list was a hornpipe, and the one who took the most steps was to come off victor." Suse Bryant, the thinner of the two dancers, entered the ring first and gave her walk-around by making "three courtesies to the spectators who formed three sides about her." Then "the negro fiddler struck up Fisher's Hornpipe, and Susan commenced—and the way she put in the big licks was a 'sin to Moses.'" Because the audience knew the dances, "shouts of applause rent the air, whenever she changed a step." The author praised Bryant for her grace and rhythmic skill: "Her limbs moved as if guided by machinery." (Juba's steps would be compared to a chronometer.) She ended her hornpipe with "the heel and toe business—and done it to a *nail*. . . . Every one shook her hand and congratulated her on her success—when a voice was heard from among the crowd, crying: 'Make way for old Nance, she'll make some of you howl.'"

"'Yes indeed,' . . . " cried Nance Holmes, the heftier dancer, as she entered the ring. "'Come strike up,'" she called to the fiddler, who asked what tune to play.

"'Why, the same to be sure, I ain't going to give that gal any advantage,' quoth Nance.

'Well, I only thought you were goin to put in your fancy licks on de Ellsler music,'" he retorted, showing they had worked together before.

"'No, no, keep them back,' said she, 'so here goes.'"[40]

According to the reporter, "Every step the Bryant took, Nance repeated—and all conceited that it would be hip and thigh between them, which is a tie. 'If the Holmes can only last,' cried out one of the idlers, and as the words fell on our ears, she dropped, not flat, no indeed, but in a position which looked much like a squat—when she was forced to take the step which was to decide all, and which was no more or less than the famous 'Taylor's Hop.'"[41] Champion dancers often ended their turn by "the cutting of such acrobatic steps as *léim an bhradáin* (the salmon leap)."[42] Holmes chose the tailor's leap, which is described in Carleton's account of the Irish champion, who flung his heels one after the other against his inner thigh. An early engraving captures Master Diamond about to cut that same leap onstage (fig. 2.1). The position of the legs in the air resembled the way a tailor sat as he worked.

After Holmes's dramatic finale, both parties "took a recess" to refresh themselves with gin and cakes before tackling the finishing dance, which they would perform at the same time until one or the other gave out. Both women reentered the arena "in fine spirits," the fiddler struck up the "Camp Town Hornpipe," and the dancers struck the wharf. "It was hard to decide who was to come off victor," but "the knowing" offered odds in favor of Bryant. "From the Camptown the tune was changed to the Grape Vine," with no effect on them, and then to

> "Take your time Miss Lucy," [usually danced by a man impersonating a woman] and the way they went it was a caution—even the change to
> "Where did you come from, knock a nigger down,"
> and "Jenny get your hoe cake done my lady,"
> did not effect [sic] them—the sweat run down their faces, as if all within was on fire; . . . now came the tug of war—the tune was changed to one of Sandford's jigs—"Go it Nance," "Go it Suse," came in from all sides. They danced—the sweat poured, and now the fatigue of the delicate Nance became apparent, but amid the cheers of her friends she yet kept pace with the Bryant; but she couldn't stand it much longer, and after one of the closest contested dances on record, Nance Holmes gave out, and the Bryant came off victorious![43]

Suse Bryant won the match by superior stamina. The two women danced equally well, but she held out longer.

Like their male peers, female dancers faced off because that is what champion jig dancers did. Holmes and Bryant performed to the same music and danced the same steps as male champions and, according to some spectators, even excelled them in the end. "The names of Rice, Smith, Williams, Sandford and Diamond are heard no more," testified the *Whip and Satirist*. "Instead of Napoleaon Bonnett's or Bunker Hill Monuments you now hear of *Bryant* slippers and Long Wharf."[44] Even if spoken tongue in cheek, such comments suggested that women were recognized and recognized themselves as superior dancers.

Men left women out of the story on purpose. In theory, one's status was based on merit in the American republic. No one inherited their station in life, they earned it; no one, that is, except African Americans, who held a station below whites, no matter how respectable they were or how far up the ladder of achievement they climbed. Nor was women's status based on achievement. A Black woman's station was determined by her race and gender. A white woman's station was determined by her virtue, the only achievement worth merit. The more intellectual or physical acclaim a woman achieved, the more she teetered on the brink of respectability. One step too high and down she fell. Virtuous Black women and competitive white women threatened the social order. It simply did not serve the interests of white men to recognize them. But if Dickens's picture and the *Libertine*'s narrative bore any semblance to reality, Juba's cohort was up against some pretty stiff female competition.

Hostile Reception

American Notes for General Circulation received its first reviews in the American press in November 1842. Its reception was not warm. Americans read Dickens's "judgement" of their institutions, democracy, and manners and lashed back in book reviews, letters, verses, and plays.[45] A review in *Spirit of the Times* called the book "the most *trashy* of all the publications ever issued in relation to the United States."[46] New Yorkers were perturbed that their chapter mentioned none of the balls thrown in Dickens's honor, the speeches he heard, or the writers he met. Instead, complained the *Flash*, "the 'lion' of 'penny-a-liners'" gave a graphic description of his enjoyable time "in the society of the dusky ones of the 'infested regions.'"[47] A Southern reader complained that Dickens mistook foreign wretchedness in New York ("foreign paupers being thrown in such number into the port of our commercial emporium") for American pauperism, although "there may, it is true, have been an abundance of 'vice' at the negro dance he attended."[48]

Nativists were appalled at the excitement Dickens's visit elicited. "LAFAYETTE, FANNY ELSSLER, and CHARLES DICKENS, all received in the United States . . . with the same apparent enthusiasm!" grumbled the *Newark Daily Advertiser*. "Would it not be in better taste to suffer an European . . . to travel unnoticed through our country as he would through other countries?"[49] *American Notes* also roused in white Americans a proprietary claim to the depiction of African Americans. One *Spirit of the Times* correspondent, miffed by the attention Dickens paid to his Black coach driver, sent in "African Notes for General Circulation," a poem ostensibly written by the driver. Dickens had seen "a kind of insane imitation of an English coachman!" in the driver's worn-out and oddly matched clothes and heard America's get-ahead national character in his cry of "Go Ahead!" to the horse. Dismayed that the great "Massa Boz" would not ride inside but perched upon the coach box beside him, "Driber John" took the measure of the man and declared Dickens and his offerings "mighty small."[50] Similarly, when Dickens left New York, the *Whip and Satirist* warned his prospective readers that Boz "can never do a nigger. It needs a native to do up a Virginia Negroe or a Western Indian."[51]

Ironically, just as *American Notes* was taking a literary thrashing, "Dickens's visit to the Points" became a favorite walking tour. The famous author's description of New York's "East End," its degradation and vitality, sent people scurrying to Five Points to see what he saw. Officer Stephens was the first to make a business out of escorting flocks of "slummers"—missionaries in search of misery and woe and "gay fellows" seeking the pleasures of low life—through the Sixth Ward. Among them was newspaperman Nathaniel Willis, who engaged "the Boz officer" to take "a distinguished party" to "Dickens's Hole at the Five Points."[52] They approached the "grand subterranean Almack's" by way of Anthony Street, through an alley between Center and Orange Streets, and down a flight of stairs. The ballroom seemed clean and cheerful, noted Willis. "It was a spacious room, with a low ceiling, excessively white-washed, nicely sanded and well-lit, and the black proprietor and his ministering spirits were well-dressed and well-mannered people." The dancing hour had not yet arrived, however, so Willis's party "proposed to look in again after making the round of the other resorts."[53]

Willis and company then entered several drinking places thronged with people "who looked over their shoulders very significantly at the officer" and one or two tidy barrooms kept by women "(though in every clean place the hostess seems a terrible virago)." He did not see Juba dance that night, but in "a cellar crowded with negroes" he did see a professional dancer: "one very well-made mulatto girl playing the castanets, and imitating Elssler in what she called the *cracoveragain*" (see fig. 2.4 again). Apparently, blacked-up boys were not the only dancers imitating famous ballerinas. Eve Schnaffer, who owned a tavern on 21st Street between Broadway and the railroad, engaged a girl to "dance in the house on Sunday's [*sic*] like Fanny Elssler, to music played on the premises."[54] When the theaters wouldn't hire them, these "Elsslers" found work toeing the boards in places unfamiliar to middle-class audiences.

Dickens had his imitators too. On December 30 a *New York Sporting Whip* correspondent took the Dickens tour with some Canadian dragoons. Guided by the facetiously named "Officers Fallen and Tappen," they squeezed through an eight-inch alley and entered a rookery at the rear. What they found was not exactly what they expected, however. The first door opened onto the "decent" apartment of "a colored man and his wife." The next door, up a narrow flight of stairs, led to a room where "three negroes" sat around a charcoal furnace enjoying the fire. Ascending still higher, they entered a garret shared by an old crippled "black fellow" and "an Irish girl who was seated on a heap of rags holding in her lap the head of a black wench, who slept so soundly that our presence and conversation did not wake her." When asked how she came to be there, the white girl replied that she came to warm herself. This camaraderie disappointed white punters seeking squalor and immorality. The only scene of real destitution they found was in the cellar abode of an Irish family whose mother tried to give them her baby and whose father flippantly inquired "how Mrs. Boz was."[55]

The *Whip* writer modeled his scene inside Almack's on Dickens's description, altered to provide a local sporting man's perspective. Situated beneath a carpenter shop in Orange Street, his Almack's was "a large square room lighted up by some twenty lamps. There was a quadrille on the floor when we entered," he reported, "and one of the females, quite a light mulatto, we recognized as the barber's daughter, who had such an enormous rape committed on her by some rowdies who rushed in and dragged her from her father's shop, at least, so says the Herald, yet she has been a strumpet for three years. At this moment young Juba entered, and a purse was soon raised, when he took his station upon the floor, and we never saw such dancing before."[56] A "purse" meant bets were taken on whether Juba or the person in the opposite "station" would dance a better breakdown. But who was his opponent? The *Whip* writer pictures the dancer alone, but his vulgar offhand comment about the rape suggests that Juba's rival was the quadrille-dancing barber's daughter.

Here was the truth in all its ugliness. Any woman who danced for her own purposes (pleasure, competition, status) risked being defiled. As the "light mulatto" daughter of a barber, Juba's partner belonged to the Black middle classes. But respectability did not protect her. With no real recourse to the law, Black women were easy marks. So too was any young woman who acted independently. Two weeks earlier, Ann Murphy, an eighteen-year-old Irish immigrant, had accepted John Underhill's offer to take her to his sister's house to obtain the directions she was seeking. Underhill led her instead to a Broadway porterhouse where she was raped by several men.[57] Behind every allowance made for the female sex lurked the threat of violence. The mulatto dancer had not been violated by the "enormous rape committed on her," implied the *Whip* correspondent, because she was already sexually active.

America's sporting men brought Juba into the fold by first despoiling and then erasing his female rival. Her existence was irrelevant, since the point of the article was to foment a rivalry between males. The moment Juba entered, a purse was raised, and he took his station upon the floor, "and we never saw such dancing before. Why his feet were like the movements [of] a chronometer, so regular did they keep time. Talk about your Diamonds, why they are no comparison to the dancing we witnessed there."[58] With that taunt to the "Diamonds," a young Black dancer was entered into a strictly male circle of competitors. A man and woman competing was a fascinating amusement but not a sport.

Dickens's description of Almack's changed people's view of Juba but not of the women dancing in the room. To bind men together, the sporting press had to downplay, ridicule, or disappear female competitors, to depict them as men's property—wives or paramours—not as individuals. This erasure began the process of turning mixed-sex games into masculine sports and Juba into Diamond's number one opponent.

Diamond's Return

If he hadn't heard about it before, once he reached the North, Diamond learned that Juba had caught the public's attention. Dickens had visited Philadelphia after leaving New York in March, and his presence lingered. At Francis Courtney Wemyss's American Theatre in June, Diamond danced between *Tom and Jerry* and "Farce of Boz; Or, the Strange Gentleman." *The Strange Gentleman* was Dickens's first play—a two-act comic burletta of cross-wooing and jealousy written in 1836.

"Farce of Boz," featuring a Mr. Richings as "the Strange Gentleman" and a Mrs. Laforest as "Juba-Dobbs" (Julia Dobbs in the original), burlesqued the burletta.[59]

Diamond and Sanford made their way north in the spring of 1842, when theatricals were dull.[60] In April Philadelphia's Arch Street Theatre hired them to dance "to the house" and at a benefit in aid of Texans preparing to repel Mexican troops from San Antonio, "yet the houses were only tolerable."[61] Dwindling receipts may also have convinced Barnum to bring Diamond to New York to dance at his new venue, the American Museum. One year previously, Barnum had purchased Scudder's Museum at Broadway and Ann Streets, added to the collection of curiosities filling the building's several stories, expanded the lecture room into a large theater, and set the admission price at twenty-five cents to view everything. Barnum's Museum "was all the go then," recalled one contemporary; "the girls and boys used to go meet each other in the 'Lecture Room,' and enjoy themselves generally." According to that source, John Diamond agreed to perform there after Barnum promised to pay him a "good salary" and make him "a kind of star."[62]

If Diamond did agree, it didn't work out. "Master John Diamond, the great and original negro dancer, whose renown has induced others to assume his name, has just returned from a two years' absence at New Orleans," announced the museum's ads on May 23, 1842.[63] Of course, most of those Master Diamonds had been Barnum's employees. This particular Diamond was encored a dozen times on his first night and supposedly reengaged the next week to dance with banjoist William Whitlock. But by June 4 John Diamond had bolted, and Whitlock's partner was an impersonator. "Whitlock is quite equal if not superior to [banjoist] Sweeney; and off the stage he is a gentleman, and is respected by all who know him," commented the *Herald*. "His pupil, Master Frank, is quite as good a dancer as Master Diamond, and possesses none of his bad habits."[64] That comment identified Diamond and Sweeney as rough circus performers and Master Frank (Kent) and Whitlock as smooth theater performers. But it didn't matter. On June 11 Diamond was back in Philadelphia dancing with Sanford and fiddle player Richard Myers.[65] There is no evidence that he ever danced for Barnum again.

Unruffled by Juba's emerging renown, Diamond stayed in Philadelphia, where Masters Coleman and Chestnut joined him and Sanford in a grand trial dance for Diamond's benefit.[66] In August he danced with two other juveniles, Masters Saunders and Reed, on the steamboat *Hudson*, which took excursions up the Delaware River to Dunk's Ferry and back on Saturday evenings.[67] Then he partnered up with Irish American Barney Williams, who patted his legs while singing "'Miss Lucy Long,' and 'War did you come from,' with heel and toe accompaniments, by Master Diamond."[68]*

---

* Dialects written for Black and Irish characters shared words such as "war" (where), "dar" (dare, there), and "clare" (clear), and the "Hibernian darky" became a blackface character.

In October "Messrs. Diamond and Williams" took their show on the road. At Boston's National Theatre they traded intervals with American ballerina Julia Turnbull, whose rivalry with Mary Ann Lee had inspired the Holmes-Bryant match on Long Wharf, and performed "Bumpology," a farce lampooning the new science of phrenology (measuring bumps on the skull to predict character traits), a fad spread by phrenologists traveling with circuses.[69] In New York they shared the stage with jig dancer Great Western, and in Baltimore they reconnected with fiddler Richard Myers.[70]

Diamond returned to circus work in the late winter of 1842. Welch's Olympic Circus, a formidable combination of Welch and Mann's and Rockwell and Stone's companies, had taken over Philadelphia's National Theatre on Chestnut Street.[71] On Christmas Eve, that circus presented an afternoon performance featuring an "Equestrian Masquerade, Master Diamond, and other performances adapted to youth."[72] Then they packed up and headed to New York City, where Rufus Welch had fitted up the Park Theatre with rich decorations, new backdrops, and an indoor dirt ring.[73] The building, which was 187 feet deep and 76 feet wide, had three tiers of boxes and a gallery that seated two thousand patrons. Welch billed his company as the first ever "refined and genteel circus, which [fashionable families] can attend with propriety, and without loss of *caste*."[74]

A circus at the Park (New York's Old Drury) worried some critics, nonetheless. "We have no doubt, but that tears will fall from [veteran actor Sarah Wheatly's] eyes when she beholds the boards . . . sullied by the rude and uncouth dancing of a Diamond or a Pierce; but what of that?" inquired the *Whip*.[75] The circus was going to save the Park from ruin. "Welch has certainly struck a vein, and a rich one too, and well does he work it," noted the *Herald* on January 7, 1843. "We have noticed here what is not always seen at a Circus, and that is the ladies," as well as "gentlemen of every class and profession . . . and what is more, they all seem delighted. . . . Welch is carrying the town—Old Drury is on its legs again."[76]

Rather than damaging the theater's reputation, Diamond's dancing helped to repair it. The dancer developed two new acts that winter: "Negro Sayings and Doings" (spoofing a current dramatization of Theodore Edward Hook's *Sayings and Doings* [1824–1828], a collection of stories representing fashionable life) and "a series of Negro dances, songs, &c., entitled COMIC, BUT NOT COMMONPLACE, by Master John Diamond, whose celebrity is every where acknowledged. Assisted by Hoyt, the Negro Comedian, and W Chestnut the great Banjo Player." An immense congregation attended the Saturday matinee on January 23 "to witness" the daring bareback stunts of Cadwallader and Master Glenroy, the pretty Misses Wells' ballet steps, and Mr. Nathan's clever black pony, reported the *Herald*. "But probably no part of the performances gave them more delight than the negro dancing, in which the original, veritable, simon-pure, and inimitable John Diamond took a part."[77] Diamond's act was so admired that a reviewer attending

FIGURE 7.7. In dance, "attitude" refers to the arabesque position, in which one leg is lifted to the back with the knee slightly bent and one arm is raised above the head. In this theatrical print, the dancer poses in the arabesque or "attitude" position with upright posture as seen in Greek statuary and ballet. In the "Statue Dance," the dancer "attitudinized" (took one pose after another) in time with the music. *Dancing for eels at Catharine Market N.Y.: A scene from "New York as it is" as played by Chanfrau and Winans, at the Chatham Theatre N.Y.* (James Baillie, 1848), Library Company of Philadelphia; *Flying Mercury*, by G. Bologne, Florence, Italy, [William Henry] Goodyear Archival Collection (S03_06_01_020 image 2551), Brooklyn Museum Archives.

an evening show recommended "to Mr. Hoyt the propriety of remaining in the back ground and silent while John is dancing. His buffoonery is not needed at those times, though it is well enough at others."[78]

Among the "numerous tribe of negro singers, dancers and players, with which we are now blessed," explained the *Whip*, "[t]he favorites are now the dancers, and he who can cut, shuffle, and attitudanize with the greatest facility is reckoned the best fellow and pockets the most money." To "attitudanize" meant to strike poses (fig. 7.7). John Diamond supplied the Park Theatre Circus with all the attitude it needed from January to March 1843, while a few blocks away, Nathan Howe's Bowery Amphitheatre Circus employed nine jig dancers in January alone.*

Diamond was only so interested in attracting genteel spectators, however, so he also danced at the Cornucopia, an eating and drinking establishment next door to the theater at 28 Park Row. The Cornucopia had a ground-floor refectory (a room used for common meals) and a second-floor bar and concert saloon reached by an outside staircase in the back. Its customers tended more toward the artisanal classes than the bon ton.[79] In November a customer had tried to start a fight by striking one of the Cornucopia's owners with a brickbat and punching a barkeeper

---

* Frank Kent, Richard Pelham, Frank [Lynch] Diamond, Joe Miles, James O'Connell, Master Pierce, Frank Brower, John Daniels, and Dan Gardner.

in the eye.[80] Diamond appeared in the saloon as a competitive jig dancer and in so doing "diverted from the Park Theatre a certain class of its patrons," including the sportsmen and gamblers following Juba.[81]

Excitement Among the Sporting Community

The patrons attracted to Diamond's saloon shows recognized and promoted jig dancing as a betting sport. "Match dances are very frequently got up, and seem to give general satisfaction, if we are allowed to judge from the crowds who throng to witness them," remarked the *New York Sporting Whip*.[82] On January 19, 1843, "Mr. Daniels, the negro dancer," took his benefit at the Franklin Theatre "and was gre[e]ted with a crowded [house] from floor to ceiling. The performances were concluded with a match dance between Miles and Daniels for $50 a side, in which Miles came off victor," reported the *Whip*. "The excitement was great and glorious—women as well [as] male bipeds enjoyed the sport with a relish keen and delightful."[83] Joe Miles was working at the Bowery Amphitheatre at that time, and John Daniels was at the Franklin Theatre, which made the night a win for both. Although Miles took home the fifty dollars, Daniels was well compensated by his share of the receipts on his benefit night.

The *New York Sporting Whip* was one of the few papers that published the results of dancing matches. Its editor, George B. Wooldridge, began his journalism career in 1841 writing saloon gossip for the Sunday *Flash*. Wooldridge was familiar with Diamond and Juba's home turf. His father ran a bathhouse and refectory on Chambers Street near City Hall, and after he died, his widow ran the Court Lunch in the home she shared with her son. Wooldridge joined the family business in 1840 as proprietor of the Elssler Saloon, an oyster house on Broadway that sold alcoholic drinks, raw oysters, and apple cobbler. Oyster cellars were a step down (literally and figuratively) from first-floor refectories and restaurants. Wooldridge's saloon had curtained booths where people could sit without observation, giving the aspiring journalist access to "unseemly" gossip and providing a refuge for pugilists and working-class politicos (fig. 7.8). Wooldridge quit the *Flash* in 1842 and founded a rival weekly, the *Whip and Satirist,* which featured a new "Wants to Know" column of questions sent in by readers. That paper survived for nearly fifteen months (until March 1843), during which time Wooldridge renamed it the *Sporting Whip* and expanded coverage to include brothel fashion, firemen's activities, theatricals, balls, prizefighting, and other betting sports.[84] While the popular press generally endorsed the status quo, the flash press sanctioned alternative ways of living.

On January 21, 1843, the *New York Sporting Whip* ran an article entitled "Negro Dancers" assessing "the merits of some of the many 'heel and toe-ologists' now

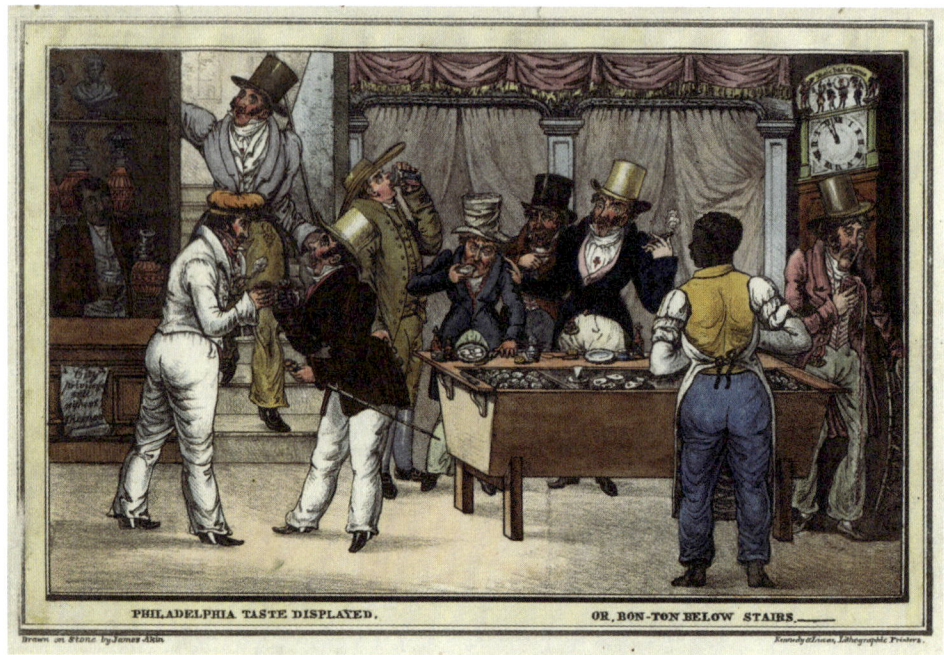

FIGURE 7.8. Oyster cellars (or saloons or houses) served drinks and raw and cooked oysters. They were run by Black and white proprietors and attracted middle- and working-class patrons. In his oyster cellar print, Atkin depicts the trunk-like table in which raw oysters were kept fresh on top of ice and the curtained booths at the back that offered patrons privacy. The Woodville painting provides a close-up view of the goings-on inside one of those booths. James Atkin, *Philadelphia Taste Displayed or Bon-Ton Below Stairs,* ca. 1830, media graphics collection Bb 38 097, Collection of the Historical Society of Pennsylvania; Richard Caton Woodville, *Politics in an Oyster House,* 1848, oil on fabric, gift of C. Morgan Marshall, 1945, Walters Art Museum, Baltimore, MD.

in this city." John Diamond headed the list of best white appropriators of Black culture. According to the *Whip*, Diamond kept his jigs fresh and authentic by "freely" spending his money and time in the company of Black dancers. "His style of dancing is peculiarly his own, having ever since his first appearance made the habits of the negro his study." R. W. Pelham, Diamond's first opponent, came next on the roster, but the *Whip* maintained that his dancing had fallen somewhat behind the times: "His steps are good but out of fashion ... too old to take in this age of modern improvement." Frank Brower, "scarcely known" as yet, was reckoned "a good fellow and excellent extravaganzist." Billy Chesnut was deemed "one of the steadiest boys in the profession," and Frank Kent, "who for a long time was favorably known as Master F. Diamond, [but now] again appears under his own name, thus showing that he does not wish to 'stand in the way' of *the* Diamond," was touted as "a good dancer and no mistake, and with the exception of John Diamond, there are few, if any, who can compete with him." Contrarily, the *Whip* warned John Daniels, a Boston dancer, that "blowing [your own horn] will gain you no reputation." Daniels may be well enough at home, "but abroad he is 'no go.'" Great Western (James Western), who ended the list, took his stage name from the Great Western Railway, which linked London to the west of England: "He is, indeed *the* 'locomotive nigger.' He has some original and peculiar steps and his fortune is made."[85] Oddly, several champion dancers, including Joe Miles, whose win was covered in the same issue, did not make the list.

Most notable among those absentees and someone certainly on the mind of the *Whip*'s readership was Juba. He showed up in the next issue, however, very much in the running. A month earlier, the *Whip* writer who took the Dickens tour to Almack's in search of "the greatest dancer known" had thrown down the gauntlet, declaring Juba a brighter star than all the "Diamonds." A response to that challenge was published on January 28, 1843, under the headline "Excitement among the Sporting community—Match between John Diamond and Juba." On the strength of his legs and the power of the press, Juba had leaped the entire queue.

America's sporting world did not routinely welcome African American athletes into the fold, but the best among them were often acknowledged. Ignoring a Black athlete who was so much better than everyone else would have discredited the sporting community's authority. Since Diamond acquired his craft in a Black-Irish community, he could only prove he was the best at jig dancing by competing with the best African American dancer. That dancer was Lane, who staked his claim in champion dancing when he chose the stage name Juba, a synonym for Black jig dancing.[86] By taking that name, Lane seized the advantage his heritage gave him.[87] As Juba he defined the dance, one-upping all those white dancers who called themselves the "king of Juba dancers." Pitting Juba against Diamond would give challenge dancing credibility as a genuinely African American and therefore authentically American sport.

The proximity of the stages on which John Diamond and William Lane were performing and the publicity Lane had garnered in the press brought the two dancers together as opponents in late January. "We have not had a *real*, scientific, out-and-out trial of skill since that between Dick Pelham and John Diamond at the Chatham," reported the *Whip*, "but it appears we are soon to have another of these refined and elevating exhibitions. A match has been made between John Diamond and a little negro called 'Juba,' by some of the sporting community." The time and place of the contest were not yet decided but would be announced in the next issue. "The stake is large and an unparalleled display will be the result," declared the *Whip*, which also predicted that Diamond would "conquer" his opponent.[88]

8

PARTNERS IN TIME

On most nights, when he'd finished his acts at the Park Theatre, John Diamond went next door to the Cornucopia to eat his supper and dance for drinks and extra cash. But one night in February 1843, he joined a gang of his friends outside the stage door and walked instead up to the Sixth Ward.

They made their way along side streets where the snowdrifts were several feet high. The weather had been nasty, one storm after another covering the roads and sidewalks with snow and ice. Walking was treacherous, particularly over the slippery iron grates and trapdoors that ventilated basements.

At the corner of Leonard and Orange, the party came up against a high board fence, lifted a latch, and headed down a flight of stairs.[1] Diamond led the way. He pushed open a door at the bottom, spilling out a slant of light, and sauntered into Pete Williams's tavern. He'd come to dance a match with Juba.

The place was crowded when Diamond's gang arrived. They entered a room heated by a cast-iron stove, about twenty-five feet square, with wooden benches along the walls, a bar at one end, and a raised platform where musicians perched on sugar boxes.[2] About one dozen set dancers were still occupying the floor at 10:30, so Diamond and his friends "took dinner all round." Juba was there too, surrounded by his friends and supporters, "who jested him about the match" when they saw Diamond arrive "and told him to go in and do his best."[3]*

---

* The only surviving account of Diamond and Juba's 1843 tavern match—"The Great Match-Dance—Barnum's Museum Against Pete Williams' Dance-House"—was written and published after the Civil War. The teller was a white concert saloon proprietor who described himself as equally fond of "colored people" and "burnt-cork people," "this bein,' perhaps, the only case in which I am as fond of the make-believe article as of the genuine."

While the dancers were eating, "'Boss' Harrington came in to look at the match, and he was warmly greeted by the boys, for the Boss had lots of friends," recalled an eyewitness.[4] The appearance of the white bare-knuckle boxer increased the excitement already circulating the room. Bets began to be made, and the money was placed in the hands of Williams, the Black proprietor, who acted as bookmaker.

The aroma of dancing bodies still lingered in the air when the two young men stood up from their suppers and took off their coats. We don't know what they wore exactly, but each dancer's clothes would have accentuated his physical strengths and attractiveness.[5] A competitive jig dancer announced his expertise through style. "He posed about attired in a velvet coat, flashy, flowing necktie, glazed cap, tight pants, patent leather shoes with old copper pennies fastened to the heels."[6] Juba usually wore knee-high boots and tight-fitting trousers that emphasized the size and shape of his thigh muscles; Diamond wore low-cut, high-heeled boots and white stockings that directed attention to his feet and calves; and both probably sported a workingman's blousy shirt, marking their peer group affiliation. All the same, each dancer knew "it was his movin' and not his lookin' that did the business."[7]

When the dancers rose, the crowd, noisy with last-minute bets and drink orders, lined the walls to clear the dance floor. The competitors would perform in the center of the room surrounded by the spectators, who paid close attention to their footwork and called out encouragements. No judge would preside at Diamond and Juba's match, as the winner would be determined by who danced the longest with the greatest variety of steps. Five fiddlers and a tambourine were on hand that night, not for volume but because bouts between champion dancers could last several hours, and a single musician could hardly have kept up momentum for that long. The fiddlers passed off the tunes, one to the next, like a relay race baton.

The match began at about eleven o'clock.

Juba danced first.

The fiddler struck up a reel, and Juba "went at it with a will," declared our narrator. He began his dance with a three-corner bow, then "he shuffled, and twisted,

---

I really like colored people, as I have said elsewhere, and I like those who can take 'em off, provided they imitate 'em well." The account, which appeared in a reminiscence of prewar minstrelsy, reveals as much about the context in which it was written as the event it documents. For example, it mentions no women at the match, despite its being held at a dance-house. This omission reflects the fact that by the 1870s, taverns and sporting venues had become decidedly male spaces. The narrator also identifies John Diamond as Barnum's "man," but Diamond was no longer working for Barnum in 1843. Notwithstanding these inaccuracies, the account provides rare and telling details about the match that I have combined with contemporary sources to create this scene.

and walked around," contorting his torso this way and that while his feet battered out steps forte and piano. Single shuffle, double shuffle, cut and crosscut, rattle and roll, he spun about on his toes and heels, each step timed with machine-like precision. Then he slowed down, circled the floor in each direction, and "danced on." This time he incorporated more "Negro" moves, snapping his fingers, rolling his eyes, and turning in his knees as he beat out a hornpipe with heel and toe in a musical counterpoint that emanated from inside his body. Then the tune changed, and he walked around again to signal a new set of steps.[8]

Everyone went wild over Juba's dancing, their shouts of approval spurring him on. He leaped and bounded, marched and twirled, dancing with wooden legs and spring legs—"all sorts of legs and no legs," as Dickens had put it. At last, he rolled through a final flourish and "brought his left foot down with a bang," perfectly matching the last note of the tune. (Clean entrances and exits were part of the competition; they showed that the dancer knew where he was in the music.) An explosion of cheers filled the room as Juba walked calmly to the bar and called for a drink. He had danced for one hour and fifteen minutes by the clock.[9]

"Diamond didn't pretend to care much, but he did, for all his careless way," observed our onlooker. The stakes had not been announced in the *Sporting Whip*, but they were far more than financial for the dancers. This contest had personal, group, and professional significance. Champion dancers established their supremacy at informal private matches. "Johnny Diamond thought a heap of himself," and no doubt Juba thought a heap of himself too. Each opponent had his name and status to defend. Each had supporters and employers to impress. And both had a sport to dignify. "Jig-dancers have their pride like other people, and Jack had his position to maintain, and he knew that the match would get wind among the boys."[10]

Jig dancers shared a boisterous pride in physicality with artisans and journeymen, who were suffering from financial degradation and social disrespect in an industrializing society. "There is nothing disreputable in being a mechanic," noted the *Flash*. "On the contrary, the man who earns his honest livelihood by the exertion of his skill and industry by the sweat of his brow, deserves as much consideration in society as any other man. But there is an inveterate prejudice against mechanics."[11] Despite repeated references to the "Art" and "Science" of their trade, jig dancers remained working class. After all, they supported themselves with their bodies and sweat. Champion dancer Joe Miles was "one of the roughest chaps, but with a soft heart under his hard hide," said one contemporary. "He was quite a jig-dancer, and very proud of his legs; as well he might be, for those legs of his made him his livin.'" Expert jig dancing was a working-class art, an expression of a man's virility and self-sufficiency. "So, when it came Diamond's turn to dance, he danced."[12]

It was one o'clock in the morning when Diamond took the floor. To win the match, he would have to dance longer than Juba had without repeating a single step (a step equaled sixteen bars of music). Going second gave him two advantages: The second contestant knew exactly how long he had to dance to outstep the first, and he got to see his opponent dance. A good dancer could acquire new steps from watching another dancer's feet. Sometimes a panel was placed between the dancers during contests to keep the second contestant from memorizing and adding the first dancer's steps to his own for the win, although a really good dancer could learn just by listening. Such imitative talents would underpin Juba's later successes and reputation.

Diamond began slowly, executing his first steps in a neat and careful fashion. Then he complicated the footwork, "puttin' in all the fancy touches and the funny business" with ease. He crossed his shin eleven times, shuffled and hopped, kicked from the knee, circled the room on his heels, jumped forward and skipped back, buckled his ankles from side to side, and soared through the air with his feet tucked under his thighs and a grin on his face.[13]

Putting in the "funny business" was a competitive tactic in challenge dancing. A difficult, out-of-the-ordinary move, like Juba's wooden-leg step or Diamond's heel run, communicated humor and, if it provoked laughter, could tilt the balance of support in a dancer's favor. American competitive dancers incorporated Irish crosscuts into African jubas and African hip thrusts into Irish jigs to provoke hilarity and vanquish their opponents. For them, serious dancing was not humorless; in competitions, humor made a serious point. It said, See how easy this is for me. I can do it upside down and backward.

Both Diamond and Juba excelled in the combining of skill and wit, swaying the spectators at Williams's place from one to the other. "The negroes around had gone wild over the dancin' of Juba, and they had bet all their coppers on their champion. Many of the white folks present, too, thought that the colored boy would win," reported our eyewitness. But then "Jack never danced so well as he did that night. It was quantity and quality both. He outstepped Juba, and then he put in a lot of fancy work besides, put in lots of fine touches."[14]

After dancing for an hour, Diamond set to rattling, adding extra beats to familiar rhythms as he battered the floor. Somebody asked him if he didn't feel tired yet, and Juba moved in closer to hear his answer, but Diamond saw him looking "and called out, smilin', to Boss Harrington, 'Why I ain't more than begun yet.'" At which point "Juba wilted," according to our source, and Diamond danced on.[15]

One by one, people began to doubt their choice. "Even the negroes gave Juba the go-bye soon, and [figuratively] threw up the sponge, and wished they had their money back." Pete Williams, who was counting on Juba to carry the day, was taken all aback. "'There's no use talkin',' he said to somebody standin' by, and he didn't say another word till it was all over." It was well after two o'clock when Diamond started playing with the cadences, speeding up to treble time, slowing down, scraping the ground, and crossing the downbeat with rippling taps, until, at last, when he'd beat Juba's time, he "gave a hop, skip and a jump, a yell and a bow, and as they say in the papers, 'retired amid loud applause.'"[16]

Diamond and Juba's first recorded dancing match ended there, but their association did not. This private match laid the foundation for public matches that would follow. It turned the two opponents into collaborators and linked their names in the public mind. Their rivalry would renew and elevate the sport of challenge dancing, setting "jig, reel, and trial" dancers apart from other professional dancers. It would also give Juba an entrée into the commercial entertainment world and help Diamond dissociate himself from Barnum's fake challenges.

Making the Match

The January 28 announcement in the *Sporting Whip* had promised to give the date, place, stakes, and "other particulars" for Diamond and Juba's match in the next week's edition. But no details were forthcoming, so we don't know exactly what day the event took place. That issue instead described the "straight four"* danced the previous Tuesday by four women at Eliza Davenport's ball as "a sort of Johnny Diamond and Juba style of dancing," suggesting that the match had already taken place and that those women had witnessed it.[17] Sporting events in the 1840s usually took place within a day or two of being announced, and it seems that Diamond and Juba followed that custom.

The *Whip* also failed to disclose the location selected for the match. The venue needed to be open to Black and white dancers and spectators and to gambling on the premises. Pete Williams's cellar dance-house served mostly African American patrons and some local working-class whites. But it became "one of the show places or sights of New York," drawing customers from outside the neighborhood, after Dickens had "enjoyed himself" there. Williams may have hired Lane after the publication of *American Notes,* when people came looking for Almack's and "the greatest dancer known." Tom Read's place was only a few doors down on Orange Street. Or the dancer may have been working at both places all along. Diamond, who grew up in the Sixth Ward and tended to gravitate to integrated venues, probably knew Williams's place already.

---

* A "straight four" reel was usually performed by two couples. Forming a line, the dancers passed in and out of each other until the men were facing the women, whereupon they "set" before each other (also called "jigging it off"), with the men "exhibiting all their skill" and the women "dancing as quietly as possible" for eight bars of music. At Davenport's ball, Miss S. Austin, Mary Williams, Mary Yates, and Harriet Sillman danced both parts, and either all four women "set to" with "all their skill" or two of them "jigged it off" while the other two quietly vamped.

One other "particular" never published was "the amount staked." Dancing matches figured into a much larger world of games and sports in antebellum America. "In the old times dancin'—jig dancin'—was thought to be a big thing, as it was," recalled one aficionado, "and bets used to be made on favorite jig-dancers, just as they are now on favorite horses or walkers."[18] Those bets turned jig dancing into a sport. Sports were physical games with winners and losers. That same aficionado said that Diamond and Juba's match "made quite an excitement," referring to the "flutter" or large number of bets made. Betting on a match or contributing to large stakes added to the excitement of the dancing. The thrill came from wagering money on someone you thought and hoped would win.

Diamond's and Juba's supporters bet briskly on the match. The *Whip* weighed in by stating its "steadfast and unmovable belief" that Diamond would prevail.[19] But people came with their own ideas about whose dancing to place their money on.

Dancing matches figured into the culture of reciprocity that sustained working-class communities. Betting at a local contest was an expression of loyalty to one's neighborhood and friends, not just a personal profit-or-loss decision. Winnings moved around the room when poor people gambled among themselves in honest games.[20] And when a sport's contestants, spectators, and promoters were all tied to the community, money stayed in the local economy. At Diamond and Juba's match, both dancers' factions supported Williams's tavern with purchases of food and drink before, during, and after the match. In exchange for this business, Williams held the stakes and provided an honest, comfortable space for the contest. This give-and-take ethic competed with other business models. The wage labor system that separated work time from leisure time stimulated the growth of more commercialized drinking and betting venues that operated on the profit motive.[21] At gambling saloons where individuals bet against the house, winnings did not circulate as freely or equitably.

Like the *Sporting Whip*'s announcement, "Boss" Harrington's arrival lent honor and manliness to the match and cemented the relationship between boxing and dancing. Apart from obvious differences, such as battering the floor instead of pummeling your opponent, challenge dancing paralleled bare-knuckle boxing. Both involved a kind of combat with the body as the sole weapon governed by a set of rules that set it apart from no-holds-barred competitions.[22] The *Whip* called Diamond and Juba's match a "*real*, scientific, out-and-out trial," words ordinarily saved for prizefights. It also compared jig dancing to "sparring" by suggesting (somewhat ironically) that the match to come would be "refined and elevating."[23] Like gloved boxers in a sparring match, the competitors would demonstrate "the science of the Art" rather than simply attempting to win the battle through brute force.

The two sports shared a vocabulary and a history, as the pictures of "pugilists, sprinters, and clogdancers" hung side by side in the male-only saloons of a later era would attest.²⁴ The term "bout," which refers to a short period of intense activity, was a synonym for a round of boxing and for a session of step dancing in Ireland: *babhta rince*, a "bout of dance." Similarly, a boxing match was called a "set-to," which is taken from the jig-off or breakdown at the end of a set dance. Both sports developed as local recreations that attracted neighborhood rivals who worked in other trades—carpenters, drivers, printers, blacksmiths, grocers, shoemakers, day laborers. Their competitions ranged from informal bouts got up on the spot to prearranged contests with carefully outlined terms of engagement. Challenges could be oral or written, with the latter appearing in newspapers or on posted handbills advertising the match. Anyone could challenge anyone else to a boxing or dancing match, but champions waited for a purse to be raised before toeing the mark. It was also common in both sports for friends to sponsor matches and trustworthy local businessmen to "hold the stakes."*

Harrington reframed what people saw at Diamond and Juba's match. "In his time and way he was a noted personage," reported *Harper's* in 1868. "For several years he was a leading authority on sporting matters, and was better known and more generally respected than any man of his class."²⁵ A butcher by trade, William "Liverhead" Harrington became the Boss in 1832 when pugilist James Sanford lost to Andrew McLane and enlisted Harrington to take on his conqueror. Although each boxer was a hero on his home turf (amateur fights often began as personal disputes), some people considered Harrington's set-to with McLane a contest for urban superiority.²⁶ Diamond and Juba's match acquired a similar significance when the Boss showed up.

Harrington's attendance at the dancing match may also have served the boxing community. Illegal in many states, prizefighting had suffered a severe blow a few months earlier when Irish-born boxer Thomas McCoy was killed in the ring at Hastings, New York, by English-born boxer Chris Lilly. As in a dancing match, the length of a boxing match was determined by the skill of the contestants, who fought until one of them could no longer stand. On Tuesday, September 13, 1842, in front of thousands of spectators, McCoy was beaten to death by Lilly in a bout that lasted for 119 rounds. Harrington's interest in the art of competitive dance might have helped to counter the ensuing charge that McCoy's death had been caused by a brutal instinct inherent to all boxers. Twenty years later, Harrington was remembered as an amateur pugilist who "retained his gentlemanly instincts" and never evinced the brutality that "disgrace[s] the supporters of the prize-ring."²⁷

Obviously comfortable in Williams's dance-house, Harrington belonged to an international "pugilistic corps" that had long included Black champions.²⁸ As

---

* At boxing matches, wagers were literally placed in a sock (socked-up) or purse and hung from the corner posts (stakes) that marked out the ring.

a formal sport, bare-knuckle boxing migrated from Britain to America at the turn of the nineteenth century. Few prizefighters were American born at that time; most contenders came from England or Ireland. However, among those few were several African Americans. The first US-born boxers to compete for the English championship were Bill Richmond (born on Staten Island in 1765) and Tom Molineaux (born in Virginia around 1784). Molineaux, who began his life enslaved, may have taken the (Norman Irish) surname of his young former master, Algernon Molineaux, to identify himself as Black Irish. He began his boxing career in New York, made his way to England, where he trained with Richmond, and battled the white champion Tom Cribb. He eventually moved to Ireland, where he died in 1818. These two pioneers were followed by a number of "colored champions" in England and the United States (fig. 8.1).[29]

In May 1835 the English-born boxer John Sheridan presented an exhibition of the "art of self-defense" in Boston that included trials of skill between C. Ottignon,

FIGURE 8.1. The international "pugilistic corps" had long included Black champions, and, as can be seen at this fives court sparring match, the boxing crowd (or fancy) was characterized by racial and class mixing. In America the jig-dancing community both paralleled and interacted with the boxing community. Charles Turner, *The Interior of the Fives Court. With Randall and Turner Sparring*, London, Sept. 1, 1821, aquatint, hand-colored. Paul Mellon Collection, Yale Center for British Art.

J. Hudson, and Sheridan ("commonly designated the Phenomenon") and a kind of boxer's "imitation dance" during which Sheridan displayed "the positions of the following celebrated pugilists; Jem Ward the Champion of the London ring; Wm Fuller of N. York; Molineaux the Slave Fighter; McCane the Philadelphia Pet; Flanagan the Irish Pugilist, acknowledged by all as the Champion of the United States; [and] Joe Battas the African Boxer."[30] This company of white, Black, and immigrant prizefighters paralleled and interacted with communities of jig dancers, the best of whom demonstrated their rank by imitating their colleagues' moves.[31]

Juba was not an anomaly in the sporting world. Besides boxers and dancers, Black jockeys (enslaved and free), wrestlers, and pedestrians (walking racers) could be found competing in public (fig. 8.2). African American handlers pitted their dogs and cocks against those belonging to other men. And Black people supported sports as trainers, grooms, and fans. To understand Juba's position, these "exceptions" need to be accounted for. Racism kept their numbers small, but Black athletes entered arenas where genuine wagers and trials of skill trumped segregation.[32]

In prizefighting, enthusiasm was often drummed up by opposing athletes with dissimilar ethnic backgrounds or national allegiances, such as Irish McCoy and English Lilly. News coverage of the 1811 championship contest between white English boxer Tom Cribb and Black American boxer Tom Molineaux suggests

FIGURE 8.2. A small but substantial number of Black athletes, from jockeys and foot racers to boxers and dancers, penetrated antebellum sporting arenas. Edward Troye, *Tobacconist, with Botts' Manuel and Botts' Ben*, 1833, oil on canvas. Paul Mellon Collection, 85.646, Virginia Museum of Fine Arts, Richmond.

that Molineaux's Americanness troubled the English boxing fancy far more than his color. "It appeared somewhat as a national concern," reported Pierce Egan. "ALL felt for the honour of their country, and were deeply interested in the fate of their Champion, TOM CRIBB. *Molineaux* was viewed as a truly formidable rival" (fig. 8.3).[33] Differing backgrounds elevated the importance of matches between equally skilled opponents. Diamond's whiteness and Juba's blackness similarly turned their dancing match into a battle for the "champion" title.

Race mattered, but it mattered differently in the South, where the entire society was geared around racial slavery, and in the North, where most Black people were not enslaved. It mattered differently to white middle-class people who only encountered Black people in their capacity as servants or laborers and to white and Black working-class people who rubbed shoulders on a daily basis. Even in a society where white dominance over Black was the norm, proximity enabled alternative relationships.[34]

The barman who recorded the scene at Diamond and Juba's match located its racial antagonism primarily in the two types of venues that hired challenge

FIGURE 8.3. British news coverage of the championship match between white Tom Cribb and Black Tom Molineaux suggests that Molineaux's American origins troubled the English boxing fancy far more than his color. Attributed to George Cruikshank, *The Battle Between Cribb and Molineaux, September 28, 1811* (Walker and Knight, Oct. 3, 1811), gift of A. Hyatt Mayor, 1969. Metropolitan Museum of Art, New York.

dancers rather than among the competitors and spectators: "You see it was not only a case of Barnum's Museum against Pete Williams' dance-house, but it was a case of white against black."³⁵ The match took place during a transitional period when popular entertainments were being increasingly commercialized and democratized, making one's choice of venue an indicator of class (or at least social pretension). Despite the fact that both dancers worked in both contexts, Diamond represented Barnum's museum, where the audience was segregated by race and separated from the dancing by a stage, and Juba represented Pete Williams's dance-house, where Black and white dancers and spectators mingled and everyone participated in the action. The battle lines inside Williams's dance-house were far more amorphous than "white against black."

Even our onlooker recognized that race did not determine status in a context where everyone danced the same steps. After witnessing Juba's success, "Diamond went at his dancin' with double energy—first, for his place, next, for his color." Diamond doubled his game to keep his place at the top of a corps of competitors that, as far as he was concerned, had always included African Americans. He knew that Juba could take that place away from him. Both Black and white gamblers thought that Juba would win that wintry night, and both "changed their tune" after seeing Diamond dance for a while. During the match, "one of the colored boys yelled out 'He's a white man, sure,' lookin' at Diamond, 'but he's got a nigger in his heel.'"³⁶ Challenge dancing realigned people who shared the same activities and conditions. It served as a medium for competition without conflict.

In these circumstances, Diamond and Juba represented an excellent matchup in terms of age, size, and training. Both were teenagers in 1843. Juba was short, slight, and spry. Diamond was also small in stature but more dexterous than sprightly. Both had learned to dance as children in a Black and Irish neighborhood and continued to pick up steps and ideas from dancers down the block. By accepting each other as opponents, Diamond and Juba placed white and Black on the same plane while at the same time posing and begging the question of who owned the steps. According to their contemporaries, they both did. "Diamond and Juba originated everything that has ever been done in jig dancing," acknowledged minstrel dancer Billy Birch in 1891, "and much of what they did has never been done since nor ever will be."³⁷ The two men had similar physiques, different strengths, and equal abilities, making the course their rivalry would take as yet undecided.³⁸

After the Match

The 1843 match did not catapult Juba onto the commercial entertainment stage, but it did bring him within striking distance. It placed him on a level with Diamond that opened doors. Williams's dance-house became a place where circus dancers and musicians congregated. "The best in the profession danced there," recalled one minstrelsy chronicler, "as well as Juba."[39] White tavern-keepers catering to the sporting crowd also hired him to perform in their houses. As "the colored boy, Juba," Lane had entered the privileged domain of professional athletes and sportsmen; now he needed to find a way into the public limelight. Diamond would provide his ticket.

The sporting press did not print the results of the 1843 match, but on February 11, the *Spirit of the Times* commented that "Master John Diamond, the dancer, is 'a great cat' just now."[40] Diamond kept dancing at the Park until April, when half of Welch's company, renamed New York Circus, headed out of Manhattan. Their first stand was Brooklyn's Military Gardens, where "the original John Diamond and J. Mills" danced a match for the benefit of the gardens' proprietor.[41] In September Diamond moved to John Tryon's Independent American Circus at the Bowery Amphitheatre, where he headlined off and on until December.[42]

Lane/Juba may have continued to work at Williams's place until the first week of May, when "Master Rattler, the Ethiopian Dancer," reappeared in the newspapers. Echoing Dickens's words, Rattler's advertisements described him as "universally allowed by common consent to surpass all other competitors—he is the greatest dancer in his line America ever produced."[43] By performing under several stage names, Lane may have been following a theatrical expedient that allowed him to work at more than one place at the same time. Or he may have used particular names for particular venues. It is also possible that, as "Juba" was known to be Black, he changed his stage name when working at white venues that wanted to hide his race.

At Peale's New York Museum and Picture Gallery, Lane/Rattler was back in P. T. Barnum's employ, although he did not work for Barnum directly. In 1842 Henry Bennett, the manager of Peale's museum, had launched a campaign to outdo Barnum's American Museum by reducing the price of entry to twelve and a half cents and burlesquing whatever Barnum produced. For example, when Barnum presented the Orphean Family of talented vocalists, Bennett presented the Orphan Family; and when the American Museum advertised the Feejee Mermaid, Peale's museum advertised the Fud-gee Mermaid. The gimmick stirred up interest in both museums for a time, but eventually Bennett lost money and had to close down. Seizing his chance, Barnum secretly purchased the museum from its owner and engaged Bennett as his agent. For the next six months, posing as adversaries, Bennett and Barnum ran a spirited competition that profited both establishments and gave Lane a semipermanent gig as Rattler.[44]

In the summer of 1843 Lane moved between stages and employers, dancing as Master Rattler at both Peale's museum and Vauxhall Gardens, where James W. Bancker's circus was stationed. The week of July 4, he shared Peale's stage with vocalists honoring American independence and a "GIANT GIRL, six years old, four feet seven inches high, weigh[ing] 240 pounds." Later that month, Vauxhall's show included Master Rattler's "Camp Town Hornpipe" and "break-downs" by Miss Josaline and others in "the Negro Extravaganza of Love, A La Mode." Rattler also faced Mr. Smith in "a grand match dance" for William Manning's benefit.[45] In August, Barnum's museum presented "Master F. Diamond, the greatest extravaganzist and Negro dancer in the world," and Peale's museum advertised someone called "Master Diamond, the unrivalled banjo player and Ethiopian Dancer."[46] One of those Diamonds may have been Lane, who switched his stage name to fit the bill (although neither Lane nor Diamond played the banjo). After that engagement, Lane receded from the "Amusements" columns until December, when he reappeared to dance a match with John Diamond under the presumptuous stage name Master Champion.

In mid-December Diamond performed "his eccentric heel and toe exercises" between the play and "the new leg spectacle of the Irresistibles" at the recently renovated Chatham Theatre, assisted by Barney Williams, who "patted juba" as accompaniment.[47] "Master Diamond has opened with renewed vigor and is better than ever," reported the *Herald* after his first night. However, "a new and powerful rival in his line has sprung up, and challenged [Diamond to] a trial of skill, which the latter has accepted. . . . [L]arge sums have been staked upon the result, and much interest is manifested among the respective partizans."[48] That match took place on December 20, 1843, Diamond's benefit night.

Diamond may have suggested the trial of skill to William S. Deverna, the Chatham's manager, who was trying to offset another "big cat" in town that winter, a good-looking fiddle player from foreign parts who brewed up a concoction that made everyone go music mad. In the ad for Diamond's benefit, Deverna announced "the grand new drama of the Bohemians," described by the *Herald* as "so effective" that "Ole Bull, Vieux Temps, and Ariot, will be thrown into the shade when viewed comparatively," and "the great prize dance of $500 a side between Master Diamond and Master Champion."[49]

Like Elssler, thirty-three-year-old Norwegian violinist Ole Bull had left his imprint on the nation's budding culture. Bull arrived in the United States in November 1843, followed shortly thereafter by a twenty-three-year-old Belgian violinist named Heinrich Vieuxtemps, who vied with Bull in the press and onstage. The young men's musicianship and rivalry stimulated poetry and editorial commentary in the press:

> Two fiddlers have come, of skill and renown,
> Whose merits respective have crazed half the town.
> The Yankees all stare, and stoutly declare,
> Ole Bull is superb, is delightful, sublime;
> While the Frenchmen all swear, he cannot compare,
> But is vastly excelled by his rival Old Time. [*Vieux Temp].[50]

Two more foreign violinists entered the lists in December, the Belgian Joseph Artôt and Irish-born Australian Vincent Wallace. Despite their classical training, these four savvy musicians attracted audiences by dueling each other in cities across the country. "The violin is producing wonders in every way," observed the *Herald*. "We should not be surprised if it were to decide the next presidency."[51]

But it was blue-eyed Ole Bull who stole the hearts of Americans with his "genius, wonderful enthusiasm and skill." Bull enlivened his farewell concerts by asking his audience to write down on pieces of paper songs they would like to hear him play and pass them forward: "Much amusement was created when Mr. Timm called out the names of the favorite melodies deposited in the urn," the *Herald* reported. "Among [them] were, 'Old Dan Tucker,' 'The Devil among the Tailors,' 'Dance, Boatman, Dance,' . . . 'Oft in the stilly night,' 'The Exile of Erin,' 'Hail, Columbia,' and numerous airs from popular operas. Ole Bull seemed to enjoy this part of the business exceedingly, joining in the laugh" over some of the suggestions. He concluded his concert at New York's Tabernacle "by executing a Grand Fantasia" on the two favorites, "'Home, sweet Home,' and 'Yankee Doodle.' . . . It was listened to with breathless silence, and . . . could have kept the audience there . . . till this moment, had he continued to play. But he ceased—bowed repeatedly in his own fascinating way, and retired evidently almost overpowered with excitement."[52] Diamond and Champion's match took place the night after Bull's farewell concert.

Bull's influence was felt across the nation. According to memoirist James Thomas, "[Bull's] success in Europe had caused the [American] people to feel anxious to hear him. They had never heard anything fine. The Scotch reels, hornpipes, and any of those [tunes], the product of American fiddlers, were their delight."[53] Almost immediately, American musicians began adding Ole or Ole Bull to their stage names. In December Tryon's Circus advertised "Negro Songs, Choruses, &c. by 'Ole' Whitlock." Philadelphia fiddler Richard Myers took the name Ole Bull Myers and never gave it up. And, at least once, Juba would cast himself as Bull's dancing counterpart.[54]

The *Herald* identified Master Champion as a "new aspirant" in Diamond's "line," but evidence indicates that he was Lane/Juba dancing under yet another stage name. In subsequent ads and playbills, Juba would claim that he had danced with John Diamond at the Chatham Theatre for $500 and "pocketed the 'rocks,'" and there is no other such match on record. The $500 wager was also a clue that Master Champion was Juba. The high stakes indicated that a matchup between Diamond and Champion would be well worth watching. The dancers probably did not make the wager, nor did the winner take home $500. The purpose of announcing the stakes was to pack the theater. The real windfall on such occasions was the door receipts, which Deverna would split with Diamond on his benefit night and on the prospect of which Diamond and Lane would have made a financial arrangement.

Rematch!

For the first six months of 1844, Diamond worked again at the Bowery Amphitheatre with Tryon's circus. He also traveled with a band of singers and musicians who called themselves Virginia Serenaders. That June Master Rattler was listed among "the ordinary performers" (singers, actors, and ballerinas) who shared the stage with "living curiosities" ("Dwarves, Giants, Giantesses and Fat Girls") at Peale's New York Museum.[55] That dancer may or may not have been Lane, since "Juba" was working on Broadway with a band that also called itself Virginia Serenaders. On June 28 Diamond danced a match at the Knickerbocker (Bowery Amphitheatre) with a Ruthven Jones for ten dollars a side, a fair wager, since Jones was unknown.[56] Presumably, Jones did not prevail, as he did not appear again. Or he was simply overshadowed by all the excitement stirred up three days later when Diamond accepted a "CHALLENGE TO THE WORLD" made by Juba.

The timing of Juba's challenge could not have been safer. From May to July, religious and nativist xenophobia overtook antiabolition as the major stimulus for mob violence in the United States. The targets were Mormons and Irish immigrants. In June the Mormon prophet Joseph Smith was charged with instigating a riot after he destroyed the printing press of his disaffected followers, whose "libelous newspaper" accused him of practicing polygamy and planning to declare himself a theocratic king, then shot to death by a mob of locals who stormed the jail in Carthage, Illinois, where Joseph and his brother Hyrum were awaiting trial. Meanwhile, in Philadelphia riots between native-born Protestants and naturalized Irish Catholics broke out. In May a group of Irish allegedly broke up a rally being held by members of the Native American Party (a nativist political party) in Kensington, a Northern suburb with one heavily Irish ward and several Protestant wards. In response, the *"natives"* regrouped a few days later in the mostly Irish district of Southwark, inciting animosity, violence, and bloodshed. In July twenty thousand nativists marched in honor of American independence, inspiring someone to send a letter to St. Philip Neri Catholic Church threatening to burn down the building. The priest took the threat seriously and brought in arms to defend his church, provoking an anti-Irish, anti-Catholic riot that seized Philadelphia by the throat and throttled it for two days.[57] The Irish were blamed for provoking both assaults. In this atmosphere, a public challenge made by a Black jig dancer in New York hardly raised an eyebrow.[58]

Almost everything about Diamond and Juba's 1844 contest conveyed authenticity. The challenge took the customary form used by pugilists. It began with an exchange between the two dancers' seconds (promoters, endorsers) published in the *New York Herald* the first two days in July. That exchange suggested that the original challenge had been made orally by J. S. Masset, the proprietor of the Concert Saloon, where Lane/Juba was currently working.[59] He would "match the colored boy Juba for $100 against any other Break-down Dancer in the world." To instigate a match of any kind, an athlete or his friends made a challenge, which another athlete accepted, countered, or refused. Acting as Diamond's second, George B. Wooldridge, former editor of the now defunct *New York Sporting Whip*, accepted Juba's challenge on Monday and specified his terms: "I will match John Diamond against him for the above sum, in a Jig and Reel; one Judge to be selected by each party, they to select a third. If danced in private, the expense to be divided; if public, the winner of the match to have all receipts over actual expenses. The dance to come off within one week from this date." J.S.M. accepted Wooldridge's offer on Tuesday: "This is to certify that I am ready to stake the above sum, or any amount he wishes to bind the wager at the Concert Saloon 74 Chambers street, and the match to come off on Monday, 8th inst., either private or public, and at any place hereafter agreed upon" (fig. 8.4).[60] These preliminaries identified the dancers as serious athletes.

The explanation of how the expenses would be divided was an important authenticating detail. A $100 wager put up by each promoter (for the dancers) meant the dancer who won the match would get $200. A $200 stake was large but not excessive, signaling genuineness. The private or public nature of a match also determined the winnings. If the match was private, meaning danced for friends and fans at a tavern or saloon where no tickets were sold, the expenses would be shared by the two parties, no matter who won the wager. But if the match was open to the public, meaning danced at a theater or amphitheater where tickets were sold, the expenses (hiring the room, printing the tickets, providing refreshments) would be paid for by the winner, who would receive both the wager and leftover ticket money. These terms differentiated matches from "mere speculations," wherein both sides received back their stakes and split the expenses and the profits no matter who won. "These sort of humbugs" were looked down upon by the sporting community.[61]

The promoters who negotiated the terms placed the match squarely in the sports world. Wooldridge, Diamond's second, had covered and promoted boxing and advertised Diamond and Juba's tavern match while he was editor of the

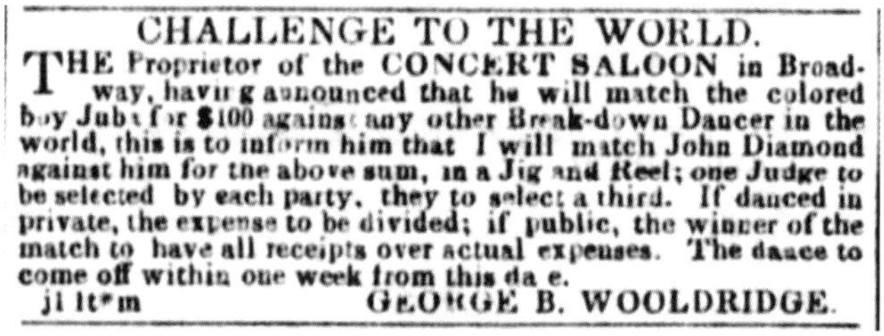

FIGURE 8.4. In this newspaper clipping, George B. Wooldridge, acting as John Diamond's second, accepts the challenge and terms laid down by the proprietor of the Concert Saloon, J.S.M., who is acting as Juba's second. "Challenge to the World," *New York Herald,* July 1, 1844, 3.

Sporting Whip.⁶² Juba's endorser (and employer), J. S. Masset, was also connected to the sports scene. In the 1840s some working-class drinking places began reflecting gender divisions in the industrial workplace. "Concert saloon" was the generic name for a spacious tavern that offered nightly shows along with drinks and food. Unlike neighborhood taverns, these saloons were designed for male sociability and supported a boisterous masculinity. Women were not barred from entering, but where they did enter, they were excluded from the rituals of working-class camaraderie, such as treating. Saloons were designed to attract workers with similar occupations, ethnic backgrounds, or interests.⁶³ At 74 Chambers Street, J.S.M.'s Concert Saloon occupied the same building as Hudson & Ottignon's Gymnasium and Pistol Gallery, where the boxer Charles F. Ottignon gave "instructions in the noble Art of Self Defense."⁶⁴ (Tiffany, Young & Ellis jewelry was on the first floor, and Chickering restaurant was in the basement.) The Concert Saloon inhabited the second floor, and Ottignon's gymnasium was on the top floor, each providing its neighbor with patrons and bringing dancers and boxers together.

Juba designed his dancing exhibitions at the Concert Saloon to attract the sporting crowd. Boxers such as Ottignon and John Sheridan advertised their abilities, gyms, and prizefights through "Art and Science" displays, trials of skill, reenactments of famous bouts, and demonstrations of their opponents' moves. The ad for Juba's show on July 4, 1844, promised similar enticements for six and a quarter cents at 10:00 a.m. and 1:00, 4:00, and 8:30 p.m. (Four shows a day required considerable strength and stamina.) "The celebrated, unrivalled, and yet to be beaten Negro Dancer, Juba . . . will dance some of his most popular jigs, reels and break downs, and will likewise give his inimitable imitations of all the celebrated Negro Dancers in the United States, and in particular the celebrated Master John Diamond, who is now matched to dance with Master Juba for $100. This will be a good opportunity of witnessing some of Master Juba's unrivalled steps."⁶⁵ Like a boxer, Juba generated excitement for the upcoming match by showing off his capabilities and imitating his opponent's. Anyone undecided about whom to support could come to the Concert Saloon and see him dance beforehand.

On July 7 the *New York Herald* detailed the particulars of the match: "GREAT PUBLIC CONTEST BETWEEN the two most renowned dancers in the world, the Original JOHN DIAMOND and, the Colored Boy JUBA, for a Wager of $200, on MONDAY EVENING, July 8th, at the BOWERY AMPHITHEATRE, which building has been expressly hired from the Proprietor, Mr. Smith, for this night only, as its accommodations will afford all a fair view of each step of these wonderful Dancers." The match was open to the public, and the price of admission was affordable for almost anyone: "On this occasion—Boxes 25 cents: Pit 12½ cents. Tickets for sale at the Concert Saloon . . . and at the Theatre during Monday." This match was not a part of Tryon's circus program. The dancers would not appear in blackface. This was a stand-alone sporting event for which spectators would need a separate ticket.

The terms of the match had been finalized in private negotiations. The contestants would "meet and Dance three Jigs, Two Reels, and the Camptown Hornpipe. Five judges have been selected for their ability and knowledge of the Art, so that a fair decision will be made." The rules affecting the judging were also laid out: "Rule—Each dancer will select his own Violin and the victory will be decided by the best time and the greatest number of steps." Anyone who danced would have been familiar with these terms and rules. Jigs, reels, and hornpipes were the tune changes in any set dance. They had different rhythms and feels and required different skills. The choice of violin over banjo reflected the variety of steps the dancers would exhibit—Irish, Scottish, English, and Negro. It also paid tribute to the popularity of Ole Bull and his rivals.

Each dancer brought his fiddler with him, because a dancer's speed and accuracy depended on the musician's ability to anticipate his moves. Dancers preferred musicians who knew how to move their feet, and musicians liked working with dancers who could play an instrument. Good dancers did not just follow the music; they embellished it with their rhythms. They played a duet with the musician. Nor did good musicians just keep time for the dancer; they responded to the steps, inserting rhythmic and melodic passages of their own. A few years later, the spectators at one match blamed a dancer's poor showing on "the musician misunderstanding him" and at another on the audience clapping so loud the dancer could not hear the musician and vice versa.[66] The names of the fiddlers who played on July 8 are lost to history, but the synergy between musicians and dancers can be seen in the lithograph of banjoist William Whitlock and Master Diamond performing together (fig. 2.1). As Diamond mounts a dynamic "tailor's leap," Whitlock poises his hand in the air, his eyes fixed on the dancer's feet, preparing to strike the banjo strings at the exact moment the dancer lands and continue without missing a beat. Rhythmic clarity and synchronicity demonstrated the musical proficiency of both dancer and musician. Choosing the right fiddler could win the match for the dancer.

Judges with "ability and knowledge" were dancers themselves. Diamond and Juba's match was adjudicated by five judges instead of the usual three, signifying the importance of the contest. Two judges were chosen by each dancer, and one disinterested party was enlisted in case of a tie. They all watched and listened, counting and marking down in chalk the dancer's steps and any missteps or breaks with the rhythm.

No record of the judges' decision at Diamond and Juba's match has survived, but here is an example of a decision given at a $200 match danced in Chicago in 1856:

Time—Joe Brown fifteen minutes and one-fourth second, making ninety-nine movements, and breaking time at three different periods.

Time—R. H. Sliter nineteen minutes, making one hundred and twenty-three movements, and breaking time at two different periods.

For ease and grace of dancing, we, the judges, think that Mr. Sliter is far superior to Mr. Brown, and therefore decide in favor of Mr. R. H. Sliter.[67]

The spectators also took part in the judging by closely following the steps, cheering and applauding their favorite dancer, and assessing the judges' choice, all of which made the clear view of the stage at the Bowery Amphitheatre important on July 8.

Diamond and Juba's promoters presented the match as a championship: "The fame of these Two Celebrated Breakdown Dancers has already spread over the Union, and the numerous friends of each [have] claimed the championship for their favorite." Like boxers, any number of dancers could be named the champion. No official organization or championship tour had been established. Therefore, Diamond and Juba's friends "anxiously wished for a Public Trial" to determine which should be called (in typical boxing hyperbole) "Champion Dancer of the World. The time to decide that has come."[68]

The popular press offered no postmatch coverage of the 1844 contest, but Juba's subsequent playbills claimed that he had prevailed. This silence has led some scholars to speculate that James Gordon Bennett, editor of the *New York Herald*, was too racist to print the result. Others take it to mean that all dancing matches were fakes. But the outcome of a dance match was rarely reported unless the result was disputed. That Juba won and no one challenged the decision says something interesting about jig dancing as sport. It didn't matter that the winner was Black, so long as the dancing convinced the spectators that he deserved to win. What mattered was superiority in the field, and Juba knew that he had demonstrated that. In 1845 he christened himself "the Wonder of the World JUBA Acknowledged to be the Greatest Dancer in the World. Having danced with John Diamond at the Chatham Theatre for $500, and at the Bowery Amphitheatre for the same amount, and established himself as the King of All Dancers!!" (fig. 8.5).[69] Diamond never disputed that claim, nor did he give up his own title. There was room at the top for both. Diamond was the American champion, Juba the African American. Tied together in the public mind, they boosted each other's glory.

Lane triumphed in more ways than one on July 8, 1844. With Diamond's help, he launched a career in commercial entertainment as an African American star. By facing and conquering Diamond in the sporting arena, Juba gained a kind of prominence that he could not have acquired through blackface performance alone. As a Black dancer in America, he had to enter the limelight through competition.

Both dancers gained from their rivalry. It placed them on top and made them celebrities, which helped them secure regular employment. But Juba would prove

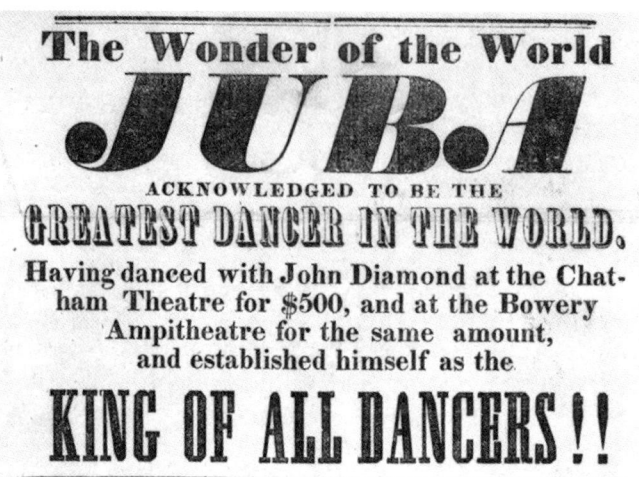

FIGURE 8.5. Juba's playbills and advertisements affirmed that he had won the 1844 match at the Bowery Amphitheatre. They also suggest that he was the "Master Champion" who danced against Diamond at the Chatham Theatre in December 1843. Detail from Georgia Champions playbill, Portland, Maine, June 18, [1845], MS Thr 1848, box 14 (Juba, Master), Houghton Library, Harvard University.

better at deploying his success than Diamond. A dancer's image was key to his status as a professional, and Juba quickly mastered the art of publicity and self-promotion. Diamond, who endlessly lost control of his name and his temper, did not. The structure of opportunity in antebellum America was built to privilege white people over Black people. But in this instance, Lane turned the tables.

9

GROSS IMITATORS

On June 8, 1845, African American dancer Edward Gray waited inside the pavilion in Boylston Garden at the bottom of the Boston Common. A native of the city, Gray announced his expertise in his stage name—Boston Rattler. The Sable Harmonists, a recently organized quartet of white male singer-musicians, were onstage performing in blackface.[1] During the first part of the program, they sang a variety of popular songs, glees, refrains, and choruses dressed, according to their playbill, "as Dandy Niggers of the Northern States." An established blackface character based on the young urban sporting male, "the Dandy" displayed the tailored clothes, polished manners, and courteous ways of a gentleman but was actually an insincere pretender ignorant of the values associated with that elevated social station.[2] The program's second part, comprising harmonic versions of popular "Negro" songs, they described as "Saturday Afternoon in Old Virginia, representing the Corn Huskings and Merry Meetings of the Slaves of the South." Engaged for four nights only, Gray's job was to conclude the concert with a "Grand IMITATION DANCE" in which he gave "correct imitations of all the principal Dancers in the United States": Jim Sanford of Philadelphia, Dick Pelham of New York, John Smith of Albany, Frank Brower of New York, and Frank Diamond of Troy, New York. And finally, Gray imitated the three champions: John Diamond, Master Juba, and himself (fig. 9.1). By all contemporary accounts, Gray was an outstanding dancer who belonged among the champions.[3] His imitation dance proved that. He leaped onto the platform and knocked the audience out with his accurate reproductions of his rivals' steps and demeanor. But Gray's act was itself an imitation of Juba's imitation dance.

A highly specialized art form, imitation dancing set champion dancers apart from other dancers working with blackface minstrel troupes. Unlike generic or stereotyped parodies of race and gender, the imitation of a specific individual,

FIGURE 9.1. The imitation dance set champion dancers like Juba and Edward Gray apart from other dancers working with minstrel troupes. Unlike the generic and stereotyped parodies of blackface minstrelsy, imitation dancing required the dancer to replicate the steps *and* reveal the physical personality of each dancer being imitated. Juba's imitation dance may have been the inspiration for a grand jig-dancing tournament that reportedly took place at Boston's Boylston Garden in the summer of 1845. "Boylston Garden" playbill, June 8, [1845], MS Thr 1848, box 12 (Gray, Edward), Houghton Library, Harvard University.

especially a well-known performer, was a comedy of proximity. The imitation dancer identified the person being imitated by name—Elssler, Diamond, Pelham, Juba—then drew out and exaggerated a prominent characteristic of his or her subject. Rather than performing "a type," where only general accuracy was needed, imitation dancing had to be precise; the dancer had to "get inside" and reveal the physical personality of the person being copied.[4] For the audience, the pleasure of watching imitations came from knowing the style and disposition of the subject being imitated. Dancers such as Juba, Diamond, and Gray imitated their opponents with these audiences in mind. In contrast, the Sable Harmonists portrayed gross stereotypes that ill-informed audiences could recognize.

Juba developed his imitation dance in a cultural world rife with borrowing, impersonating, thieving, caricaturing, and appropriating, the most popular example being blackface minstrelsy. In early 1843 circus and tavern musicians began forming bands and blacking-up to sing African American songs and other popular tunes in four-part harmony. A typical troupe included four or five white male singer-musicians and a jig dancer. An extension of the "Negro extravaganza," blackface minstrelsy began as a set of songs performed as an entr'acte or final act at saloons, circuses, and theaters. Over time, these acts were combined into full-length, stand-alone vocal and instrumental concerts divided into parts and interspersed with dances and exaggerated parodies of Black people's repartee and culture.

Blackface was the gimmick by which these musical quartets set themselves apart from other vocal ensembles. In most of their lyrics and skits, blackface minstrels presented free Black people as vain and ridiculous and enslaved Black people as ignorant and happy. These stereotypes became more degrading when slavery's proponents began defending enslavement as a positive good compared to the uncertainty and destitution caused by wage labor under capitalism.[5] In 1848 African American abolitionist and newspaper editor Frederick Douglass called blackface minstrels "the filthy scum of white society, who have stolen from us a complexion denied to them by nature, in which to make money, and pander to the corrupt taste of their white fellow-citizens."[6] Blackface troupes marketed their concerts by appealing to people's racial prejudice and curiosity. But that appeal did not guarantee success. To get their business off the ground, blackface minstrels needed a jig dancer.

Minstrel troupes relied on champion dancers to draw audiences to their shows, and jig dancers worked with minstrel troupes to stay employed and spread their names. Each benefited from working in conjunction with the other. However, minstrels needed jig dancers much more than jig dancers needed them. "Without the champion jig dancer," noted minstrel-manager Frank Dumont, "the minstrel show was a ship without a rudder. He was the star of the troupe. If he signified his intention of quitting the show the entire troupe would [beg him on] bended knees [not to] leave them to their fate."[7] Blackface minstrels were at sea without a champion dancer because 1840s America was overflowing with musical troupes. This competition gave stars such as Diamond and Juba considerable leverage when choosing which minstrel bands to work with, demanding a level of payment, and deciding the nature of their acts.

For Diamond and Juba, minstrelsy provided opportunities and imposed limitations. Juba traveled with minstrels to New England, where free Black people were relatively safe, quickly mastered the art of publicity, and asserted his champion status by imitating his blackface rivals. Diamond mostly toured with circus minstrels, was constantly troubled by impersonators, and asserted his champion status by challenging his peers onstage and off. Each dancer bolstered blackface minstrelsy's popularity while also disrupting its message. White people ate up the stereotypes but were also treated to some awesome dancing at minstrel shows. Minstrelsy banked on the subjugation of Black people and women but also provided a platform on which individual dancers could challenge their place in the social order. Edward Gray's claim to champion status represented one such challenge. Diamond's penchant for trial dancing over comic roles represented another. Juba's triumphs in the minstrelsy business potentially flipped that social order on its head.

Minstrelsy's Rudder

Both Diamond and Juba figure into minstrelsy's origin stories. African American memoirist James Thomas placed Diamond at the center of minstrelsy's evolution. When John Diamond first came to Nashville, recalled Thomas, he danced to the circus band. "When he came again, he had a fiddler in back to sit on the ring along the side [of] the board. They soon added a banjo player, then tambo[u]rine, in a few years they had formed troupes."[8] This trajectory from extravaganza act to musical band fits the reminiscences of William Whitlock, who said he got the idea of combining the banjo* with other instruments in 1840 while performing with Master Diamond in Philadelphia: "I practiced with Dick Myers, the violinist, and on our benefit night we played the banjo and violin together for the first time in public."[9]

Juba's dancing talents fueled minstrelsy's rise as well. "After practicing for a while, [four of us] went to the old resort of the circus crowd—the 'Branch,' in Bowery—with our instruments," recalled Whitlock, "and in Bartlett's Billiard room performed for the first time as the Virginia Minstrels." The band, which consisted of Whitlock on banjo, Daniel Emmett on violin, Frank Brower on bone castanets, and Richard Pelham on tambourine, first performed onstage at Pelham's Chatham Theatre benefit on January 31, 1843. The next day, they appeared with

---

* Banjos would displace the violin as minstrelsy ossified into a few stereotypes.

Nathan Howe's circus at the Bowery Amphitheatre, where they also performed the "rich, racy and original" one-act burlesque entitled "Boz at the Five Points, or American Notes for English Circulation," with Pelham acting and dancing the part of Black Bill, or Juba.[10]

After seeing their Bowery performance, continued Whitlock, "the proprietor of the Cornucopiae, next door to the Park Theatre, prevailed on the party to appear in his saloon nightly, in conjunction with the jig-dancer John Diamond." They opened there in February, thus, claimed Whitlock, diverting patrons away from the Park and forcing "Gen. Rufus Welch, whose circus was then occupying that theatre," to engage them. "Diamond did not go to the Park with them," he maintained, "as both Pelham and Brower were dancers, and would brook no opposition." What Whitlock failed to mention, however, is that Diamond was already dancing for Welch at the Park.[11]

Minstrel troupe musicians liked to think that their songs and comic patter were the heart of their entertainments, with the jig dancing introduced by way of variety. But what placed one company above another was not the singing or acting, insisted one manager; it was the jig dancer and banjo. That "negro element . . . was the most relished part of the programme."[12] All the early minstrel troupes formed around challenge dancers. Ballad singer Edwin P. Christy gave his first minstrelsy entertainments in Child's Alley, Rochester, in union with three young jig dancers: Dick Sliter, John Daniels, and John Perkins (whom one chronicler identified as African American).[13] From the beginning, the challenge dancer's exhibitions of prizewinning steps were the highlight of minstrel troupe programs, a fact articulated in the size of the print and length of the prose describing them.

Without a champion jig dancer, blackface minstrel troupes were just another version of "Music for the Million." American minstrelsy rose in tandem with an international movement to democratize harmonic vocal music that swept through the United States in the early 1840s. It began with Joseph Mainzer, a German priest and composer who sought to ameliorate the miseries of the poor through music. Forced to flee Germany in 1833, Mainzer took his system of training "masses of people" to read musical scores divided into parts for the different voices—bass, tenor, alto, and soprano—to Brussels, Paris, and London. His classes were largely attended by teachers, who carried the art to working-class people in their home districts. The name of the movement came from a suggestion offered by Mainzer's students when the storefront he taught them in overflowed. If each of his pupils, "which would, ere long, amount to a *million*," subscribed a shilling, they said, they could raise enough money to build a hall they could call their own.[14]

By 1843 Mainzer's manual *Singing for the Million* (London, 1841), the "shilling concert" idea, and untold volumes of vocal scores had immigrated to North America, inspiring thousands of people to join together to sing harmonic renditions of traditional airs, popular tunes, opera choruses, and "Negro" songs.

Hundreds of vocal troupes formed, among which white male bands of blackface minstrels were only one type. In January 1844 the *New York Herald* called the four-part harmony of a blackface troupe "a new era . . . in negro music."[15] The white Hutchinson Family Singers (three boys and one girl, "all of them very pretty and quite young"), who traversed the country seeking middle-class audiences for their close harmonies, mountain melodies, and abolitionist songs, represented another type.[16]

The democratizing impulse behind the Million movement helps explain Juba's participation in minstrelsy and acceptance as a minstrel. White male musicians may have predominated, but Blacks and women emboldened by the movement also formed professional singing troupes, blackface and otherwise. In 1844 the Shilling Concerts at Concert Hall in New York were produced by male and female performers and attended by audiences of "700 persons, 500 of whom were ladies." The Sable Sisters—Annette, Angeline, and Pauline Garson, and sometimes Rosina—introduced themselves as "ladies of musical education . . . Talent and Ability, in both the instrumental and Vocal Departments," and banded together with the five members of the Ethiopian Minstrels under the banner "Music for the Million" to perform solos, duets, quintets, and choruses in Boston and New York for "the reduced price" of twelve and a half cents (one shilling). In 1845 F. S. Myers formed the Johnson Family of Ethiopian Serenaders with his wife and daughter in Philadelphia, the Tabernacle in New York presented harmonic concerts in which all the performers were "of the colored race," and an "Ethiopian company" joined the Million by washing their blackened faces and giving "capital vocal concerts at Franklin Hall."[17]

Male and female dancers exploited the market opened up by the Million concerts. In October 1845 dancing women surrounded Juba in Hartford, Connecticut, where blue laws still proscribed thespians from performing. However, "this week we have had, at one hall, negro dancing, (and, of course, the wonderful 'Juba,') and singing," reported a *New York Herald* correspondent. "Another company of female dancers (white) &c. followed them."[18] In March 1846 jig dancer and tambourine player John Brown formed a little company in Providence with Irish jig dancer Fanny Hutchinson, nautical hornpipe dancer James O'Connell, and a comical singer.[19] In this environment, an African American youth such as Juba, with dancing laurels and singing abilities, could steer a minstrel troupe's course.

Both Juba and Diamond began working with minstrel troupes between their 1843 tavern match and their "Grand Public Contest" in July 1844.[20] Juba danced in New York with the "celebrated band of Virginia Serenaders, consisting of Sam Johnson, Fluter, Glancell, [and] Harmony." Juba was the star and the Serenaders were his accompanists at the Concert Saloon on Chambers Street, where he gave "his inimitable imitations of all the celebrated Negro Dancers" and made his challenge to the world through the saloon's manager. Diamond danced in New

England for a different troupe of Virginia Serenaders ("Messrs. Myers, Sanford, White, Edwards and Carter"), accompanied by the Green Mountain Boy on violin. George Wooldridge, who would sponsor Diamond when he accepted Juba's challenge, acted as agent for the band.[21]

Diamond's Serenaders were in Bangor, Maine, and Juba's Serenaders were at the Concert Saloon when another band of Virginia Serenaders opened at the Chatham Theatre.[22] Chroniclers of minstrelsy say that Philadelphia violinist Richard ("Ole Bull" Dick) Myers led *the* Virginia Serenaders and list John Diamond, James Sanford, and several others not named above as his associates. But that selection simply represents an attempt to impose order on a chaotic enterprise.[23] "Performers were constantly changing around and troupes disbanding, but the original names . . . were continued by other parties," recalled one theatrical manager.[24] "While the salaries paid were small the rivalry that existed between the various managers was great, the result was a performer would leave the company he was engaged with for a larger salary offered by another manager. On this account you would oftentimes find the same performer advertised as a member of one or more companies."[25] Champion dancers were even more mobile than musicians. They also commanded better pay.

As star performers, Diamond and Juba aligned themselves with minstrel troupes rather than disappearing into their ranks. Diamond's likeness never appeared in any troupe's group portrait. Neither did Juba's, until he performed in England a few years later. For example, Diamond was not included among the band members on the cover of a songbook that served as promotional material for the Virginia Serenaders' tour in 1844. Casting himself as a band member would have undermined the independence he wielded as a celebrity.

After the Bowery match in July 1844, Juba took advantage of touring opportunities opened up by minstrelsy. That fall he headed north as the star of a show that included a duo of "posturers" (juggler-acrobats) and the Georgia Champions, a minstrel band consisting of A. F. Winnemore, an African American vocalist and composer, and Harmony and Fluter from the Concert Saloon's Virginia Serenaders.[26] Harmony may also have been Black, but his identity is lost. Fluter was the stage name of white banjoist-composer Thomas F. Briggs. The little company rode into town on the heels of departing equestrians, cashing in on a long-standing circus practice. On their days off, acrobats, musicians, and other nonequestrian circus performers would band together to present what they called "stage or hall show turns," during which they took turns presenting their acts in a hotel parlor or other rentable room and then split the proceeds. Minstrel troupes venturing out on their own turned these venues into circuits.

Juba's company opened at the Melodeon, a concert saloon attached to Boston's National Theatre, in late November 1844.[27] Savvy about promotion, he did not identify himself as the dancer described in Dickens's *American Notes*, as that might have impinged on the reception of his performance. Dickens's tour of Five Points had already been lambasted in print and burlesqued by blackface minstrels. Instead, he advertised himself as the equal of every current champion. "OLE BULL *vs.* JUBA" buzzed the *Daily Bee*, invoking the violin prodigy's departure from Boston to promote Juba's arrival in that city. "No sooner is one wonder gone than another comes, in the person of JUBA, the young man who danced against John Diamond in New York.... [O]ur readers, no doubt, as well as thousands of others, will be on the *qui vive* to see him, as his friends in New York challenge the world for from one to ten thousand dollars to produce his equal.... It is said he far exceeds Diamond, Brower, Smith, Chestnut, Sanford and all of the other dancers."[28]

Juba's Melodeon ads reached out to dance enthusiasts on both ends of the spectrum. He appealed to the sporting crowd by issuing challenges, calling himself "without exception the greatest Dancer in the World" and assuring the public that "there is not one point of deception in this announcement. Any person proving that such is the case, will on application to me, with such proof, receive for 25 cents paid, the sum of five dollars." This "precocious boy who has become the observed of all observers" (after Dickens) also tempted more "respectable" theatergoers by reserving the front seats or gallery "expressly for the Ladies and Families," charging half price for children, and guaranteeing that "a competent person will be in attendance to seat the audience and preserve order."[29]

"Ladies and Families" was not a euphemism for white-only audiences in Boston. In December Juba and the Georgia Champions moved (without the jugglers) to Washingtonian Hall, where antislavery fairs and functions were held, gentrified their ad copy, and performed for white and Black houses (fig. 9.2).[30] At his benefit on December 13, "Little Juba . . . will do his prettiest and introduce some of the tallest specimens of dancing ever witnessed," announced the *Daily Bee*, meaning his most exquisite and his most humorous steps. The Champions reserved their last entertainment at Washingtonian Hall, a Saturday matinee, "for the convenience of the colored population."[31] Saturday was also Juba's last performance with that particular quartet of singer-musicians.

Imposters and Unreliable Sources

While Juba danced in Boston, Diamond negotiated engagements in the mid-Atlantic states. In his unpublished "Personal Reminiscences," Samuel S. Sanford claimed that John Diamond "played the bones" for Sanford's minstrel band at Palmo's in New York, then traveled with them to Philadelphia in late November 1844.[32] Like the tambourine, wooden or bone castanets were a percussive, rhythmic instrument often played by dancers. The problem with Sanford's story is that according to the papers, "The celebrated and original Master JOHN DIAMOND"

FIGURE 9.2. Washingtonian Hall and Amory Hall, where Juba's minstrel troupes performed in Boston, were public buildings open to African American performers and audiences. In this poster, the language and props of competitive sports are employed to attract an antislavery crowd. The "Colored Citizens" of Boston presented white abolitionist William Lloyd Garrison with a "Silver Pitcher" to indicate that he was "Champion of Universal Emancipation." The "farewell meeting" was also a benefit night for Black abolitionist and writer William W. Brown, who was departing for Europe. *Presentation and Farewell Meeting!!,* July 16, 1849, Colored Citizens of Boston Collection: Anti-Slavery Collection, Rare Books Department, Boston Public Library.

had arrived at Baltimore's Front Street Theatre with Welch's circus in early November. Several band members from Diamond's Virginia Serenaders were also with the equestrians, including Master Edwards, who danced a grand trial dance with Diamond on November 7 for the benefit of a proponent of "second sight" who gave lectures on mesmerism. "Come early if you want a Seat!" recommended the *American and Commercial Advertiser*.[33]

Whether Diamond traveled to Philadelphia with Sanford or the circus or some other company is unknowable: "Performers of that time were not adverse [*sic*] to appropriating the names of their more successful rivals. In this manner a half dozen shows might have simultaneously claimed Johnny Diamond as their own champion."[34] When Sanford's Ethiopian Serenaders played Commissioners' Hall in Southwark the last week in November, they claimed as their champions "the Original JOHN DIAMOND . . . and last, not least, the Original SANFORD." Inaccurate reminiscences reflect the nature of memory and the chronicler's purpose in writing, which in this case was to demonstrate his own importance to minstrelsy's "rise and progress." Sam Sanford wanted to mark his band as the first minstrel troupe and himself as the first "Sanford" to play in Philadelphia. He even announced that he, "the Original Sanford," would "dance a TRIAL DANCE with the Original Diamond," purposefully mixing himself up with James Sanford, Diamond's opponent in Philadelphia in 1840.[35]*

Diamond did dance with Sam Sanford's band in December 1844, when the Ethiopian Serenaders moved to Temperance Hall in Philadelphia's Northern Liberties. "Master J. Diamond will, during the evening, give imitations of all the great dancers of the present day," announced the *Public Ledger*.[36] That imitation dance and the public's response indicate that this dancer *was* John Diamond. Despite Sanford's self-promotion, the dancer overshadowed the minstrels. "On Christmas night they were obliged to discharge over five hundred persons who could not witness their Grand Concert," reported the *Ledger*. "Why don't they come in the city, so the elite may see that wonderful Master John Diamond, who created such a sensation in this city some three years ago?" Instead of moving downtown, on New Year's Eve the Ethiopian Serenaders took someone called "the *Original John Diamond*, Banjoist and Dancer," to Manayunk, outside Philadelphia.[37] Who was that dancer? Other Diamonds played the banjo, but not John, who only played percussive instruments such as the tambourine and castanets.

Imposters stalked Juba as well. "Look out for counterfeiters," the *Boston Daily Transcript* warned Juba's patrons in November 1844, "as he will not appear before being regularly announced through the press in conjunction with the Champions."[38] Antebellum entertainment was rife with deceivers, who were publicly exposed as cheats when people found them out. The quality of the show usually gave the imposters away. In May 1845 at least two minstrel companies toured the Northeast with a quartet of female singer-musicians advertised as the Sable Sisters. When the fake Sable Sisters played Hartford, the audience showed its disapproval by "joining in the entertainment," which in contemporary parlance meant making noise, throwing food, and being generally disruptive.[39]

Diamond had lost control of the stage name Master Diamond early in his career, and with the rise of minstrelsy, he lost control of John Diamond as well. In January 1845 "the original John Diamond, the greatest Dancer in the world and Tambo[u]rinist" performed "his imitation of the Locomotive at full speed" with a band of minstrels that included someone called Ole Bull Myers and "J.

---

* Sam Sanford also failed to note that the "Ole Bull Myers" who accompanied the match "on his talking fiddle" was "Will" or "Bill" Myers and not "Dick" Myers. There were three Ole Bull Myerses: J. Richard, William, and F. S., the latter considered "one of the most useful actors" on the Philadelphia stage. Sam Sanford claimed that when people talked about Temperance Hall in 1844, he and Ole Bull Bill Myers were always confounded with either Dick Myers or Jim Sanford, neither of whom (he said) had ever played there previous to July 1845.

Sanford" (the italicized *J* suggesting this name was borrowed) at Philadelphia's Masonic Hall. Meanwhile, another band of minstrels led by another Ole Bull Myers played at F. S. Myers's saloon in the Union Building. "As many are led to believe that it is not Ole Bull Dick Myers' Band," cautioned the manager, "they can convince themselves that it is by calling and judging."[40] To confound things further, on January 20 John Diamond was also advertised at both venues. The following day, the *Public Ledger* published "A CARD" signed "J. DIAMOND" protesting that he was not even in Philadelphia: "We see an announcement in the Sun and Ledger, stating that the Original John Diamond was back to his old Quarters, Union Building, but I, John Diamond, is with the Great Ethiopian Serenaders, and perform in Harrisburg, this week, by invitation of many citizens in that place."[41]

Snagging the real Diamond was a boon and a bane for managers. The day before his card was published—a preinaugural night of "drunken revelry" in Harrisburg—Diamond let down his Ethiopian colleagues. Identifying him as "the bone end" of the company, someone later reported that John Diamond "got into an altercation with and stabbed a night watchman. Diamond was arrested and lodged in Harrisburg jail," forcing the company's agent to replace him with another performer, after which his name vanished from newspaper advertisements in Philadelphia.[42]

No doubt Diamond's alcohol consumption added to his rowdy behavior, but it was no anomaly. Between 1790 and 1830 Americans consumed on average, per capita, on the job and off, 3.9 gallons of absolute alcohol a year. By 1840 temperance (abstinence from alcohol drinking) crusades, which began in the late 1820s, had been taken up by manufacturers hoping to keep their workers sober, churchmen who correlated poverty and destitution with alcoholism, and the respectable and propertied classes. Some working people climbed on the temperance wagon as well, but far "larger numbers remained attached to their traditional drinking habits and customs."[43]

Diamond resurfaced in Philadelphia two months later and, according to the *Public Ledger*, accepted a challenge to dance a "trial of skill" with an unspecified "Sanford" at Temperance Hall on March 15, 1845.[44] In April some "Great Ethiopian Serenaders" led by "Ole Bull Myers" played in conjunction with "the Original John Diamond, the best dancer in the world" at Carpenter Hall.[45] Perhaps fed up with sparring imposters and battling "Ethiopians," Diamond then headed over to Chesnut Street, where Welch, Mann & Delavan's National Circus was packing up, secured a job, and climbed on the wagon train.[46]

Juba set himself apart from his blackface counterfeiters by imitating the imitators. In January 1845 the Georgia Champions reorganized in Providence, Rhode Island, with Juba at the helm. The quartet now consisted of H. Ryder on violin,

Earle Pierce on castanets, Fluter on banjo, and Juba on tambourine. The Champions toured Massachusetts and trekked through Maine's rugged terrain for six months, stopping in the same towns and cities where Diamond and the Virginia Serenaders had performed the previous year. The *New York Herald* kept its readers apprised of their movements, noting on January 11 that "the celebrated Georgia Champions, and that astounding prodigy, Juba, are giving entertainments at Taunton."[47] The company attracted attention by introducing Juba as "the ninth wonder of the world," announcing on their playbills that he had won two $500 matches against Diamond, and concluding every show in every town with Juba's "Imitation Dance."[48]

Juba set the tone for the company's performances. The Georgia Champions appeared in "their new and splendid Georgian Costumes" and described their show as an "innocent amusement" played to "fashionable audiences" with "brilliant success" "in all the principal cities in the United States."[49] Mr. Russell, "the Celebrated Accordionist, Of Boston," added elegance to the evening program with solos of stylish new dance tunes—quicksteps, waltzes, gallopades—and requests for popular airs.* But it was Juba's vocal and dance solos that propelled the Champions' olio of traditional, folk, opera, and "Negro" music.[50]

The Champions' June 1845 entertainment in Portland, Maine, had three parts separated by two ten-minute intermissions. (The songs were shuffled around on subsequent nights, but Juba's dances remained in place.) During Part I Master Juba sang "My Old Dad." In Part II he sang "Colored Gentleman (from Opera of Amile)" and as a finale performed the "Grand Statue Dance," an updated eighteenth-century stage dance usually performed by a woman who assumed static poses in time to the music.[51] Part III began with the only act on the program described in blackface lingo: "Grand Overture of the money musk!!!—in imitation of the slocomotive bullgine, dat at de fust ob de beginning is very moderate, den as de steam rises de power of de circumvolution exaggerates itself into a can'stopimization, and runs clar ob de track." Juba performed the "Boatman Dance" with the chorus as the fifth song, after which came banjo and accordion solos and the evening's grand finale: "Imitation Dance *by Juba* In which he will give correct imitations of the principal Ethiopian Dancers throughout the United States, ending with an IMITATION OF HIMSELF,—then you see the vast difference between those who have heretofore attempted Dancing and this truly wonderful young man. No conception can be formed of the variety of beautiful and intricate steps exhibited by him with ease. You must see to believe."[52]

---

* Russell probably played an early diatonic accordion, a small, single-row buttoned, free-reeds instrument operated by bellows (also called a Melodeon). Manufactured in Germany and played by women and men, accordions spread in popularity alongside the polka in antebellum America.

Swelling of the Ranks

The jig dancer could make or break a minstrelsy show. So long as there were people in the audience who danced themselves, jig dancers had to be innovative and versatile. As minstrels turned their acts into full-length shows and lost contact with other entr'acte performers, their songs, repartee, and skits became stale. But competition kept the champion dancer's acts fresh, unpredictable, and worth coming to see. Minstrel musicians took note. They copied the dancers by billing themselves as unrivaled champions and imitating them on their instruments. During his "Grand Challenge Solo," John Brown replicated the rattler's "bullgine lecture"* on the tambourine. He claimed that his version sounded like a locomotive running off the tracks and bursting its boiler, "rattling cannon in the distance," and the "rattlings of a Cotton mill and machinery."[53] Minstrels also advertised trials of skill between individual musicians and whole troupes. In June 1845 Vauxhall's resident blackface troupe tried to drum up interest by challenging "any other Band to Play, Sing and Dance for the sum of $1000" before falling back on a sure thing and presenting the troupe's champion dancer in a match for the same amount.[54]

Following Diamond and Juba's "Great Public Contest" in 1844, "many of the leading companies claimed the world's champion dancer," noted theatrical manager Michael B. Leavitt, "and this emulation made an interesting feature of the minstrel business in its then stage of development, for competing contests were of frequent occurrence, causing the utmost excitement wherever held."[55] Some of these dancers were extravaganza dancers turned minstrels, while others were newcomers. Wherever they traveled, circus and minstrel troupe dancers found contenders anxious to try their luck, earn some cash, or break into the big time. In 1844 Joe Brown, a thirteen-year-old from Buffalo, challenged Master Pierce to a match, won it, and entered the circle of professionals; Mr. Price of the Southern Band of Minstrels faced Joe Miles in a $400 match in New York; and in July 1845 "Master Thomas Tcaser, from Troy" accepted a challenge made by the manager of the Vauxhall Gardens saloon to "dance a Grand Match Dance with Jerry Bryant for $1000, the Audience to be the Judges."[56]† Minstrelsy almost guaranteed that outstanding jig dancers could find a place to work.

Juba's imitation dance may have been the inspiration for a grand jig-dancing tournament that reportedly brought seven of those dancers to Boston's Boylston

---

* A "bullgine" was a steam engine: "bull" (as in uncastrated male cow) plus "-gine" (as in engine).
† Thomas Teaser was probably Jerry's brother Dan. Jerry, Dan, and Neil O'Brien were Irish American jig dancers from Troy, New York, who took the stage name Bryant when they migrated to New York City as minstrels.

Garden in the summer of 1845. Like boxers, the contestants identified themselves with a leading city rather than a particular minstrel troupe. "When a general tourney was held, as frequently happened, the public, moved to a high pitch of sectional pride, applauded its favorites with a prodigality that was indeed stirring," explained Leavitt in a section of his autobiography entitled "When Jig Dancing Was Considered an Art." At Boylston, New York City was represented by Dick Pelham and Frank Brower, Philadelphia by Jim Sanford, Troy by Frank Diamond, Albany by John Smith, Providence by Master Juba, and Boston by John Diamond and Ned Gray.[57] To cover the "art" as well as the "science" of jig dancing, style and execution were added to the length of time danced and the numerical advantage in steps as the elements to be considered by the judges.[58]

The cities the dancers represented were only partially determined by their minstrelsy connections. New York native Dick Pelham and Baltimore native Frank Brower danced for New York because that was where they had organized the Virginia Minstrels. James Sanford represented Philadelphia, where he was adored and currently working with the Virginia Serenaders. Frank (Lynch) Diamond danced for his hometown of Troy, where Barnum had found him. And John Smith danced for Albany, where he and Master Coleman were working for Spaulding's North American Circus.[59]

Juba danced for Providence because that was where he reorganized the Georgia Champions. Providence contained a fairly large free Black community. Gradual emancipation began in Rhode Island at the end of the Revolution, and by 1840 the number of African Americans in Providence had risen to 1,301, despite an exodus following a riot in 1831. That riot took place when mobs of white outsiders torched the houses of Black people living in Snow Town, a racially mixed neighborhood in northern Providence where poor people concentrated their residences.[60]

Edward Gray, referred to by one chronicler as "Ned Gray, (colored man) known as the Boston Rattler," claimed Boston, which also had a substantial free Black population. By 1790 the federal census recorded no slaves in Massachusetts, but no law or amendment to the state constitution ending slavery was ever passed. "Some masters manumitted their slaves formally and arranged to pay them wages for continued labor." Others "freed" their slaves but restricted their freedom by retaining them as indentured servants for extended periods. By 1830 free people of color made up 3 percent of that city's population, and by 1850 Boston was home to five Black churches, a publicly funded school for African American children, and an internationally renowned abolitionist community.[61]

Dancing for Boston was a strategic move on John Diamond's part, since it was the city in which the tournament was taking place. Boston also contained about thirty-five thousand Irish immigrants, representing one-fourth of the population in 1845.[62] Aligning himself with their city no doubt ingratiated him with many spectators. According to Leavitt, John Diamond won the tournament, but what the contest was like, when exactly it took place, and how the audience responded to the dancing can only be imagined. Leavitt's account and a list of the participants scribbled on a scrap of paper are all that remain.[63] No ads or coverage appeared in newspapers, leaving one to wonder if this tournament was extrapolated from posters announcing Juba's or Ned Gray's imitation dance.

The Colored Gentleman and the Jailbreaker

Whoever wrote Juba's publicity, whether Lane himself or his agent, knew what they were about. The young African American dancer came off just cocky enough to please his peers and eloquent enough to pique the curiosity of bourgeois audiences. This was not the case for Diamond, whose promotional gestures seem clumsy in comparison (for example, his ungrammatical "but I, John Diamond, is . . . "). Lane may indeed have had more schooling than Diamond. Campaigns for free public education in New York City coincided with the founding of the manumission society, whose purpose, among other things, was to give African Americans "the elements of education." In 1820 a privately funded facility enrolled about seven hundred students; Black teachers replaced its white teachers in 1832; and by the time "the African Free School" was integrated into the public school system, it had educated thousands of girls and boys in seven buildings in different neighborhoods. These schools inspired the organization of the Free School Society under the presidency of Mayor De Witt Clinton, who wanted to "furnish free education for the many children whose parents could not afford to pay for it" and whom church schools did not reach.[64] Yet poor parents often resisted sending their children to school rather than out to work. Apprenticed to Barnum at twelve, Diamond likely received little formal education, public or Catholic. He seems to have learned to read and write, but his itinerancy limited his schooling.

Lane's awareness of how to succeed grew as he toured. Every 1845 advertisement promoted his prowess and respectability with market savvy. "Juba, who danced against John Diamond . . . and pocketed the 'rocks' . . . Juba himself has been here!" raved a paper in Gardiner, Maine, which described him as enthralling "crowded and fashionable houses . . . by the astonishing skill and ease with which he executed some of the most difficult performances."[65] He also knew to stay away from circuses, which even boxing reviewers found too lowbrow to recommend: "A display of the noble science of Pugilism . . . might enlighten our ignorance," argued New York's *Knickerbocker Magazine*, but the Park Theatre Circus "presented exhibitions that were not altogether replete with mind. The workings of the intellect . . . were not apparent; and for this reason, we repeat, we did not 'cotton to' the circus."[66] Shrewdly, Juba identified himself as a sportsman and elevated his dancing above physicality with intelligence.

Conversely, Diamond's actions revealed a disregard for social rank and self-preservation. Circus work was certainly harder than touring with minstrels. Welch, Mann, and Delavan's "mammoth circus" set up, had a show, broke down, and moved on to the next town almost every day in the summer of 1845. They passed through Pennsylvania and New York State, along the Erie Canal to Buffalo, and back through Pennsylvania to Washington, DC, typically performing at six principal towns and villages every eight days, with the "far-famed" Diamond dancing the finale every evening accompanied by a "Comic Band of Negro Minstrels."[67] The fatigue of circus employment may have fed the dancer's belligerence and indifference to authority. In September 1845 Diamond was arrested and imprisoned in Chambersburg, Pennsylvania, "for cutting one of his fellow Ethiopians." A few days later, he escaped from Franklin County prison in the company of a "well known Jail-bird" named Donnelly. Attempted and successful escapes from "round-top" prison, nicknamed for its domed roof and cupola, were common. "The Sheriff of Franklin county offers a reward for [Diamond's] apprehension," a correspondent informed the Philadelphia Dollar Newspaper. Donnelly, who was caught first, defended his fellow jailbreaker by saying that "Diamond *cut* his acquaintance, after they had got outside of the borough." Diamond was apprehended in New York in October. He may have been kept in round-top's "dungeon cells," which according to legend also served as a hiding place for runaway slaves on their journey to the North.[68] He did not reappear until late November.

Whether ill or well behaved, Diamond and Juba faced social scrutiny simply for being dancers in the 1840s. Polite society considered jig dancing and the drinking and brawling that often accompanied it antisocial behavior not to be tolerated in any caste.* Blackface minstrels buttressed these sentiments in skits about sexual rivalry leading to fights at colored people's balls.[69] In fact, dancing of any kind was suspect. A strident antidancing campaign arose after the waltz and polka, which required couples to embrace, gained popularity among middle-class youths. Some reformers insisted that the physical pleasure derived from such exercise was an enticement to immorality.[70] Even watching dance could lead to violent passions. Ballerina Emma Ince caused a brawl in 1845 when one "midshipman threw a ring on the stage for her, and another a rag baby. The first middy got mad at this," according to a Boston paper, "and called the second middy 'no gentleman,'" prompting a fight at a chance meeting later on.[71] Abolitionists came down on both sides of the dancing debate. Some claimed that whenever Black people danced, they reinforced racial stereotypes; others declared dancing a nonissue compared to slavery.[72] Black musicians and dancers whose livelihoods depended on white

---

* The verb "to brawl," meaning noisy fighting or quarrelling, is derived from the name of a French dance.

patronage had no choice but to make their middle-class allegiance clear. For example, African American band leader Francis Johnson published "A CARD" in the newspapers thanking "the Ladies and Gentlemen of Philadelphia and its vicinity" for their "very liberal patronage" and informing them that he had "just received from Europe, a large and well selected collection of Quadrilles."[73] Danced by four couples forming a square, quadrilles were considered more respectable than waltzes or polkas. White dancers and musicians had more leeway to ignore middle-class mores.

Opposite class ambitions tempered by race and personality shaped Juba's and Diamond's relationship to minstrelsy. Lane's choices led him away from other Black performers; Diamond's kept him in an integrated milieu. Juba sang and danced in town halls with white musicians; Diamond danced under circus tents with Black musicians, some of whom had previously worked with Juba. In the summer of 1845 the core of Welch, Mann, and Delavan's nonequestrian show was a trio composed of "Mr. Jameson, the Comic Singer and Banjo Player; Mr. Winnemore, the colored Vocalist; [and] Mr. John Diamond." A. F. Winnemore also took part in "An African Concert" with Hoyt, Edwards, Kelly, and Major. Kelly and Major, who do not appear in circus or minstrelsy histories, were probably Black. J. W. Bancker, who had managed Lane and Davis at Vauxhall, was Welch's agent. This mixed-race cast performed throughout New York and Pennsylvania under a pavilion capable of holding three thousand persons.[74]

Diamond may have gravitated to circuses because their public was also Black and white. In December 1845 Philadelphia's Temperance Hall was "crowded nightly . . . by the Ladies" when he and Jim Sanford "(two of the greatest dancers in the world)" appeared with some minstrels and other "Black Stars."[75] But when that show ended, Diamond took his talents to G. W. Smith's Old Dominion Circus in North Baltimore, which advertised a "Colored Gallery."[76]

Juba's race bound him more geographically than professionally. His primary performance city was Boston, where more Ethiopian minstrel companies were organized between 1843 and 1850 than in all the rest of the major cities put together.[77] Juba worked with four of them in 1845. After the Georgia Champions, he appeared at Washingtonian Hall with the African Troubadours and the Sable Harmonists in September.[78] Then he moved to Amory Hall (another abolitionist meetinghouse) and danced with the American Chimers. While not identical, all these bands contained one or more of the same people. As a nightly act in September, Juba danced a "trial of skill" with Frank Diamond (who knew Lane from the Vauxhall Gardens saloon) and with John Brown in November.[79] Juba and the Chimers also performed in Music for the Million concerts at Amory Hall and Springfield's Masonic Hall, where for Juba's benefit "the Sable Sisters and Brothers [sang] some of their best songs, assisted by the wonder of the world, Mast. Juba," whose imitation dance was the inevitable finale.[80]

When Juba left them in December, his fellow band members tried to fill his position. They had the versatile Black minstrel H. Ryder (Jake Hunter)—"self-taught banjo player and A. No. 1 of the Colored Race"—lead Juba's songs and dance a "Windmill Pigeon Wing," and white banjoist A. L. Thayer added a "Statue Dance" to his "Jim Along Josey."[81] But without Juba, they were forced to end their program with singing.

The Last Match

Both Diamond and Juba were in New York in the spring of 1846. Diamond appeared at Concert Saloon in March, and according to one chronicler, Juba was working at Pete Williams's dance-house. That source says that Williams placed a doorman (with a plain wooden soap box as his box office) at the end of the hallway that led to the tavern and charged people a shilling to see "this phenomenon, 'Juba,' imitate all the dancers of the day and their special steps." Occasionally, ringmaster Bob Ellingham (Robert White) acted as interlocutor, announcing the names of the dancers Juba imitated, until finally addressing the dancer directly: "'Now, Master Juba, show your own jig.' Whereupon he would go through all his own steps and specialties, with never a resemblance in any of them to those he had just imitated."[82]

In May Diamond toured Massachusetts with John Brown's Ethiopian Minstrels, which now included Juba's former colleagues Fluter, Ryder, and Thayer. The company's Fall River playbill clarified Diamond's relationship to the band. Printed in the largest, boldest type, his name dominated the center of the poster and his "Grand Match Dance" with Brown ("audience to decide who is the victor") served as its masthead.[83] Diamond called that act a match rather than a trial of skill (which did not demand a victor) for the same reason Juba danced his imitation dance: to reinstate his position at the top of the pack of minstrel dancers.

Diamond played castanets for the band, but they relied on him more as a dancer than a musician. His dances were interspersed strategically throughout the nine-part program. He performed his "Locomotive Lecture" as Part II, his "Camp Town Hornpipe" as Part V, and his "Grand Match Dance" with Brown as Part VIII. The final act, Part IX, was "the laughable After-piece, entitled the Rival Darkies." Diamond played "Peter Williams, the dancing pet," who had no speaking lines.[84] His job was to show off during the four-handed reel and dancing brawl that closed the skit so that people would stay to the end of the program.

When Diamond and Brown's Ethiopians arrived in Boston in June, it was clear that conditions were ripe for a showdown with Juba. Neither dancer had performed recently on Boston's stages. Welch and Mann's circus and Van Amburgh's Grand Caravan of big cats had rolled into town, bringing circus workers and spectators from throughout the vicinity to the city center. And a string of pugilists from New York, Philadelphia, and Boston, including Boss Harrington and T. Belcher Kay, had recently offered sparring exhibitions at Amory Hall, adding to the competitive atmosphere.[85] "NOW COMES THE TUG OF WAR!" boomed the *Boston Daily Atlas*. "Grand Match Dance by the two greatest Dancers in the World, Master JOHN DIAMOND, and the Wonder of the World, JUBA, both from New York."[86]

The contest took place on Saturday, June 20, 1846, at Graham's Olympic Saloon on Court Street. Graham's place, which styled itself "for all the boys," was situated in the old Concert Hall building, which had over the years housed meetings, parties, and a dancing and fencing academy.[87] "The public are respectfully informed that these two celebrated Dancers are to decide a wager of $500 a side, on which occasion judges will be chosen to decide who is the victor." The match was held in a saloon rather than a theater to emphasize its status as a sporting event. The layout inside Graham's resembled a boxing arena, in which the opponents performed on a raised dais surrounded by two concentric circles of seated spectators flanked by people standing on their feet. "First and second circle" at this match cost twenty-five cents, and the "parquette" behind the seats cost twelve and a half cents. "The ETHIOPIAN MINSTRELS will be in attendance to enliven the audience," noted the *Atlas*, and it is likely that both dancers chose Fluter or another musician from the troupe to play for them.[88] But the minstrels were just a warm-up act for the main event.

The grand tug-of-war at Graham's Olympic Saloon was the last time Diamond and Juba presented a public contest. No one bothered to record the event, and the winner was not announced in the papers. (Dancing is so ephemeral.) But subsequent events suggest that Juba had won again, an outcome that was integral to what each dancer did next.

A Puff of Smoke

The day after the match, Diamond was smoking a cigar in the square outside Graham's saloon when a couple of women walked up Hanover Street toward him. As the women passed, Diamond bumped into one of them and blew a cloud of cigar smoke into her face. Smoking in public was illegal in 1840s Boston. It was also a Sunday, which in that puritanical city exacerbated the infraction. It is possible that the woman had reprimanded him for smoking outside, causing him to rebel in this way. It is also possible that he was flirting with her. Either way, his actions led to his arrest. As always seemed to be the case when Diamond did something stupid, two policemen happened to be close by, and "before John had got over chuckling at the bold feat he had accomplished," reported the *Boston Post*, "the hand of the officers were upon his shoulders. He affected to believe he was only taken because he was smoking in the street, and begged pardon, saying he was a stranger in the city, and not acquainted with its customs. The officer concluded that, if he was indeed a stranger, he would like to see some of our public institutions and conducted him to jail; and in the morning carried him to the court house, where he was made practically acquainted with our forms of judicial proceedings." On Monday Diamond was sentenced to pay a fine of fifteen dollars: seven dollars and costs "for the insulting assault on a female" and two dollars and costs "for violating the ordinance against smoking in the streets."[89]

Notices of Diamond's arrest ran in papers across the country alongside war news from Mexico. The *Times and Compiler* of Richmond, Virginia, a tobacco-growing region, added a moral to its story: "Smoking in the streets of Boston is, therefore, a costly luxury." But the Northern papers had no sympathy for the dancer. "Served him right," announced the *Hartford Courant*. "Good," echoed editors in Vermont and Rhode Island.[90] John Diamond's rough behavior and lawbreaking had become as identity defining as his jig dancing.

Diamond paid his fine and remained in Boston but did not change his habits. A few weeks later, he stood again before Judge Cushing in the police court, alongside twenty-eight males and three females arrested on complaints of drunkenness and other minor infractions. "He was arrested near the head of Hanover street, having previously attracted the attention of the watchmen by his noisiness in the Verandah," reported the *Boston Daily Bee* on August 18. Brawls were common at the Veranda tavern, which served a lower-class, predominantly Irish neighborhood. "The City Marshall made some remarks concerning the rum-mills in [that] vicinity . . . and said that knowing it was the worst place in Boston, he had stationed extra police men there." Diamond either was fighting in the bar or resisted arrest, for he "exhibited some severe wounds about the nose and eyes, and was fined $3 and costs, and if not paid to be imprisoned in the House of Correction."[91]

The dancer may have served a short term in jail this time, as he did not return to New York until late September. There he worked at the newly opened Greenwich Theatre on Richmond Hill, where the manager, who usually produced Shakespeare and popular melodrama, called him "the first, best, greatest and most original Nigger Dancer in the World." Diamond danced a breakdown, a grapevine twist, and his "bullgine lecture" between the play and the farce, and the well-known "excelsior"* balladist Emma Leslie sang at his benefit. More variety arrived on October 6 with Miss Lenite Robinson, dancer, and "the Ethiopian Minstrels and Sable Sisters."[92] When Miss Leslie and the Ethiopians combined into a touring company later that month, Diamond joined them. They called themselves Music for the Million.

Music for the Million played at Temperance Hall in Charleston, South Carolina, the last week in November 1846. Besides Diamond, the artists who appeared

---

* Excelsior was used to identify a performer of the highest attainment.

included Mr. R. W. Smith, comic singer and tambourinist; Mr. J. Hallett, Ethiopian melodist; Mr. T. Fluter, banjoist; Mr. B. Baresford, violinist; and "MISS LESLIE. Together with the Ethiopian Minstrels and Sable Sister, Angelique." Emma Leslie headlined.[93] For a week, their advertisements announced "PRICE REDUCED," as if they were giving a shilling concert. (Tickets actually cost twenty-five cents.) Their program featured a solo act by each performer during the first part and the male musicians in blackface with Leslie as their Sable Sister in the second part.

Diamond danced at Emma Leslie's farewell concert on November 28, but when Music for the Million played for white and "colored" audiences in Augusta, Georgia, the first week in December, he was no longer with them.[94] For the next year and a half, John Diamond left no professional trail. Some people assumed he had died, which could easily have been the case. He had volunteered to fight in America's war with Mexico.

Going for the Cup

There is no record of Lane's movements immediately after the match at Graham's Olympic Saloon. He may have replaced Diamond and gone off with his friend Tom Fluter's band. In February 1847, after Diamond went missing, Juba performed at the Boston Museum, where he was billed as "the greatest dancer now living." The program included "Ethiopian Minstrels," a mechanical diorama of "the Battle of Bunker Hill," "Italian Fantoccini," and Mr. Davis, the "Comic Conjurer."[95] The next time he appeared in the papers, he was back in New York, acting in blackface dramatics and performing his champion dances at White's Melodeon.

Performer-author-manager Charles White wrote a one-act skit entitled *Going for the Cup* to feature the teenaged Lane's amazing dancing and White's own favorite character, an old man who puts one over on younger men (White was twenty-six) (fig. 9.3). The play opens with two blackface characters engaged in conversation. "Knowall (a consequential Darkey in a fancy shirt and high hat)," played by Dan Emmett, and "Jack Danger (an ordinary negro)," played by Neil Hall, were gamblers looking for some action. Enter Old Mr. Rogers, played by Charley White in a long vest, loose pants, old white hat, and large slave shoes, carrying a wagon driver's bamboo cane, looking for people to transport to a dance at Old Mrs. Williams's house. When Knowall and Danger hear that Rogers intends to compete for the silver cup being awarded to the best dancer at the ball, Knowall bets him five dollars he won't beat Ikey Vanjacklen. Enter Ikey, the barber's boy, played by Master Juba in a fancy jacket and shirt, knee breeches, striped stockings, low quarter shoes, gay necktie, and neat straw hat. As Ikey happens by, Rogers asks him, "Does you want to go ober to de ball? I got a wagon outside; only three cents; de roads is bad, and I'm off in a couple of minutes." "Not now," Ikey replies. "I've got a carriage of my own if I want one. By de way, what are you going to de ball for?" Rogers answers that he plans to win the cup, and Ikey, looking at Rogers's enormous feet, wagers five dollars that he won't. They decide to compete right then and there for the best out of three dances. Rogers finagles it so that he is holding everyone's stake money, which he puts in his purse. He also names himself referee and judge. Then he and Ikey go at it while Knowall and Danger watch. Despite the youngster's superior dancing, the old man gives himself the winning chalk mark after the second bout. "Gemmen, dat settle de question—two chalks and de money," Rogers says, and Ikey starts to cry. Knowall convinces Rogers to give the boy one more chance, then secretly soaps the floor so Rogers will slip, which he does. While Ikey dances his two minutes on the soaped floor with artful aplomb, Rogers secretly removes the stake money and leaves his empty purse on the bench for Knowall and Danger to steal. After Ikey ends his dance, the gamblers entreat him to go to the ball with them, and the three begin to leave just as Rogers pretends to "discover" that his purse is gone. The others call out, "Who's got the pocket-book?" as they wave it in the air. "Yes," he says, fingering the bills, "an' who's got de money?"[96] Although rivalry between the generations was the play's driving theme, the play also demonstrated White's respect for his younger colleague's expertise.

FIGURE 9.3. Charles White championed serious dancers such as Juba and Diamond in his advertisements and his venue. White's Old Mr. Rogers costume and character were less caricatured than those of other blackface performances. "Going for the Cup," the skit he performed with Juba, commented more on the generational than the racial divide. Charley White daguerreotype, TCS 38, Harvard Theatre Collection, Houghton Library, Harvard University; *Portrait of Charles T. White in blackface, as a minstrel character,* Portraits of Actors, Rare Book & Manuscript Library, University of Illinois at Urbana-Champaign.

Lane/Juba began working at White's Melodeon in August 1847. The room on Bowery Street was long and about thirty feet wide, with a gallery at one end. White called it the Melodeon after the saloon connected to Boston's National Theatre, where Juba's first minstrel troupe had played.[97] The Melodeon's entrance fee and entertainment reflected White's democratic management style. For a time, he offered what he called "free" concerts. The price of admission was actually a shilling to the pit and sixpence to the gallery, but with a shilling ticket came either a drink or a cigar.[98] White concluded his "highly miscellaneous" shows with a farce written by himself.[99] He did not print playbills or run advertisements at first. He relied on word of mouth. However, once Lane arrived, the *Herald* began "noticing" the large numbers attracted to the Melodeon "every night to hear White's Negro Minstrels, and to see Master Juba's dancing feats."[100]

Juba helped White establish the Melodeon's reputation. Dozens of singers, dancers, comics, and instrumentalists (male and female, foreign and native-born) made their earliest successes working for White. But the Melodeon was "especially noted for the number of first-class dancers who made their reputations on its boards." White brought out "R. M. Carroll, or 'Master Marks,'" whom Tony Pastor considered "probably, the best jig dancer of them all, after 'Juba,'" Master Williams, who jigged on a peck barrel, Joe Miles, Pete Lane, Miss Leroy, William Hedden, Billy Quinn, Joe Brown, Mickey Warren, and other trial dancers.[101] What White paid Juba is unknown, but according to a different manager, in those days most minstrels received "from $6 to $12 per week, with a few exceptions like T. D. Rice and John Diamond, who received $50 each per week. . . . [T]he next highest salary was $25 paid to Charley Jenkins, a fine buffo-singer, who accompanied himself on the banjo."[102] In America, even an exceptional Black dancer-singer-actor such as Lane could not have demanded a salary of fifty dollars, but his fame and popularity might have supported the next highest.

Juba moved between two saloon theaters in the winter of 1847–1848. When White faced financial trouble and temporarily closed the Melodeon in December, Juba moved to Greeley's Broadway Odeon, a prosperous little variety theater that patrons entered through Pinteaux's Saloon. Juba's frenetic movements contrasted with the latest fad on the Odeon stage: "Poses Plastiques by Model Artists,"* the motionless reenactment of famous scenes by living persons (mostly female) in costume. On "these cold nights, a punch and oysters, at Pinteaux's saloon, and a visit to the Odeon afterwards, is an agreeable way of passing the evening," remarked the *Herald*. "At least many seem to think so, as it is crowded nightly. [Greeley's] model artists are as plump as ever."[103] No

---

* *Poses plastiques* (flexible poses) were music hall renderings of *tableaux vivants* (living pictures), an old soirée entertainment revived in London and Paris in the 1830s and transported to America by imitators of European fashions.

doubt the poses of "model artists" enriched the "statue" dances of Juba and others.

In February 1848 White recouped his funds, reopened the Melodeon, and rehired Juba, who astounded audiences.[104] "I used to think I was no small jig dancer," recalled Billy Birch, who was sixteen when he first saw Juba's Melodeon act. "I would spend hours at a time trying to perfect myself in the art. But one night I went to see Juba, and it broke my heart. There never was a man like him, nor ever will be. He would appear at the rear of the stage on his toes, and come rushing down toward the footlights with a whirr. Then he would dance in the wildest, cleverest, and most unapproachable style, and before you could collect your scattered senses he had spun himself off the stage."[105] Lane, champion imitation dancer, had pilfered pointe work and pirouettes from ballerinas. With his feet encased in leather-soled boots, he glided across the floor as if it were soaped. No wonder other minstrel-managers came looking to steal him away.

On March 12, 1848, a fire closed down the Melodeon again. It started in a chair maker's shop in back, destroying some of White's property, but it did not burn the concert saloon itself. Most of the damage, breakage, and loss of scenery was "occasioned by the water," noted White in a letter to the Sunday *Courier*, hastening to add his thanks to Engine Company No. 15 and Hose Company No. 9 for their "prompt exertions in subduing and extinguishing the flames." Firemen were his patrons, after all. White took the opportunity to remodel the Melodeon's interior into a theater that accommodated eight hundred people, with boxes for "ladies as well as gentlemen." Juba did not wait to see the results. "In a note addressed to Charley White," T. Allston Brown averred, "Juba informed him that, when next he should be seen by Charley, he would be riding in his own carriage."[106] He was on his way to England with a couple of speculating minstrels. Ikey would beat Old Mr. Rogers yet.

The skill, knowledge, and finesse needed to become a challenge dancer made the jig dancing of early blackface minstrels an imitation (a sincere form of flattery) rather than a caricature (a cruel exaggeration). A champion like Master Juba, John Diamond, or the Boston Rattler did not simply mimic his peers. He got inside them and in so doing danced "in a style peculiar to himself."[107] In June 1849 Frederick Douglass would attend an evening performance of Gavitt's Original Ethiopian Serenaders in Rochester, New York, "partly from a love of music, and partly from curiosity." "The Company is said to be composed entirely of colored people, and it may be so," he wrote in the *North Star*, but because they wore burnt cork and large painted lips, "the better to express their characters and to produce uniformity of complexion," it was hard to be sure. Douglass was not impressed by the troupe's singing, which "was but an imitation of white performers, and not even a tolerable representation of the character of colored people," or by their "attempts at wit," the lack of which "gave their audience a very low idea of the shrewdness and sharpness of the race to which they belong." Still, he did not criticize Black performers for organizing minstrel troupes. "It is something gained when the colored man in any form can appear before a white audience," he argued. "But they must cease to exaggerate the exaggerations of our enemies; and represent the colored man rather as he is." Only one member of the troupe did that, according to Douglass. The dancer "B. Richardson is an extraordinary character. His Virginia Breakdown excelled anything which we have ever seen of that description of dancing." Let performers like him "bring around themselves persons of equal skill" and cater more to "the refinement" than "the vulgarity" of the public, Douglass advised, "and they may do much to elevate their race in popular estimation."[108]

Lane's performances as Juba had begun that process. It's a shame Douglass never got to see him dance.

III

FALLING GIANTS

10

JUBA ABROAD

It rained the first night William Lane and Tom Briggs crossed over the low arched bridge connecting London to Vauxhall Gardens in June 1848. And it kept raining from Monday to Friday, making the unfamiliar streets muddy and the dreary nights darker. A railway station opposite the Grand Entrance was due to open in a month. They might come that way in the future. Passing through the gardens' Bridge Street turnstile, the two young men immediately turned left into a column-lined walkway that ran along the edge of the Grand Quadrangle. The grounds were seldom empty, despite the weather. Beneath the colonnades couples strolled arm in arm, the women's skirts dragging a little with the weight of the wet, while supper parties of boisterous men feasting on "cold chickens and champagne" spilled out of airy boxes facing the empty pavilion and garden paths, where thousands of variegated wax lamps winked amid the wet, shimmering foliage.[1]

That first night the fire bell clanged as Lane and Briggs reached the Rotunda, signaling that it was time to view the entertainment. But it wasn't their signal, not yet. Their show began "at a Quarter to Ten precisely." Inside, the arena overflowed with steaming bodies, its air thick with the pungency of musty sawdust covering wooden floors sticky with spilled arrack punch and the pounding of equine hooves beneath the strains of human voices and brass trumpets. The audience was mixed, with young bloods in abundance, but the ratio of respectable ladies, shopkeepers, and ministers was still high. Knots of young women, thatched and cosseted by bonnets and shawls, sat down front directly behind the ring boards.[2]

They were waiting for him, the "phenomenon" described by Charles Dickens. He was "Boz's Juba" now, "a copper-coloured votary of Terpsichore,—the Monsieur Perrot* of Negro life in the southern states; [who] possesses the additional

---

* A reference to celebrated ballet dancer Jules Perrot.

attraction of being a 'real nigger,' and not a 'sham,' like his vocal associates."[3] It was all so amazing. Not that people came to see him or that the troupe's leader had agreed to his terms, brought him to England, and placed him up front. He'd come to expect that. It was that these English were excited to see him because he was Black, not despite it.

Lane found Britain's entertainment milieu welcoming. People were not race blind, but in the United Kingdom Black people moved freely, and performers of his quality could obtain well-remunerated employment and attention. Between 1848 and 1854, Juba toured England, Ireland, and Scotland as the star of a seven-person band known as the Ethiopian Serenaders, as a member of a three-person troupe, as the leader of his own band, the American Serenaders, and as a solo act. Performing as "Boz's Juba," he gained celebrity and became a measure of excellence for others. He also grabbed the reins of his career and his life.

The historical record of Juba's years across the Atlantic is rich and various. Newspaper advertisements plotted his movements. Theatrical journals extolled his merits. Investigators enumerated his audiences. And, years later, a handful of contemporaries passed on hearsay about his actions. But the dancer left no personal archive. Taken together, these materials do not constitute a full biographical narrative. However, they do portray a multifaceted figure of popular appeal.

Although Juba was removed from the social forces that menaced Black people in the slaveholding United States, his professional choices abroad were limited by his race, only differently. Frederick Douglass, novelist William Wells Brown, and other African American travelers and exiles commented on the relative absence of racial prejudice in the British Isles and the liberating effects of that absence.[4] Juba shared some of that experience. His dancing and singing talents drew audiences from the highest to the lowest classes. He interested people because he was American and Black, young and handsome, and because his art was fresh and exciting. British people perceived Lane's performances in diverse ways—as superlative entertainment, as demonstrations of authentic American and slave culture, as proof of the benefits of English abolition and free labor ideology, as an ethnic exhibit, and as a mild threat to the status quo. He exemplified what happened when Black people became too famous. Despite their history of colonization and empire, the British saw themselves as less racist than Americans, and Juba benefited from that self-congratulation. In Britain he was a "living example" of Black genius, a testament to the power of dance, and a figure that "Ethiopian" pretenders had to contend with.

To London

While Juba was in New York moving between the Melodeon and the Odeon, a young minstrel named Gilbert Ward Pell returned from England looking to organize a company (fig. 10.1). Pell had been a member of James A. Dumbolton's Ethiopian

Serenaders, who first appeared in New York. Finding the competition thick and success elusive in 1846, Dumbolton packed up his troupe and left the country.[5] Well equipped and performing "splendid selections of songs with harmonized voices," the all-white Ethiopian Serenaders "lost no time in securing a footing in London." Their "headquarters" for twenty months became St. James's Theatre. According to Sam Sanford's reminiscences, Dumbolton's Ethiopians had uninterrupted success until "our party" (Sanford's New Orleans Ethiopian Serenaders) appeared and divided the question. "[We had] the advantage with instruments," claimed Sanford, and "we introduced jigs and Banjo solos [and] Lucy Long in character." Troupes "superior in singing" but without banjo and jig dancer were deficient.[6]

Pell must have agreed with Sanford. Immediately after his return to the United States, he set out to find a dancer and banjo soloist of his own to take to England. Gilbert was the younger brother of Richard Ward "Dick" Pelham. He took Pell as his stage name so as not to be confused with his brother, who had also performed in England.[7] Back in New York, Pell stopped in at White's Melodeon to see Master Juba. Then he hunted down the only banjo player who could match him, Thomas F. Briggs (a.k.a. Fluter).

Close in age and temperament, Lane and Briggs worked well together. As T. Fluter, Briggs had played in almost every band (African American and white) that

FIGURE 10.1. In 1848 Gilbert W. Pell (Pelham), a twenty-three-year-old bones player and comedian, recruited William Lane to perform with his minstrel troupe in England as Boz's Juba. Like Lane, Pell had begun his career as a child performer. His older brother Richard Pelham was Master Diamond's first stage opponent. *G. W. Pell, Ethiopian Serenader, Bones*, T. H. Maguire, lithographer, John Mitchell Publisher, 1847, MS Thr 1848, box 5, Houghton Library, Harvard University.

Juba danced with between 1844 and 1846. Handsome even when blacked-up, he was considered "a kind and gentle spirit, he was shy, modest and reserved, and free from the hard habits which characterize most of his class," recalled a former flash press editor. "He had a great notion, too, of being a gentleman, and instead of hanging about taverns and passing his time in vulgar pleasures, he devoted himself to elegant attire, good company, and that laborious practice which is the mother of improvement."[8] His banjo manuals are still consulted today.

On April 26, 1848, a steamboat towed the packet ship *Sir Robert Peel* to the Southwest Spit off New York City, where she lay anchored until setting sail.[9] On board was Gilbert Pelham, but his dancer and banjoist did not appear on the manifest. Black passengers were proscribed from securing first-class berths on American ships.[10] They probably sailed from New York directly to Liverpool, a cheaper transatlantic passage that averaged five weeks. Pelham disembarked in Dover on May 19; Juba and Briggs arrived in England on May 26. Two days later *The Era*, a London-based theatrical journal, announced: "Mr. PELL, the celebrated bone player, . . . has arrived in London with a new party of Ethiopian singers and delineators of American eccentricities, among whom, we understand, is a first rate dancer."[11]

The Original Vauxhall

From June to September 1848 Pell's Ethiopian Serenaders (Pell on bone castanets, Juba tambourine and vocals, Briggs banjo and vocals, M. C. Ludlow vocals, J. H. Irwin vocals, J. W. Valintine vocals, and J. H. Everton violin and vocals) played in the Rotunda Theatre of London's Royal Gardens, Vauxhall (fig. 10.2). The band's London agent was John Mitchell, who managed entertainments at St. James's Theatre and the Royal Gardens. In 1848 Mitchell sold tickets for the Rotunda's private boxes at his music "Library" on Old Bond Street.[12] He also arranged for Juba to appear at the St. James's Theatre in June for "the younger branches of Royalty."[13]

On English stages, Lane was known as Master Juba, Juba, or Boz's Juba. Twenty-three-year-old Pell called his castanet-playing stage persona Old Bones. They announced their first engagement in London's *Morning Post:* "The inimitable 'Juba' of the immortal Boz (vide his 'American Notes') with 'Old Bones' and his highly-talented corps, have arrived in England, and will APPEAR, for the first time, at the Royal Gardens, Vauxhall, on MONDAY next, June 12, and every evening except Saturday."[14]

The gardens' Rotunda became a refuge for Juba and the company, as London was inundated with rain and wind the entire summer season. Fewer "holyday makers" and "*habitués*" than usual prowled the gardens on June 12, but the rain did not curtail the indoor performances. "Notwithstanding the unfavourable state of the weather," noted *The Standard,* "a considerable number of persons assembled to witness Juba's first appearance, all of whom were delighted and astonished at

FIGURE 10.2. From June to September 1848 Juba and Pell's Ethiopian Serenaders played in the Rotunda of London's Royal Gardens, Vauxhall. To create uniformity, they all wore dapper black cutaways, black trousers, striped shirts, white or yellow waistcoats, tight curled wigs, and burnt-cork makeup. Pell and Juba altered their costumes slightly to set themselves apart and identify their expertise—Pell, the comedian, with "a yard of shirt collar and frill" and Juba, the dancer, with knee-high boots. Detail from Royal Vauxhall Gardens poster, W. J. Dailey, lithographer, 1848. Courtesy of the British Library.

his extraordinary evolutions."[15] The Rotunda was an indoor amphitheater with a dirt arena surrounded by a circular ring fence. Behind the fence the "pit seats" were flanked on either side by two tiers of box seats and one large balcony facing a plank stage and narrow orchestra pit on the opposite side. Pell's Ethiopian Serenaders shared the Rotunda with Gauthier's French equitation troupe; Wallett and Moseley's English Corps of Equestrians, vaulters, and tumblers; T. Barry the clown; and others. The Serenaders' concert was the closing act.[16]

Pell's minstrels replicated the style and format introduced by Dumbolton. The musicians sat on chairs in a semicircle as they sang American "Songs, Glees, Choruses, [and] Refrains" interspersed with "Ditties, Burlesque Lectures, &c." To create uniformity, they all wore dapper black cutaways, black trousers, striped shirts, canary-yellow waistcoats, tight curled wigs, and burnt-cork makeup. Dumbolton's troupe had had no dancer. Their concerts' variety came from their range of songs and the bones and tambourine players, who demonstrated physical skill and humor in their manner of handling their instruments and their facial expressions. Juba's and Briggs's acts represented the only significant difference between the two troupes.

Juba performed his dances wearing the same attire and blackened visage as the musicians. Only his flowing necktie and knee-high boots set him apart. He danced alone on the stage and down in the ring, which gave the ladies in front

"JUBA," AT VAUXHALL GARDENS.

FIGURE 10.3. The *Illustrated London News* depicted Juba dancing in blackface makeup in the ring of the Rotunda at London's Vauxhall Gardens for a predominately female audience. *"Juba," at Vauxhall Gardens,* from the *Illustrated London News,* Aug. 5, 1848, 3.

a better view and afforded full scope to his dancing (fig. 10.3).[17] "It is the most wonderful conglomeration of every step that was ever thought of," proclaimed *The Era* during Juba's second week, "and reminds the spectator more of one of the 'dancing dervishes,' or fabled willis, than anything else he can think of."[18]* Juba's dances punctuated the vocal numbers performed by the troupe and always concluded the show. "The effort baffles description," noted several newspaper editors who tried to describe it anyway. "It is a combination of almost every

---

* Dervishes are a sect of Sufi Muslims who whirl and dance ecstatically as a form of dhikr (remembrance of God). The "fabled willis" are the female ghosts who appear in the second act of the ballet *Giselle*. They are the elementary spirits of brides who died before marrying and for whom "the old passion" for dancing still burns in their hearts and feet. At midnight they rise and assemble on highways, where they surround young men and make them dance until they fall dead.

quality in the art,—from the graceful movement of 'The Minuet' to the highest pitch of terpsichorean illustration—and something more. There is such energy, such rapidity as is quite novel even in the annals of dancing."[19]

Juba combined genres to appeal to the spectrum of visitors seeking entertainment at Vauxhall's Royal Gardens. Besides the Rotunda Theatre, the grounds featured a covered stage called the Ballet Theatre in among the trees (with no seating), a two-story pavilion in the Grand Quadrangle from which vocalists and musicians gave concerts and provided music for balls on fine nights, covered arcades and supper rooms for dancing and dining, grottos and mazes to explore, and outdoor exhibitions such as balloon launches and, weather permitting, a nightly fireworks show at eleven o'clock (fig. 10.4). All classes of holiday seekers enjoyed the Royal Gardens, which were open to the public without charge. However, the shows required tickets, which meant more working-class Londoners saw Juba dance after the price was lowered from two shillings and sixpence to one shilling later in the season.

Vauxhall's advertisements appealed to the fashionable, and reviews suggest that Juba drew them in. Three weeks after he arrived, London's *Morning Chronicle* gave Juba credit for Vauxhall's "Unprecedented Success.—The most brilliant assemblings of rank and fashion have nightly honoured the gardens, to witness the extraordinary and unparalleled performance of JUBA." As proof of their own gentility, Juba and

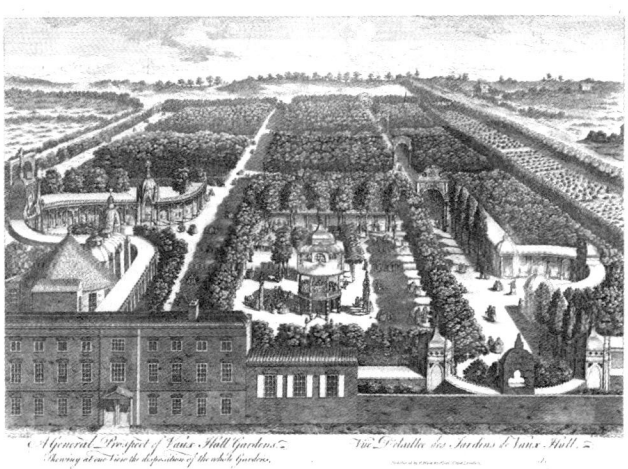

FIGURE 10.4. Juba's appearances with Pell's Serenaders in the Rotunda (left side behind the covered supper boxes) at London's Vauxhall Gardens brought the dancer to the attention of all classes of holiday seekers. The garden entertainments were free, and a ticket to the Rotunda show was lowered to one shilling at the end of the season. Samuel Wale, del., *A General Prospect of Royal Vaux Hall Gardens,* ca. 1751, published by Francis West, London, ca. 1830. ©The Trustees of the British Museum.

the Serenaders gave "gratuitous performances in the Rotunda" in July. At "a Brilliant Fete Al Fresco" held on the grounds in aid of the Distressed Needlewomen's Society, "the celebrated Juba proved that the wants of the needlewomen could excite him to the most extraordinary exertions in the cause of benevolence," reported *The Times* of London. And on Juvenile Night of the Licensed Victuallers' Asylum Fancy Fair, he entertained the asylum orphans, who were "accommodated with seats to witness the Scenes in the Circle, and the performances of Juba, which, from their uproarious merriment, appeared to afford them unfeigned delight."[20]

Juba's enormous appeal lay in his youthfulness, his physical charms, and his versatility, as well as in his energetic dancing. The *Caledonian Mercury* declared that "the interest is much increased by the youth of the performer, who is only in his seventeenth year, but who has for several years drawn immense audiences in his own country."[21]

Young Juba was a pleasure to look at, "with a joyous expression of features" (fig. 10.5). "He is small in stature, though tightly, trimly built, with an abundance

FIGURE 10.5. Admired for his youthful beauty, Juba also charmed British audiences by performing with "a joyous expression of features." Detail from Royal Vauxhall Gardens poster, W. J. Dailey, lithographer, 1848. Courtesy of the British Library.

of muscular power." His "happy cast of countenance 'that doth denote him truly,' prepossesses the audience in his favour."[22] It is noteworthy that in this abundance of praise, none of the newspapers racialized his features. (However, one illustration survives that caricatures both Juba and Pell. It portrays the dancer with large, exaggerated lips and the bones player with a devil's pointed ears and tail.)[23]

Juba also surprised audiences with his versatility. From the packed Newburgh Rooms in Brighton, a correspondent to *The Era* reported that "Master Juba, sings, plays, and dances well, the tambourine being his instrument."[24] "From it he produces marvelous harmonies," added the *Illustrated London News*. "We almost question whether, upon a great emergency, he could not play a fugue upon it." In addition, his singing was singular: "His enunciation is both powerful and distinct, and astonishes at the same time that it amuses."[25] Juba "sings the nigger songs with a rich gusto not to be imagined by those who have not heard him. His volubility is astounding, and his perfect enjoyment of his own efforts is quite delicious," admitted the *Morning Post*. "He trills, he shakes, he screams, he laughs, as though possessed by the very genius of African melody. . . . But his dancing casts into the shade all previous choreographic efforts."[26]

Juba's aesthetic feats did not impress everyone. *The Puppet-Show,* a satirical London weekly, expressed its disapproval by offering a negative sketch of his dancing:

> Juba's talent consists in walking round the stage with an air of satisfaction and with his toes turned in; in jumping backwards in a less graceful manner than we should have conceived possible; and in shaking his thighs like a man afflicted with palsy. He makes a terrible clatter with his feet, not owing so much to activity on his part as to stupidity on the part of his boot-maker, who has furnished him with a pair of clumsy Wellingtons sufficiently large for the feet and legs of all the Ethiopians in London: besides this, he sometimes moves about the stage on his knees, as if he was praying to be endowed with intelligence, and had unlimited credit with his tailor. As a last resource, he falls back on the floor.[27]

Even as it mocked his dancing, *The Puppet-Show* confirmed Juba's tidal wave of approval by singling out the same elements that other writers praised: his facial expressions, unusual movements, and execution of steps. When translated into the language of dance, the description offers a motion picture of Juba's act. In typical hornpipe fashion, he began his dance with a walk-around, promenading in a circle for a few bars of music before facing the audience and launching into his steps. The novelty of his dancing came from his combining of humorous and startling moves with intricate, precise, and rapid heel-and-toe work: "His pedal execution is a thing to wonder at, if his flexibility of muscle did not confound us. He jumps, he capers, he crosses his legs, he stamps his heels, he dances on his knees, on his ankles, he ties his limbs into double knots, and untwists them as one might a skein of silk, and all these marvels are done in strict time and appropriate rhythm—each note has its correspondent step and action." And each step and action had its correspondent meaning. Juba's "plantation dance" is an "illustration of Collins's 'Ode on the Passions,'" noted a *Morning Post* reviewer: "Now he languishes, now burns, now love seems to sway his motions, and anon rage seems to impel his steps."[28]

Juba's "wonted spirit and indefatigable energy" were catching. In the same issue as its lampoon of Juba's dancing, *The Puppet-Show* ridiculed an unemployed journalist for imitating Juba ("under the influence of champagne"). "He behaved so ridiculously that he may actually be said to have surpassed him," gibed the writer. "When we addressed him (for, in spite of his conduct, we are still on speaking terms with him), he assured us that if he were not Our Discharged Contributor he would be Juba!"[29] Juba aroused the flattery of imitation.

Juba's achievements were validated at the end of July 1848, when the troupe played in Brighton, a beach resort fifty-four miles south of London, for a few days. The dancer probably missed out on cooling his feet in the sand and sea, however, for despite being midsummer, "the weather was extremely boisterous and wet during the week." Instead, he and the Serenaders gave performances at the Newburgh Rooms in Cannon Place, one block from the seashore, where among their audience on July 23 was the bachelor Duke of Devonshire with a large party of friends. William Spencer Cavendish, sixth Duke of Devonshire, was a Whig nobleman, connoisseur of the arts, and friend of Charles Dickens. "Pleased to express his high admiration of Juba, the Banjo, and the Bones," the duke invited the company to perform at his house, No. 1 Lewes Crescent, in Brighton's Kemp Town.[30] A few days later Pell received a letter from Charles Coote, pianist to His Grace, expressing how pleased the duke had been with the performances and adding his own "testimony to the excellence of your amusing and harmonious entertainment." Pell would milk that letter for all it was worth in future advertisements.[31]

"The Real Article"

In mid-August the manager of the Rotunda made Juba and Marie Macarte, "equestrian enchantress," the featured acts in a show of entertainments from the United States. The two stars shared the bill with another American attraction: "Van Amburgh, THE LION KING, with his unrivaled collection of lions, tigers, leopards, &c" (fig. 10.6). In England Juba was described as introducing "the NATIONAL SONGS and DANCES of his country."[32] "The only national dance that we really believe in, as a fact," wrote *The Era*, "is that of the Niggers." Fanny Elssler's "Cachucha" was never known in Spain nor Carlotta Grisi's "Truandaise" in Paris, agreed the *Illustrated London News*, and "hornpipes are entirely confined to nautical dramas and pantomimes, or the square bit of board or patch of carpet

FIGURE 10.6. The upper right-hand illustration of this poster depicts the interior of the Rotunda (looking out from the stage), which in August 1848 featured an all-American show for one shilling: Boz's Juba performing with G. W. Pell's Serenaders on the stage, and equestrian Marie Macarte and Van Amburgh's lions performing in the ring. Royal Vauxhall Gardens poster, W. J. Dailey, lithographer, 1848. Courtesy of the British Library.

of the street dancer; . . . [however,] [t]he 'Virginny Breakdown,' or the 'Alabama Kick-up,' the 'Tennessee Double-shuffle,' or the 'Louisiana Toe-and-Heel,' we know to exist. If they did not, how could Juba enter into their wonderful complications so naturally?"[33] In England, Juba's dances were not just examples of African American culture, they were American culture. Yet the compliment also belittled Juba's talent by naturalizing it.

British emancipation shaped Juba's reception in England. In 1833 Parliament passed the Slavery Abolition Act, which ended slavery in the British West Indies on August 1, 1834, and up until the 1860s, much of the popular interest in blackface minstrelsy in the United Kingdom came from a conviction in the public mind that John Bull was the natural protector of the slaves. Ironically, this attitude prevailed even in textile-producing regions that relied on slave-grown cotton.[34] In the United States, by contrast, minstrelsy's ludicrous stereotypes reinforced the proslavery argument that Black people were not suited to liberty.

The antislavery sentiment and a diminishing Black population propelled blackface minstrelsy in England. White people came to minstrel shows because they were curious to know what Black people were actually like.[35] Nineteenth-century censuses never classified residents by race, but anecdotal evidence suggests that the number of Black British dwindled from an estimated fifteen thousand enslaved Blacks in the 1770s to a much lower number of free Blacks in the 1840s. There was no identifiable Black community. The descendants of eighteenth-century slaves had mostly intermarried with the indigenous population and joined the cosmopolitan poor of London and the seaports. Other than a few exceptional visitors from Africa, the West Indies, and the United States, the only Black people middle-class whites encountered were members of the lowest segment of English society—dockworkers, cart drivers, laborers, hucksters, humble street entertainers, and beggars.[36] By the time Juba arrived, this scattering of individuals had mostly blended into the already racially mixed population. Even in Liverpool, where sailors of African heritage frequently sojourned, a dark-skinned Black person was rarely seen, and mulatto people were seldom noticed. This scarcity increased the appetite for "Ethiopian" characterizations like Pell's Old Bones, which mid-Victorians deemed realistic portrayals of African American life.[37] What people really wanted to see, however, was not these "industriously clever" mimics, as Dublin's *Freeman's Journal* put it, but "the real article."[38]

Juba's blackness thus added significantly to his appeal in England. "Juba is a youth of colour—'a real genuine Nigger, and no mistake,'" swore *The Era* in 1848, using two contemporary idioms for African Americans.[39] The phrase "youth of colour" was derived from "Man of Colour," used in Britain to describe famous American-born Black men such as prizefighter Tom Molineaux, "*The Tremendous Man of Colour.*"[40] "Nigger" was a xenophobic term that usually referred to someone of African ancestry but at midcentury was increasingly applied to anyone with a complexion darker than Anglo-Saxon whiteness.[41] Juba was "a real genuine" African American, not a "sham" or blacked-up white man. "As for Juba," stated a Scottish newspaper, "he is a coloured serenader, which is rather a rarity."[42] The N-word certainly had a derogatory connotation, but Black people in Britain did not suffer from universal racial intolerance. Discrimination aggravated rather than caused their hardships. Some lodging houses and employers turned them away, but as a group they were not segregated. Black people mixed reasonably freely as individuals with others of their class and were subject to the same economic uncertainties.[43] Juba rode in the same trains and carriages and ate and drank in the same public houses as his white companions. This kind of racialism made the United Kingdom warmer terrain for the dancer.

Juba was also advertised as the "only" youth of color to ever come "before the Public" in England and Ireland.[44] That claim was simply hype. Black thespian Ira Aldridge was eighteen years old when he debuted at the Royalty Theatre in

London in 1825. And it is unlikely that that fact was forgotten, since Juba's Vauxhall debut followed Aldridge's well-publicized return to London in March 1848 after fifteen years in the Northern provinces.[45] Rather than the first Black youth to perform on the British stage, Juba was the first African American to perform there with a minstrel troupe. His managers counted on that novelty to draw in audiences and on his youthful beauty and dancing skills to bring them back again and again.

English audiences even saw Juba's "wench" dancing as a portrait of America.[46] On August 21, 1848, the dancer added "his celebrated character of Miss Lucy Long" to his Rotunda performance.[47] In the States, Juba had sung and danced to "Lucy Neal," a typical British ballad about a sweetheart dying, played in $\frac{2}{4}$ or hornpipe time, with lyrics by James P. Carter. In Carter's version the sweetheart is a "yaller gal," or mulatto slave, with an Irish name. The same was true of "Mary Blane," another "slave's lament" sung by Juba in England in which a lover marries his sweetheart, who is sold away by her master, after which he lays himself down and dies. Written in $\frac{4}{4}$ time with verses and chorus, "Mary Blane" was published in the English compilation *Singing for the Million*.[48] Juba sang the verses solo, and the troupe harmonized the chorus.

Banjoist Joel Sweeney introduced "Lucy Long" as a solo extravaganza at New York's Bowery Amphitheatre in January 1842, and by May stores were advertising the sheet music (fig. 10.7).[49] Miss Lucy, performed by a male dancer in female attire, catches the eye of the smitten singer, who extols her beauty and dancing skills through outlandish comparisons. But when he asks her to marry him, she says "she'd rather tarry [wait]." He vows to wed her anyway, and if she proves to be a scold, then he'll sell her down the river. (The male singer was also in blackface, making the song's misogyny outshine its racism.) Like other blackface tunes brought to Great Britain by Americans, the lyrics to "Lucy Long" were easily altered to include allusions to current events.[50] However, the $\frac{2}{4}$ rhythm, eight bars of instrumental music, and verbal promptings emphasized the dancing. The musicians sang as Juba's Lucy circled the stage preparing to take flight during the instrumental interlude, which was repeated as many times as needed:

> Oh! take your time Miss Lucy
> Take your time Miss Lu-cy Long
> Oh! take your time Miss Lucy,
> Take your time Miss Lu-cy Long.

Juba's Lucy Long, "attired in a most ladylike mode," was "full of life and broad fun."[51] "With a most bewitching bonnet and veil, a *very* pink dress, beflounced to the waist, lace-fringed trousers of the most spotless purity, and red leather boots,—the ensemble completed by the green parasol and white cambric pocket handkerchief,—Master Juba certainly looked the black demoiselle of the first

FIGURE 10.7. Banjoist Joel Sweeny had introduced the song "Lucy Long" to British audiences five years before Juba performed his Lucy at Vauxhall Gardens in 1848. Although the lyrics privileged the male character's point of view, Juba's Lucy stepped in front of the singer and stole the show with her ultrafeminine costume, loveliness, and dancing antics. Front cover of music sheet for "Lucy Long" as sung by J. W. Sweeny at the Theatre Royal English Opera House, illustration and lithograph by George Edward Madeley (D'Almaine and Company, n.d.), Gabrielle Enthoven Collection, Theatre and Performance Collection. Museum no. S.25–2012. ©Victoria & Albert Museum, London.

ton to the greatest advantage."[52] Juba's youthful good looks and lithe body made his gaudy costume oddly attractive: "He is a perfect *black-amour*—no 'coloured geleman' [sic] could resist the ebony coquette—the mincing gait and the ultra gracefulness are things to be witnessed."[53]

Impersonating a woman gave Juba the opportunity to combine genres of dancing. "Promenading in a circle to the left for a few bars, till again facing the audience, he then commenced a series of steps, which altogether baffle description, from their number, oddity, and the rapidity with which they were executed," reported the *Morning Post*. "The highland fling, the sailor's hornpipe, and other European dances, seemed to have been laid under ... and intermixed with a number of steps which we may call 'Juba's own,' for surely their like was never before seen for grotesque agility, not altogether unmixed with grace. The promenade was then repeated; then more dancing; and so on, to the end of the song."[54]

European dances were specialties of female theatrical dancers. The ultraflounced dress and lace-trimmed bloomers that turned Juba's walk-around into the promenade of a comic coquette were, on the other hand, garments more typically worn by men impersonating women. What set Juba's Lucy Long apart from other "wench" dances was the way he performed the role. "The character is not exaggerated as we generally see such attempts on the stage, and consequently there is nothing offensive, however absurd it may be," reported the *Manchester Times*. "He dances in this disguise in a very peculiar style, such as Taglioni or Elsler [sic] would find difficult to imitate, and the whole is a piece of excessive drollery."[55] A young man dressed in lace performing, in his own way, dances made popular by famous ballerinas—that was funny. But something even more interesting happened when this particular dancer refused to mug to the crowd. He transformed a Black woman into America. "Juba reigns still pre-eminent, and his portraiture of the new world—famous Lucy Long—is alone worth a visit," declared the *Morning Post*. "Far above the common performances of the mountebanks who give imitations of American and negro character, there is an ideality in what he does that makes his efforts at once dramatic and poetical, without losing sight of the reality of representation."[56] Male and female, ideal and real, American and Negro, what more could he offer?

Alongside "Lucy Long," Juba introduced his own characterization of the male plantation slave in holiday clothes, which was entirely new to British audiences. In these acts, Juba "illustrated the dances of his own simple people on festive occasions" accompanied by "BRIGGS, on the native Instrument, the Banjo."[57] The "grotesque element, in the character of the steps," and the dancer's great "physical exertion" were even "more extraordinary" than in "Lucy Long," declared the *Manchester Guardian*. By "grotesque element," the newspapers referred to Juba's invention of "eccentric and unaccountable movements." Toe dancing; going stiff in the limbs and then rubbery; landing, sliding, and running on his knees; walking on buckled ankles; falling down and dancing on the ground; jumping up and dancing in the air; "it is all the same to Juba."[58] With these unprecedented steps, Juba turned "authenticity" into individuality, a move that was particularly appreciated in Britain's industrial North.

To the Provinces

Juba's engagement in London ended when the Royal Gardens closed the last week of September 1848. During the winter season, stock companies returned to theaters, and visiting luminaries toured England's provinces, Ireland, and Scotland. Juba's tour began in the West—in medieval Bath and maritime Bristol, where he and Pell's Ethiopian Serenaders performed entr'actes at the Theatres Royal, managed by Mrs. Macready, stepmother of actor William Charles Macready.[59] The name Theatre Royal indicated that the playhouse had a royal patent, without which performances of serious plays were illegal. The Theatres Act of 1843 ended the monopoly on spoken drama held by large patent theaters, thereby increasing the number of smaller playhouses able to obtain licenses to put on plays. Nevertheless, Theatres Royal remained at the top of the heap in terms of status, enabling managers to charge more for seats and pay higher salaries. Playing in them gave Juba and Pell's company a patina of respectability.

There was a definite social hierarchy of entertainment venues in the United Kingdom. In general, royal theaters were patronized by the nobility and upper classes; minor theaters, music halls, and Free Trade Halls by the middle classes; and concert rooms in hotels and taverns by the working classes.

The people in different regions were struck by different aspects of Juba's performances. From Bristol, the troupe took the train 160 miles north to the textile-manufacturing city of Manchester. They opened at the Free Trade Hall on October 16 and stayed four weeks. Advance advertisements lauded Juba as the dancer "immortalised by 'Boz'" and "a genuine son of the southern clime." But during his stay, Manchester's journalists made their own assessment. "The company has with it a coloured youth, who has been . . . associated with a passage from Dickens' 'American Notes,'" reported the *Manchester Courier & Lancashire General Advertiser*. "Whether this be the same Juba that Boz there alludes to we know not, but certainly the feats of the present claimant of the name appear to be quite equal to him in . . . agility and marvelous flexibility of body."[60] Four newspapers covered the company's well-attended nightly entertainments. The *Manchester Guardian* favorably compared Juba's physical attributes to Pell's ludicrous makeup, costume, and "grimaces": "He is apparently about eighteen years of age; about 5 feet 3 inches in height; of slender make, yet possessing great muscular activity. His head is very small, and his countenance, when at rest, has a rather mild, sedate, and far from unpleasing expression."[61] Juba "was decidedly the lion of the evening," decided the *Courier,* "and though the songs of the vocalists were frequently encored, and the jokes of the two speakers, old as many of them were, heartily laughed at, he has done the most to secure those good houses."[62]

Despite Juba's London advertisements, Northern journalists did not presume that Juba was the son of Southern slaves. Instead, someone interviewed him. "This youth was born at New York in the year 1830, and commenced his career as a dancer in the year 1838," reported the *Manchester Times,* establishing dance as Juba's trade.[63] Then it interpreted race relations in the United States through class relations in England.[64] Juba's birthplace determined his training. "American people of colour," noted the interviewer, "are all great lovers of, and noted for their singing, whistling, dancing, fiddling, tambourine and banjo playing, whether it be in New York among the free negroes or in the South among the slaves." But they did not learn or practice their arts under the same conditions: "The slaves have a strong natural love for the dance and song; compelled to retire at nine o'clock and forbade to leave their huts after that time, should there be communicated an intimation of a distant plantation dance, they steal away after the overseer has visited them, dance all night and return in the morning, nearly exhausted, to pursue a daily toil."[65] True, but not Juba's story. He was a free man, born in the North, living proof of the "free labor" argument (promoted by abolitionists during debates over emancipation in the West Indies) that liberty induced "a spirit of industry and achievement" in people.[66]

> In the city of New York the free labourers of colour meet at nights for similar social amusement, each one trying to excel in what they call "the glorious art;" they do not appear at any public place [by which the interviewer meant legitimate theaters], this being against the social laws of the Free Country. It is from amongst such that Juba has sprung; having been seen by many people in private, he ... was introduced on the stage,—being the only performer of colour that has ever found such a distinction in the United States.[67]

The interviewer made a pitch for Juba and appealed to Manchester's residents by taking a jab at America, that "Free Country" across the Atlantic where judicial laws protected the ownership of enslaved labor and social laws thwarted the ambitions of free African Americans. Juba's appearance at the Free Trade Hall was an example of the heights free people of color could achieve.

Audiences in England's Northern provinces appreciated Juba's charm and creativity, but they prized more his rhythmic sense. "To us, the most interesting part of the performance was the exact time, which, even in the most complicated and difficult steps, the dancer kept to the music," wrote the *Manchester Guardian.*[68] This skill was particularly noted in areas with their own percussive dancing traditions.[69] Competitive clog dancers near the Lancashire cotton mills, for example, included "timing" in their matches. A dancer in Ashton-under-Lyne specified his terms as "scutch and patter, truth and time, or three turns, three steps and shuffle off to each turn, hornpipe, jig, and waltz, for £5 or £10 a side."[70] Juba knew the value of "truth and time."

A master dancer of color might make the audience laugh, but he could not afford to be seen as a clown. Juba didn't pull gags to gain audience approval. He kept to the music. That's what distinguished his dances from other minstrelsy acts. "The two legs appear entirely independent of each other, performing the most curious and opposite acts at the same moment," gushed the *Manchester Times*, "whilst, in the most extraordinary rapidity of action, the true, marking of the time is really wonderful."[71] Appreciation for this element of Juba's dancing led Pell to add an addendum to the company's advertisements outside London: "Mr. Pell would take it as a great favour if the Audience will keep as quiet as possible during Master Juba's Dances; by doing so, they will hear the exact time he keeps with his extraordinary steps."[72] Exact timekeeping made Juba's uncanny movements thrilling. "From his most frenzied movement to the most subdued demeanour possible," reported the *Birmingham Journal*, " . . . all is in character, all in keeping, and in exquisite time."[73]

Juba and the Serenaders appeared at the Free Trade Hall rather than a Theatre Royal in Manchester. This change of venue altered the character of Juba's "good houses," from mostly upper-class to a mixture of middle- and working-class patrons. By 1848 Manchester was densely populated by rural families who had come to the city for the wages offered by mills and factories and were now living in dire conditions caused by poverty, overcrowding, and cholera epidemics.[74] A trades hall was a meeting place open to the members of any trade pursued without restrictions. Manchester's Free Trade Hall had been built during the previous decade's protests against the Corn Laws, which united textile industry workers and employers. Those laws protected the interests of "rapacious and plundering" landowners by levying taxes on imported wheat, thereby raising the price of cereal products at a time when food supplies were short and wage cuts and irregular employment plagued industrial workers.[75] Manchester thronged with minor theaters, music halls, concert rooms, saloon theaters, and penny gaffs, places off-limits to ministers, tradesmen, shopkeepers, mechanics, and their wives and daughters, who abided by a middle-class code of moral conduct that separated them from both the proletariat and the aristocracy.[76] However, trades halls were not off-limits to these people, and performing in them did not jeopardize Juba's elevated status.

From Manchester, Juba and the Serenaders took the train to Sheffield, where they changed venue type again. Their two-hour show at "Music-Hall, Sheffield," cost two shillings for ground-floor seating in the "saloon," one shilling for gallery seats, and "Children with their Parents or Guardians, Half-price."[77] Music halls were large, purpose-built buildings that were very like minor theaters.[78] However, the two became discrete after the 1843 Theatres Act distinguished playhouses from other entertainment premises by denying the latter "the privilege of staging the drama" but allowing "the running sale and consumption of drink and tobacco in the auditorium."[79] In other words, if you put on plays, you couldn't sell liquor during the show, and if you sold liquor during the show, you couldn't put on plays. This distinction gave even small regional theaters a higher status than music halls while making music halls more generally popular.

Celebrity

After four nights in Sheffield, the company played the Theatres Royal in Liverpool, Birmingham, Leamington, Wolverhampton, and eventually Doncaster. Mr. Simpson, the region's theatrical manager, respectfully informed the "Nobility, Gentry, and Public in general" of Juba's arrival to each city. Recognizing that "this bronze genius" was the show's main attraction, Pell began publishing the times of Juba's acts in the papers. Doors opened at half past seven and the program commenced at eight, with "Juba's Lucy Long, at Half-past Eight," "Juba's Festival Dance, at a Quarter to Ten," and "Juba's Plantation Dance, at Ten o'clock." Juba's final act probably lasted fifteen minutes, as carriages arrived to take people home at quarter past ten.[80]

To encourage attendance during their monthlong stay in Liverpool, Pell added "a Fashionable MORNING CONCERT" on Fridays at 2:00 p.m. for women and children from "the *elite* of Liverpool and its vicinity" who could not attend the evening performance at the Theatre Royal in Williamson Square. He also announced an award of a silver cup to two people who came up with the best new conundrum (a riddle with a pun in the answer) for the troupe to perform. All entries were to be sent, prepaid, "to the Committee, at the Liverpool Mercury-office" by December 2. The cup, "a neat little thing" valued at "about four guineas," was kept on display for inspection "at the Mercury office, daily, from 9 a.m. until 7 p.m." Best of all, the prize conundrums would be named "and the Cups presented by G. W. Pell and Boz's Juba, in the Theatre, at the end of the Second Part of the Concert" on their respective benefit nights.[81] As hoped, the contest enlarged the audience on both nights, but the prospect of winning at the dancer's benefit attracted more participants. "For Juba's prize cup, on this occasion, there were many more candidates, and the conundrums were, many of them, of a better order."[82] Boz's Juba had become the celebrity people wanted to get close to.

In January and February 1849 Juba extended his appeal in Manchester, Liverpool, and Newcastle by impersonating "the Swedish Nightingale, in the song of the 'Daughter of the Regiment.'"[83] Swedish soprano Jenny Lind (Johanna Maria Lind), one of the most highly regarded opera singers in Europe, had performed in London during the 1848 summer season when Juba was at Vauxhall and like him was currently touring the provinces.[84] Juba sang Lind's song as Part Second's closing act every night and on Saturday afternoon at the Lord Nelson Street Concert-Hall in Liverpool, where a short distance away Lind was singing Felix Mendelssohn's oratorio *Elijah* at the Collegiate Institution.[85]

Pell had other gimmicks for drawing in spectators. In and around Newcastle, he announced that the Serenaders would perform "several Pieces as Sung before Her Majesty Queen Victoria, H.R.H. Prince Albert and Suite at Arundel Castle." (Pell had performed in Scotland with Dumbolton's Serenaders in 1846.) He also approached the military men at Fenham Barracks and in February produced a show at Grainger Street Music Hall "by Desire and under the Distinguished Patronage of COL. POLE And the OFFICERS of the 63rd Regiment." Newcastle's Music Hall was long and narrow with balconies on the sides, providing a tunnel for sound. Expecting a raucous crowd of soldiers, colliers, ship builders, and their partners, Pell repeated his request that the audience withhold their applause while Juba danced so that everyone could hear "the exact Time he keeps with his extraordinary Steps."[86]

Although the program varied little, the prices were modified from place to place. In March Juba and Pell's Serenaders played at Newcastle's Music Hall and "the Theatres" in South Shields and North Shields (suburbs on opposite banks of the River Tyne), then journeyed two hundred miles south to Birmingham's Theatre Royal. At the Music Hall, reserved seats cost two shillings, back seats one shilling, and gallery sixpence. At the Theatre Royal, lower boxes cost three shillings, upper boxes two shillings, pit one shilling, and gallery sixpence; dress boxes could be secured in advance at higher prices. However, after Part Second, the price of all box seats was reduced by half to accommodate patrons who only wanted to see Juba dance to Briggs's banjo in Part Third (and, presumably, to refill those seats vacated by patrons who only came to hear the Serenaders sing).[87]

Humble Venues

When Juba and Pell's Serenaders returned to London after seven months in the provinces, they discovered that engagements were harder to come by. At the Royal Surrey Theatre, where they performed the entr'acte for three weeks in April 1849, they billed themselves as "the bona fide Original Serenaders" and "the inimitable and unconquerable Juba," likely because both British and American minstrels had converged on London. At the Royal Standard Theatre, Shoreditch (London's East End), someone called "the great American Prize Juba Dancer" was performing "Lucy Long" with the Lantum Serenaders, and Dumbolton had returned to the St. James's Theatre with a new company of minstrels starring Jerry Bryant as dancer and "bones." According to Sam Sanford, Dumbolton's engagement was a "fizzle."[88] But the competition he represented might explain why Juba and company appeared at the Concert Rooms in Horns Tavern (near Vauxhall) and the

Music Hall in Bedford Square in mid-May rather than at a theater. Not until June did they book the Royal Sadler's Wells Theatre for two weeks while the resident company was in Brighton and repeat the practice of lowering the price of admission at nine o'clock, when Juba and Briggs took over the stage.[89]

Pell's Serenaders left Horns Tavern quickly because concert rooms did not share the prestige of purpose-built music halls or theaters. Principally the domain of the working classes, these venues grew from the practice among tradesmen and workmen of crowding into a private room in a tavern to sing glees (songs with verses and a chorus) while drinking a pint. Concert rooms were often very modest affairs with a few tables and an upturned dais from which a notable local vocalist led the songs (fig. 10.8). Observing that singing had a capital effect on drink sales, some proprietors knocked out the wall between two rooms (hence the plural "concert rooms") to provide space for as many patrons as were attracted to these open harmonic meetings. Over time, more entrepreneurial proprietors raised a backyard shed or bought an adjacent property and extended the room even farther, dropped the rule that all who attended must participate in the singing, obtained a music license, hired a professional musician and one or two "room singers" of metropolitan quality, and set down a program.[90]

By 1840 the title "concert rooms" described a plain, oblong hall with an open platform at one end, two fireplaces, and a narrow balcony along each side or at

FIGURE 10.8. Juba performed across the social hierarchy of entertainment venues in the United Kingdom, from humble tavern concert rooms like this one to crowded music halls to elegant Theatres Royal. George Cruikshank, original sketch, ca. 1845. ©Victoria & Albert Museum, London.

the back. Drinks and food were sold at a bar under the back balcony or in the adjacent tavern, and the auditorium contained benches and tables where people drank and ate during the performance. The ease and convivial atmosphere of the tavern remained even after proprietors added decorative features to give their rooms a genteel ambience when the sweethearts, wives, and daughters of male patrons began attending. Men and women singing ballads, comic songs, glees, and character songs accompanied by piano or violin remained the staple entertainment, with the occasional dancer, acrobat, or living statue thrown in for variety. Juba and Pell's Serenaders filled the role of metropolitan-quality talent.

While they were stationed in London, Gilbert Pell's brother took over as manager of the troupe. Richard "R. W." Pelham was familiar with British theatrical circuits, having toured the provinces with the Virginia Minstrels and his own companies from 1843 to 1847.[91] Despite this experience, Pelham was probably not the best choice for an agent. In May 1849 he was arrested for "committing a violent assault" on "C. L. Smith, a professional singer of Yankee songs" who had recently published a songbook in which he claimed that Pell's Serenaders were shams: "[Pell advertises his] party of black minstrels . . . as chosen by himself in America," alleged Smith. "This, however, is not the case, and I wonder that Mr. P[ell] after the kind manner in which he has been received at the St. James's Theatre, would attempt to foist a lot of penny slang [low-class counterfeit] negroes upon the public as Americans. Were Dumbolton the managing man instead of the fellow they have [Pelham], things would be far different."[92]

Smith was correct that Ludlow, Irwin, Valintine, and Everton were not Americans, even if Pell, Juba, and Briggs were. Pelham knew Smith, who had played in one of his British companies. So when he caught sight of him "leaving the stage door of the Surrey Theatre, [he] cried out 'Oh, I've caught you now, and I'll give it to you,' and immediately struck him a blow on the side of the head that knocked him down." Smith tried to run away, but Pelham, a powerful man, overtook him and knocked him down a second time "by a blow on the mouth, which broke one of his teeth," and in falling Smith's trousers were torn and his watch was smashed. Pelham's lawyer attempted to show how his client, the defendant, was provoked by Smith, the complainant, who had not only attempted to injure his professional reputation but also endeavored to steal away some of Pelham's company the previous year. Smith admitted that he had been engaged by Pelham for twelve months and that he left him in Dublin after two months and induced "a Mr. Randall" to do likewise "in consequence of the defendant not paying him his salary" or providing his company with "the necessary garments to appear on the stage. . . . [A]nd the reason was this[,] that the speculation in Ireland proved so unsuccessful, and the Irish people seemed to have such a distaste for Yankee performances, that nightly there was nothing but empty benches."[93]

Pelham did not deny that he had assaulted Smith, but he would not agree to the level of "violence asserted" or the claim that he had not paid him punctually. Pelham considered his actions an appropriate response to Smith's "scurrilous writing against him." The magistrate disagreed. Notwithstanding the alleged persecution, "by law the defendant was not justified in the assault." He therefore fined Pelham fifty pounds: "two sureties of 25*l*. each, to keep the peace" and to pay for the damage sustained by the complainant's trousers and watch.[94] The charge of nonpayment for services rendered would plague Pelham for the next three years and may explain why Pell's Serenaders dwindled down to dancer, banjo, and bones under his management.

Celtic Exhibits

Riding against the tide of emigration, Juba, Briggs, and Pell's Serenaders took the ferry to famine-ridden Ireland in June 1849. They opened at Dublin's Music Hall on June 22. As advance advertising, Pelham published a series of questions meant to catch the eye: "Have U seen Juba?—Y have U not seen him?—R U going to C Juba?—U should C Juba?—Y should I C Juba? Because he is the Greatest Wonder of the Age!!! Juba! the inimitable Juba! immortalized by 'Boz.' He is a perfect phenomenon!"[95]

Since 1845 the Emerald Isle had suffered hard times. Consequently, the Music Hall's manager, Mr. Mackintosh, had not been "accorded" the public support he deserved for bringing in artists of merit, according to Dublin's *Freeman's Journal and Daily Commercial Advertiser*. Mackintosh hoped this new attraction would change all that. And if Juba's write-ups and the company's six-week engagement are any indication, it did. "Boxes, Pit, and side seats—all were crowded" on June 25, reported the *Journal*.[96] "Such peals of applause as greeted the performance of Juba we never heard before at any previous concert in the Music Hall."

Nevertheless, Dublin's patronizing newspapers transformed Juba's Blackness and singing into a kind of ethnic exhibition. The *Freeman's Journal* described him as "a sable beauty of undoubted Gambian origin, requiring no artificial negritude to give an ebon hue to his features, which shine in the true glossy sable of his race, and bear the never-to-be-mistaken marks of his decided Ethiopian origin." When he sings, "Juba is a true African Apollo—his voice is clear and peculiar—and his laugh, joyous and ringing, seems to embody the very spirit of thoughtless fun and merriment."[97] The population of Africans in Ireland had never reached more than one thousand in the eighteenth century, and by 1849 most Black residents had married or otherwise assimilated into the white population. Interest in the African race was therefore high in 1847 and 1848, when a "scientific" exhibition of "bushmen" or "Bosjesmans" (two men, two women, and a baby "from the

Interior of South Africa") appeared at Dublin's Portobello Gardens. According to the *United Irishman*, when the price of admission was lowered to one penny, a crowd collected that was so large that few could get a sight of the Africans, and a considerable row broke out in which lamps were broken and a wooden Mount Vesuvius demolished.[98]

While his skin and singing seemed clearly "African" in origin, Juba's dances were not so readily placeable. "What on earth can his dancing be compared to?" asked one newspaperman. "Why, to nothing under the sun that we have ever seen or witnessed before. His dancing is an affair *sui generis*." To back that claim, the *Freeman's Journal* revived the comparison between "Juba, the veritable nigger, and his mock sable *confreres*." "It is our belief that no man—much less youth—of European birth and habitude could, by any possibility, achieve the wonders of simultaneous muscular exertion, [or] sustain it for quarter the time which Master Juba occupies in getting into good humour with himself and his performance." With "perfect command of his lungs" and "muscular power," Juba was a phenomenal individual yet still "a curiosity."[99]

One wonders how these racialized descriptions affected Lane's self-perception. His actions certainly show that he knew how to succeed as a professional entertainer. Competition for music patronage was formidable in Dublin in July. The popular Monsieur Jullien and his orchestra were at the Rotondo accompanying the Italian soprano Madame Persiani, and *The Beggar's Opera* was being performed at the Queen's Royal Theatre. To steer people to the Music Hall, Pelham revamped Pell's command performances for "the Nobility in the three kingdoms."[100] And Juba helped out by performing "for the first time in this City" two new songs ("I's gwine on de old Pedee" and "Way up in Alabama") and "two original dances" whose titles evoked Irish steps done the African American way ("The Cotton-picking Reel" and "Corn-husking Jig").[101] Mackintosh kept them on for two more weeks.

After his Music Hall benefit on August 2, 1849, Juba's professional circumstances changed. He arrived in Scotland at the end of the month accompanied by only Pell and Briggs. He was also treated as the leader of the trio. The manager of Edinburgh's Adelphi Theatre engaged "Juba and his companions" for one week to perform their show in three truncated parts between and after the plays. The trio received good reviews. The *Caledonian Mercury* marveled at Pell's dexterity and variation "on what are esteemed to be very monotonous instruments. Having exhibited his skill on the four bones, he reduces the number to two, and eventually to one. How he performs a solo on the remaining bone, we leave to be seen, but its accomplishment excites not a little mirth." And "Mr Briggs plays the banjo with extraordinary facility and power, producing either the sweet sounds of the guitar, or the more boisterous accompaniments to negro melodies." As for the "coloured serenader" Juba, well, his singing, tambourine playing, and dancing received four times as much copy as the other two combined.[102]

Juba outshone his two colleagues wherever they performed. While in Edinburgh, the trio became acquainted with actor John W. Anson, who took them on the Dundee circuit through Scotland's mountainous northeastern region. From September to November, Anson opened theaters in Perth, Stirling, Dundee, and Aberdeen for "a short season" (from a few days to two weeks) and provided the public with "a treat of a very rare and novel kind . . . the inimitable Juba, whose dancing and singing is of that wonderful nature so richly described by Boz, and highly eulogized by the London press," reported the *Dundee Courier,* which then added almost as an afterthought, "Pell, the far-famed 'Bones,' and T. F. Briggs, the banjo player, are in their way pre-eminent."[103]

Rivals and Posers

Juba's success encouraged emulation. While he was at London's Vauxhall Gardens in 1848, a "happy-looking fellow" calling himself "'Ceda,' the inimitable and renowned dancer," debuted across the River Thames. Advertised as "Juba's Double," Ceda claimed that he had won a "great Trial Dance" against Juba at New York's Chatham Theatre and that Boz had witnessed the match. Ceda danced with a band of "real Virginian Harmonists" from the United States (Messrs. Winnemore, Hooley, Christie, Wilson, and Raymond). Never given a surname, Ceda may have been African American, and Winnemore, who acted as "leader or jester to the band," was probably "Mr. Winnemore, the laughable colored vocalist" who had worked with Diamond at Welch's circus. They played the Hanover Square Rooms, Harmonic Hall, New Royal Victoria Theatre, and Cremorne Gardens from June to September, then Ceda traveled to the provinces. Ceda may have been one of Juba's Black rivals employing (and stretching) that fact as publicity, just as Juba had invoked his rivalry with Diamond in his ads.[104] Other dancers were not so bold. In 1849 another American named John Millicent toured with Dumbolton's Ethiopian Serenaders billed as "a wonderful dancer, second only to Juba."[105]

Imposters also followed Juba into the provinces. On October 1, 1849, a troupe advertised as the "Original ETHIOPIAN SERENADERS, (From St. James's) Messrs. Stanwood and Germon, In conjunction with BOZ'S JUBA," opened at Sheffield's Music Hall. They presented themselves as "under the patronage of the Queen," consequently attracting "a pretty good muster in the gallery and some company in the salon." The first surprise came when only two performers appeared on the stage, "the programme having announced several performances by the 'Band' and the 'Company.' The thing went on however, to the last performance of the second part, set down as the 'Great Juba Dance,' by Juba. The audience had been very skeptical before," reported the *Sheffield & Rotterham Independent,* " . . . but this dance satisfied them completely that the dancer was no Juba; and then their indignation rose to a high pitch." The gallery gods made their way to the orchestra and fetched the men out by force. "One of the unlucky serenaders acknowledged that he was not the person whose name he had assumed, and laid the blame on his colleague," causing "a considerable scuffle," after which the imposters were escorted through the streets and "deposited at the Tontine, their instruments having suffered considerably."[106]

Another troupe of "Ethiopian delineators" took over the Oddfellows Hall in Manchester in November, but "hardly anyone came so they skipped town," reported the *Manchester Examiner and Times,* leaving "the hall-cleaner, with whom they had lodged, minus their board, and the bellman of the town without his fee for announcing their astonishing performances."[107] Juba's popularity stimulated imitation while making impersonation difficult.

Juba, Pell, and Briggs played "the Country Rooms" in Aberdeen in late October, said goodbye to Anson, and returned to Glasgow, where they gave "a series of their queer performances" at the trades hall on Glassford Street from November 1849 to January 1850. An extensive rail system built to service the surrounding mill towns made it possible to punctuate that long stay with short stands in Greenock, Paisley, Port Glasgow, Johnstone, Lochwinnoch, and Beith.[108] But when Monsieur Jullien arrived in Glasgow the second week in January, they bid farewell to their fans.

A flamboyant conductor and composer, Louis Jullien's aim in life was to widen the audience for serious orchestral music, and to that end he may have engaged Juba at some point.* Jullien was renowned for his colorful Concerts Monstre, which combined major symphonic works with lighter pieces, including his own compositions and arrangements of popular songs. He directed the orchestra at Vauxhall for several years, but by the time Juba arrived he had moved to the Royal Surrey Zoological Gardens.[109]

From Glasgow, Juba, Pell, and Briggs took the ferry to Northern Ireland, where Pelham took over again as manager.[110] In mid-January, they played two nights "at the Music-Hall" in Belfast, followed by one night each in Armagh and Lurgan. While they were away, a review of their Belfast performance appeared in the *Banner of Ulster.* The journalist judged the "'hash-up' of stale Nigger Melodies, and common place Conundrums, to have been a positive failure. The Serenaders, who, by the way, are said to have been for a length of time connected with the Music Saloons of our town, threw the company into a state of sickening *ennui.* The only, to a certain extent, redeeming feature of the evening was 'The Plantation Dance,'

---

* Sam Sanford claimed that Jullien took over Juba's management and introduced him in a "Bone solo, together with his jig Dancing" in front of his orchestra. The maestro did compose orchestral arrangements for jig-dancing tunes, and his engagements overlapped with Juba's in London, Liverpool, Dublin, and Glasgow. But I have found no evidence that proves Sanford's claim.

and 'Miss Lucy Long' (in character), by Juba." An enraged Pelham responded by offering to give "500 POUNDS STERLING!! To the Author, if he can prove" that either Boz's Juba, G. W. Pell, or Briggs were ever in Belfast previous to January 13, 1850, "on which morning they arrived from Glasgow; or if he can prove one, or any of them, ever played in any Music Saloon in England, Ireland, or Scotland." He then rehearsed the troupe's past itinerary at Theatres Royal, trades halls, and minor theaters in large towns and cities. "Between the above-named places they gave Entertainments at a number of small towns," he granted, "but always in the First Rooms." Pelham sidestepped the reviewer's disclosure that local musicians were performing as Pell's Serenaders and the fact that they *had* performed in concert rooms in London the previous April. He also ignored Juba's separate and more positive review. Instead, the calculating Pelham bent his rebuttal into self-promotion, signing the $500 challenge "Director of Pell's Serenaders and Boz's Juba" and naming the hotel where he could be found.[111]

The trio responded to the review by moving to Belfast's Theatre Royal when they returned on January 2 and by pushing Juba to the front. This venue switch was necessitated by "the Music Hall not being large enough to give full scope for Boz's Juba's Dances," they informed the public, underlining Juba's preeminence with a pronoun: "He, in conjunction with G. W. Pell [and] . . . T. F. Briggs . . . will appear at the above Theatre." If the intention of the move was to erase the troupe's association with second-class music saloons, it did so by elevating the dancer above his fellows.[112]

The dancer responded individually as well. For whatever reason, Lane/Juba appears to have tired of the trio's company, or of Pelham's management, or both. After the engagement at Belfast's Theatre Royal, he left the troupe.

11

ASSERTIONS OF INDEPENDENCE

Brilliant spectacles greeted the US soldiers returning home from Mexico in the spring of 1848. Officials and residents in cities across the states sponsored parades, speeches, twenty-one-gun salutes, and banquets in their honor. Bareback rider John Glenroy observed one such reception on his way to St. Louis to join Dan Rice's circus. He traveled by boat, he recalled, stopping at Cincinnati to rest for a day, "and there we met our Home Volunteers returning from the Mexican War. The men were in a destitute condition, their clothing being in rags and hardly a boot on their feet; but the people of Cincinnati had an immense reception provided for them, the streets being profusely decorated and all the Clothing stores being thrown open free to the men, so that the soldiers would get something to wear, and that same evening a banquet was tendered to the men."[1]

No such reception greeted John Diamond, who may have spent the final months of the war in a New Orleans prison. Two accounts of Diamond's military service written sixty years apart—a letter to the *Baltimore Sun* and a minstrelsy chronical entry—agree that the dancer had volunteered to fight in Mexico and that he exited the war in a disgraceful state. John T. Ford, who employed Diamond in 1853, attributed the dancer's postwar condition to the treatment of volunteer soldiers in general: "This much in justice to Mr. Diamond I will say, that when war was declared he sacrificed all his ties of house and affection, and a business yielding him over $100 per month, *to take up arms at the miserable pittance allowed a private soldier.* When he returned, he was penniless in pocket and much injured in health."[2] T. Allston Brown, who published his version in 1912, blamed Diamond's postwar circumstances on his character. "Diamond was of a revengeful and passionate disposition," he declared. "Having enlisted in the American army, he made an attack on his superior officer; for this he was sentenced to be shot; but, fortunately for Diamond, the treaty of peace saved his life."[3] Whatever the cause of his postwar problems, Diamond's soldiering experience affected the rest of his life.

The Mexican-American War set in motion processes that would touch Juba's life as well. Postwar politics turned the United States into an utterly inhospitable place for Black entertainers, many of whom sought refuge overseas. Juba played it safe and stayed in the United Kingdom, while Diamond roamed around America getting into trouble. Otherwise, Diamond's activities between 1848 and 1852 mirrored Juba's. Blackface minstrelsy remained a lucrative venue for challenge dancers, and both dancers would try leading their own company before going solo. Economic and geographic expansion had amassed workers outside capital cities, providing each dancer with a ready public. Juba's most appreciative audiences were factory workers in England's industrial North; Diamond's became the immigrants in America's river port, mining, and mill towns. Both felt and asserted their independence, made friends and enemies, and were warned to watch their step.

To War

It is unclear where Diamond signed up for military service. Enlistees from Northern and mid-Atlantic states mustered at New Orleans and departed for Mexico by sail.[4] Registration cards from numerous cities bore the name John Diamond. But the soldier whose profile fits Brown's story was a private named William Diamond, age twenty-five, who enlisted in Pittsburgh on December 1, 1846. That Diamond appeared on the muster roll of Company J of the First Regiment of Pennsylvania Infantry until February 1847. However, on January 14, 1847, he was "Delivered over to Civil Authorities on account of assault & Riot & left at New Orleans."[5] This may have been the man Brown heard about. Was he our Diamond? It is possible that he was. But he was not the only infantryman to riot or assault an officer during the war.

The United States' war with Mexico was a blatant land grab. Many US citizens believed they had a moral responsibility to develop the continent, but they disagreed on the form that imperialism should take. Whigs saw the nation's mission as setting a democratic example through expanded trade and Protestant values. Democrats favored conquest. The war did not represent an American consensus. Mexico was a young republic, considerably weakened by a divided government. Even military men recognized that President Polk's administration had fabricated Mexican aggression at the Texas-Mexico border. "We have not one particle of right to be here," a US lieutenant colonel wrote in his diary in 1846. "It looks as if the government sent in a small force on purpose to bring on a war, so as to have a pretext for taking California and as much of this country as it chooses."[6]

As a twenty-five-year-old Irish American, Diamond fit the demographic of the war's common soldier. The violence permeating the lives of working-class city youths made many eager to join up and fight. According to one municipal judge, Philadelphia suffered from an "increase of juvenile offenders" in the 1840s, "resulting from the various associations of young men that throng the street corners, and find shelter in engine and hose houses, and who are banded together to commit crime." "Gangs of hooligans" with names like the Killers, the Stingers, the Shabs, the Crusers, and the Buffers, terrorized Southwark and other racially mixed neighborhoods, ransacked market districts, and committed "downright acts of piracy along the Delaware" (fig. 11.1). These attacks declined as gang members joined the Mexican War.[7]

FIGURE 11.1. Gangs of street toughs like the Killers terrorized Philadelphia neighborhoods and ransacked markets along the Delaware River. They also peopled Diamond's audiences, as the poster advertising Dan Rice's circus attests. These outrages declined when Diamond's generation volunteered to fight the Mexican War. *Two of the Killers,* ca. 1848, lithograph by J. Childs. Library Company of Philadelphia.

Many volunteers were enticed by the wages, bounties, land warrants, and pensions promised as recompense by the government. But it is unlikely that Diamond joined up for the money. Even the poorest-paid minstrel made double what a private made. In May 1846 Congress set a soldier's pay at $8.00 per month. Infantry privates were promised $7.00 a month plus $3.50 for clothing, bread, and other staples. However, paymasters were often tardy, making foraging, pilfering, and outright robbery common. By volunteering, Diamond descended into the enlisted soldier's destitution.[8]

Young men were also enticed by the honor and excitement attached to soldiering. But the majority of volunteers who rushed to join local regiments did not fight in a single engagement. Grueling marches, unsanitary camps, communicable diseases, and heavy drinking constituted their shared experience. They also endured servile military discipline and witnessed displays of punishment that defied their understanding of American liberty. Courts-martial regularly doled out public whippings and other corporal humiliations to enlisted men for minor violations, while courts of inquiry showed leniency to officers who injured or killed unruly soldiers while inflicting cruel and severe punishments.[9]

Diamond's Irish heritage probably fueled his enlistment and fouled his military experience. More than two hundred thousand people fleeing agricultural blight and starvation in Ireland and political persecution in Germany arrived in the United States during the war years. Enlistment became a pathway to citizenship and steady wages for many of these immigrants. But Irish volunteers, immigrant and American-born, were treated as inferior soldiers by most officers. They were given the most unpleasant jobs, punished severely for small infractions such as drinking and negligence of duty, denied promotion, and refused requests to attend Catholic services.

Such experiences created angry and disheartened soldiers, some of whom expressed their frustrations through violent aggression. They had come to defend white "American liberty" against an invasion (heathen, colored, and Catholic) that prowar propagandists claimed had begun. But the fact that the Mexicans had founded a republic on democratic principles troubled some US soldiers. Recognizing the contradiction, a small but significant number of Irish, German, British, and American-born troops joined the Legion of Saint Patrick (Batallón de San Patricio) and fought for the Mexican Republic.[10] Thousands of others, fed up with stark conditions, harsh discipline, and the privileges of rank, deserted and disappeared. And a few more, possibly including Diamond, turned to outright confrontation with their officers.

The Dead Alive and the Lost Found

Ailing and bereft of cash at the war's end, Diamond stumbled back onto terrain that had shifted while he was soldiering. Challenge dancing was still a distinct act, with young champions emerging. But one rarely saw a jig dancer outside a minstrel show. For the troupe playing at Philadelphia's Temperance Hall in January 1847, Master Stickney danced a match against the "far-famed" Master McFarland, "only eight years old," whom competent judges designated "the best Dancer in the world, not excepting John Diamond."[11] Those judges could claim McFarland's superiority because Diamond had been missing in action since the previous year and, effectively, stayed missing for eight months after the Treaty of Guadalupe Hidalgo was signed. Over thirteen thousand Americans died in the Mexican War, and for a time Diamond was counted among them. "*John Diamond, the great negro-dancer . . . who was reported dead some time since, has again come to life and at the last accounts was creating a considerable excitement at St. Louis*," declared the *Louisville Daily Courier* in October 1848 under the arresting headline "The Dead Alive and the Lost Found."[12]

Diamond's opening gambit was a challenge dance at New Orleans's Olympic Theatre in July 1848. Between the plays, "John Kelley will draw a long bow [tell tall tales], and John Diamond will dance a dozen of the thickest planks clear out of the middle of the stage, on a challenge of $500," announced the *Daily Delta*. In August Diamond and Kelley formed a quartet called the Ethiopian Melodists with two other dancers, John Stickney and Tom Coleman, after which Diamond, Stickney, and Coleman danced with a band known as the Sable Melodists. Tom Coleman was Master Coleman, who billed himself as Master Diamond's equal in 1840, and John Stickney was "Master Stickney, the celebrated Light Dancer from the Southern Theatres," circus proprietor S. P. Stickney's son. At the end of the month, Diamond and Stickney formed a trio with banjoist T. Wilson, then Diamond, Coleman, and Wilson headed up the Mississippi to join Kneass's Burlesque Opera Troupe.[13]

A capable actor, opera singer, and composer, Nelson Kneass organized his first Troupe of Burlesquers in 1845. In April 1848 he directed John C. Benson's all African American band, the Sable Harmonists, who later traveled to the United Kingdom (and competed with Juba for audiences), and in July he took his own company on tour. That company of singers and, occasionally, corps of ballet dancers performed "the most favorite selections from the best Operas," as well as comic, Ethiopian, and Irish songs.[14] Burlesque opera troupes relied on and increased the people's familiarity with operatic music and librettos, including Black people, for whom Kneass routinely reserved places at his concerts.

Kneass engaged Diamond and Coleman "at an enormous expense" to perform trial dances, remarked the *Louisville Daily Democrat*. "We will have a 'taste of their quality' in a few days." For two months, the duo traveled with Kneass's troupe performing "their rival feats" in St. Louis, Louisville, and Cincinnati.[15] In winter Diamond and Stickney danced as "Two Rival Champions" for S.P. Stickney's Olympic Circus in New Orleans. Then Diamond hooked up with Dan Rice & Company's Metropolitan and Hippodramatic Circus, "a mighty gathering of all the singular Male and Female, Adult and Juvenile, Principal and Scenic, Equestrian, Comic, Gymnastic, Tight Rope, Herculean and Pantomimic Phenomena in the country." From May to September 1849 Rice & Company pulled into dozens of towns between Schenectady, New York, and Wilkes-Barre, Pennsylvania, on carriages drawn by "curiously caparisoned" horses, set up tents, and offered performances at 2:00 and 7:00 p.m. But in October, when Dan Rice was jailed for assaulting a newspaperman in Baltimore, the dancer moved on.[16]

Diamond was drawn to Midwestern states where employment and masculine pleasures were plentiful. In November 1849 he secured a month's entr'acte work at Cincinnati's American Theatre. He also snagged an adversary. On November 3 Richard "Dick" Sliter, "the *Champion Dancer*" and leader of "R. H. Sliter's [eleven] Empire Minstrels," advertised and exhibited "his *Celebrated Original Dances,* in all of which he *challenges competition*" at Cincinnati's Masonic Hall.[17] Diamond ignored Sliter's open challenge until his current engagement ended and Sliter approached him personally. For his "farewell benefit" at the American, Diamond danced his "celebrated DECANTER JIG," unequalled locomotive imitation, and "VIRGINIA JIG." "Now For It!" declared the *Cincinnati Enquirer* on December 1. "R. H. Sliter and John Diamond, The Two Best Dancers In The World, Will Dance A Trial Dance, at the Masonic Hall." Billed as a one-night event (admission thirty cents), the trial stretched to five nights, for which Sliter paid Diamond fifty dollars. No wager was advertised, and according to a statement made by Diamond at a later date, no winner was announced.[18]

At the end of December, Sliter followed Diamond to Louisville, Kentucky, where Diamond was dancing for William A. Lloyd's Sable Harmonists at the Odd Fellows' Hall. Sliter's Empire Minstrels appeared at the Apollo Room. Noticing the stalking, Diamond called his trial dance with a Mr. William Fish "the Grand Tar River Dance" (Sliter's signature step), and Lloyd introduced him as "Sliter's great rival."[19] But the only dancer Diamond acknowledged as *his* great rival was Juba.

The Decanter Jig

Unlike his fellow minstrels, Diamond fashioned his repertory and stage persona to suit his audiences. By 1849 the "inimitable singing, delightful music, and amusing witticisms and funnicalities" of bands like Lloyd's represented old minstrelsy fare. Diamond elevated such programs by performing dances that resonated with new spectators. The decanter jig, which he danced for "five minutes with a decanter full of liquor on his head" is one example.[20] In Ireland it was said that a well-trained dancer could jig with a pan of water balanced on her head and never spill a drop.[21] Over seven hundred thousand Irish Catholic refugees had disembarked on America's shores.[22] Northeastern port cities absorbed the largest portion of these newcomers, but countless others journeyed inland to settle along the Ohio River.[23] Diamond advertised his decanter jig as "a feat never attempted by any other dancer."[24] But the Irish in his audiences would have been familiar with the format, if not his particular dance steps.

Enslaved African Americans easily incorporated this "Irish" skill into their jig-dancing competitions, as carrying a water jug on the head was common in many African regions. There is no record of Juba's dancing the decanter jig, but Nancy Williams (b. 1851) recalled "dancing' wid a glass o' water on my head an' three boys a bettin' on me" while enslaved in Virginia.[25]

Diamond revived his locomotive dance in response to "railroad fever" and the railroad workers at his shows. In *La Bayadere* in 1840, he had invoked the Underground Railroad by mimicking with his feet the sound of a train's iron wheels clacking over railroad ties. The meaning of that sound had changed of late. The acquisition of Western territories after the Mexican War and the discovery of gold in California precipitated rampant speculation in railroad construction, manufacturing, and Western lands, turning the locomotive into a tool and symbol of American progress and social mobility. Audience reactions to Diamond's railroad imitations puzzled some reporters, nevertheless. "A wag remarked that John even *beat* the locomotive," noted the Washington, DC, *Evening Star,* "and several calls were made for 'Captain Owens,' 'Humphreys,' and 'Collins,' the polite conductors of the Washington and Baltimore road, who were humorously imagined to be following the engine with their trains—so perfect was the deception. Or, at least, such was the queer way of complimenting Mr. Diamond for his great success."[26]

Stepping High

Diamond's conduct offstage was even more baffling than onstage. From January to March 1850 he returned to Cincinnati's American Theatre, then he rejoined William Lloyd and toured cities along the Ohio, Mississippi, and Cumberland Rivers. "They Have Arrived! With The Great Champion Dancer John Diamond," announced *The Tennessean* when Lloyd's Sable Harmonists opened in Nashville on April 10. That same day, the *Louisville Daily Courier* reported that on Friday night, Diamond had fought with a man named John Buchanan at "a house of ill-fame" in St. Louis. Several shots were fired, and a bullet went through Buchanan's arm, "but this was the only damage done." The dancer was not arrested or charged, prompting New Orleans's *Picayune* to comment: "John Diamond, who shot a man at St. Louis and took to his heels, is announced at Nashville, where, like the man with the cork leg, he is still progressing."[27] Ironically, by the time that article appeared, Diamond and Lloyd had been indicted in Nashville "for common assaults, on Thomas Buckly and others." The two men submitted their cases in court on April 23: "Lloyd was fined $45 and costs—Dimond [*sic*],

$65 and costs." Both gave security and were discharged, suggesting that their tour had been lucrative enough to pay the fines.[28]

Louisville, Kentucky, became the site of Diamond's next scuffle with the law. In May he joined the American Circus Company, which arrived in Louisville on the steamer *Daniel Boone*, circled through Kentucky and Ohio, and returned in August 1850.[29] Diamond had friends in Louisville, a swiftly expanding steamboat port on the Ohio River with a thriving sporting community. One-third of the city's thirty-six thousand white inhabitants were Irish Catholic (and German Lutheran) immigrants who had arrived in the last decade.[30] Louisville also housed the largest whiskey distillery in the world.

Flush with money and unemployed, Diamond and his friend Tom Dickson got drunk on August 7, "went down to Madame Royston's, and behaved very badly right in the presence of the modest old woman!" reported the *Louisville Daily Courier*. Royston was a successful businesswoman who kept a hotel boardinghouse, bar, and brothel downtown. The popularity of her house showed in its size (the building was converted into an orphan asylum a few years later) and the frequency of its mention in the papers. Arrests of Madam Royston's male and female customers for drunkenness and fighting made the news, as did the "shines" perpetrated against her by spirited young men, who once drenched Royston's "on-fire" house with cold water.[31]

Diamond and Dickson were arrested "for disorderly and riotous conduct" and arraigned the next day. "The court required bail in the sum of $500 each for one year, and the b'hoys travelled out to the cave, where it will not be diamond cut diamond," jested the *Courier*, "but Diamond cut granite, unless some of John's Ethiopian brethren interfere in his behalf." The Cave was Louisville's workhouse, a large, publicly funded edifice built on a tract known as Cave Hill Farm. All persons convicted of misdemeanors—drunkenness, disorderly conduct, vagrancy, prostitution—were confined to the Cave for "safe-keeping" until their fines and costs were paid or had been discharged by their labor in the nearby rock quarry at the rate of fifty cents a day.[32]

Diamond's celebrity helped and hurt him in Louisville. Someone did apply to bail the dancer out, "but the city attorney contended that there were some new steps which John ought to learn."[33] Fame did not protect a working-class person with no middle-class employer to vouch for them. Bail was denied, and Diamond was likely confined to the Cave for four months, as there are no reports of him dancing again until December 1850.

Juba Takes the Reins

Juba parted ways with Briggs and Pell, and Pelham, in February 1850. It had become clear that his dancing and not Pell's bones playing scored the highest with the public. One measure of his prestige, at least among the owners of racing dogs, could be found in the "coursing" news. That month, "Mr. Begbe's Juba" was the runner-up in the Kennett Stakes, and "Mr. Laurence's brindled dog Boz's Juba beat Teasdale's white dog The Swindler" in Newcastle, after which "First to the Hare beat Boz's Juba."[34] Juba's popularity and prowess were tallied in the coursing dogs named after him.

After two years, Juba knew enough people in the UK to put together his own minstrel troupe and find bookings. "Boz's Juba, who has for some time past parted from Pell, the bones player, is now at the head of another party of Serenaders, who have been giving entertainments through the midland counties," reported *Lloyd's Weekly Newspaper* in March 1850. "On Wednesday they opened the Chesterfield Theatre," thirteen miles south of Sheffield, in Derbyshire.[35] His former partners floundered briefly. Briggs stuck with Pell for a few months, then returned to the United States.[36] Pell returned to London and cobbled together a new troupe of "original Ethiopeans" (Pell, Ledger, and De Brenner), who appeared at Cremorne Gardens in 1851 with "Redmond, the far-famed Juba Dancer."[37]

From February to April 1850, Juba and the American Serenaders (also called "his company of Americans" and "a party of Serenaders") danced and sang in town halls, tavern assembly rooms, small theaters, and mechanics' institutes. Either Juba booked their appearances (which ranged from one-night stands to three-week engagements) or he hired someone else to make the arrangements and print out the programs to hand out at performances. On February 25 Juba and his band appeared at the town hall in Liverpool's St. Helen's district. They stayed "positively for one night only," as they were set to perform at the Lion Hotel's assembly rooms in Warrington the next day.[38] During his travels with Pell, Juba had gained a sense of where he would be most welcomed and how extensive an audience he could count on in each town.

From Warrington, Juba's party worked their way north to Bradford, one of Yorkshire's industrial boomtowns. In 1850 cities and towns in England's Midlands were linked by an extensive system of railroads and canals. The textile cities of Bradford (wool), Leeds (wool and flax), and Manchester (cotton) had swelled in population and area far beyond the older market towns of Bristol, Norwich, and York. Juba booked the lecture hall at Bradford's mechanics' institute for two nights in mid-March and reached out to "all Classes." Reserved seats to the "Artiste's Fashionable Entertainment" cost two shillings, and "second seats" cost one shilling. Other halls called that arrangement "Working Class half price."[39] As word got out, spectators from towns nearby came for the show, so Juba and "his Company of Americans" stayed another week.[40] In mid-March they took the train to Sheffield for a one-night stand, then continued south to Nottingham, opening at the mechanics' hall on Milton Street, where back seats cost only sixpence. The band performed there for seven nights, diversifying their entertainments with "some superior solo playing on the violin and dulcimer" and closing with Juba's benefit on March 30. Then, having whetted the appetite of surrounding districts, they hopped on another train and traveled the thirty-eight miles back to Sheffield.[41]

From years working as a professional dancer, Juba had acquired the wisdom of experience about how to promote performances. In Sheffield, "Boz's Juba" and "his Company of Vocal and Instrumental Artistes" booked the spacious lecture hall at the Athenaeum and Mechanics' Institute (fig. 11.2). Billed as "A Treat for Easter Week!" their entertainments cost only two shillings for reserved seats, one shilling for second seats, and sixpence for gallery seats. Juba also cut ticket prices in half for children and school groups and on top of that "kindly offered to Admit the Members of the Athenaeum and their Families at Half-price." The institute's directors piggybacked on Juba's largess, announcing a reduced price for joining the Athenaeum that week and describing the advantages of its "lofty, spacious, elegant, and comfortable Rooms"—a news room "furnished with the London and Provincial Papers and Periodicals," an annually augmented library containing nearly a thousand volumes, "a Smoke Room, Chess Room, and other needful Conveniences," and a coffee room where "Tea and Coffee, Chops, Steaks, &c. can also be had at any Hour of the Day."[42]

By calculating his publicity correctly, Juba extended his stay in Sheffield to a successful three-week engagement. At the end of his first week, the *Sheffield &*

FIGURE 11.2. After going solo, Juba calculated his publicity to fit each city's venue. In Sheffield, England, he and the directors of the Athenaeum and Mechanics' Institute devised a mutually beneficial scheme whereby Juba admitted members and their families to his show for half price and the Athenaeum offered a reduced membership price during Juba's engagement. *The Sheffield Athenaeum and Mechanics' Institute,* from the *Illustrated London News,* Sept. 4, 1847, 149.

Rotterham Independent proclaimed that "'custom does not stale' the performances of this extraordinary individual." To bolster attendance his second week, Juba solicited the support of influential locals. Taking his cue from Pell, he announced in advance that his benefit on April 8 would take place "Under the Patronage of COL ARTHUR and the OFFICERS of the THIRD DRAGOON GUARDS, Who will attend, together with a number of the most Influential Families of Sheffield and its Vicinity."[43] The Guards and first families of the region, who would themselves attract gapers, guaranteed Juba a full house.

Meanwhile, Richard W. Pelham began publishing advance notices stating that "Boz's Juba will shortly appear in Liverpool." When his brother's trio disbanded, Pelham decided to return to performing (after a six-year hiatus), formed his own band, called the American Delineators, booked the concert hall on Lord Nelson Street for two weeks, and engaged Juba. He advertised the upcoming show as "The Greatest Novelty ever offered to the Public of Liverpool" and ordered posters and playbills to be printed. But when April 23, opening night, rolled around, Juba did not turn up. "Boz's 'Juba' was to have accompanied Mr. Pelham to this town," reported *The Era* on May 5, 1850, "but the ebony youth failed to keep his appointment, and another gentleman was engaged for the Plantation and Lucy Long dances."[44] Pelham probably danced those dances himself, making the greatest novelty on the program "Herr Dugburgh on the Dulcimerian Lyre."[45] In 1848 Gilbert Pell claimed Juba as his "*protégé*"; and in 1850, in a similar stab at proprietorship, his brother Richard announced that Juba would appear in Liverpool under his "guardianship."[46] Both white Americans claimed authority over the Black dancer's career, and both grossly overstated their role in his life. Juba may have been seventeen when he arrived in England, but he was nobody's protégé; and as a nineteen-year-old professional, he did not require a guardian.

Going Solo in Concert Rooms

Instead of meeting Pelham in Liverpool, Juba stayed in Sheffield to dance at the Casino in the West Bar neighborhood. The name "casino" referred to a large room separated from a tavern's public bar, often with more comfortable furnishings, used for general purposes such as lectures, meetings, or dances. Like other aspiring public house proprietors, Thomas Youdan had turned his concert rooms into a tastefully ornamented, unlicensed "theatre, with drop-scenes, side wings," a gallery, and enough seats and tables to accommodate an audience of one thousand. A writer for the *Sheffield Times* visited Youdan's newly fitted-up Casino for the first time while Juba was employed there. "The body of the theatre was occupied by artizans [sic], numbering 600 at least, and we [do] not remember [having] seen better order kept by that class at any of our public places than on that occasion. The gallery was filled with a respectable, middle-class audience, composed in a great part of clerks, shopkeepers, and the better paid class of artizans; and who, if we may judge by the hearty applause given to the performers were highly delighted."[47] By catering to the working middle classes, Juba's act helped fulfill the aspirations of men such as Youdan.

Juba added to the Casino's variety from May to July 1850 as a solo dancing act. He did not take the American Serenaders with him. On May 11 Youdan presented songs by several female and male vocalists, "an excellent performance on the tight rope by the Misses Young, and dancing by Juba—the veritable laughter-provoking Juba," reported the *Sheffield Times*. "Juba is drawing large houses, and we thought that he acquitted himself better on Wednesday night than on any former occasion while in Sheffield. The 'National Anthem,' sung by the whole *corps musicale* concluded the entertainments at eleven o'clock precisely."[48]

Juba may have stayed in Sheffield because he preferred the concert-saloon environment. A few months earlier, a special correspondent from London's *Morning Chronicle* had visited Liverpool's "cheap or free concert-rooms" seeking the amusements of the people. In one of the larger houses, "the greater portion of the auditors were evidently mechanics and labourers, with their families," he reported; "but there was a considerable number of sailors, British, American, and foreign. There was also a large number of young boys, of from fourteen to sixteen years of age, of whom there was scarcely one without a pipe or a cigar in his mouth."[49] The age of employees at concert rooms was not much older. At the City Tavern, where Juba worked in Dublin, for example, the proprietor employed "a respectable Lad, from fourteen to twenty, to take charge of one of the Bars."[50]

Drinking (for all) and smoking (for males) were part of the entertainment at tavern concert rooms, where a three-penny ticket entitled the visitor to enjoy the musical entertainment and a glass of ale or porter besides. At some houses no admission was charged, "the proprietors depending solely upon the sale of their liquors for the payment of their performers." In larger concert rooms, the audience sat "on benches, in front of small tables, or rather ledges, with just sufficient room before each person to place a bottle and a glass. Men, women, and children mingled together. A dense cloud of tobacco-smoke filled the room." The boys in the audience enjoyed themselves with abandon: "Their applause rang loudest. . . . [T]heir commands to the waiters for drink were more frequent, obstreperous, and rude" (fig. 11.3).[51]

Most concert rooms geared their décor and shows toward a working-class temperament. In one house, the walls were frescoed with "gigantic full-length portraits of celebrated prizefighters, all in boxing attitude." A stage was set with moveable scenery, in front of which men and women sang sentimental and comic songs, danced hornpipes in nautical garb, exhibited risqué tableaux vivants, and performed husband-and-wife skits abounding in double entendres. In houses nearer the docks, where the number of sailors and Irish families was bigger,

FIGURE 11.3. At tavern concert rooms and music halls in England's industrial and port cities, Juba was expected to descend into the crowd between his acts and socialize with the patrons. Concert saloon audiences were dominated by artisans and laborers and their families and young single male and female workers, all mingled together. A three-penny ticket entitled the visitor to enjoy the musical show and a glass of ale or porter besides. Smoking was an additional entertainment. *The Green Gate Tavern, City Road,* print from an engraving by T. H. Shepherd, about 1854, London. Museum no. S.981–2017. ©Victoria and Albert Museum, London.

dancing supplied a larger portion of the entertainment "and included 'nigger dances,' the sailor's hornpipe, and the jig, and in one house a dance in pattens [wooden-soled shoes], by a woman with her face blackened, to personate a negress, and in another an imitation of Boz's Juba."[52]

During Juba's engagement, Youdan renamed his business the Royal Casino. In June he presented "the usual stock company of singers," studding the program with one or two stars, including the American Barlow, who "provided a pleasant Nigger Entertainment, in conjunction with the celebrated Boz's Juba." Juba's tenure proved so successful that in July, when the dancer suddenly left him, Youdan only allowed that "Boz's Juba had closed here for the present."[53] In fact, Juba was on his way to Manchester, having received a better offer from the Colosseum. Once again, the African American dancer took advantage of his freedom in Britain to make and break a contract. Youdan was not happy about that.

Manchester's Colosseum constituted a step up professionally from the Casino, but it also represented a step backward for Juba, from solo performer to member of a minstrelsy company. Established regional concert rooms such as the Colosseum (where Juba remained until August 10) and the Bermondsey Hotel in Bradford (where Juba would perform in December) were large (seating at least a thousand people), professionalized, and commercialized venues that advertised in the London papers. The Colosseum's proprietor, T. Towers, also managed the well-known Polytechnic Concert Hall and Tavern in Salford.[54] Juba "jumped over" to Towers's

Colosseum on July 8, 1850, "tripped it on the fantastic," and exercised "the genius of his toe and heel" with a "grace and lightning rapidity" that was better "credited and admired than described." His act became part of "a beautiful pictorial novelty and Ethiopean spectacle," which London's *Theatrical Journal* credited "to the ability of the manager, and the execution of the company in their individual personations." By joining that show, Juba participated in the rapid development of England's music hall entertainment. In the 1850s and 1860s unprecedented numbers of performers flooded the profession, including dozens of English comedians who banded together in small groups, "called themselves 'funny blacks,'" and stressed the superiority of their acts over ordinary vulgar music hall fare.[55] On this circuit, Juba's authenticity as an African American was again emphasized. "We understand, he is a genuine grit negro, from the far-west," confirmed the *Journal*, "and not one of those domestic manufactured piebald abortions of Ethiopians."[56]

Jumping Fast

Juba had been dancing at the Colosseum for a month when the *Theatrical Journal* compared him to the African American turned British actor Ira Aldridge: "We have two distinguished darkies enlightening us just now, one with the genius of his heels, and the other with the genius of the brain." "The Ethiopian tragedian (Aldridge), or better known as the African Roscius,"* had just returned to London after two years of touring regional theaters, where he attracted great notice not only for his Othello and other Shakespearean roles but for his full range of melodramatic characters—the noble and self-sacrificing, the wily and villainous, the fiendish and half-mad, the comic and absurd. "There is no denying the fact that this black diamond possesses great abilities," opined the *Journal*.[57]

Aldridge also attracted attention for his flashy dress and equipage and for riding through the streets of London inside a carriage with Margaret Aldridge, his white wife (fig. 11.4). The *Journal* recalled sighting Aldridge two years earlier "on a fine and sunny day on the Manchester race course; his dress on that occasion, we remember, made him stand out in bold relief—a white hat, green coat, white trowsers, and a shepherd's plaid slung around him." Was Juba aware of the comparison of Aldridge and himself? Probably. Which begs the question: When did Juba write the note telling Charley White he would be riding in his own carriage the next time White saw him? In 1850, being spotted riding in your own carriage signified not only fame but also its concomitant wealth, since it required owning a horse and carriage, a coach house, and a stable and employing a coachman and groom. Was he thinking about Ikey in *Going for the Cup* when he wrote that line or about Aldridge's carriage? Probably both.

---

* Roscius was the name of a great Roman actor.

FIGURE 11.4. In 1850 London's *Theatrical Journal* compared Black dancer Juba's "genius of the heels" to Black actor Ira Aldridge's "genius of the brain." Aldridge attracted attention for his exquisite acting, his flashy dress, and his equipage and for riding through the streets of London inside a carriage with his white wife, Margaret Aldridge. *Ira Aldridge, the African Roscius!*, TCS 1.249, Houghton Library, Harvard University.

Juba was "jumping very fast at the Colosseum, but too fast is worse than too slow," warned *The Era* on August 4, 1850, "and we advise him to be wise in time. It is easier to jump down than to jump up."⁵⁸ By "too fast" *The Era* might have been referring to his intention to leave the Colosseum, or to his fast life off the stage, or to his expectations regarding salary. Among the "good things flying about," Sam Sanford recalled, was the rumor that Juba "got $50 per night" and "'what for,'" asked the man who told Sanford. "'Why to kill himself 50 dollars to[o] much money for a col'd man.'"⁵⁹ While surely expecting more than the usual salary, it is doubtful that Juba asked for that large a sum. He may have asked for fifty pounds per week or eight to ten pounds per night. In 1848 the Surrey Theatre paid Aldridge sixty pounds for a five-night engagement or twelve pounds per night. But even eight pounds a week was much higher than most concert saloons paid performers. According to an 1849 police report concerning performers employed at concert rooms in Liverpool, typical salaries earned by the 218 musicians and singers interviewed were six, nine, twelve, fifteen, or eighteen shillings or one pound per week. Only the best performers received "a very high salary," noted one proprietor, "up to £2 per week" to keep them from moving to a competing venue.[60]

Whether or not the salary was the problem, Juba "jumped away" from the Colosseum the following week. *The Era* offered "an earnest yet friendly caution, let us hope that he will not throw himself away. Be wise in time is a wholesome motto."[61] Aldridge had been given similar advice three years earlier. Some theater managers took advantage of the Black actor by not compensating him properly, and Aldridge sought redress by publicizing those swindles in the papers. *The Era* interviewed Aldridge about one such matter in 1847 and came down firmly on his side. However, it also advised him to proceed no further, as it might damage his reputation, which was at present "above suspicion." If Juba, a Black dancer, left the Colosseum of his own volition, whether due to unfair payment or to pursue something better, he would be faulted with unwisely throwing his talent away.[62]

What Juba did do was go back to Sheffield, work at the Casino the last week in September, and get arrested on October 9 for assaulting Youdan. According to a court reporter, "The inimitable Juba was placed in the dock along with a young man, named Thomas Carroll, whose general appearance betokened him to be a follower of the Thespian art, on a charge of assault. . . . The quarrel which gave rise to the charge . . . appeared to have originated from an ill feeling which exists between Juba and Mr. Youdan, his late employer."[63] Where that ill feeling came from was not recorded. However, after Juba left him in July, Youdan added a tier of private boxes to the Casino and dubbed the building the Surrey Music Hall.[64] The argument might have been a salary dispute caused by those changes. Juba may have asked Youdan for more money to dance in the music hall, prompting Youdan to insult him and Juba to retaliate. Carroll, Juba's friend and possibly his musician, was discharged. Juba was ordered to pay a fine of two shillings sixpence and costs. The trivial fine suggests either that the assault was minor or that the grievance behind it was valid. The next man who came before the magistrate, charged only "with neglect of work" by his employer, was committed to jail for a month![65]

Youdan, who held a grudge against Juba for at least eight months, took a few jabs at the dancer in a plug for his new show in May 1851: "'Boz's' Juba is rivaled by Mr. J. Millicent, whose powers, unlike Juba's, bear a nightly repetition without palling the senses. He is talented and industrious."[66] According to those statements, Juba was boring, untalented, and lazy, and Millicent, who had been declared "second only to Juba" eighteen months earlier, had moved into first place. But even then,

Youdan wasn't finished punishing Juba. In 1912 T. Allston Brown kept alive a vindictive and racist rumor about a Barnumesque hoax undoubtedly set in motion by Youdan after Juba died. "It has been stated," repeated Brown, "that his skeleton was on exhibition at the Surrey Music Hall, Sheffield, Eng."[67] Such a claim could not have been made about a white man's bones. "Be wise in time," *The Era* had warned Juba, because if you jump down, your enemies will keep you down.

Diamond Finds His Feet

While Lane was facing the magistrate in Sheffield's courthouse, Diamond was counting the days in Louisville's workhouse. He emerged from the Cave in December 1850, formed a minstrel troupe of his own in Cincinnati, and took them on the road. Diamond's Band of Sable Melodists appeared at Thatcher's Athenaeum Hall in Chillicothe, Ohio, at the end of January 1851. He informed that city's "citizens" that tickets could "be had at the door of principal Hotels" and that "front seats [were] reserved for ladies." The "*levees* of John Diamond" drew "enthusiastic, admiring crowds," according to the *Daily Scioto Gazette*. "It was evident that the fee of two bits . . . was considered cheap, in exchange for [the] real fat fun, of witnessing a white man shuffle his feet a half hour with the 'hairstrokes,' and hearing others sing and talk more negrofied than so many Congoes themselves." The *Gazette*'s reviewer recognized that Diamond and his troupe were adept at what they did, but he was unsure as to why people would brave the cold and pay twenty-five cents to watch them do it. Why not attend instead the Philosophical Society's free lectures on astronomy at city hall, he inquired of "all who are fond of variety." Those first-rate discourses are "too valuable to be neglected."[68]

Like Juba's American Serenaders, the members of John Diamond's Melodists were never identified in the papers. Their purpose was to accompany Diamond's thirty-minute dancing act and round out the show. The troupe was not even mentioned in February, when Diamond supplied the entertainments at two "prize concerts" given by Thomas Finegan at Cincinnati's mechanics' institute. (At prize concerts one's admission card served as one's ticket in a lottery for advertised prizes, in this case $650 worth of jewelry.) "The great attraction of the evening" on February 5, previous to the drawing, was John Diamond and Otto Burbank in a trial dance. "John Diamond's Minstrels" played a final engagement in April at Pittsburgh's Lafayette Hall. Diamond described himself as having "no rival as a dancer." He verified that statement by performing his decanter and locomotive dances and a grand trial of skill with "a gentleman of this place" and by dancing "'Sliter's Jig,' in imitation of Dick Sliter," who was performing in Buffalo as "R. H. Sliter, the Champion Dancer."[69]

After one season wearing the manager's cloak, Diamond disbanded his troupe and went solo again. Juba had done the same in England. Why were dancers such reluctant managers? One contemporary offered an answer in a biographical sketch of Philadelphia dancer James Sanford: "Jim couldn't be depended on much as a manager. He was like a good many of the men they call managers in those days, and didn't care particularly about a contract or an engagement. He did what suited Jim Sandford [sic], and if it didn't suit other people, why so much the worse for the other people, that was all."[70] As celebrities, Diamond and Juba did not need to work with minstrels to draw an audience, so they had little incentive to take on the responsibility of providing livelihoods for a band of performers. A good *manager* was proficient at arranging and fulfilling engagements and at collecting and distributing the money accrued by the performers' labor—skills respected in a time-oriented business world. Successful *dancers* concentrated on developing their physical abilities and maintaining control of their time and the money generated by their talents—skills valued in the task-oriented artisanal world being undermined by industrial capitalism.

As a solo act, Diamond could work in any class of performance venue and with all sorts of performers. In April 1851 he "executed some of his most difficult dances" after the play *David Copperfield* at the Buffalo Museum. In May he shared the gaslight at Albany's New Museum Saloon with the actor-playwright Frank S. Chanfrau and "the fascinating actress and danseuse" Miss Albertine, both of whom he had worked with before. Son of a French naval officer turned Bowery eating-house proprietor, Chanfrau was best known for his vernacular character Mose, the "fire laddie" and Bowery b'hoy from *The Mysteries and Miseries of New York* and other plays based on Benjamin Baker's 1848 *A Glance at New York* (fig. 7.7). Miss Albertine played Mose's girlfriend, Eliza or Lize, and split the entr'actes with Diamond, whose dancing also figured in the play.[71] In June Diamond jumped over to White's Melodeon in New York, and in July he danced at a circus in Philadelphia.[72]

To advertise his return to Eastern cities where other dancers still used his name, Diamond announced the number of years he had been absent and specified what his "unequalled dances" would be. At Philadelphia's National Theatre and Circus, he performed a medley of jigs—"SMOKEHOUSE JIG, PAS DE AFRICAN REEL, WALKING AND STEP DANCE, GRAPE VINE TWIST"—and what had become his three signature acts—the locomotive engine, the decanter jig, and the trial dance, in this case, "his inimitable *Virginia Breakdowns,* in which he challenges the world."[73] In August someone called "John Diamond, the great dancer" appeared with "his able assistant Ole Bull Myers" at Barnum's Museum in Philadelphia, but that Diamond was probably an impersonator, as he did not name his dances.

Impersonators were not the only impediments to Diamond's comeback. He also ran up against cultural barriers generated by political and economic divisions. After the Mexican War, the few freedoms enjoyed by Black Northerners were further curtailed by the Fugitive Slave Act, part of the postwar Compromise of 1850. The act, which required that runaway slaves be returned to their owners even if apprehended in a free state, caused strong revulsion, as it denied the alleged fugitive any right to a jury trial and exposed formerly enslaved and free Black people to injustice. It also empowered federal marshals to demand that citizens aid them in the enforcement of the act, making whites who helped runaways subject to legal sanction. The compromise also bolstered the Free Soil Party (1848–1854), which opposed slavery's expansion into the territories acquired by the Mexican War so that that land might be reserved for free white labor. This campaign divided the urban working classes into opposing factions: those who supported slave-free states versus those who feared that restricting slavery would threaten their elevated status as white men. On top of that, women's campaigns for equal rights following the 1848 Seneca Falls Convention triggered gender animus across the classes. At the same time, an economic boom increased the number of people anxious to be identified as middle class.[74] To placate these various interests and markets, minstrel companies increased in size, standardized the structure and content of their programs, and ramped up the racism, nativism, and sexism in their shows. Diamond's acts occupied a precarious position in this environment, betwixt and between blackface minstrelsy's attempt to control and repress the culture of Black people and women and jig dancing's reliance on race and gender mixing.

Diamond was pulled into this melee in October 1851, when J. C. Rainer's Original New Orleans Serenaders secured his services for a Northeastern tour. Rainer was a discerning manager who altered his program according to location. When his eight-member company reached Troy, New York, at the mouth of the Erie Canal, Rainer courted the region's largely immigrant textile and iron workers by heralding John Diamond's "Challenge to the World for $1,000."[75] In Boston (Juba's old stomping ground), he announced that "the ORIGINAL JOHN DIAMOND, the Greatest Dancer Living," would appear "in his Plantation Dance, introducing 120 different steps, also his celebrated character of 'Miss Lucy Long' a la Bloomer," dances associated with Boz's Juba.[76] Juba's triumphs in the United Kingdom were rarely remarked upon by the American press. But Rainer had seen Juba's show in England in 1848 and knew those dances pleased white middle-class audiences.

The subtitle "a la Bloomer" gave Diamond's Miss Lucy Long a contemporary American twist. It referred to the reformed female costume—trousers gathered at the ankles worn under a dress that fell to just below the knees—designed by health and religious crusaders contesting women's cumbersome apparel. (In the 1850s, middle-class women wore ankle-length skirts made of numerous layers of fabric over a metal hoop suspended from the waist to the skirt's hem by canvas straps, a separate tight-fitting bodice worn over a laced corset cinched at the waist, and long hair pinned into a bun amplified by hair pieces.) The new "freedom dress" was donned by a group of women's rights advocates in April 1851 and labeled "the Bloomer" in September after Amelia Jenks Bloomer, editor of

FIGURE 11.5. Amelia Jenks Bloomer, editor of *The Lily*, published an engraving of herself wearing the new "freedom dress," dubbed "bloomers" afterward. Diamond's act "'Miss Lucy Long' a la Bloomer" was both an imitation of Juba's Lucy Long and a parody of women's rights advocates and health reformers who promoted the outfit in 1851. The dress was criticized by people who challenged the wearers' morality and femininity, ridiculed them in jokes and cartoons, and pelted them with mud and jeers. *Amelia Jenks Bloomer,* daguerreotype (ca. 1852–1858). Courtesy of Seneca Falls Historical Society.

The Lily: A Monthly Journal, Devoted to Temperance and Literature, published an engraving of herself in the costume to show her readers "just what an 'immodest' dress we are wearing and about which people have made such an ado" (fig. 11.5).[77] The voluminous skirts and lacy undertrousers of Juba's Lucy had caused the English to pronounce her "an ebony coquette." Diamond's costume was read quite differently. Lucy "a la Bloomer" was a danced equivalent of the blackface act "Lecture on Women's Rights," which ridiculed intellectual women's calls for equality.[78]

Having tried on his rival's costumes, Diamond left Rainer the last week in December to dance for John P. Ordway's Aeolian Vocalists, the resident troupe at

Boston's Harmony Hall. The Aeolians presented a standard "middle-class" minstrel show of "White and Ethiopian" songs, but Diamond did not dress as Lucy Long for them. As female caricatures became an expected feature of minstrelsy, Diamond dropped all "wench dancing" from his repertory, although probably not out of some growing respect for women. His subsequent actions suggest he sought to embody in his dances the kind of masculinity that other men achieved through sport and combat. To that end, he danced solo in his champion dancer attire and replaced the "Plantation Dance" with "his famous Rattlesnake Jig and step dance, in which he performs 120 different steps, and defies competition with any dancer living."[79]

Between January and June 1852 Diamond infused his acts with Irish elements. "Step dance" was the Irish name for a dancing challenge. For Ordway in Boston, he performed a blackface skit with Jerry Bryant called "Grand Step Dance," which featured a match dance between the two performers. When Bryant left, Diamond danced the same act alone, giving burlesque imitations of his opponent. Across the river at Charlestown's city hall, for "Mead's [twelve] Euterpean Vocalists,"* he performed "two of his Principal Dances": "Ethiopian Jig, in which he stands unrivalled" and "Irish Jig, Introducing Rory O'More, danced only by John Diamond."[80] This addition was a smart move, as well over one-quarter of Boston's population was now Irish. Diamond "seems to have lost none of his former elasticity, or sprightliness of *heel and toe*," noted the *Boston Herald*. "This week has proved him *the* John Diamond of other days."[81] The champion "Negro" dancer revived his career by reclaiming his Irish heritage.

Greatest Dancer Living

Variety theaters and music halls gave Diamond other opportunities to reestablish his champion status. These venues differed from minstrel houses in that blackface performances represented only a fraction of their programs. In the summer of 1852 Diamond returned to New York City to work for George Lea, who had leased Charley White's Melodeon at 53 Bowery. Lea opened in June with some serenaders, several female dancers, and a ventriloquist "wizard lecturer." Diamond joined them in July, after which Lea "challenged Sliter or anybody to compete with this dancing genius." In August he added living model statuary to the show, thereby turning the Melodeon into a typical American music hall in which male patrons were entertained by mostly female performers and served by "waiter girls." Lea's

---

* The casual use of the word "Euterpean," from "Euterpe" the Greek Muse of music and lyric poetry, shows how the classics had percolated down to and through ordinary people's culture in antebellum America.

next exhibition, "Palace of Beauty," starred ballad singer Mlle Louise Jerome and the Bloomer Company, "each lady in different costume."[82]

Later in 1852 Diamond helped Charley White launch White's Varieties, his new venture on the Bowery (near Chatham Square). Diamond "made lustrous" the evenings alongside White's blackface Serenaders, the young actress Lora Gordon, and Frank Chanfrau's theatrical company.[83] In turn, White helped Diamond maintain his station. Every evening in October, White's eclectic show concluded with a grand trial dance between John Diamond and another dancer, among them the new jig-dancing prodigy Master Marks (Richard M. Carroll) (fig. 11.6).[84] Carroll became Diamond's understudy, and on those occasions "when Diamond had looked upon the wine when it was red," recollected White, Master Marks filled his shoes "most competently."[85]

Diamond looked to his friends for continued employment. That winter, he danced for former Virginia Serenader Bob Edwards, now stage manager at Philadelphia's

FIGURE 11.6. Master Marks (Richard M. Carroll) was hired by Charley White after Juba left for England in 1848. He also filled in at White's Melodeon when Diamond was too drunk to dance. His portrait demonstrates that youth continued to be a valued characteristic of champion jig dancers. *MAS.ᵀ MARKS, THE CELEBRATED DANCER*, detail from *Ethiopian Melodies of White's Serenaders* (1849), Sheet Music—Negro Minstrels. Courtesy of the American Antiquarian Society.

Masonic Hall, whose proprietor wanted to build "a good A No. 1 company of Performers, to have the best Hall, to have the best Audiences, to give better satisfaction and finally, DEFY COMPETITION."[86] On New Year's Day, he and Charles Jenkins put on a show upstairs in Trenton, New Jersey's Temperance Hall. A few months later, Diamond moved with Edwards to the Chinese Museum on George Street, where adult tickets to the lecture room cost "25 cents. Children 12½ cents," and "Boxes for Boys, 15½ cents," which meant that, for three cents more, as many boys as could fit were allowed to squeeze into a box. Edwards also touted "the only Female Serenaders in existence," Miss Lamertine and Miss Rose Taryon. While hardly the only women minstrels around, Lamertine and Taryon represented novelty in a genre now dominated by white men.[87] Diamond's appearances in variety venues rather than minstrelsy houses made him a novelty as well.

Diamond's activities after 1848 paralleled Juba's undertakings abroad. Both dancers starred for minstrel troupes, tried their hand at managing, and chose the independence of solo work. With the association between them still strong in the public mind, Rainer had presented Diamond as Lucy Long, Mead had billed him as the greatest dancer "in this or any other country," and the *Boston Herald* had declared him "without any exception the best Ethiopian Jig Dancer living." All of these acts and boasts alluded to Juba, whose absence spawned malicious rumors. Lane had stepped off the British stage at the end of 1851, and unsubstantiated reports of his demise circulated abroad. Chroniclers of minstrelsy would later claim with authority that Juba died in England during the 1851–1852 season.[88] They were wrong.

Juba Slows Down

In late 1850 Lane/Juba was in the provinces enjoying a string of engagements and favorable notices. In November he danced between the drama and the ballet at the New Theatre in Huddersfield, a small city in West Yorkshire known for social and industrial unrest. "Boz's Juba is starring here in his nigger melodies, Festival and Plantation dances, each evening during the week," announced *The Era*. "Business is great." Despite the theater setting, Juba did not court the fashionable or revive his Lucy Long. He played to the cheap seats, which were packed with male and female factory workers. "The performances of Boz's Juba have created quite a sensation in the gallery, who greeted his marvellous feats of dancing with thunders of applause, and a standing *encore*," reported the *Huddersfield Chronicle and West Yorkshire Advertiser*.[89]

In December young workers also dominated Juba's audiences at the Bermondsey Saloon in Bradford.[90] In Huddersfield these fans were confined to the balcony, but at Bermondsey the gallery gods descended to Earth. We know this because concert saloons and beer houses became the subject of campaigns for factory reform in the 1840s and the target of religious and temperance reformers in the 1850s. In nearby Leeds, for example, an investigator touring "the low places of resort of the working classes" found them "crowded with lads and girls" from the factories. Those places in which a fiddle or some other instrument was played or where a dance was held in a good-sized room upstairs "were thronged as full as they could hold." Very few of the patrons were "above 20 or 21 years of age, and most of them 16 or 17." Among them were "professed thieves" and "a sprinkling" of prostitutes, he claimed, but these were "easily distinguished from the factory-girls by their tawdry finery and the bareness of their necks."[91] England's dancing workers were Juba's peers in age and interest, if not in background.

Bradford's Bermondsey Saloon matched Sheffield's Casino and Manchester's Colosseum in size and popularity but exceeded them both in dissolution, according to visiting Baptist missionaries. The persons entering Bermondsey Saloon between 7:00 and 10:00 on one Saturday night, they reported, included "males, apparently above the age of sixteen, 491; under sixteen, 169; females, 99; total, 759." "Each person has to pay 3d. for entrance, which is returned in the shape of some kind of liquor. The consequence is, that most of the money is spent in intoxicating liquor, which, combined with the grossly immoral songs, recitations, and indecent exhibitions displayed on these occasions, are inculcating lessons, and implanting habits amongst youth of our town fearful to contemplate."[92]

As part of the entertainment, Juba figured into the indictment.[93] Yet he was a youth himself and therefore in danger of learning the same fearful lessons as his audience, for at concert rooms stage performers were expected to descend to the floor and socialize with the patrons.

Where Juba worked in January 1851 is not clear, but in February he returned to the West Midlands. He performed at the concert hall in Hanley, one of the six towns that make up the Potteries in Staffordshire.[94] Besides Juba, the only performers were Mr. Baker the Red Man of Agar, Vining the comedian, and a husband and wife who exhibited tableaux vivants using all the company as props. In smaller venues like Hanley's, which accommodated from forty to fifty people, the performers and audience were invariably on "the best of terms." Until they were summoned to appear onstage, both male and female performers were required to drink and socialize with all who invited them and when done with their act to return to the floor and mingle with the guests again. These requirements made work in concert rooms somewhat disreputable for single females, as a young woman explained to a London correspondent in Liverpool:

> Singing in such houses is hard work, and altogether our kind of life is very disagreeable. I should be glad to exchange it for any other. But what can I do? I do not know a note of music. I sing altogether by ear, and if I left my present situation, I should either have to take in needle-work, or go into the streets. At needlework I could not earn 5s. a week, and I gain 18s. a week at this. So you see it is good pay,

and though disagreeable for some reasons, it is better than needle-work, and more respectable than the streets.⁹⁵

Unlike this woman, single males like Juba may have enjoyed the stipulation that performers fraternize with the patrons. It gave a young peripatetic and possibly lonely Black dancer an opportunity to make friends. England's pottery fields and factory towns were alive with communities of competitive dancers who may have enjoyed getting to know Juba as well. When he "jumped down" from theater stages to tavern concert rooms, Juba jumped into an environment full of Irish immigrants and native-born English people who danced for fun and money.

English Challenges

Challenges published in England's sporting press offer a picture of what the competitive dancing scene was like in the regions where Juba worked. By 1850 *Bell's Life in London and Sporting Chronicle* had replaced Pierce Egan's *Life in London and Sporting Guide* as England's number one weekly sports paper. Like America's *Spirit of the Times, Bell's Life* devoted most of its pages to horse racing and other turf sports. But when the founding editor's son took over in 1852, the paper began following more working-class sports. Dancing challenges usually appeared in a short column dedicated to local matches in sports such as wrestling, curling, donkey racing, fencing, shinty, mouse singing,* skating, ploughing, and pigeon flying. The challenges and matches of more prominent regional dancers were advertised in a separate column.

Although England's dancers were dispersed across the provinces, their challenges paint a picture of tight circles of friends and competitors congregated near industrial centers. Up north, "W. Wheatler of Cassop, near Durham," challenged "any man within 50 miles" to dance "the Old English hornpipe, i.e., three steps and a half and shuffle, for £10 or £15 a side." Just south of Leeds, "William Craven of Hunslet" offered to "dance any man in Yorkshire three steps and a half and shuffle of the toe, for from £1 to £5 a side."⁹⁶ While dancers such as Wheatler and Craven made open challenges, other dancers and their seconds directed theirs at particular people: "Felix Thaker of Lane Delph has got a man named Daniel Stanfield that will dance William Harrop of Ashton-under-Lyne, for £10 or £20 a side, or any man in Ashton or the Potteries. Money ready at the Dragon Inn,

---

* "Shinty" (or "Camanachd" in Gaelic) is a Scottish game similar to hurling or field hockey. "Mouse Singing" seems to have been a form of music-making using an actual mouse: "W. Cook will sing his mouse against any other mouse, for the most changes of song, for from £1 to £5. A match can be made at Mr Wightman's, King's Arms, Notting Dale, Notting Hill" (*Bell's Life in London,* Jan. 21, 1855, 7.1).

Fenton." Thaker also offered to pay the opponent's expenses "to dance in the Potteries."[97]* If competitive dancers were at Juba's concerts, he may have engaged with them in spontaneous matches. And even if he did not, by dancing in the concert rooms of regional taverns he entered their sporting world.

A small Midlands concert hall may also have been where Juba met the woman he reportedly married. T. Allston Brown's 1912 minstrelsy chronicle claims that Juba "was married" in England "to a white woman."[98] Although scanty, evidence from Lane's years in the United Kingdom make Brown's claim seem likely. Interracial marriage was not illegal in England in the 1850s, nor was it unknown. A married man named Henry Juba appears in the census records collected on March 30, 1851, in Dudley, a large, unhealthy, slum-ridden industrial town near Birmingham. Dudley had a "Concert-Room" on Hall Street where male and female "Negro Melodists and Juba Dancers" appeared, so it is possible that Juba danced in Dudley.[99] The census lists twenty-six-year-old Henry Juba, who identified himself as a "Professor of Dancing," and his twenty-five-year-old wife, Sarah Juba, as lodgers in the home of John Preece, a tailor, and his family on King Street. The census taker listed Henry Juba's place of birth as "J Barbades" and Sarah Juba's as "n k" (not known). Lane may have taken the surname Juba and given it to his wife because that was the name he was known by in England. And he probably named the British colony Barbados as his birthplace to obtain the rights of British citizenship.[100]

Juba may have stayed close to home teaching dancing lessons for a few months after his marriage or picked up work at small houses throughout the region after leaving Hanley in February 1851. Or he might have taken up some other type of employment until mid-June, when he appeared in Birmingham. "Boz's Juba, the delineator of Negro Life and Character, is creating quite a furore" at Birmingham's Standard Concert Hall, reported *The Era* in London.[101] Juba may have been working less, but he was still national news when he played big-city venues.

African American Competition

Meanwhile, other African American performers followed Juba into Britain's entertainment circuits. In July 1851 a "celebrated Troupe of Real Sable Harmonists, consisting of seven real negroes," opened at Gothic Hall, No. 7 Haymarket, in London. The troupe traveled to England under the direction of John C. Benson, who took advantage of the crowds attending the Great Crystal Palace Exhibition of 1851 to launch their United Kingdom tour from London. Their publicity claimed that they were "Real Darkies from the South" performing entirely "new and original Negro Melodies, Quartette Choruses, Parodies from the Opera,

---

* No dancer identified himself as Black in these notices; however, Black boxers, whose "money was always ready" at one tavern or another, did make challenges in *Bell's Life*.

Burlesques, Dances, &c." In Dublin in 1852 they travestied "MONS. JULIA-ANN'S PROMENADE CONCERTS" with an "Orchestra consisting of something less than One Hundred Performers." They also played London's Royal Gardens and a number of assembly rooms and music halls before heading out to the provinces as "Mr. Henry Box Brown's troop of Sable harmonists from Vauxhall Gardens."[102]

Henry Box Brown, an African American abolitionist, lecturer, and performer, may indeed have been working in conjunction with Benson's troupe. Born enslaved in Virginia, Brown had resolved to escape to the North after his pregnant wife, Nancy, and their three children were sold to a Methodist preacher in North Carolina. In March 1849 he conspired with a Massachusetts-born white man, who, for a sum of money, agreed to ship a wooden box with Brown hiding inside to the Pennsylvania Anti-Slavery Society in Philadelphia. Following this daring escape, Brown took Box as his middle name, published his *Narrative of Henry Box Brown*, and toured New England telling his story and singing songs he had composed. In 1850 he settled in Boston and created a panorama painting that gradually unwound to reveal scenes from his personal experience and the history of the slave trade. Meanwhile, Congress passed the Fugitive Slave Act, so Brown moved to England, where he continued his performances and promoted American abolition by staging reenactments of his escape. For example, he had himself shipped in a crate from Bradford to Leeds. In 1855 Brown married Jane Floyd, the daughter of a Cornish tin worker, and in later years toured on both sides of the Atlantic in a family act with his white wife and their three children.[103]

In Dublin the Real Sable Harmonists faced more racist publicity in 1852 than Juba had in 1849: "It was little dreamt of that a trained and practiced company of real *Niggers*, with genuine woolly heads, and skins of sable that could not be washed white, could be imported from the rice and cotton fields of America, to exemplify not what the 'bondaged darkies' were like, but what they really were," declared Dublin's *Freeman's Journal*. The attention given to the troupe members' physiognomy may have stemmed from the ethnographic exhibitions of Africans that also toured London and the provinces during and after the Crystal Palace exhibition. The "musical company of real Negroes formed one of the great attractions at M. Soyer's Symposium," continued the *Freeman's Journal*, "and now, that all the world has, for a time, left London, the niggers, ever aping the fashions of the white man, have commenced a tour."[104] Ethnography ripped away the expertise of African American performers, turning them into natural history specimens and exhibits. Even a performer as revered as Juba confronted such prejudiced perceptions.

Juba's minstrelsy competition increased as well. A new dancer and blackface troupe called Rattler and the Southern Delineators debuted in Liverpool in August 1851, then followed the provincial trades and concert hall circuit pioneered by Juba. The *Liverpool Mercury* considered the show old-fashioned: "The dancer is a very curious specimen of humanity, 'half India rubber, half gutta percha,' and presents us with a humorous sort of burlesque on the poetry of motion." (Masters Diamond and Juba were also compared to rubber.) "There is nothing to offend the most delicate taste, though we cannot say we have much sympathy with the entertainment. The roars of laughter and the vehement applause gave, however, testimony that we were in a very serious minority."[105] Outside that theater, the minority opinion was spreading. "We are fond of music," acknowledged a self-appointed spokesman for London's working classes interviewed by reformer-journalist Henry Mayhew in 1851. "Nigger music was very much liked among us, but it's stale now. Flash songs are liked, and sailors' songs, and patriotic songs."[106] Despite being out of date, blackface companies persisted. As a singer and a dancer, Juba was affected by both new competition and the change in fashion.

Juba's reputation was directly challenged in Dublin in August 1851, when John Byrne's Tavern and Concert Hall announced that "T. Parkinson, a Nigger melodist and dancer, is performing here, and surpasses Juba." In September the public got to judge the truth of that statement when Juba himself arrived in Dublin.[107] For two weeks, Boz's Juba appeared at Byrne's Concert Hall alongside male and female ballad singers and dancers and a husband-and-wife-led band of instrumentalists. Neither Juba's performances nor his race were remarked upon by the press. Benson's Real Sable Harmonists followed Juba to Bryne's place in December and informed "their imitators, who use cork to black," that "they wish it to be distinctly understood, that individually or collectively, they challenge the world."[108]

Even as he stepped away from England's entertainment realm, Juba remained the measure for all "Ethiopian" dancers.[109] In October 1852 London's Royal Marylebone Theatre advertised "the great American Wonder," Richard Pelham, in "the Negro Interlude of the Masquerade Ball." Pelham played Sambo, the doorman at a millionaire's party who unknowingly admits a host of famous, fashionable, and disreputable characters.[110] The *Sunday Times* called Pelham's acting "dry, tame, and ineffective" and his dancing "a very wretched imitation of Juba's style of dancing." Pelham responded immediately in print. He was particularly miffed by the reviewer's assumption that he was a Juba imitator, stating that "he can prove by the American press the fact of his having danced before the public in his own style years before Juba was heard of."[111] Pelham had, of course, danced against Master Diamond several years before Juba was introduced to the white public. However, since then the young Black dancer had taken the art to a level the older Pelham could never reach.

Staying Abroad

Ten months after his Dublin appearance, Boz's Juba gave his last advertised performance. The occasion of his appearance was the benefit of Mr. William Brown at London's Adelphi Theatre on July 16, 1852.[112] That beneficiary may well have been the African American novelist, playwright, lecturer, and fugitive slave William Wells Brown. From 1849 to 1854 Brown toured the United Kingdom, giving hundreds of speeches describing his experience of slavery, denouncing the Fugitive Slave Act as unconstitutional, and calling for international unity among abolitionists. He also spoke of his love for his nation. Brown sailed back to America in August 1854 after his British friends raised enough money to purchase his freedom.[113] But where Juba went after July 1852 is lost to history.

William Henry Lane never returned to the United States. He may have remained in Dudley, the polluted environmental conditions destroying his health. But he probably moved to Liverpool, where he entered the fever ward at Brownlow Hill workhouse infirmary in early 1854. As England's largest west coast (transatlantic) trade and immigration port, Liverpool had absorbed people from across the globe, making it easier for Lane to blend in.

There were many reasons why a freeborn African American might choose to live out his life abroad. In the United Kingdom, Juba could journey anywhere he wished. In America, his movements would have been confined to Northern free states. In England, everyone, from the nobility to his working-class peers, respected his art. In the United States, his Blackness prevented his dances from receiving equal respect. In the United Kingdom, a Black man could ride in his own carriage with his white wife without risking his life. In America, the Fugitive Slave Act and increasing Negrophobia made every Black person vulnerable to violence. Lane did not escape racism in 1850s England, but he did escape the grimmer reality faced by Black performers back home.[114] Marginalized in England, oppressed in America, and surrounded by African American refugees, the free dancer decided to stay where he was.

These explanations are conjecture. Lane left no record of what he did after 1852 or why he did it. But that does not mean his story ended there, for even his absence had a palpable effect on challenge dancing. Despite taking place on a different continent, historical events conjoined Diamond's and Juba's destinies one more time: Back in the United States, Diamond had fought in the war that instigated the fugitive slave law that clinched Juba's decision to make England his home, thereby robbing Diamond of the only dancer he considered a worthy opponent.

12

ABOVE ALL PUNY RIVALRY

On Monday, June 20, 1853, Diamond stood uncharacteristically still at the front of a deep stage. He was backed by a small contingent of young men, all of them facing three tiers of packed seats at Baltimore's Holliday Street Theater. Outside, torrents of rain, flashes of lightning, and mutterings of thunder bombarded the roads and sidewalk awnings. Inside, Baltimore's Independent Fire Company had interrupted the evening's program to award Diamond "a splendid belt, with a silver plate" for being the "Champion Jig Dancer of the World." To gratify his friends, Diamond donned the belt and launched into his "Champion Jig."[1]

Three blocks away, at the Baltimore Museum, Dick Sliter opened with Sam Sanford's New Orleans Opera Troupe billed as "the Greatest Dancer in the World." That claim appeared in advertisements and the museum's program, which stated that Sliter had won the "Dancer's Champion Belt" in Cincinnati after a trial of skill with Diamond. "That assertion . . . is a paltry evasion of truth," countered an appalled Diamond in the *Baltimore Sun* the following week. "I danced with Mr. Sliter in Cincinnati while he had an Ethiopian Company, five evenings, *for which I received FIFTY DOLLARS*. NO ALLUSION WAS EVER MADE TO A BELT, OR DID WE EVER DANCE FOR ONE." Provoked by what he called the "Cincinnati fabrication," Diamond then issued Sliter a challenge: "I WILL DANCE WITH HIM AT ANY HALL IN THE CITY. . . . The Dances are: TWO 'JIGS,' TWO 'REELS,' and a 'WALK AROUND,' the victor to receive the BELTS and the WAGER that may be decided upon." He signed his letter "Respectfully, JOHN DIAMOND," then added a postscript in boxing parlance: "This is plain, blunt and palpable. So come up to the scratch."[2]

Diamond turned twenty-eight the year he received his champion belt. He had been on the stage for fourteen years. Professional longevity impacted his dancing career. He was well known and respected, but he was aging as a dancer. Structural forces also impinged upon his life and art. Economic hard times, vast Irish immigration, capitalist production, and political agitation over slavery were altering the society that had supported his style of dance, the venues in which he performed, and the meaning of his jigs. But rather than accepting comedic blackface dance as his next step, he leaned into his renown as a challenge dancer and eked out a living without wagering a penny.

At Ford's Theatre

Diamond found an advocate in John T. Ford, manager of the Holliday Street Theatre. Something of a prodigy, the twenty-four-year-old Ford had already developed a successful strategy for attracting audiences to his theaters (fig. 12.1). He engaged an established star as his chief attraction, created an appealing environment for middle-class audiences, remained open after competing theaters had closed for the season, and encouraged controversy in the press.[3] Diamond gave him plenty of material to work with.

Most theaters went dark in the summer, but the acquisition of Diamond enabled Ford to keep his doors open. He designed his ads to appeal to different classes of theatergoers. To attract respectable middle-class people, Ford needed to establish his playhouse as socially above reproach. To that end, he referred to the theater's minstrels, Kunkel's Nightingales, as "talented and gentlemanly" and to Diamond as "an Artiste," "the very first of American dancers," "the highly distinguished Dancer," and "the professor of his art." After Diamond arrived, Ford also promised there would be "polite ushers in attendance." (He did not post the

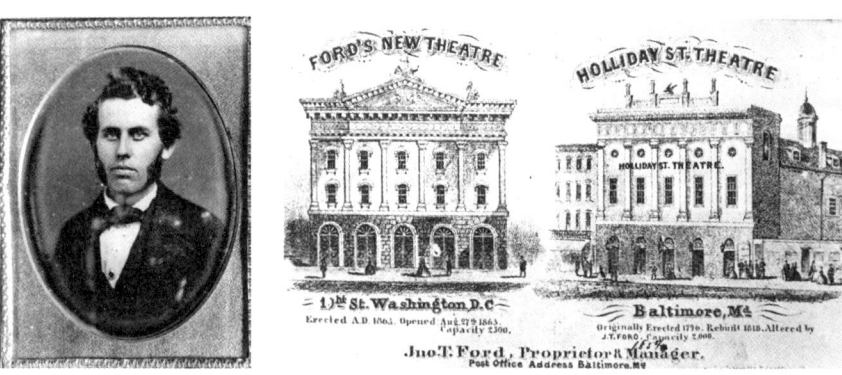

FIGURE 12.1. Diamond received his "Champion Jig Dancer of the World" belt at Holliday Street Theatre in Baltimore. The theater's young proprietor, John T. Ford, would operate several theaters during his lifetime, including the Ford's Theatre in Washington, DC, where President Lincoln was assassinated in 1865. *John T. Ford* and *Ford's New Theatre (Washington, D.C.) Holliday St. Theatre (Baltimore, Md.)*. National Park Service.

more usual and alarming statement: "An efficient police will be in attendance to preserve strict order.")[4]

Despite a month of pelting storms, an animated assembly of "fashion and beauty" attended Ford's theater every night in May and June to witness "the Nightingales and that master spirit of Terpsichore, Mr. Diamond."[5] No one was dissuaded from attending. Admission was twenty-five cents for all, except "gentlemen to the dress circle, unaccompanied by ladies," who had to pay an extra twelve and a half cents. The third tier had been "elegantly refined and enlarged" to accommodate "the respectable Colored residents of Baltimore who wish to witness the entertainments." (Newspaper advertisements for the theater's new "Colored Dress Circle" and for slave sales were printed on the same pages of the *Baltimore Sun*, a not uncommon juxtaposition in slave states with large free Black populations.) Everyone found "the Invincible Dancer" pleasurable and inoffensive. "Even the ladies applauded his inimitable dancing," noted the *Sun* on May 27, encouraging Ford to offer matinees "for the accommodation of children and ladies unable to attend at night."[6] Diamond danced every performance that season, enabling him to later brag that he had danced his champion jig in Baltimore for 130 consecutive nights.[7]

To attract Baltimore's sporting community, Ford's advertisements reproduced Diamond's confrontational lingo and radical claims. "After an absence of seven years, MR. DIAMOND returns to Baltimore with as an extensive a fame as a WONDERFUL DANCER, As an Artiste, that ever appeared before an American public. He now stands ABOVE ALL PUNY RIVALRY, as the very greatest of that class of Dancing which is PURELY AMERICAN. As Jig Dancing originated in this Country." The words written in uppercase letters were not randomly chosen. They painted a portrait of Diamond as a refined, trash-talking, nationalist figure.

The dancer walked the line between the ethereal and the material in his publicity. Diamond's dances are "neat, clean and graceful, combining, *with extraordinary muscle*, elegance and dexterity," reported the *Sun*. "The ease and elegance of his movements *defy competition*, all who see him admit his superiority."[8] Notwithstanding the elegance of his art, Diamond saw himself first and foremost as a superior athlete whose jig dancing deserved the accolades and awards given to the most manly of contestants. His opponents were "puny" weaklings in comparison. Insulting or boastful speech intended to demoralize one's opponents was the lingua franca of masculine sports. In the absence of Juba, Diamond's competition on the dance floor seemed paltry.

What Diamond did when not onstage is mostly a mystery. However, the final phrase of his ad suggests he was acquainted with the proponents of workingmen's politics and the Young America cohort of passionately democratic writers (journeymen turned journalists such as Irish-born Mike Walsh and American-born Walt Whitman) intent on creating a new self-consciously "American" literature.[9]

When Diamond called jig dancing "purely American" he identified his art with that movement, thereby appealing to that contingent in his audience.

It is also noteworthy that he called his "class of Dancing" simply "jig dancing" rather than "Negro" or "Ethiopian" dancing. His dancing "originated in this Country," but not as a blackface enactment of middle-class racial fantasies. It encompassed the sport as practiced by working-class Irish Americans and African Americans, whom nativism and Negrophobia were alienating in the 1850s. This understanding of the term "jig dancing" helps explain Diamond's response to Sliter's counterchallenge.

Counterchallenge

Although in the end Diamond and Sliter would not face off, a close reading of their newspaper challenge illuminates the significance of Diamond's champion belt and the way blackface minstrelsy undermined challenge dancing's reputation as a serious sport. Sliter's "Challenge Accepted" notice appeared in the same issue of the *Sun* as Diamond's challenge: "Having noticed in the papers of this city a CHALLENGE . . . of from ONE HUNDRED to ONE THOUSAND DOLLARS to embrace TWO JIGS, TWO REELS, and a WALK AROUND . . . I hereby respectfully accept the same on the following conditions and specifications, to wit That the Dance shall consist exclusively of Jigs, or else extend to the entire professional ability of the competitors."[10] Sliter's terms were meant to tip the balance of the competition in his favor. Every challenge dancer developed a repertory of dances with which he became identified. Diamond excelled at jigs and reels, but his real forte was the intricate downbeats and syncopations of percussive hornpipes (called "walk-arounds" in the States). He therefore named all three dances in his challenge. Sliter was also an expert at "Ethiopian" jigs. But in 1853 his specialty was wench dancing. In fact, his advertisements in the *Baltimore Sun* read: "R. H. SLITER, the Champion Dancer of the World—who will imitate all the celebrated female dancers who have appeared in this country."[11] So Sliter countered that he would accept Diamond's challenge so long as they danced only jigs or opened it up to every dance in the profession, meaning wench dancing.

Diamond had danced the Black *bayadère* for Barnum and performed Lucy Long for Raynor's company, but wench dancing was no longer in his repertory. Nor did he consider such "character dances" as challenge dance material. On the night of the belt presentation, Diamond performed his "Champion Jig," "Inimitable Drumming Feat," and "Cotton Pod Reel," and Tom Moxley (a.k.a. Master Floyd) appeared as Miss Fanny in "Lucy Long."[12] If Diamond agreed to dance only jigs, his "Cotton Pod Reel" and "Drumming Feat" would have been excluded. And if the dances were extended to the competitors' "entire professional ability," Sliter's female imitations would have changed the judging criteria, making humor and novelty as important as speed, dexterity, and numerical advantage in the decision. Diamond responded by calling Sliter's terms "a subterfuge" gotten up to hide his deficiencies and save his "sinking fortunes." Jigs, reels, and walk-arounds are "dances we both do every night and belong legitimately to the Ethiopian Business," he reminded Sliter. "I reiterate my challenge, and dare him to an open and fair trial. If he is the victor, my be[l]t is his."[13]

In his initial challenge, Diamond underscored the difference between dancing for wagers and dancing for wages. Both could provide a dancer with much-needed income, but more was at stake in the former. Diamond refused to consider his Cincinnati trial of skill with Sliter a dancing match because Sliter paid him ten dollars a night to dance and because no belt had been mentioned. In a similar scenario, jig dancer Mickey Warren indignantly pulled out of a dancing tournament after the organizer asked if he "would be satisfied to take $20" in lieu of the publicized prize: a gold watch. Warren considered the switch "a complete swindle," explained fellow jig dancer Hank Mason. "Had the prizes been there Mr. Warren would have competed for them, as he is, and was, ready to dance any man in the United States for $300 or $500."[14] Wagers and matches represented more than income to jig dancers. They measured the contender's social and cultural worth. "I will pay FIFTY DOLLARS for *Proof* of the triumph of Mr. Sliter over me in Cincinnati," Diamond vowed, "or for the evidence of our dancing for a belt."[15]

By staking his belt along with the monetary wager, Diamond vouched for the sincerity of his challenge and the authenticity of the coming match. Champion belts were invented by boxing enthusiasts. With no sports federation behind them, boxers (and dancers) received belts paid for by local subscribers, who designated the boxer champion of a particular city or state. The national belt was also an unofficial production. In July 1842 the *New York Sporting Whip* announced that "five dollars will be given for the best design for the [boxing] Champion Belt of America; to be purely American in its bearing; and the ornamental part to be characteristic." "Lovers of the Ring" in New York City wanted a symbol of prestige to uplift the sport in their country. The next week they opened the subscription for donations.[16]

Awarded after a series of matches or at special ceremonies honoring the competitor's career, regional champion belts were valuable objects made with precious metals by skilled artisans. They were also nontransferable. In other words, the belt's owner decided whether or not to stake his (or her) belt in a bout. Conversely, a national or "world" champion belt was transferred. Unlike city or state champion belts, the national belt moved from champion to champion. In 1842, when Ben Caunt wore the Champion of England belt for prizefighting, William Thompson (a.k.a. Bendigo) challenged him to a match, adding that he possessed "a belt which he will tie to the stakes against the transferable Champion's Belt, and fight Caunt for the brace of them."[17] Bendigo's city belt was like any wager or prize in that it belonged to the athlete awarded it, whereas Caunt's championship belt belonged to whoever was champion at the time.

Champion jig dancers, female and male, adopted this boxing belt tradition. When Naomi Porter accepted Julia Morgan's challenge in Boston in 1862, she proposed that instead of the $100 to $500 stake they "dance for a SILVER CHAMPION BELT, of the value of $100, to be awarded the winner" of three out of five dances in a match extending over five evenings. When the match took place, Morgan danced as the "Boston Pet" and Porter as the "New York Favorite," thereby turning the match into a national championship and rendering the belt transferable.[18]

Diamond followed this precedent when he proposed that both his belt and Sliter's be added to the wager. Diamond's silver belt had been paid for and awarded by Baltimore's firemen, who designated him "Champion Dancer of the World" in honor of his almost fifteen-year competitive dancing career. They also saw the dancer as representing their interests. Diamond had regularly volunteered at fundraisers for firefighters, including a benefit for Baltimore's Independent Fire Company in May.[19] As the most long-term and loyal portion of his audience, firefighters assumed the right to award the belt. Sliter claimed to have received his "Dancer's Champion Belt" from the citizens of Cincinnati. However, each dancer considered his own the championship belt and the other's a local champion's belt. So Diamond suggested they dance for the two belts and a wager, after which there would be no mistaking who wore the championship belt.

Sliter's counterchallenge authorized Sam Sanford to act as his "agent to settle the preliminaries for said contest." Diamond was to meet Sanford the following afternoon at the Baltimore Museum to decide where to hold the match, settle the amount of the wager, and deposit their forfeits. Diamond had offered to dance against Sliter at any hall in the city, but "not in the museum, to fill the coffers of his manager." He knew what happened when managers rather than dancers controlled the division of the proceeds. Ford's theater had greater seating capacity than the museum to be sure, but Diamond also refused to dance there out of fairness to his opponent.[20]

All dancing matches were entertainments, got up to draw in spectators who would spend money on entrance fees, drinks, food, or bets. The differences between a trial of skill and a real match were the risks taken by the performers. To demonstrate they were serious, contestants who made a match had to forfeit a portion of the stakes in advance as a deposit. If one of them failed to put his money down, he was pronounced a braggart and not taken seriously.[21] *New York Clipper* editor Frank Queen put it like this: "If both parties mean match making, they can have no objection to making a show of the dimes, before making a show of themselves."[22]

But instead of negotiating with Diamond at the proposed afternoon meeting, Sanford placed a "CARD" in the *Sun* complaining that "some malicious scamps of no character" had defamed his reputation by accusing his company of assuming the names of Rainer's New Orleans Serenaders and lying about Sliter's champion belt. He also scoffed at Diamond's allegation that holding the match at the museum would simply amount to putting money in Sanford's purse. Such a statement "comes with a very bad grace and shows the ingratitude of *certain individuals who have themselves been the recipients of my charity when in a state of destitution*," confided Sanford. His "liberality" was "too well known to be questioned," he added, as was his opposition to schemes got up solely for the purpose of money making: "If the parties challenging wish to test their skill with my Troupe, or Mr. Sliter, a wager may be made, and I will guarantee to give the proceeds to the poor." However, "I will not desert my Hall. My Troupe is there, and may be found when wanted."[23]

Indignant at having been played, Diamond redirected his challenge to Sanford, daring him to prove his "reckless" assertion that Sliter had won the "Dancer's Champion Belt" in Cincinnati. "I declare such an intimation unfounded in truth, and ... to show my confidence in your equivocations, and my own truthfulness, I will deposit $50 in the hands of any prominent man, if you will do the same, and if we never danced for a Belt, your money shall be divided among the Orphan Asylums. If, on the contrary, we [did,] then mine shall be divided. Now, sir, this is plain. *Face the music*, or retract your insinuations."[24]

Ford defended Diamond in the following day's *Sun*. He chided Sanford for "blowing his own trumpet" as a philanthropist and in the same breath reproaching Diamond for accepting his benevolence. "With Mr Sanford's charities, or Mr Diamond's destitution, I have nothing to do, nor will I make a *display of that virtue which loses its sacredness by being trumpeted*. This much in justice to Mr. Diamond I will say, that when ... he returned [from the Mexican War] he was penniless in pocket and much injured in health, now, if destitution is crime, John Diamond, is criminal."[25] Having exposed Sanford's ploy to turn Diamond and Sliter's match into a mere speculation and Diamond into a bum, Ford then bowed to Sanford's suggestion that Baltimore audiences judge the qualities of each troupe in their separate venues.

On June 28 an ad in the *Sun* used a play on words to inform the public that Diamond and Sliter had not come to terms: "The champion Dancer, the REAL Diamond, Will give his Famous Reel, That acknowledges no MATCH."[26] The 1853 challenge was not the first time Sliter had tried to piggyback on Diamond's fame. After their trial dance in 1850, Sliter's publicity claimed that he could "outdance John Diamond."[27] Unprovoked, Diamond had ignored him. And when Diamond was in Buffalo in 1851, Sliter tried again to make a match. "Those 'mysterious rappers' with the heel and toe, John Diamond and 'our own' Dick Sliter, are kicking up considerable ... dust at Rochester," reported the *Buffalo Daily Republic*. (The clairvoyant "table-rapper" Miss Martha Loomis was also in town.) "A challenge has been given and accepted by these champions of loose joints, and a regular break down is to decide to which dancer belongs the victor's laurels."[28] No match followed, exposing the announcement as a fishing expedition. "We have no knowledge that John Diamond and Dick Sliter ever danced a match dance together," Frank Queen, editor of the *New York Clipper*, told a reader in 1858, "and those who are 'in the business' say they never did."[29]

The *New York Clipper* became America's most popular weekly sporting journal after its founding in April 1853. Modeled on *Bell's Life in London*, the *Clipper* covered all kinds of games and sports, accompanied by biographical sketches of sportsmen and actors. Dancing matches were not as numerous as prizefights or pedestrian races in the journal, but editor Queen treated them exactly like other sports. He printed challenges made by dancers or their sponsors in the "Challenges" column (or, if overseas, in "Sports Abroad"), published letters negotiating the terms of matches, publicized and covered important face-offs, and recorded results. Queen also held the stakes for competitors, answered readers' queries regarding champion dancers, printed letters disputing results, and denounced "humbug" or fixed matches. Before the advent of sports associations, the *Clipper* acted as sounding board and arbiter for all sporting matters.

No one minded that a number of cities (and minstrel troupes) claimed champion dancers, but the national title—whatever that might be—became a contentious issue after Diamond challenged Sliter. With no institution to back their claim, any dancer could adopt the moniker Champion Dancer of the World. And several did. "This championship of jig dancing reminds me of an article in the CLIPPER last winter, in relation to the [boxing] championship . . . between Morrissey, the Benicia Boy, and Hyer," confessed jig dancer Hank Mason in 1858. "They all three claimed the championship, but neither one had the honor of contesting for it." "The only man who ever wore a champion belt in this country for jig and reel dancing was Master John Diamond, who is now deceased," insisted Mason, "unless others purchased them for themselves privately."[30]

It is possible that Diamond and Sliter's contention was staged from the beginning as mutual publicity. But more likely, Sliter and Sanford saw no professional benefit in dancing a match under Diamond's terms. In the end, each dancer kept his belt. Diamond's belt was never transferred, nor was his American champion title.[31] Sliter lost his belt to "Champion Prize Dancer" Joe Brown in 1856.[32] Brown took the belt and the title "Champion Dancer of the World" to England in 1857, whereupon he was immediately challenged by the Lancashire champion John Booth for assuming the international title without dancing for it.[33]

Artiste-Athlete

After his encounter with Sliter, Diamond cultivated the dual identity of artiste-athlete. Industrialization had just begun to divide working people into distinct classes by separating mental work (design) from manual work (execution).

Diamond straddled that boundary. In August 1853 he danced at the Odd Fellows Hall in Washington, DC, during a spate of hot weather that prompted the proprietor to provide the audience with ice water and fans during Diamond's performance. He called the dancer an "astonishing artiste," while reviews of the show underscored his physicality. "John Diamond surpassed himself in his really surprising feats," reported the *Evening Star*: "Such a toe-tapping, heel-rapping, foot-battling, floor and drum-rattling . . . must satisfy the most fastidious admirer of the dance-ethiopian or athlete."[34] Diamond's dancing satisfied two classifications: art ("dance-ethiopian") and labor ("athlete").

Diamond's new signature step added to his dual allure. In the 1840s Master Diamond was associated with the quirkily rhythmed "Camp Town Hornpipe," a dance tune of Black and Celtic heritage. That tune (which had no lyrics) fit the energetic dancing style that he and Juba developed as boys. But 1850s audiences were less attuned to instrumental dance music. Diamond's new signature dance became "Wait for the Wagon," a popular "Ethiopian" song with a catchy tune, inoffensive lyrics, and a simple $\frac{2}{4}$ (hornpipe) rhythm that provided unobtrusive support for his fancy footwork. "Diamond's dances are really elegant," reported the *Boston Investigator*, "particularly his 'Wait for the Wagon.'" That song moved easily between settings. At New York's National Theatre, for example, Diamond danced it as part of "a Parlor Entertainment."[35]

Economic downturns impacted entertainers like Diamond no less than other workers. Unemployment rose in Northern cities after 1853 as America's financial markets began a precipitous decline. In 1854 Diamond performed with a cast of unknowns at Newark, New Jersey's Washington Hall Theatre, splitting the entr'actes and sharing benefit nights with two other dancers, a Miss Harrison and a Mr. J. S. Turner.[36] He also appeared in a number of grand prize concerts (for "Eighty Dollars worth of Jewelry") put on by a troupe called the Minstrel Brothers. These engagements seem a bit of a comedown. Diamond was bellwether to a new cohort of dancer-athletes who challenged each other in the *Clipper* but whose daily bread-and-butter depended on work provided by theaters and minstrel troupes.

To distinguish himself in a market saturated with minstrelsy, Diamond led with his athletic foot. "John is to dance a fancy jig, 'Wait for the Wagon,' which gained for him a Silver Belt in Baltimore, and gave him the title of Champion Dancer," announced the *Boston Investigator* on Diamond's return to Ordway Hall in May 1854. "He will wear the belt during his dances." That champion belt and its fire company provenance became integral to Diamond's promotional and personal identity. "None can say they do not get their money's worth at Ordway's," the *Boston Herald* reassured its hard-up readers, where every night for three months the program included Ordway's Aeolians, John Diamond in his "splendid" belt, comedian Eph Horn, and Juba's former partner Tom Briggs on banjo. In July

Diamond danced at Briggs and Horn's farewell benefit "previous to their California tour," then moved to Purdy's National Theater. Meanwhile, Briggs took sick on the road to California and was unable to play. He died in San Francisco on October 23, 1854, at age thirty, leaving behind a score of dance tunes, an unpublished banjo primer, and an unsullied reputation as a fine, sober fellow.[37]

New Partners and Opponents

Among Diamond's opponents that year was a Native American dancer named Okatewaula. In November Diamond danced at the Howard Athenaeum in Boston, a variety house that presented plays and farces, bel canto operas, operatic ballets, and a range of specialty acts, including a sparring exhibition accompanied by orchestral music. Two companies dominated the entertainments that month: Professor Risley and his "Family" of acrobats, including the "Infant Prodigy" (rolled into a ball), whom Risley juggled with his feet, and the Monasco Indian Troupe of "Real Indian Performers," who exhibited tribal "Manners, Rites, Customs, Ceremonies, Indian Tragedies, Historic Scenes, Scalpings, Rejoicings, Burlesques, and all of the Indian Dances."[38] Diamond joined the Native Americans' show.

Native dancers had been touring the country for over a decade. In 1843 Barnum hired "5 Indians, 2 squaws, and a little [papoose] five or six years old besides the interpreter" to dance in his museum.[39] The Monasco Indian Troupe, one of several Native American companies that predated Buffalo Bill's Wild West Show, had been performing under a large pavilion for several years. They entered towns and cities in a circus-like parade, the chiefs and their warriors "riding through the streets on horseback, dressed in their Indian Costume, painted and fully equipped for war," preceded by the Monasco Brass Band.[40] The performers numbered from eight to ten in total—two women, six men, and one or two stars, all hailing from tribes and nations in the Nebraska Territory and west of the Rocky Mountains. In August their show featured "the celebrated Indian chief, Kawshawgance, from the Walaitpu nation, accompanied by Okatewaula, a chief from the Callapoohas tribe."* Kaw-shaw-gance was an Indian orator who had been educated "*at the first schools in the states*" and who acted as master of ceremonies. The company maintained that their performances were "not for speculation, but for the purpose of procuring means to complete the education of this family of Aborigines."[41]

Okatewaula's style of dance is impossible to recreate, but it may have included a circular stomping motion to signify "flattening the grass," by which a dancer produced a stage for his performance.[42] Wal-ait-pu was the Native American name

---

* Their early appearance suggests they wore their native garb rather than the generic "Indian chief" outfit worn by Buffalo Bill's performers and adopted by whites "playing Indian."

for Cayuse, an Indian nation in what is now eastern Oregon. White Protestants established a mission among the Cayuse at Waiilatpu (Place of the Rye Grass) in 1838. Callapoohas was an alternative spelling for Kalapooya/Kalapuya, a tribe from southwestern Oregon. The ritual traditions of the Kalapuya people included dances celebrating catching salmon, preparing for war, and receiving dream gifts. When someone dreamed of something repeatedly, that person would sing it in front of the people, recalled one tribal member, and "if the song good enough, the people dance with it for five nights." Or a dream spirit would give a child a song, chant, or dance that they would share with their village.[43] Okatewaula, who may have been one of those gifted dreamers, would later lead his own troupe of Native dancers.[44]

The Native American entertainers at Boston's Athenaeum added three new features to their show after Diamond arrived: "Target Shooting" for "a *Gold Watch*," "shooting an apple from the head of Okatewaula," and "JOHN DIAMOND and OKATEWAULA in a Match Dance."[45] "Two of the greatest dancers in the world are announced this evening," reported the *Boston Herald* with enthusiasm on November 8. This program was sure to draw audiences. Indian removal and extermination had made Native Americans a rare sight on the East Coast, causing many whites to conclude that Indians were becoming extinct. People were therefore curious to see their "vanishing" culture. And even audiences who had already seen the Monasco troupe returned to witness "the well-known" John Diamond face off with "the ninth wonder," Okatewaula.

There were historical precedents for bringing together jig dancers and Native American dancers. Music-making and dancing (which Native Americans imbued with political, social, and spiritual value) figured into the trade networks of tribal nations.[46] Whites seeking sovereignty in the West took advantage of this Indian practice. During their reconnaissance of the Louisiana Purchase in 1805, Lewis and Clark sent fiddle players and jig dancers into Mandan villages to begin détente with their chiefs. "I found them much pleased at the Danceing of our men," Clark wrote in his diary. "I ordered my black Servent to Dance which amused the Croud verry much, and Some what astonished them, that So large a man Should be [so] active."[47] Enslaved African and Native tribal people traded and adopted each other's and their oppressors' music and dance. As late as the 1930s, the enslaved son of a "full-blood African" father and "pure-blood Indian" mother remembered the dance tune "Fisher's Hornpipe"* as "an Indian song" whistled by his Choctaw mother when she was angry.[48] Thus were hornpipes merged with Choctaw identity, and "Kitefoot shuffles" incorporated into set dances at Raynor's tavern, and the different flat-foot reels of Okatewaula and Diamond compared in Boston.

---

* Link to "Fisher's Hornpipe": http://www.youtube.com/watch?v=6NyJRohR3Po.

No follow-up of the November match appeared in the papers, suggesting its function was to draw spectators, not determine a winner. But Diamond revealed something about himself by dancing the match, even if it was a money-making gimmick. Master Diamond's stage debut had been filling the interludes of the anti-Indian drama *Nick of the Woods*. This staged competition placed Diamond on a par with Okatewaula and vice versa and for one night at least made jig dancing commensurate with Indian dancing.[49] Yet it also erased one incommensurable aspect of each man's dance: its vernacular meaning, thereby reducing both to entertainment for an uninformed audience.

Best in His Line

The 1854–1855 season was bad for all theaters. "Signs of distress were quite visible at the Bowery—as at the National, when a circus invaded the precincts of the drama," lamented an early New York stage historian.[50] Diamond worked in New York most of 1855. At Charley White's Opera House in February and March, he danced solo and in trials of skill opposite Irish American jig dancer Mickey Warren as an extra attraction. Warren figured prominently in the circle of professionals and amateurs who made and accepted challenges in the *New York Clipper*. Diamond did not publish challenges in the *Clipper*, nor was he ever challenged in its pages. When a correspondent asked the *Clipper*, "Is John Diamond the best dancer in New York?" the "Recognized Sporting Journal of America" responded that "in his particular line we believe he is."[51] In April Diamond and a male-female duo danced in their "particular modes" at Purdy's National Theatre, and in May he returned to White's Opera House, where Charley paired him with the veteran actor T. D. Rice as "the greatest Ethiopian features in existence." But by the 1850s "Jim Crow" had become "a relic of former popularity," reducing Rice to "a filler-in."[52] Only Diamond was retained.

Diamond survived that summer by reeling from one New York venue to another.[53] Anticipating the winter season, in late August he journeyed back to Philadelphia, where he found his former partner-opponent James Sanford sick and disheveled in the Blockley Almshouse. Sanford died on September 2, 1855, at age forty-one.[54]

Hard times forced even former enemies to make peace. Toward the end of September, Diamond worked for the other Sanford, who had just completed the construction of a "burlesque opera house" in downtown Philadelphia. Like other theater owners, Sam Sanford had to look for ways to keep his business afloat during the financial downturn. As soon as his doors opened on September 20, Sanford ran advertisements informing "Associations, &c. desirous of having Benefits" that they could hire his establishment and blackface troupe on reasonable terms by "applying to the Box Office" and that he had secured Diamond's services for a "brief season." Sanford sublet his opera house for a benefit to aid sufferers of yellow fever in Norfolk and Portsmouth, Virginia, on Friday, September 28, but the animosity between Diamond and Sanford had not abated, and the "far-famed . . . Star Dancer" cut his engagement down to one night.[55]

Diamond spent the next few months working for Sanford's competition. In October the Southwark Opera House on Second Street was opened by Diamond's friends from former times: Henry Mestayer (who also deserted Sanford), Bob Sheppard, and their minstrel troupe. In November Bob Edwards took over as manager and engaged Diamond as the headliner for his minstrelsy and variety show.[56] Every Southwark advertisement identified Diamond as "Champion Dancer of the World."

That all-encompassing title was observed by an immigrant dancer in Philadelphia. In March of the previous year, Phil Gannon had introduced himself to the American public through a challenge in the *New York Clipper*: "The undersigned will dance any man or boy one Irish Jig and one Irish Reel, single, double, or treble, in public or in private, for the sum of One Thousand Dollars. Money and man ready at T. Scroggy's Segar store, 443 Vine street, Philadelphia. P. J. Gannon, *Champion Dancer of Ireland*."[57] By July 1855 Gannon was well-enough known to receive a grand testimonial benefit at the Baltimore Museum, where he was billed as "the young *Comedian and Champion Terpsichorean Artist*."[58]

Immigrant dancers like Gannon reconfigured the composition of American challenge dancing. For example, in answer to an open challenge made by Dick Sliter in the *Clipper* in 1856, Mickey Warren stated that he would dance a match with Sliter "for from $100 to $500. The dance to be a jig, straight reel, Irish reel and Irish jig. What says Sliter?"[59] By adding Irish steps to his challenge, Warren added immigrant dancers and spectators to his supporters.

Phil Gannon tried to enter the top ranks of America's jig dancers by announcing that he and Diamond would hold "a Match Dance for a Silver Goblet" at Philadelphia's Assembly Buildings on November 26, 1855. The Irish champion may have intended that declaration to serve as a challenge, or he invoked Diamond's name as a publicity stunt. Either way, he misjudged his mark. That very day, Diamond published his own "Notice to the Public" in the *Ledger*: "Seeing my name posted through the city, for the benefit of a Mr. GANNON, and not having given my consent, this is to certify that I will not appear on any such occasion. JOHN DIAMOND, Southwark Opera House."[60] As the recognized champion, Diamond could refuse a challenge without losing caste. He was not averse to dancing with newcomers, although he may have been wary of facing a dancer whose steps were unfamiliar to him. More importantly, he expected competition protocol to be followed.

Dancing for Boxers

Diamond and Gannon may have met before, since both belonged to Philadelphia's overlapping boxing and dancing community, which encompassed American-born and immigrant athletes. In the spring of 1856 Diamond circulated in that community rather than performing onstage.[61] In February he danced at boxer Matthias "Matt" Rusk's sparring exhibition at Franklin Hall. On that occasion, "Rusk set to with a young American, J.B.B.," and offered to spar "in a friendly manner with any gentleman" present, after which the "champion dancers" John Diamond and William Sparks exhibited their sport.[62] Gannon would dance at Franklin Hall in February 1857 at a benefit for boxer "Young Bendigo," where the participants hailed from America, Wales, Belfast, and southern Ireland.

Correlations between the two sports became more pronounced in the 1850s. Both boxers and dancers gave themselves aliases and regional affiliations. "The Center Market Novice"; Dan Smith, a.k.a. "Young Bendigo"; and "Scotty of Brooklyn" were boxers. "Hank the Mason"; Johnny West, a.k.a. "Young America"; and Michael Cunningham, "better known as the Albany Fat Boy," were dancers.[63] They wore similar outfits onstage and in the ring: black shoes, white stockings, short pants, and champion belts (fig. 12.2). Both camps made challenges, held matches, and exhibited their champion moves in public venues. And both considered body size when making a match. New York "Light Weight" Johnny West, for example, specifically challenged "any boy of 90 lbs . . . to dance a 40 stepped Jig, on time, for any amount they wish to stake."[64]

Professional and journeyman dancers exhibited their art at boxing events. What's more, some boxers danced! African American sportsman Aaron Molineaux danced his "great Decanter Dance" for the boxer J. E. Taylor's benefit in Boston in 1854 and at exhibitions held in his own establishment, Molineaux's Gymnasium, in Worcester, Massachusetts, in 1856. A century later, heavyweight boxer Muhammad Ali would include dancing footwork in his training regime. After jig dancers Mickey Warren and Hank Mason performed for the crowd at boxer Barney Aaron's sparring exhibition, the pugilists Johnny Aaron and Johnny Sweetman joined them in "a regular Virginny breakdown." According to the *New York Herald*, "The pugs seemed to be as much at home with their feet as their fists."[65]

A newspaper account of Young Bendigo's benefit made it plain that dancers and boxers were cut from the same cloth. According to "George," who covered the event for the *Clipper*, the fourth sparring match that night was "a teaser, hot and heavy. . . . They are both good hitters and quick on their legs, and made a good display." Gannon came next. He "danced a jig in very good style. It was encored, and he repeated the operation in a hornpipe style, and in good taste, as to time and steps. Hugh Smith followed in a jig, [and] a hornpipe, both well danced, and

FIGURE 12.2. Like boxers, competitive jig dancers wore black shoes, white stockings, short pants, and, if winners, a champion belt. The female champion's costume echoed the male's, except for its lace-trimmed trousers, which fulfilled expectations regarding femininity. *A Striking view of Richmond,* 1810, New York Public Library Digital Collections; *Frank Converse and Tommy Peel,* MS Thr 1848, box 27, folder 30 (Mixed Materials), Houghton Library, Harvard University; *Kitty O'Neil, Celebrated Jig Dancer,* ca. 1870, box 67, Series II: Actors, Card Photograph Collection, Performing Arts Collection, Harry Ransom Center, University of Texas at Austin.

in a remarkably easy manner." Two more sparring matches followed the dancing, then Gannon's pupil Master Warren "came forward and danced a jig. . . . [H]e really did remarkable well. . . . [B]efore long 'Jack will be as good as his master.'" The next two boxers' "showings" were "well-given": "Hit and hit, first one, then the other. . . . [I]t was rat-a-tat-tat on both sides." Gannon sang two Irish songs between those matches. Then came the evening's "wind-up," a boxing "set-to" between the beneficiary and Mr. Lee of South Wales, who "in our opinion, was overmatched."[66] Clearly, "George" and the others present felt comfortable judging boxing *and* dancing for themselves.

The journeyman's league of challenge dancers included "some noted Jig Dancers ['all very good'] who were well known to the community but never figured much professionally," recalled a *Clipper* editor some years later.[67] Diamond's partner-opponents in 1856 belonged to that list. In April he danced "a Trial Jig Dance" with Bob Dudley (Dudly) in Baltimore at a "Grand Festival. Equestrian, Dramatic and Musical" that included a firefighter's one-mile race against time. German American Dudley, who had volunteered the previous week for the Independent Fire Company's benefit at the Holliday Street Theatre, may have been a firefighter himself.[68] By choosing Dudley, William Sparks, and other local champions as his partner-opponents, Diamond satisfied a desire for peer-group approval. The sporting community also provided him with much-needed employment during the economic downturn.

Female Champions

One large group of dancers unable to exploit the sports world in 1856 was women. Jig dancing was not a particularly boyish or girlish activity when done as an amusement. But when a game entered the realm of sports, the male sex claimed it. Sports gave men of different ethnicities and classes an arena in which to unite and compete.[69] But nonwhites remained on the fringes of the circle, and a class hierarchy persisted among working-class participants and upper-class spectators. Athletes might become public celebrities, but they were never really accepted into the middle class. To maintain the semblance of equality, sports promoters portrayed athletic competition as an exclusively male profession and pastime, whether or not women were present. But men's claim on the sport of jig dancing did not preclude women from competing in their own way.[70]

A cluster of female challenge dancers emerged in the late 1850s alongside the spread of commercial music halls that employed large numbers of young women to dance jigs onstage. Star dancers distinguished themselves from this untrained chorus by adding "champion" to their stage names and promoting their matches and tournaments in the popular press. Like male dancers, some female challengers launched their professional careers by burlesquing the opposite sex. Actor-dancer Julia Morgan, a.k.a. "the Boston Pet," exploited her role in "Three Fast Men" (a farce containing a scene in which two women impersonate white male blackface dancers) by challenging Tommy Peel, Dick Carroll, Hank Mason, E. Bowers, "'OR ANY OTHER MAN,' or female in the country" to a dancing match for a stake of $100 to $500.[71] "Lightning jig dancer" Naomi Porter, "the New York Favorite," accepted Morgan's challenge, followed by prize-cup winner (and New York saloon-keeper) "Kate Stanton, the Invincible," who took on all comers, and a Miss Lizetta King. No male responded. Nevertheless, the Boston tournament between four "young ladies, who are by common consent admitted to be the most eminent jig dancers of this (or any other) country," was advertised on mammoth placards, well attended, bet on, and covered by newspapers as far afield as Sacramento, California.[72]

Diamond no doubt encountered this cohort of women champions at White's Opera House, where he worked again in the summer of 1856. White's stage was the platform on which "first-class dancers" of every sort—"not, by any means, all 'blackface'"—were introduced to the public.[73] English clog dancers, female jig dancers, and juvenile "peck-measure" dancers established their reputations there. Charley White was possibly the only minstrel manager who treated jig dancing and blackface minstrelsy as different, if intersecting, categories of entertainment.[74] And as he had done with Juba in 1848, he billed Diamond as his counterpart: "Charley White, the old favorite together with John Diamond, the wonderful dancer."[75]

"Challenge Dance" Burlesque

For Diamond, dancing in a variety house differed from dancing in a full-length minstrel show. In early October 1856 he appeared with the Campbell Minstrels, led by "those great humorists Bryant and Mallory," at the Empire Hall on Broadway billed as "the famous Ethiopian dancer." "It is seldom that such dancers as Dan Bryant, Ben Mallory and John Diamond all appear on the stage together," exulted the *Herald* after two nights.[76] Bryant and Mallory were considered two of the best "negro dancers" in the business; but, seeking respectability for their blackface performances, both had left the sport of jig dancing behind. At their establishment, Diamond performed as a fellow artist, not an athlete.

A hierarchy developed among America's entertainment venues in the mid-1850s, when playhouses and minstrel companies began refurbishing their auditoriums to accommodate middle-class audiences. At the Bowery Theatre, "the pit was transformed into an orchestra with cushioned seats, the first and second tier benches gave place to chairs, while the old third-tier gallery was done away with completely."[77] These physical changes did not reflect the existing class structure; instead, they participated in its creation. Working people who felt unwelcome in theaters that required all patrons to sit together and behave themselves went instead to music halls, variety houses, and circuses.[78]

Racial segregation accompanied theater renovations. In Boston no laws prevented African Americans from attending the theater, but in 1857 a middle-class Black man who sat as usual in the family circle at the Howard Athenaeum found himself hissed, "for which he brought suit against the manager." The case went to the superior court, reported the *Clipper*, which "decided that he must confine his company to those of his own 'persuasion.'" Such rulings barred Black people from any theater that had eliminated its third tier or gallery, where they and the poorer class of white patrons were previously seated.

Changes onstage fortified audience divisions. Blackface minstrels who gentrified their playhouses made their skits more crudely racist to identify themselves as observers of rather than participants in "Negro" culture. As they had been in the past, these acts were informed by working-class social relations. Unlike their predecessors, most of the Irish Catholic immigrants who flooded American cities in the 1850s distanced themselves from African Americans. Faced with de-skilling and competing with free Black workers for employment, they defended their jobs and rights as white men.[79] The political debate and violence surrounding the expansion of slavery into the territories reinforced this construction of a white working class. Antislavery proponents wanted Western land reserved for white males, not for plantation owners and their slaves, free Blacks, or Indians. In this environment, mixing with Black people placed Irish and other immigrants in an underclass rather than demonstrating working-class assertiveness.

Challenge dancing played a part in this process of class formation. In 1857 Dan Bryant and his brothers formed a thirteen-member company called Bryants' Minstrels, turned New York's Mechanics Hall into a minstrelsy theater, and introduced a blackface skit called "Challenge Dance" to their program.[80] Played by "two speaking Dancers," the sketch was a send-up of challenge dancing's Black-Irish origins. "Ill-Count McGinnis (a Hibernian Darkie)" is headed to a ball in a local hall, where a silver cup will be awarded to the best dancer, when he meets "Farmyard Sam (an Ethiopian Exquisite)," who challenges him to a match for ten dollars a side. The humorous bits of dialogue and action are blocked out in the stage directions, but when the competition begins, the script simply says: "new steps introduced."[81] Those new steps were meant to placate working-class spectators who knew what good jig dancing looked like, while the play's counterfeit nature (and the Irish dancer's blackface) made watching the contest acceptable entertainment for middle-class audiences. Described as a "Prelude to Dance," the "Challenge Dance" skit maliciously mocked the rivalry of Irish American Diamond and African American Juba and positioned all such interracial partnerships in the preindustrial past.

With fewer knowledgeable jig dancers in their auditoriums, blackface minstrels rid themselves of a critical segment of their audience: people who understood and relished challenge dancing's technical aspects, its mixed history, its risk taking. Without that core audience, anything could be passed off as "Negro dancing."

Diamond danced with Bryant and Mallory for two weeks, then returned to White's Opera House, with its diverse entertainments "in cork" and otherwise. In mid-October 1856 he costarred with nineteen-year-old Billy Quinn (Quin), a jig and clog dancer from the British Isles.[82] Clog dancing was a kind of social and competitive street dancing that resembled Diamond's flat-foot style; it was practiced by workers in Lancashire, Yorkshire, and other mill and mining regions in England. Performed in the wooden-soled shoes worn by those laborers, clog dancing was dubbed "toe and heel" because that was where all the action took place. The dancer held his or her arms in set positions (characteristic of sailors and other stage characters) and focused on producing intricate rhythms with the feet. After migrating to the United States with stage dancers such as Quinn, clog dancing was incorporated into popular dances in the American South, where clogging became synonymous with white people's breakdown dancing.[83]

With two brilliant dancers in his theater, White decided to sponsor a tournament. "Great dancing week, to test the superiority of the best Negro Dancers in the world," he promised his patrons. "Look out for the Grand Trial Dance, for a silver cup, which takes place on October 23. All the Champion Dancers in New York have entered their names."[84] Ads for the tournament featured Diamond and Quinn, but the names of the other contestants were not posted, indicating they comprised jig dancers well known to the dancing community but not the public. Who got the silver cup was also not announced. Diamond stuck around nevertheless, suggesting tacit approval of the competitive format of the dancing acts at White's place.

Last Days

The 1856 economic recession culminated in bank and business failures across the United States and Europe in August 1857. The boom-and-bust economy had thinned out audiences, noted the *New York Clipper*, forcing many theaters to adopt "the 'two-third salary' system, hoping thereby to be able to scud through the storm in safety."[85] White's Opera House provided Diamond a shelter through December, but in January it burned down. White rebuilt quickly with the aid of friends and reopened in February 1857, but by then Diamond had settled back into Philadelphia's Southwark Opera House. Residual effects of the financial panic eventually induced White to vacate his East Side venue and work under someone else's management for two years.[86]

Economic hardship also stimulated the flurry of dancing challenges and matches announced in the *Clipper* from August 1856 through 1857. Diamond was pointedly absent from the field and the ads. In March a correspondent asked the *Clipper* where the dancer was at present. He wanted to know because two dancers representing themselves as John Diamond and Mickey Warren had just been arrested and charged with stealing clothes from a hotel in Cleveland. "There have been so many 'John Diamonds,' and originals, too, that it is a difficult matter to keep track of them all," admitted the writer, who thought the original was in Philadelphia. The editor replied that Warren had been in New York "ever since his match dance" and that Diamond was performing at Philadelphia's Melodeon (fig. 12.3). Warren, "fearing that many who are unacquainted with me personally might labor under the impression that it was myself," set matters straight in the next edition. "I have never been in Cleveland," he told the *Clipper*, "and when those parties were arrested, I was fulfilling engagements in Albany and Troy."[87] Diamond did not respond personally. For him it was nothing new.

His celebrity among Philadelphia's working classes kept Diamond afloat that spring, but just barely. In April he and champion jig dancer Peter Lane volunteered to dance together for a benefit performance at the National Circus on Walnut Street.[88] For the rest of the month he danced at the concert saloon in Military Hall on Library Street amid a "Grand Galaxy of Talent" supported by Prof. Slack at the piano. The stars in that galaxy were "JOHN DIMOND [*sic*], the only Champion Dancer in the World," and local celebrities Dan Lewis, the comic vocalist, and Jim Lewis, "in his Negro Eccentricities and Burlesque Dances, assisted by Bill Bloomer, the Monarch of the Banjo, and his talented Company of male and female artists." On April 25, 1857, Diamond danced a "Grand TRIAL

FIGURE 12.3. American music halls such as the Melodeon, where Diamond danced at the end of his life, were often expansions of taverns situated next to playhouses. A step down from their conjoined theaters, music halls featured variety shows dominated by troupes of female dancers. *Chestnut Street Theatre, Chestnut Street at 6th,* ca. 1855. Courtesy of the Free Library of Philadelphia, Print and Picture Collection.

DANCE" with Jim Lewis, who also circulated in Philadelphia's boxing and dancing community. Admission was "only 6 cents," half the typical price. It was his last publicized event.[89]

According to the "Answers to Correspondents" column in the *Clipper*, Diamond danced at Philadelphia's Melodeon once more in May. His name did not surface again until October 3, when the *Clipper* apprised another correspondent that "John Diamond is alive, but we cannot give you his present whereabouts." The question prompted the editor to look into the matter, however, and he elaborated on his previous answer two weeks later: "At that time we were unable to furnish the information, but a friend has since informed us that Diamond is now lying very low, said to be in the last stages of consumption, in one of the public institutions of Philadelphia."[90]

CONCLUSION
Forgotten Legacies

William Henry Lane, a.k.a. Juba, Boz's Juba, and Masters Juba, Rattler, Diamond, and Champion, died on February 3, 1854, in the fever ward of Brownlow Hill workhouse in Liverpool, England. He was described on his death certificate as "Bois Juba" ("Boz's" misspelled), a thirty-year-old musician born in the United States. Probably less abandoned when he died than the press's lack of notice suggests, Lane/Juba was buried in the free part of St. Martin in the Fields cemetery, Liverpool, on February 6.[1] John Dimond, a.k.a. Diamond, Master Diamond, and the original John Diamond, died three years later on October 29, 1857, in the charity hospital of Blockley Almshouse in Philadelphia "after a lingering illness." Death notices in Philadelphia newspapers said he was "in the 34th year of his age" and invited "relatives and friends of the family" to attend the funeral. A wake was held for Diamond at Raymond House, a hotel and gambling house near the Walnut Street Theatre in the residence of its proprietor, William "Buck" Greer. He was buried outside the city at Cathedral Cemetery alongside other Irish Americans.[2]

Both dancers succumbed to consumption (now called tuberculosis) in what was considered early middle age. Waves of epidemic disease—yellow fever, cholera, pneumonia, and the "captain of death," tuberculosis—swept through urban populations in America and England in the 1850s, filling almshouses and workhouses with the sick and dying (fig. C.1).[3] Private hospitals were few and expensive (four to five dollars per week) at that time, and the home environment was considered more conducive to recovery. Almshouses took in people with no family or friends to nurse them; patients with contagious, chronic, or incurable diseases; and people deemed morally unworthy, such as prostitutes and alcoholics. During

294 · CONCLUSION

FIGURE C.1. The workhouse in Liverpool where Juba died and the almshouse in Philadelphia where Diamond died were similar public institutions. Sickness and destitution were related in the nineteenth century, in that a recovered almshouse patient might be put to work rather than discharged, and a workhouse inmate who fell ill would be sent to the in-house infirmary rather than home. *Blockley Almshouse, Opposite Philadelphia*, 1857. Barbara Bates Center for the Study of the History of Nursing, School of Nursing, University of Pennsylvania.

epidemics, public officials often rounded up poor immigrants whether or not they were sick and took them to almshouses, where many became ill and died. Few people, no matter how poor, voluntarily entered an almshouse, where "the virtuous and the vicious" were treated indiscriminately. Dying in an almshouse suggested abandonment by family, employers, and community, which translated into bad character within prevailing social assumptions.[4]

Itinerant dancers were particularly susceptible to illness. Late hours, repeated heating and chilling during and between performances, inhalation of tobacco smoke and lamp fumes, exhaustion, and constant exposure to contagious diseases from crowded audiences all contributed to the likelihood of their early deaths. Pete Lane, Billy Quinn, Tommy Peel, Ben Mallory, Jerry Bryant, Earl Pierce, and Dick Sliter all died between the ages of twenty-five and thirty-six. Jig dancers were also prone to joint injuries and rheumatism, which helps explain their fondness for alcohol, one of the few pain relievers readily available at the time. But rather than blaming their drinking and early deaths on the exigencies of their profession, chroniclers of American minstrelsy claimed that Diamond and Juba were done in by "dissipation and riotous living."[5]

Juba and Diamond died as workers, not celebrities. The fame each enjoyed as a dancer became the explanation for his demise. "Juba achieved the success which shortened his life," remarked T. Allston Brown.[6] "He could command any salary he wished," added Sam Sanford, but "the bottle became his favorite and his duration was then only a limited time. It was a race but bottle got the best, and 'Juba the Great' now lies in a grave in London."[7] After leaving Barnum, "Diamond accepted engagements on his own hook, and reaped considerable profits from the speculation," noted his *New York Clipper* obituary. "Through his fame, and successes, his life became a continued round of pleasure, [which] led him to disregard the great laws of health, and even while he rioted in luxury, the fell destroyer was slowly gnawing at his vitals, and preparing him for an early grave."[8] "P. T. Barnum picked him up, and made a great deal of money with him," claimed a later chronicler. "Diamond, however, was a rascal, and was sent to prison for theft, and finally died a drunkard."[9] More than just unkind assessments, these recollections turned Diamond and Juba into convenient explanations for why some white and all Black people did not deserve fame and fortune: They did not know how to handle it.

There's no denying that Diamond drank and brawled. Juba probably imbibed as well. What needs to be explained is why they were sidelined by minstrelsy's proponents. The obvious reason is that neither dancer followed the advice or example of his "betters." Both remained jig dancers who labored with their bodies and prized their physical abilities. Both continued to socialize across the color line after becoming famous. Both dumped their managers, opting for independence over economic stability, and stayed the course under deteriorating conditions. And both died poor in an almshouse. Their contrariness kept their dancing fresh, increased their popularity, and padded their pocketbooks, but it also kept them out of respectable society. Not only their race and ethnicity but also the work they chose, the way they lived, and where they died made them objectionable representatives of American culture.

As a consequence, neither man enjoyed real social mobility. Because he was white, one might say, Diamond's possibilities were vast. He could have "had it all" (or at least middle-class security) if he had just behaved. But Diamond stayed in the sporting milieu, where he could count on an audience and had a social standing. There he could make his jigs as Black as he liked without costuming up, but that choice kept Diamond and his dancing working class. Because he was Black, Lane's possibilities were more limited than Diamond's. He could not have joined white middle-class society in any case. But Juba's race also enabled him to reach the jig dancer's ultimate prospects. Because he was smart and could dance and sing and act, blackface minstrelsy gave him a pathway to a different life. It got him to England, where he not only charmed middle-class audiences but also received aristocratic and royal patronage. His blackness set him apart, but outside of minstrelsy that authenticity counted for little.

Both Lane and Diamond were revered by their working-class peers. The Black-Irish origins of challenge dancing made each a contender for the championship title. As a jig dancer, recalled Juba's fellow performers, "the world never saw his equal." He was "the greatest his race ever knew." Diamond was likewise remembered as "the greatest jig dancer . . . that the world ever knew."[10] A few days after he died, Bryant's Minstrels announced that the receipts from their performance would be given to erect a tomb to Diamond's memory. And twenty years after Lane died, a jig-dancing specialist acknowledged that "though John Diamond stood without an equal there was really his superior, and that man was Juba, a colored jig dancer mentioned in 'Dickens' Notes.'"[11] These comparisons were possible because the two dancers were fundamentally separated by race. Racism prohibited a direct comparison between Black and white, but it enabled Juba to reign supreme alongside Diamond without fully triumphing over his opponent: Juba danced for his race, Diamond for the world. These comparisons recognized challenge dancing's origins in the mixing of Irish and Black dance, origins that enabled Diamond and Juba's rivalry and partnership and, in the end, erased them from our collective memory.

* * *

In the decades after Diamond's and Juba's deaths, the spaces in which white and Black people came together to dance were greatly curtailed. Public markets remained important sites of exchange, but in the 1860s municipal officials began the process of consolidation. Street vendors were more closely regulated, market sheds demolished, and privately owned, off-street market houses proposed, making ferry docks and market squares less lucrative sites for busking dancers.[12] The number of children hawking their talents in the streets of American cities fluctuated with the economy, immigration, and migration. Their incomes remained essential to lower-class families, but few of these children were "discovered" by entertainment entrepreneurs. At times, child street traders (called "the newsboy class" by one such boy) were so ubiquitous that they went unnoticed, or they were placed among "the dangerous classes" and targeted by middle-class reformers intent on saving them from the likes of hunger, abuse, and crime.[13]

White and Black people continued to socialize in some leisure venues. But in the late 1850s liquor licensing laws, police raids, and temperance reformers besieged economically marginal tavern operators, especially the female and Black proprietors of grog shops and neighborhood dance-houses who provided safe places for young men and women to mix. The rise of saloons and barrooms aimed at the industrial working classes promoted solidarity among men with similar interests rather than the community as a whole.[14] Men, women, and children did not meet and compete as equals on the dance floor of these masculinized spaces (few barrooms had one anyway).

At the same time, the division of labor and dominance of white male capitalists made it possible to convince white workers that their financial distress and skill degradation were caused by the people below them rather than by their employers.[15] The practice of replacing the lowest paid white laborers, especially Irishmen, with even lower paid Black laborers prompted more whites to riot against Blacks than to channel economic and racial tension into jig-dancing competitions.[16] This racial animosity was exacerbated during the Civil War, when casualties, unfair draft quotas, and job competition with African Americans weighed most heavily on already hard-pressed working-class Irish Americans. Yet the Civil War and Reconstruction were also times when white and Black people fought together to end racial slavery and advance equality.

After Reconstruction and well into the twentieth century, deepening racism and class polarities in American society limited people's interactions and the cross-pollination of cultural forms. The "shared public culture" that had enriched Diamond's and Juba's dancing gradually split into highbrow and popular entertainments, male and female pursuits, and white and Black art forms performed in separate physical spaces.[17] Playhouses no longer hired circus performers to fill their entr'actes, challenge dancers and ballet dancers appeared on different bills, sporting events moved to their own halls, social dancing became a feminine art and athletics the province of men, and blackface minstrelsy ossified into a middlebrow genre that no longer incorporated the latest musical or dancing styles.

The process of separating culture into "white" or "Black" categories accelerated when segregationists "nabbed the name of what they censored" and called the legal and quotidian separation of the races "Jim Crow," a blackface theatrical character who was himself produced by Black-Irish mixing.[18] After emancipation, white people for whom racial slavery had rationalized white supremacy had difficulty figuring out where African Americans should fit into American society. This discomfort was expressed through the violent suppression of Black people's rights and the proliferation of blackface minstrelsy, which spawned weirdly contradictory messages and depictions of Black Americans. Minstrel shows featured entire orchestras of blackface musicians in tuxedos and chorus lines of corked-up males in identical clog-dancing outfits, as well as skits from former times that caricatured Black men as unthreatening buffoons and natural performers. In this realm, the exhilarating and unstable "Negro jigs" of challenge dancers gave way to the "nice and easy" style of soft-shoe tap-dancing teams. Soft-shoe tap, which grew from the same soil as challenge dancing, was accepted as a white middle-class version of Blackness even when performed by African Americans, while dances with elements deemed too wild, crazy-legged, or acrobatic for elite taste became Black. The color line made it easier for Americans to believe that there never was or ever could be a time or place in which white and Black people mixed their cultures together willingly.

English colonialism and calls for Home Rule stimulated a similar aesthetic segregation in Ireland. In 1893 the Gaelic League (founded to preserve the Irish language) began the work of purging Irish culture of any "foreign influences." In 1929, after British rule ended in most of Ireland, the Irish Dancing Commission (An Coimisiún Le Rincí Gaelacha) began searching for an ancient Celtic dance tradition. In the countryside and port cities such as Dublin, Cork, and Limerick, it found instead plebeian communities "whose music and dance appeared wild and uncouth." Later dubbed *sean nós* (old style), this vernacular dance was rejected by the commission, which sought to promote a middle-class Irish dance aesthetic. *Sean nós* is a vigorous close-to-the-floor style of stepping performed with relaxed arms held away from the body, very like American tap. These energetic exhibitionist competitive dancers had absorbed and subtly altered "un-Irish" movements and rhythms (African and otherwise) and whole dances to create a personal style. Their *tradition* valued precisely those elements that the commission considered "alien" or "spurious dancing."[19]

All of these impulses toward separation and hierarchy were present when Diamond and Juba were alive, but they never completely controlled people's activity. They were mixed in with traditions, tastes, and aesthetic dispositions whose roots would lie deep and dormant thereafter, emerging only in rough stages, decades apart, when people separated by prejudice found common ground in culture.

* * *

Despite their fading into obscurity, Diamond and Juba left a legacy. It was passed on when female dancers infiltrated music halls during the Civil War and challenged any comers to a match. And after Reconstruction, when elder dancers circulated their steps by exchanging tap-dancing dares with young people at home, in city bars, and at roadside juke joints (fig. C.2). And when the children of professional dancers surpassed their parents by watching from the wings and soaking up whatever they saw on the vaudeville circuit. And when formerly enslaved women proudly described their youthful dancing feats to New Deal folklorists. And when couples of both races turned the Lindy Hop's swing-out into a competition. And when duos such as the Nicholas Brothers and Gregory Hines and Savion Glover took their taps and taunts to Broadway and the silver

FIGURE C.2. A youngster learns his grandfather's "licks" in the 1870s. Thomas Eakins, *The Dancing Lesson,* 1878, watercolor on off-white woven paper. Fletcher Fund, 1925. The American Wing Collection. Metropolitan Museum of Art, New York.

FIGURE C.3. Acrobatic tap dancers Harold and Fayard Nicholas in the 20th Century–Fox film *The Great American Broadcast* (1941) were costumed as railroad porters, an employment dominated by African Americans in the first half of the twentieth century. Courtesy of the E. Azalia Hackley Collection of African Americans in the Performing Arts, Detroit Public Library.

screen (fig. C.3). And, even more recently, when Black and Hispanic kids turned their break dance battles into remunerative work on the streets of America's impoverished cities.[20]

The twenty-first century is rife with class and race antagonisms, yet challenge dancing persists. It surfaces every time young people from across the globe meet up to share and show off their steps and moves, as they do at Irish dance competitions, breaking championships, and hip-hop cyphers. They offer their spectators thrills akin to the excitement felt when Diamond and Juba faced off. Like *their* matches, today's contests point to the possibilities generated whenever people of diverse races, classes, genders, and generations come together to dance, whether it be for pennies, prizes, or publicity or just for the pleasure it brings.

ACKNOWLEDGMENTS

I'd like to acknowledge the many people and institutions who have supported me in so many different ways as I researched and wrote this book.

I was fortunate to receive financial recognition from the Houghton Library at Harvard University, which awarded me a John M. Ward Fellowship in Dance and Music for Theatre in 2005; American Philosophical Society, which gave me a John Hope Franklin Research Grant in 2006; American Antiquarian Society, where I held the Kate B. & Hall J. Peterson Fellowship in 2008; Shelby Cullom Davis Center for Historical Studies, where I was a "Cultures and Institutions in Motion" Fellow in 2008–2009; Humanities Institute at Stony Brook University, where I was resident fellow in the spring of 2015; National Humanities Center, where I held the John G. Medlin, Jr. Senior Fellowship in 2015–2016; Stony Brook University's Fine Arts, Humanities, and Lettered Social Sciences (FAHSS) Initiatives and United University Professions (UUP) Individual Development Awards, which together funded the project five times between 2005 and 2019; and SBU's history department, which awarded me a Marker Faculty Research Award in 2021.

For passing along references, insights, and information, I thank Nicholas Carolan, Patricia Cline Cohen, Laura Flanagan, Robin Cohen, Susan Hinely, Catherine E. Foley, Jay Cook, C. Daniel Dawson, Nancy Tomes, Rob Chase, Colin Dunne, Miriam Forman-Brunell, Mary Friel, Dror Wahrman, Louis Gerteis, William C. Jordan, John Kasson, Rip Lhamon, Mick Maloney, Kerby A. Miller, T. J. Desch Obi, Patrick O'Sullivan, Elena Schneider, Bob Stam, Julia Reid, Monique Patenaude, Alan J. Rice, Rhiannon Giddens, John Belchem, William Glenn, Shauna Vey, Kenneth Cohen, Sherril Dodds, and Steve Ward. I credit my cofellows at the Davis Center, particularly our astute director, Daniel T. Rodgers, with lending my topic gravitas. I'd also like to acknowledge the intrepid editors of academic journals and collections who published my early cracks at matters covered here.

For sharing their expertise about dance and music, I respectfully thank Emily Oleson, Greg Adams, Matthew Olwell, Stephanie Johnston, and the teachers at Ninth Street Dance in Durham, North Carolina.

I acknowledge the help of the archivists and librarians at the Irish Traditional Music Archive, Dublin City Archives, National Library of Ireland, American Antiquarian Society, Harvard Theater Collection, Houghton Library, Pennsylvania Historical Society, Library Company of Philadelphia, Harry Ransom Center at the University of Texas at Austin, New-York Historical Society, National Library of Scotland, New Castle Public Library, and public records offices in New York and New Orleans. I wish I had noted down all of your names.

I drafted the complete manuscript at the National Humanities Center thanks to its amazing staff, particularly Brooke Andrade and Sarah Harris, and my cofellows who became heartening friends, especially Nancy F. Cott, Norman Kutcher, Colleen Lye, Michelle O'Malley, Jane O. Newman, and Janice Radway.

For putting me up and tossing around ideas during my research trips, I recognize the generosity of Bríd Ní Heslín, Gail Day and Steve Edwards, John Charleton and Sally Mitchison, Gill Redfearn and Tom Woodhouse, Julia Reid and Daniel Scroop, Stephanie Johnston and Michael Newton, Molly Williams and Tom Davies. And thank you, Todd Shirley, for mapping Diamond's circus route while I was staying with you and Tammy Proctor.

For acts and words of encouragement, I thank Billie Barbara and Ric Masten, Lawrence Levine, Robert D. Newman, Eric K. Washington, Faith Childs, Ellen Masten, Alison Syring, Hiro Matsubara, Mary M. Hill, my Setauket AME friends, Mollie O'Neal, my first dancing teachers, Sharon Elliot and Mary Kay Bridges-LeValley, my history department's "second book" group, Donna Rilling, Janis Mimura, Shyam Sharma, Erin Giuliano, and the dozens of students who competed for the cake in my Dancing Through History class.

For reading and commenting on whole chapters, I acknowledge with gratitude my coffee companion Brooke Larson, Long Wharf guide Nancy Cott, ideas swapper Judith Walkowitz, "more waterfront" advocate Marcus Rediker, and North Carolina writing group—Judith Farquhar, Joy Kasson, and Jane Danielewizc, who endorsed the thick descriptions of milieu.

I stand on the shoulders of the scholars who championed the study of culture and society, particularly Herbert Gutman, who showed me that working people have a history, and Raymond Williams, whose "structures of feeling" inspired my search for structures of opportunity. I am also indebted to the authors whose books on the craft of writing, from Anne Lamott's *Bird by Bird* to Jon Franklin's *Writing for Story,* sustained and excited me as I wrote and revised this manuscript (and to Vince and Cara for introducing me to them). For the past two years, the online participants at Chloie's cowrites, particularly Chloie Piveral, Liz Levin, Nina Barufaldi, and Sam Markham, have made the tasks of revising, cutting, and preparing this manuscript less daunting. I thank them all for their cheerfulness and pragmatic advice.

    I would never have finished this book without the continual support and vision of three partners-in-time who read it all, listened to me rant about writing and publishing, and never doubted that this story was worth telling. Thank you, Cara Masten DiGirolamo—clever and generous writing coach, brilliant and delightful thinker and daughter—for writing down my ideas in the car way back when, offering increasingly sage advice about everything, and getting me through those "I'll never finish" moments; Molly Williams—gentle editor, sensitive-to-language person, and lifelong friend—for reading the entire second draft, taking me on the Juba tour, and making me happy when you said: "I don't know which dancer I want to win"; and Vincent DiGirolamo—tough editor and phenomenal wordsmith, caring and demanding reader and husband—for keeping me from sending it out before it was ready, critiquing the entire third draft, and saying, "You've got a book here." Their love and unflagging interest made writing about challenge dancers an achievable challenge.

NOTES

Introduction

1. "Excitement among the Sporting community—Match between John Diamond and Juba," *New York Sporting Whip*, Jan. 28, 1843, 4; Leslie M. Harris, *In the Shadow of Slavery: African Americans in New York City, 1626–1863* (University of Chicago Press, 2003), 7, 73, 248; Leonard P. Curry, *The Free Black in Urban America, 1800–1850: The Shadow of the Dream* (University of Chicago Press, 1981), 31.

2. Kerby A. Miller, *Emigrants and Exiles: Ireland and the Irish Exodus to North America* (Oxford University Press, 1985), 196–201.

3. "Excitement among the Sporting community," 4.

4. "Free-Trade Hall," *Manchester Guardian*, Oct. 18, 1848; "Provincial Theatricals," *The Era*, July 30, 1848.

5. "The Negro Minstrels of the Nights Gone By—Shoo-Fly, Don't Bodder Me—Shakespeare and Dumas on Burnt Cork—The Old Time Banjo-Players—The Great Match-Dance—Barnum's Museum Against Pete Williams' Dance-House," ca. 1875, HTC Clippings 13 (Bryant, Dan), Houghton Library, Harvard University.

6. MC Hammer, 1990; "Great Public Contest," *New York Herald*, July 8, 1844, 3.

7. Nuala O'Connor, *Bringing It All Back Home: The Influence of Irish Music* (Merlin, 2001), 51; Jacqui Malone, *Steppin' on the Blues: The Visible Rhythms of African American Dance* (University of Illinois Press, 1996), 13. This style was sometimes called "nigger" dancing, a descriptor that served as an epithet for the mixing of the races, one of the usages examined in Elizabeth Stordeur Pryor's "The Etymology of Nigger: Resistance, Language, and the Politics of Freedom in the Antebellum North," *Journal of the Early Republic* 36, no. 2 (2016): 203–245.

8. "The Cake Dance," *Béaloideas: The Journal of the Folklore of Ireland Society* 11, no. 1/2 (1941): 127.

9. James C. Scott, *Domination and the Arts of Resistance: Hidden Transcripts* (Yale University Press, 1990), xii; Jon McKenzie, "The Liminal-Norm," in *The Performance Studies*

Reader, ed. Henry Bial and Sara Brady (Routledge, 2016), 11; Judith Butler, "Performative Acts and Gender Construction: An Essay in Phenomenology and Feminist Theory," *Theater Journal* 40, no. 4 (1988): 519–531.

10. Marion H. Winter, "Juba and American Minstrelsy," in *Chronicles of the American Dance,* ed. Paul Magriel (Henry Holt, 1948), 39, 42; James W. Cook, "Master Juba, the King of All Dancers! A Story of Stardom and Struggle from the Dawn of the Transatlantic Culture Industry," *Discourses in Dance* 3, no. 2 (2006): 7–20; Cook, "Dancing Across the Color Line," *Commonplace* 4, no. 1 (2003), https://commonplace.online/article/dancing-across-the-color-line/; Kurt Andersen, *Heyday* (Random House, 2007); Tom Piazza, *A Free State* (Harper, 2015); Walter Dean Myers, *Juba!* (Amistad Books for Young Readers, 2015); and in Kia Corthron, *Moon and the Mars* (Seven Stories Press, 2021), the characters talk about Diamond and Juba.

11. On child labor, see Dennis Clark, "Babes in Bondage: Indentured Irish Children in Philadelphia in the Nineteenth Century," *Pennsylvania Magazine of History and Biography* 101, no. 4 (1977): 475–486; Harris, *In the Shadow of Slavery,* 80, 101, 129–130; Richard B. Stott, *Workers in the Metropolis: Class, Ethnicity, and Youth in Antebellum New York City* (Cornell University Press, 1990), 96–108; Vincent DiGirolamo, *Crying the News: A History of America's Newsboys* (Oxford University Press, 2019), pt. 1.

12. Shauna Vey, *Childhood and Nineteenth-Century American Theatre: The Work of the Marsh Troupe of Juvenile Actors* (Southern Illinois University Press, 2015); Robin Bernstein, *Racial Innocence: Performing American Childhood from Slavery to Civil Rights* (New York University Press, 2011), 6; Nan Mullenneaux, "Our Genius, Goodness, and Gumption: Child Actresses and National Identity in Mid-Nineteenth-Century America," *Journal of the History of Childhood and Youth* 5, no. 2 (2012): 283–308; Marah Guber, "The Drama of Precocity: Child Performers on the Victorian Stage," in *The Nineteenth-Century Child and Consumer Culture,* ed. Dennis Denisoff (Routledge, 2008), 63–78; Amy Varty, *Children and Theatre in Victorian Britain: 'All Work, No Play'* (Palgrave Macmillan, 2008).

13. Ann Fabian, *Card Sharps, Dream Books, & Bucket Shops: Gambling in 19th-Century America* (Cornell University Press, 1990), 40–41; Jackson Lears, *Something for Nothing: Luck in America* (Viking, 2003), 10; Roy Rosensweig, "The Rise of the Saloon," 143–147, and Pierre Bourdieu, "Sport and Social Class," 361–363, in *Rethinking Popular Culture,* ed. Chandra Mukerji and Michael Schudson (University of California Press, 1991).

14. Steven Riess, *City Games: The Evolution of American Urban Society and the Rise of Sports* (University of Illinois Press, 1989), 15; Elliott J. Gorn, *The Manly Art: Bare-Knuckle Prize Fighting in America* (Cornell University Press, 1986), 141–142; Kevin R. Smith, *Black Genesis: The History of the Black Prizefighter 1760–1870* (iUniverse, 2003); Kenneth Cohen, *They Will Have Their Games* (Cornell University Press, 2017), 236, 243–244.

15. Film critic Wesley Morris says blackface became America's popular culture by providing a nation "violently and legislatively polarized about slavery . . . [with] an entertainment of talent, ribaldry and polemics" that lent racism a stage. After the Civil War, prolonged exposure to what began as "harmless fun" normalized in the eyes of white audiences the "intended hideousness" of white performers' blackface caricatures. This normalization saddled nineteenth-century Black entertainers with the detrimental requirement that they mimic white blackface images of Blackness. It also limited the self-expression of twentieth-century

Black entertainers, for whom success with white audiences was often read as contamination by minstrelsy or selling out. Wesley Morris, "Music," in *The 1619 Project: A New Origin Story*, created by Nikole Hannah-Jones (One World, 2021), 367–368, 371–372, 374. Scholars disagree on the meaning and impact of antebellum minstrelsy. Some labor historians maintain that early minstrelsy, although drawn from African American vernacular culture, reflected and reinforced an incipient working-class racism. In contrast, some literary scholars see early blackface displaying a kind of democratic lower-class politics that was lost as minstrelsy commercialized. While harmful to race relations, minstrelsy was not intrinsically demeaning, they claim, for it relied on "common human ground" for its humor. Others blame blackface minstrelsy for generating an enduring racist ideology and stalling the development of "Negro" public arts while recognizing that "the audiences involved in early minstrelsy were not universally derisive of African Americans or their culture." Rather, blackface helped establish African American qualities as the defining characteristic of American culture. David R. Roediger, *The Wages of Whiteness: Race and the Making of the American Working Class* (Verso, 1991), 104, 117–118; Noel Ignatiev, *How the Irish Became White* (Routledge, 1995), 148–157; Alexander Saxton, *The Rise and Fall of the White Republic: Class Politics and Mass Culture in Nineteenth-Century America* (Verso, 1990), 17; W. T. Lhamon Jr., *Raising Cain: Blackface Performance from Jim Crow to Hip Hop* (Harvard University Press, 1998), 42–44; William J. Mahar, "Black English in Early Blackface Minstrelsy," *American Quarterly* 37, no. 2 (1985): 285; Eric Lott, "'The Seeming Counterfeit': Racial Politics and Early Blackface Minstrelsy," *American Quarterly* 43, no. 2 (1991): 224–225.

16. Dance historians trace American tap dancing to an amalgamation of Irish, English, and African elements but designate challenge dancing an African American practice observed and copied by white minstrels. Marshall Stearns and Jean Stearns, *Jazz Dance: The Story of American Vernacular Dance* (Da Capo, 1968), 37, 46; Mark Knowles, *Tap Roots: The Early History of Tap Dancing* (McFarland, 2002), 86–92; Constance Valis Hill, *Tap Dancing America: A Cultural History* (Oxford University Press, 2009), 12; Brian Siebert, *What the Eye Hears: A History of Tap Dancing* (Farrar, Straus and Giroux, 2015), 61–77.

Chapter 1. Out of the Mix

1. P. T. Barnum, *Struggles and Triumphs* (1869; abridged ed., Penguin Classics, 1987), 79, 90.

2. P. T. Barnum to F. C. Wemyss, Esq., "New York, Jany 21./40," document case 8, folder P. T. Barnum Collection, 1840–1890, New York Historical Society; Phineas T. Barnum, *The Life of P. T. Barnum* (Redfield, 1855), 210; Barnum, *Struggles and Triumphs*, 91; Col. T. Allston Brown, "Early History of Negro Minstrelsy: Its Rise and Progress in the United States," *New York Clipper*, Feb. 24, 1912, 5.

3. "Death of John Diamond," *New York Clipper*, Nov. 7, 1857, 226; "Juba.—The Ethiopian Serenaders," *Manchester Times and Manchester and Salford Advertiser and Chronicle* (England), Oct. 21, 1848, 5.

4. Paul A. Gilje, "The Development of an Irish American Community," in *The New York Irish*, ed. Ronald H. Bayor and Timothy J. Meagher (Johns Hopkins University Press, 1996), 74–75; Kerby A. Miller, *Emigrants and Exiles: Ireland and the Irish Exodus to North America* (Oxford University Press, 1985), 196–197.

5. G. S. Rowe, "Black Offenders, Criminal Courts, and Philadelphia Society in the Late Eighteenth-Century," *Journal of Social History* 22, no. 4 (1989): 695.

6. Jill Lepore, *New York Burning* (Knopf, 2005), 34; Leslie M. Harris, *In the Shadow of Slavery: African Americans in New York City, 1626–1863* (University of Chicago Press, 2003), 247–248; Graham Hodges, "'Desirable Companions and Lovers': Irish and African Americans in the Sixth Ward, 1830–1870," in Bayor and Meagher, *The New York Irish*, 107–124.

7. *Evening Tattler,* Jan. 25, 1840, quoted in Dale Cockrell, *Demons of Disorder: Early Blackface Minstrels and Their World* (Cambridge University Press, 1997), 86; George G. Foster, "Philadelphia in Slices," *New-York Daily Tribune,* Nov. 17, 1848, reprinted in *Philadelphia Magazine of History and Biography* 93 (1969): 40; *An Account of Col. Crockett's Tour to the North and Down East: In the Year of Our Lord One Thousand Eight Hundred and Thirty-four; His Objective Being to Examine the Grand Manufacturing Establishments of the Country, and Also to Find Out the Condition of Its Literature and Morals, the Extent of Its Commerce, and the Practical Operation of "The Experiment"* (E. L. Carey and A. Hart, 1835), 48.

8. Charles J. Kickham, *Knocknagow, Or The Homes of Tipperary* (1879), 36–37; Mary Friel, *Dancing as a Social Pastime in the South-East of Ireland, 1800–1897* (Four Courts Press, 2004), 40–41; R. Shelton Mackenzie, *Bits of Blarney* (J. S. Redfield, 1854), 299; Cockrell, *Demons of Disorder,* 104; *New York Herald,* Aug. 9, 1841; Solomon Northup, *Twelve Years a Slave* (1853; repr., Louisiana State University Press, 1996), 218–219; George G. Foster, *New York in Slices* (W. F. Burgess, 1849), 110–114; Ned Buntline, *Mysteries and Miseries of New York: A Story of Real Life* (Berford and Company, 1848), pt. 2, 81–83.

9. Roy Rosensweig, "The Rise of the Saloon," in *Rethinking Popular Culture,* ed. Chandra Mukerji and Michael Schudson (University of California Press, 1991), 127, 129.

10. Tyler Anbinder, *Five Points: The 19th-Century New York City Neighborhood That Invented Tap Dance, Stole Elections, and Became the World's Most Notorious Slum* (Simon and Schuster, 2001), 191; "The Devil Recruits in Staten Island," *The Flash* (New York), Oct. 31, 1841, 3; Foster, "Philadelphia in Slices," 40; "The Negro Minstrels of the Nights Gone By," ca. 1875, HTC Clippings 13 (Bryant, Dan), Houghton Library, Harvard University; Carol Groneman Pernicone, "The 'Bloody Ould Sixth,' a Social Analysis of a New York City Working-Class Community in the Mid-Nineteenth Century" (PhD diss., University of Rochester, 1973), 197–198.

11. "Boz at Five Points," *Whip and Satirist of New-York and Brooklyn,* Mar. 12, 1842, 2.

12. Wilbur R. Miller, "Police Authority in London and New York City 1830–1870," *Journal of Social History* 8, no. 2 (1975): 81–101.

13. *Evening Tattler,* Jan. 25, 1840, quoted in Cockrell, *Demons of Disorder,* 86.

14. "Dancing for Eels," *The Flash,* Nov. 12, 1842, 1.

15. *Longworth's American Almanac, New-York Register and City Directory* (Thomas Longworth, 1837–38), 700; Thomas F. De Voe, *The Market Book Containing a Historical Account of the Public Markets in the cities of New York, Boston, Philadelphia, and Brooklyn, With a brief Description of every Article of Human Food sold therein, The Introduction of Cattle in America and of Many Remarkable Specimens,* vol. 1 (1862), 342, 307; Edward Ruggles,

A Picture of New York in 1848: with a short account of places in the vicinity: designed as a guide to citizens and strangers (C. S. Francis, 1848), 89.

16. De Voe, *The Market Book,* 370; *New York Herald,* Jan. 31, 1843; Mabel Osgood Wright, *My New York* (Macmillan Company, 1926), 38.

17. De Voe, *The Market Book,* 370; Ruggles, *Picture of New York,* 88.

18. Frances S. Osgood, *The Cries of New-York, with Fifteen Illustrations, Drawn from Life by a Distinguished Artist* (John Doggett Jr., 1846); Vincent DiGirolamo, *Crying the News: A History of America's Newsboys* (Oxford University Press, 2019), 63, 79; De Voe, *The Market Book,* 120, 180, 323.

19. Barton Atkins, *Modern Antiquities: Comprising Sketches of Early Buffalo and the Great Lakes, also sketches of Alaska* (Courier Company, 1898), 44; Edward Le Roy Rice, *Monarchs of Minstrelsy* (Kenny Publishing Company, 1911), 35.

20. De Voe, *The Market Book,* 342, 344.

21. De Voe, *The Market Book,* 344–345.

22. De Voe, *The Market Book,* 344, 322.

23. Diamond, Dimond, and Diamon were common English translations of the Irish names Ó Déamáin, Ó Diamáin, Ó Díomáin, and Ó Maoileacáin. Immigration record: "Departed Plymouth, England arrived New York, New York, 13 May 1835: John Diamond 35; Elizabeth 30; Elizabeth 9; John 7; Sarah 5; Mary Anne 4; Nathaniel 2; Peter 1" (*Longworth's American Almanac,* 1835–1836, 215, and 1839, 208). See also Patrick Woulfe, *Irish Names and Surnames* (M. H. Gill, 1922), 94, 109.

24. Barnum to Wemyss, "New York, Jany 21./40."

25. James W. Cook, "Lane, William Henry [*performing name* Juba, Master Juba]," in *Oxford Dictionary of National Biography,* Oct. 3, 2013, https://doi.org/10.1093/ref:odnb/100407; Brown, "Early History of Negro Minstrelsy," 5; "Negro Minstrels and Their Dances," *New York Herald,* Aug. 11, 1895, Fourth Section, MS Thr 1848, boxes 20–21, Houghton Library, Harvard University.

26. Kerby A. Miller, *Ireland and Irish America: Culture, Class, and Transatlantic Migration* (Field Day, 2008), 152; Mary C. Waters, "Optional Ethnicities: For Whites Only?," in *Rereading America: Cultural Contexts for Critical Thinking and Writing,* ed. Gary Colombo et al. (Bedford / St. Martin's, 2001), 643; Cockrell, *Demons of Disorder,* 85–86; Hodges, "'Desirable Companions and Lovers,'" 123.

27. "The Cake Dance," *Béaloideas: The Journal of the Folklore of Ireland Society* 11, no. 1/2 (1941): 126–128, 131, 137.

28. Doris Green, "Traditional Dance in Africa," in *African Dance: An Artistic, Historical and Philosophical Inquiry,* ed. Kariamu Welsh Asante (African World, 1996), 18.

29. William B. Smith, "The Persimmon Tree and the Beer Dance," *Farmers' Register, a Monthly Publication* 6 (Apr. 1838): 58–61; William Howard Russell, *My Diary North and South* (O. S. Felt, 1863), 258; Lynne Fauley Emery, *Black Dance: From 1619 to Today* (Princeton Book Company, 1988), 91–92.

30. De Voe, *The Market Book,* 345; "Negro Minstrels and Their Dances"; "The Nomenclature of the West," *The Liberator,* Sept. 13, 1834, 4.

31. "Dancing for Eels," 1.

32. De Voe, *The Market Book,* 344–345.

33. Patrick Kennedy, *The Banks of the Boro: A Chronicle of the County of Wexford* (Simpkin, Marshall and Company, 1867), 147; Mackenzie, *Bits of Blarney,* 296.

34. W. Holman Bentley, *Dictionary and Grammar of the Kongo Language* (Baptist Missionary Society, 1887), 481; Pierre Swartenbroeckx, *Dictionnaire Kikongo et Kituba—Français: Vocabulaire comparé des langages Kongo traditionnels et véhiculaires* (CEEBA, 1973), 2:521, 805.

35. Herman Melville, *Moby-Dick, or, The Whale* (Harper and Brothers, 1851), 190–192; "Buried in Sweets," *Rhode-Island Republican,* Aug. 8, 1838, 3.

36. Richard Henry Dana Jr., *Two Years Before the Mast* (1840; repr., Houghton Mifflin Company, 1911), 236.

37. "BROADWAY CIRCUS," *New York Herald,* Jan. 20, 1840, 2.

38. "The Ball," *Hawk & Buzzard,* Aug. 31, 1833, 3.

39. "Dancing for Eels," *The Flash,* Nov. 12, 1842, 1.

40. Catherine E. Foley, *Step Dancing in Ireland: Culture and History* (Ashgate, 2013), 65; Arthur Gribben, *The Great Famine and the Irish Diaspora in America* (University of Massachusetts Press, 1999), 109; Seán Donnelly, "Maurice Lenihan's Account of Some Eighteenth and Nineteenth Century Dancing Masters," *Ceol na hÉirean: Irish Music* 1 (1993): 75–81.

41. Breandán Breathnach, *Folk Music and Dances of Ireland* (Ossian Publications, 1996), 50, 53; Breandán Breathnach, *Ceol agus Rince na hÉireann* (An Gúm, 1989), 178–179; Foley, *Step Dancing,* 67.

42. De Voe, *The Market Book,* 345; Pearl Primus, "African Dance," in Asante, *African Dance,* 8; John Argyle, "Dance as Social Statement," in *Encyclopedia of Africa South of the Sahara,* ed. John Middleton (Scribner's, 1997), 1:400; William Carleton, "The Country Dancing-Master, an Irish Sketch," *Irish Penny Journal,* Aug. 29, 1840, 70; Kickham, *Knocknagow,* 45; Patrick Logan, *Fair Day: The Story of Irish Fairs and Markets* (Appletree Press, 1986), 102–103.

43. William Carleton, *Traits and Stories of the Irish Peasantry* (W. F. Wakeman, 1833), 1:43–44, 55; "A Glorious Ball," *Whip and Satirist of New-York and Brooklyn,* Feb. 5, 1842, 1; "Brooklyn," *The Flash,* July 3, 1842, 3.

44. Green, "Traditional Dance in Africa," 18; Primus, "African Dance," 8; Argyle, "Dance as Social Statement," 400–401; Ivor Miller, Ken Bilby, and C. Daniel Dawson, unpublished papers presented at "Contesting Culture: Battling Genres in the African Diaspora," conference, Baruch College, New York, May 2, 2008.

45. *Silvia Dubois, (now 116 yers old.): A Biografy of the Slav Who Whipt Her Mistres and Gand Her Fredom,* ed. Cornelius Wilson Larison (C. W. Larison, 1883), 68, 93, 60; Helen Brennan, *The Story of Irish Dance* (Roberts Rinehart Publishers, 2001), 167; Foley, *Step Dancing,* 44; Mackenzie, *Bits of Blarney,* 295.

46. Foley, *Step Dancing,* 20.

47. Mackenzie, *Bits of Blarney,* 293; Foley, *Step Dancing,* 65.

48. Foley, *Step Dancing,* 75.

49. "R. M. Carroll," in Rice, *Monarchs of Minstrelsy,* 80–82; *New York Herald,* Aug. 9, 1841; "Juba.—The Ethiopian Serenaders," 5; "Death of John Diamond," 226.

50. Dennis Clark, "Babes in Bondage: Indentured Irish Children in Philadelphia in the Nineteenth Century," *Pennsylvania Magazine of History and Biography* 101, no. 4 (1977): 478–479; Harris, *In the Shadow of Slavery,* 80.

Chapter 2. Humbug's Apprentice

1. Vera Brodsky Lawrence, *Strong on Music: The New York Music Scene in the Days of George Templeton Strong* (Oxford University Press, 1987), 21–22, 60; Allan Nevins, ed., *The Diary of Philip Hone* (Dodd, Mead and Company, 1927), 1:272; Benson John Lossing, *History of New York City: Embracing an Outline Sketch of Events from 1609 to 1830, and a Full Account of Its Development from 1830 to 1884* (Perine Engraving and Publishing Company, 1884), 1:429.

2. Andrew Dolkart and Matthew A. Postal, *Guide to New York City Landmarks* (John Wiley and Sons, 2009), 204; Charles Dickens, *Bleak House* (1853), 330–332.

3. Thomas L. Nichols, *Forty Years of American Life* (Longmans, Green and Company, 1864), 369; T. Allston Brown, *A History of the New York Stage from the First Performance in 1732 to 1901* (Dodd, Mead and Company, 1903), 1:245–246, 251; National Theatre (New York) playbill, April 3, 1839, in Joseph Norton Ireland, "Records of the New York Stage from 1750–1860," unpublished scrapbook, TS 939.5.3, Houghton Library, Harvard University.

4. Henry James, *A Small Boy and Others: A Critical Edition* (University of Virginia Press, 2011), 88.

5. "National Theatre," *Evening Post* (New York), Apr. 1–3, 1839, 3; National Theatre (New York) playbill, Apr. 3, 1839.

6. Joseph Norton Ireland, *Records of the New York Stage from 1750 to 1860* (T. H. Morrell, 1867), 2:164–165.

7. "Franklin Theatre," *Morning Herald* (New York), June 27, 1838.

8. George C. D. Odell, *Annals of the New York Stage, Vol. IV: 1834–1843* (Columbia University Press, 1928), 312, 397; Ireland, *Records of the New York Stage,* 2:124, 164–165, 288; "Franklin Theatre," *Morning Herald* (New York), Apr. 16–24, 1839.

9. Arthur Herman Wilson, *A History of the Philadelphia Theatre, 1835 to 1855* (Greenwood Press, 1968), 13; William G. B. Carson, *Managers in Distress: The St. Louis Stage, 1840–1844* (St. Louis Historical Documents Foundation, 1949), 227.

10. John Buckstone to Francis Courtney Wemyss, "Philadelphia, 24 Nov 1841," box 1, folder Buckstone, John Baldwin (1802–1879), Stephen Whitney Phoenix Papers, MS 0997, Rare Books and Manuscripts Library, Butler Library, Columbia University.

11. P. T. Barnum to F. C. Wemyss, Esq., "New York, Jany 21./40," document case 8, folder P. T. Barnum Collection, 1840–1890, New York Historical Society.

12. *Longworth's American Almanac, New York Register, and City Directory* (Thomas Longworth, 1837–1838), 704; Edward Ruggles, *A Picture of New York in 1848: with a short account of places in the vicinity: designed as a guide to citizens and strangers* (C. S. Francis, 1848), 63.

13. Rosemarie K. Bank, *Theatre Culture in America, 1825–1860* (Cambridge University Press, 1997), 111.

14. *Appleton's Journal: A Magazine of General Literature* (D. Appleton and Company, 1877), 2:177; Bank, *Theatre Culture,* 48, 49; Ruggles, *A Picture of New York,* 63.

15. Lossing, *History of New York City*, 1:426.

16. Lawrence W. Levine, *Highbrow/Lowbrow: The Emergence of Culture Hierarchy in America* (Harvard University Press, 1988), 36–41.

17. Lawrence Hutton, *Plays and Players* (Hurd and Houghton, 1875), 21–22.

18. "DRAMA IN BOWERY DAYS Chief Conlin's Reminiscences of East Side Glories. When Charley White Was the Idol of the Boys—The Later Rivalries and the Well-Known Favorites," *New York Times*, Dec. 13, 1896.

19. Shauna Vey, *Childhood and Nineteenth-Century American Theatre: The Work of the Marsh Troupe of Juvenile Actors* (Southern Illinois University Press, 2015), 103.

20. "Franklin Theatre," *Morning Herald* (New York), Apr. 16, 1839; "VAUXHALL GARDENS," *Morning Herald*, Aug. 3, 1840.

21. "MASTER DIAMOND'S BENEFIT," *Daily Picayune* (New Orleans), Jan. 16, 1841, 2; "Broadway Circus," *New York Herald*, Jan. 20, 1840, 2; "MASTER DIAMOND," *Picayune*, Jan. 12, 1841, 2.

22. "DINNEFORD'S NEW THEATRE," *New York Herald*, June 1, 1840, 1.

23. Dan Redler and Benzion Munitz, *Stage Lighting: The CD-ROM* (Danor Theatre & Studio Systems, 1996).

24. Stuart Thayer, *Traveling Showmen: The American Circus Before the Civil War* (Astley and Ricketts, 1997), 15.

25. "Theatrical Costume and Agency," *Evening Post* (New York), Feb. 26, 1840, 1.

26. Master Diamond minstrel dance, in Ireland, "Records of the New York Stage."

27. James C. Scott, *Domination and the Arts of Resistance: Hidden Transcripts* (Yale University Press, 1990), 3; *The Colored American*, Mar. 6, 1841, quoted in Tavia Amolo Ochieng' Nyong'ó, *The Amalgamation Waltz: Race, Performance, and the Ruses of Memory* (University of Minnesota Press, 2009), 120.

28. Ursula K. Le Guin, *The Wave in the Mind: Talks and Essays on the Writer, the Reader, and the Imagination* (Shambhala, 2004), 187.

29. Robin Cohen, "Creolization and Cultural Globalization: The Soft Sounds of Fugitive Power," *Globalizations* 4, no. 3 (2007): 373.

30. James Thomas, *From Tennessee Slave to St. Louis Entrepreneur: The Autobiography of James Thomas*, ed. Loren Schweninger (1904; repr., University of Missouri Press, 1984), 49.

31. J. S. Bratton, "Dancing a Hornpipe in Fetters," *Folk Music Journal* 6, no. 1 (1990): 69, 66, 70–71; Eric Colleary, "Why You Should Never Whistle Onstage," *Playbill*, Jan. 20, 2018, https://playbill.com/article/why-you-should-never-whistle-onstage.

32. Helen Brennan, *The Story of Irish Dance* (Robert Rinehard, 1999), 67, 22.

33. Patrick Kennedy, *The Banks of the Boro: A Chronicle of the County of Wexford* (Simpkin, Marshall and Company, 1867), 147.

34. Daniel Defoe, *Robinson Crusoe* (1719); Marshall Stearns and Jean Stearns, *Jazz Dance: The Story of American Vernacular Dance* (Da Capo Press, 1994), 38; John Durang, *The Ball-room Bijou, and Art of Dancing* (Fischer and Brother, n.d.), 158; *The Memoir of John Durang American Actor 1785–1816*, ed. Alan S. Downer (Historical Society of York County, 1966), 11, 144; Lincoln Kirstein, *The Book of Dance* (Garden City Publishing Company, 1942), 342.

35. Samuel S. Sanford, "Personal Reminiscences," manuscript pp. [2]/1-[4]/2, Minstrel Show Collection, 1831–1859, Harry Ransom Center, University of Texas at Austin.

36. Frank Dumont, "The Younger Generation in Minstrelsy and Reminiscences of the Past," *New York Clipper*, Mar. 27, 1915 (Burnt Cork Supplement).

37. "National Theatre," *Boston Courier*, Sept. 26, 1839, 2.

38. Elizabeth Stordeur Pryor, "The Etymology of Nigger: Resistance, Language, and the Politics of Freedom in the Antebellum North," *Journal of the Early Republic* 36 (Summer 2016): 205, 212, 209; "The white *nigger* Jim Crow Rice" and "sundry white and black negroes," *Whip and Satirist of New York and Brooklyn*, Apr. 9, 1842, 3.

39. Isaac Allen, "Songs of the Sailor," *Oberlin Student's Monthly* 1, no. 2 (1858): 48–49; David S. Cecelski, *The Waterman's Song: Slavery and Freedom in Maritime North Carolina* (University of North Carolina Press, 2001), xiii; Stan Hugill, *Shanties and Sailors' Songs* (Praeger, 1969), 35; W. Jeffrey Bolster, *Black Jacks: African American Seamen in the Age of Sail* (Harvard University Press, 1997), 217; Peter Linebaugh and Marcus Rediker, *The Many-Headed Hydra: Sailors, Slaves, Commoners, and the Hidden History of the Revolutionary Atlantic* (Beacon Press, 2000), 321.

40. Albert Barrère and Charles G. Leland, *A Dictionary of Slang, Jargon & Cant Embracing English, American, and Anglo-Indian Slang, Pidgin English, Gypsies' Jargon and Other Irregular Phraseology* (G. Bell, 1897), 1:478.

41. George Cruikshank, *The Comic Almanack for 1836: An Ephemeris in Jest and Ernest, By Rigdum Funnidos* (Charles Tilt, 1836), 55.

42. Ray Andrews, *Classic English Banjo* (MTCD314), CD booklet, written by Geoff Wolfe, 15.10.01, formatting, digital editing, production by Rod Stradling (Musical Traditions Production, 2001).

43. *Baltimore Sun*, Jan. 22, 1840.

44. [scrap], H. B. White, "The origin of Ethiopian minstrelsy: Reminiscences of its early history in Boston," autograph manuscript, undated, MS Thr 1848, box 22, Houghton Library, Harvard University.

45. Aloysius I. Mudd, "The Theatres of Washington from 1835 to 1850," *Records of the Columbia Historical Society* 6 (1903): 250.

46. *Daily National Intelligencer* (Washington, DC), Aug. 23, 1839.

47. "National. Benefit of Mast. Diamond" playbill, Oct. 18, 1839, MS Thr 1848, box 10, Houghton Library, Harvard University.

48. Brown, *A History of the New York Stage*, 1:301–302.

49. Charles Hemstreet, *When Old New York Was Young* (Charles Scribner's Sons, 1902), 151–152; Vincent DiGirolamo, *Crying the News: A History of the American Newsboy* (Oxford University Press, 2019), 64–65.

50. Levine, *Highbrow/Lowbrow*, 30–31.

51. Robert Ignatius Letellier, *Daniel-François-Esprit Auber: The Man and His Music* (Cambridge Scholars Publishing, 2010), 225.

52. "Strange Vessel. . . . THE AFRICANS TAKEN," *Long-Island Star* (Brooklyn, NY), Aug. 29, 1839, 2.

53. Marcus Reidiker, *The Amistad Rebellion: An Atlantic Odyssey of Slavery and Freedom* (Viking, 2012), 99–112.

54. *Pittsburgh Gazette*, Sept. 3, 1839, 2.

55. "Bowery Theatre," *Evening Post* (New York), Sept. 2–7, 1839, 3.

56. Jennifer Homans, *Apollo's Angels: A History of Ballet* (Random House, 2010), 140.

57. After the emperor of Russia presented Taglioni with a bouquet of diamonds, the empress of Russia, not to be outdone, threw her diamond bracelets at Taglioni's feet. *Saturday Morning Transcript* (Boston), Jan. 5, 1839, 74.

58. *Columbian Centinel* (Boston), Aug. 28, 1839, 2.

59. "CELESTE, Mlle [née Kepler] (1810–18)," in *The Oxford Companion to American Theatre*, ed. Gerald Bordman and Thomas S. Hischak (Oxford University Press, 2004), 118; "Madam Céleste," *Encyclopaedia Britannica*, 11th ed. (1910), 5:599; "Bowery Theatre," *Evening Post* (New York), Sept. 9, 20, 1839, 3; *New York Herald*, Sept. 9, 1839, 4.

60. Grace Robert, *The Borzoi Book of Ballets* (Knopf, 1946), 163.

61. "American Theatre, Walnut St.," *Public Ledger* (Philadelphia), Apr. 25, 1839, 3; "American Theatre, Front street," *Baltimore Sun*, Apr. 30, 1839, 3; Madeleine B. Stern, *We the Women: Career Firsts of Nineteenth-Century America* (Schulte Publishing Company, 1963), 11–12; Lillian Moore, "Mary Ann Lee," in *Notable American Women, 1607–1950: A Biographical Dictionary*, ed. Edward T. James et al. (Belknap Press of Harvard University Press, 1971), 2:387–388.

62. "A Card," *Public Ledger* (Philadelphia), May 17, 1839, 3; "Baltimore Museum . . . Grand Trial Dance, between Miss E. Ince and Miss Gannon," *Baltimore Sun*, July 30, 1845; "National Theatre," *Detroit Free Press*, July 11, 1839, 2.

63. "National. Benefit of Mast. Diamond" playbill, Oct. 18, 1839, MS Thr 1848, box 10, Houghton Library, Harvard University.

64. Levine, *Highbrow/Lowbrow*, 31; Reidiker, *The Amistad Rebellion*, 230.

65. Odell, *Annals of the New York Stage*, 383.

66. John Glenroy, *Ins and Outs of Circus Life or Forty-Two Years Travel of John H. Glenroy, Bareback Rider, Through United States, Canada, South America and Cuba*, comp. Stephen Stanley Stanford (M. M. Wing and Company, 1885), 27; Thayer, *Traveling Showmen*, 16, 35.

67. Thayer, *Traveling Showmen*, 13.

68. Glenroy, *Ins and Outs of Circus Life*, 34.

69. Thayer, *Traveling Showmen*, 73.

70. "Broadway Circus," *Evening Post* (New York), Jan. 21, 1840, 2.

71. Glenroy, *Ins and Outs of Circus Life*, 10; "Broadway Circus," *New York Herald*, Jan. 20, 27, 1840, 3.

72. Laurent Dubois, *The Banjo: America's African Instrument* (Harvard University Press, 2016), 169.

73. "Broadway Circus," *New York Herald*, Jan. 27, 1840, 3.

74. "Amusements," *Evening Post* (New York), Feb. 13, 1840, 2; "Chatham," *New York Herald*, May 2, 1840, 2.

75. "Broadway Circus," *New York Herald*, Jan. 20, 1840, 2.

76. "Broadway Circus," *Evening Post* (New York), Jan. 21, 1840, 2.

77. "Broadway Circus," *New York Herald*, Nov. 19–20, 1839, Dec. 23, 1839, Jan. 14, 20, 1840; "Bowery Amphitheater," *New York Herald*, Nov. 21, 25, 1839, Jan. 11, 1840.

78. "Bowery Amphitheatre," *New York Herald*, Jan. 9, 11, 1840, 3; "Broadway Circus," *Evening Post* (New York), Feb. 8, 10, 1840, 3.

79. Dubois, *The Banjo*, 169; Judith Tick Matthews and Paul Beaudoin Matthews, eds., *Music in the USA: A Documentary Companion* (Oxford University Press, 2008), 116.

80. Glenroy, *Ins and Outs of Circus Life*, 28; "BROADWAY CIRCUS," *New York Herald*, Jan. 20, 1840, 3.

81. Dennis Clark, "Babes in Bondage: Indentured Irish Children in Philadelphia in the Nineteenth Century," *Pennsylvania Magazine of History and Biography* 101, no. 4 (1977): 478–479; Leslie M. Harris, *In the Shadow of Slavery: African Americans in New York City, 1626–1863* (University of Chicago Press, 2003), 80; P. T. Barnum, *Struggles and Triumphs* (1869; abridged ed., Penguin Classics, 1987), 51; Frank Keeler, *Vagabond Adventures* (Fields, Osgood and Company, 1870), 123, 125; Barnum to Wemyss, "New York, Jany 21./40."

82. Glenroy, *Ins and Outs of Circus Life*, 6, 70.

83. Thayer, *Traveling Showmen*, 98.

84. Barnum to Wemyss, "New York, Jany 21./40."

Chapter 3. Trials of Skill and Servitude

1. The Chatham auditorium description draws on contemporary accounts and images of theater audiences in New York and Boston and on the spectators addressed in Diamond's newspaper ads. "Amusements," *Evening Post* (New York), Feb. 13, 1840, 2; Walt Whitman, "About Children," *Aurora*, Apr. 16, 1842, 2; Fanny Trollope, *Domestic Manners of the Americans* (1832), chaps. 13 and 25; *American Theatre, Bowery New York, Depicting the 57th Night of Mr. T. D. Jim Crow Rice, Nov. 25, 1833*, print; Alvin Fay Harlow, *Old Bowery Days: The Chronicle of a Famous Street* (D. Appleton, 1931), 276; Nathaniel Hawthorne, *The American Notebooks,* ed. Claude M. Simpson, Centenary Edition of the Works of Nathaniel Hawthorne (Ohio State University Press, 1972), 8:501; Charles Haynes Haswell, *Reminiscences of an Octogenarian of the City of New York* (Harper and Brothers, 1896), 362; Rosemarie Bank, *Theatre Culture in America, 1825–1860* (Cambridge University Press, 1997), 92, 96, 114, 134.

2. "Chatham Theatre," *New York Herald,* Feb. 8, 1840, 3.

3. "New Chatham Theatre," *Evening Post* (New York), Feb. 8, 1840, 2.

4. "Chatham Theatre," *New York Herald,* Feb. 11, 1840, 3.

5. "Chatham Theatre," *Morning Herald* (New York), Feb. 12, 1840, 3; George C. D. Odell, *Annals of the New York Stage, Vol. IV: 1834–1843* (Columbia University Press, 1928), 383–384; Joseph Norton Ireland, *Records of the New York Stage from 1750 to 1860* (T. H. Morrell, 1867), 2:324; "Chatham Theatre," *New York Herald,* Feb. 8, 1840, 3.

6. "$500 Challenge Leroy's Specifique Francaise," *New York Herald,* Sept. 2, 1839, 1.

7. "Things Theatrical. The Chatham," *Spirit of the Times,* Feb. 15, 1840, 600.

8. Stuart Hall, "11. Notes on Deconstructing 'The Popular'" (1981), in *Essential Essays, Volume 1: Foundations of Cultural Studies,* ed. David Morley (Duke University Press, 2018), 347–361, https://doi.org/10.1515/9781478002413-018.

9. Ireland, *Records of the New York Stage,* 2:321–324; T. Allston Brown, *A History of the New York Stage* (Dodd, Mead and Company, 1903), 1:297; Mary C. Henderson, *The City and the Theater* (Back Stage Books, 2004), 60; "Chatham Theatre," *Morning Herald* (New York), Feb. 12, 1840, 3.

10. "Chatham Theatre," *New York Herald,* Feb. 11, 1840, 3.

11. "DRAMA IN BOWERY DAYS Chief Conlin's Reminiscences of East Side Glories. When Charley White Was the Idol of the Boys—The Later Rivalries and the Well-Known Favorites," *New York Times,* Dec. 13, 1896.

12. Lawrence Levine, "William Shakespeare and the American People: A Study in Cultural Transformation," *American Historical Review* 89, no. 1 (1984): 42; Bank, *Theatre Culture,* 134; Thomas L. Nichols, *Forty Years of American Life* (John Maxwell and Company, 1864), 229; Hawthorne, *The American Notebooks,* 501.

13. Harlow, *Old Bowery Days,* 276–277.

14. Bank, *Theatre Culture,* 92, 133; Christine Stansell, *City of Women: Sex and Class in New York, 1789–1869* (University of Illinois Press, 1987), 181, 256n58; Patricia Cline Cohen, *The Murder of Helen Jewett* (Alfred A. Knopf, 1998), 67–68; Timothy Gilfoyle, *City of Eros: New York City, Prostitution, and the Commercialization of Sex, 1790–1920* (W. W. Norton, 1992), 111.

15. "DRAMA IN BOWERY DAYS," *New York Times,* Dec. 13, 1896; John Bach McMaster, *A History of the People of the United States, from the Revolution to the Civil War, Vol. VII: 1841–1850* (D. Appleton and Company, 1914), 89–90.

16. Stuart Thayer, *Traveling Showmen: The American Circus Before the Civil War* (Astley and Ricketts, 1997), 74; Banks, *Theatre Culture,* 134.

17. "New Theatre" playbill, Mobile, Feb. 22, 1841, MS Thr 1848, box 10 (Diamond, Master), Houghton Library, Harvard University; "Master Diamond at Mobile," *Weekly Picayune,* Mar. 1, 1841, 10; "Bowery Amphitheatre," *New York Herald,* Feb. 1, 1843, 3; Arthur Herman Wilson, *A History of the Philadelphia Theatre, 1835 to 1855* (Greenwood Press, 1968), 25, 35; Edward Ingle, *The Negro in the District of Columbia* (Johns Hopkins Press, 1893), 47.

18. "Chatham Theatre," *Morning Herald,* Feb. 13, 1840, 3; *Evening Post* (New York), Feb. 13, 1840, 2.

19. Pierre Bourdieu, "Sport and Social Class," in *Rethinking Popular Culture,* ed. Chandra Mukerji and Michael Schudson (University of California Press, 1991), 363.

20. George G. Foster, "Philadelphia in Slices," *New-York Daily Tribune,* Nov. 17, 1848, reprinted in *Philadelphia Magazine of History and Biography* 93 (1969): 40.

21. J. S. Bratton, "Dancing a Hornpipe in Fetters," *Folk Music Journal* 6, no. 1 (1990): 68, 70–77; R. Shelton Mackenzie, *Bits of Blarney* (Redfield, 1854), 294–295.

22. "CARD," *Baltimore Sun,* Jan. 15, 1840, 2; "American Amphitheatre," *Baltimore Sun,* Jan. 16, 1840, 3; "New Chatham Theatre," *Morning Herald* (New York), Sept. 12, 1840.

23. "The Negro Minstrels of the Nights Gone By," ca. 1875, HTC Clippings 13 (Bryant, Dan), Houghton Library, Harvard University.

24. "Benefit of Master Diamond," *Morning Herald* (New York), Feb. 18, 1840, 3.

25. Andrew Davis, *America's Longest Run: A History of the Walnut Street Theatre* (Pennsylvania State University Press, 2010), 71; Charles Durang, *History of the Philadelphia Stage Between the Years of 1749 and 1855* (1856), 1:154.

26. Davis, *America's Longest Run,* 70–74.

27. Francis Courtney Wemyss, *Theatrical biography: or, The life of an actor and manager; interspersed with sketches, anecdotes, and opinions of the professional merits of the most celebrated actors and actresses of our day* (R. Griffin, 1848), 259.

28. "The Challenge Accepted!!," *Public Ledger* (Philadelphia), Feb. 29, 1840, 3.

29. This scene is drawn from accounts of the evening and images of the Walnut Street Theatre. "The Dancing Match," *Public Ledger,* Mar. 4, 1840, 2; *Philadelphia History* (City History Society of Philadelphia, 1916), 2:365–366; Samuel S. Sanford, "Personal Reminiscences," manuscript p. [8]/6, Minstrel Show Collection, 1831–1859, Harry Ransom Center, University of Texas at Austin; John Lewis Krimmel, *Nightlife in Philadelphia—an Oyster Barrow in front of the Chestnut Street Theatre,* ca. 1811–1813, Metropolitan Museum of Art; *Theatre, Walnut Street, Philadelphia,* 1831, print; the Walnut Street Theater, 1865, photo, https://www.walnutstreettheatre.org/about/gallery/?ch=2&id=11.

30. Supposedly born Blandford, Sanford (also spelled Sandford) may have changed his surname to imitate pugilist James "The American Phenomenon" Sanford, who fought English boxer James "Deaf" Burk in Philadelphia in 1836. See "The Fancy," *Public Ledger,* Aug. 4, 1836, 2.

31. Col. T. Allston Brown, "Early History of Negro Minstrelsy: Its Rise and Progress in the United States," *New York Clipper,* Feb. 24, 1912, 5; Joel Benton, *Life of the Honorable PT Barnum* (Edgewood Publishing Company, 1891), 85; P. T. Barnum, *The Life of P. T. Barnum* (Redfield, 1855), 187, 189.

32. "Broadway Circus," *New York Herald,* Nov. 19, 1839, 3; Stuart Thayer, *Annals of the American Circus, Vol. II: 1830–1847* (Peanut Butter Publishing, 1986), 264–265.

33. P. T. Barnum to F. C. Wemyss, Esq., "New York, Jany 21./40," document case 8, folder P. T. Barnum Collection, 1840–1890, New York Historical Society.

34. "Acknowledgement," *Public Ledger* (Philadelphia), Mar. 4, 1840, 2.

35. "Walnut Street Theatre," *Alexander's Weekly Messenger* (Philadelphia), Mar. 4, 1840, 3.

36. Francis Courtney Wemyss, *Twenty-six Years of the Life of an Actor and Manager. Interspersed with Sketches, Anecdotes and Opinions of the Professional Merits of the Most Celebrated Actors and Actresses of Our Day* (Burgess, Stringer and Company, 1846), 323.

37. P. T. Barnum, *Struggles and Triumphs* (1869; abridged ed., Penguin Classics, 1987), 85–86; "Brilliant Attraction!! Sig. Vivalla" playbill, ca. 1836, Somers Historical Society, Sommers, N.Y.

38. Neil Harris, *Humbug: The Art of P. T. Barnum* (Little, Brown and Company, 1973), 25; Barnum, *Struggles and Triumphs,* 86.

39. Nicholas Mirra, "Outgrowing Our Citizens: The Demise of Philadelphia's Volunteer Firefighting System" (senior history thesis, Haverford College, 2006), 4; *New York Herald,* Oct. 21, 1839, cited in Dale Cockrell, *Demons of Disorder: Early Blackface Minstrels and Their World* (Cambridge University Press, 1997), 85–86; John C. McWilliams, "'Men of Colour': Race, Riots, and Black Firefighters' Struggle for Equality from the AFA to the Valiants," *Journal of Social History* 41, no. 1 (2007): 110.

40. "Walnut Street Theatre," *Public Ledger,* Mar. 9, 1840, 2.

41. "Amusement Annals—Clipper Series, No. LXII. William M. Whitlock. The Origin of Negro Minstrelsy," *New York Clipper,* Apr. 13, 1878, 21; Bob Flesher and Rita Flesher, eds., *Historical Reprints of the Origin of Negro Minstrelsy* (Dr. Horsehair Music, 1999), 14–17; Charles Hamm, *Yesterdays: Popular Song in America* (Norton, 1979), 127.

42. P. T. Barnum to Francis Courtney Wemyss, "Boston, 16 April 1840," box 1, folder Barnum, Phineas Taylor (1810–1891), Stephen Whitney Phoenix Papers, MS 0997, Rare Books and Manuscripts Library, Butler Library, Columbia University.

43. Seymour Dunbar, *A History of Travel in America* (Tudor Publishing Company, 1937), 741, 750, 743.

44. "Grand Musical and Comical Olio," *Hartford Courant*, May 8, 1840, 3.

45. "New Theatre of Mirth and Variety . . . (late the Franklin Theatre)," *Herald*, May 25–27, 1840; "Dinneford's New Theatre," *Herald*, June 1, 1840, 1.

46. Odell, *Annals of the New York Stage*, 396; Edward Ruggles, *A Picture of New York in 1848: with a short account of places in the vicinity: designed as a guide to citizens and strangers* (C. S. Francis, 1848), 66–67; McMaster, *A History of the People*, 89–90.

47. "National. Benefit of Mast. Diamond" playbill, June 9, 1840, MS Thr 1848, box 10, Houghton Library, Harvard University.

48. "National. Diamond" playbill, June 5, 1840, MS Thr 1848, box 10, Houghton Library, Harvard University.

49. "Franklin," in Odell, *Annals of the New York Stage*, 395; Maria Amparo Ruiz de Burton, *Who Would Have Thought It?* (1872; repr., Penguin, 2009), 4; Karl Bell, *The Legend of Spring-heeled Jack: Victorian Urban Folklore and Popular Cultures* (Boydell Press, 2002), 1; Lawrence Levine, *Highbrow/Lowbrow: The Emergence of Cultural Hierarchy in America* (Harvard University Press, 1990), 33; Prasenjit Duara, "Transnationalism and the Challenge to National Histories," in *Rethinking American History in a Global Age*, ed. Thomas Bender (University of California Press, 2002), 13, 16.

50. *The Tennessean* (Nashville), June 8, 1839, 3.

51. Marlis Schweitzer, "'An Unmanly and Insidious Attack': Child Actress Jean Davenport and the Performance of Masculinity in 1840s Jamaica and Newfoundland," *Theatre Research in Canada / Recherches théâtrales au Canada* 35, no. 1 (2014): 55; T. B. Pugh, *Biographical Sketch of Mrs. F. W. Lander, Formerly Miss Jean M. Davenport, Tragedienne, with Criticisms of the Press on Her Rendition of Elizabeth, Queen of England* (T. B. Pugh, 1867), 3.

52. For example, "Cracovienne, by Master Wood . . . New Chatham Theatre," *Morning Herald* (New York), Sept. 12, 1840; Shauna Vey, *Childhood and Nineteenth-Century American Theatre: The Work of the Marsh Troupe of Juvenile Actors* (Southern Illinois University Press, 2015), 102–103.

53. Ralph Keeler, *Vagabond Adventures* (Fields, Osgood and Company, 1870), 131.

54. Schweitzer, "'An Unmanly and Insidious Attack,'" 49; Amy Varty, *Children and Theatre in Victorian Britain: "All Work, No Play"* (Palgrave Macmillan, 2008), 11–12.

55. *The Manager's Daughter*, reprinted under the title *The Young Actress: An Interlude in One Act* (Samuel French, 1868); Schweitzer, "'An Unmanly and Insidious Attack,'" 53.

56. James Orchard Halliwell, *Dictionary of Archaic and Provincial Words, Obsolete Phrases, Proverbs, and Ancient Customs, from the Fourteenth Century* (J. R. Smith, 1850), 2:744.

57. "National. Diamond" playbill, June 5, 1840. Choreographer and dancer M'lle Augusta was said to have surpassed Céleste in her delineation of Zoloe in the 1836 Park Theatre production of *La bayadère*.

58. William G. B. Carson, *Managers in Distress: The St. Louis Stage, 1840–1844* (Ayer Publishing Company, 1949), 125, 123.

59. "The Baltimore Museum," *Baltimore Sun*, Nov. 28, 1838, 3.

60. "DAILY EVENING MAIL," *Public Ledger* (Philadelphia), Mar. 5, 1840, 2; Brown, "Early History," 5.

61. "National. Diamond" playbill, June 5, 1840.

62. According to historian T. J. Desch Obi, West African battle dancers made a similar horizontal line in the sand. Thomas Hauser, "the bare-knuckle era," https://www.britannica.com/sports/boxing/The-bare-knuckle-era; and "boxing," *Encyclopaedia Britannica*, https://www.britannica.com/sports/boxing, accessed May 18, 2024.

63. *Baltimore Sun*, June 1, 1840, 3.

64. M'Arann's Garden (also spelled M'Aran or McArran) occupied the four-acre square block that today holds Philadelphia's Independence Visitor Center and its lawns. Philadelphia playbill, Monday, June 22, 1840, WorldCat.org, OCLC no. 84686081; "Great Attraction for Twenty-five Cents," *Daily Pennsylvanian* (Philadelphia), June 23, 1840, 3; *North American* (Philadelphia), June 25, 1840, 2; "The Journal of J. Warner Erwin, 1839–1854," June 26, 1840, https://losthistory.net/iconog/jwe/jweint.html.

65. "The Little Negro Dancer," *Public Ledger* (Philadelphia), June 30, 1840, 2.

66. Cohen, *Murder of Helen Jewett*, 9.

67. "City Police.—*Monday, June 29, 1840*," *Public Ledger* (Philadelphia), June 30, 1840, 2.

68. "Stealing Diamonds," *Evening Post* (New York), June 30, 1840.

69. "Master Diamond," *North American* (Philadelphia), July 11, 1840, 2; "City Gleanings," *Public Ledger*, July 10, 1840, 2.

70. "American Theatre," *Philadelphia Inquirer*, July 13–14, 1840, 3.

Chapter 4. Master Rattler

1. "Vauxhall Gardens," *Evening Post* (New York), June 17 and Aug. 15, 1840, 3; P. T. Barnum, *Struggles and Triumphs* (1869; abridged ed., Penguin Classics, 1987), 91; "Vauxhall Gardens," *Evening Post* (New York), July 13, 1840, 3; Thomas L. Nichols, *Forty Years of American Life* (Longmans, Green and Company, 1864), 369–370.

2. Leonard P. Curry, *The Free Black in Urban America, 1800–1850: The Shadow of the Dream* (University of Chicago Press, 1981), 90; Leslie M. Harris, *In the Shadow of Slavery: African Americans in New York City, 1626–1863* (University of Chicago Press, 2003), 270–271.

3. Charles Dickens, *American Notes* (Chapman and Hall, 1842; edited ed., Penguin Classics, 2000), 91–92; "Herald Building, Broadway," in Matthew Hale Smith, *Sunshine and Shadow in New York* (J. B. Burr and Company, 1868), 515.

4. "Vauxhall Gardens," *Evening Post* (New York), June 26, 1840, 3.

5. Curry, *Free Black in Urban America*, 21, 22, 293.

6. Curry, *Free Black in Urban America*, 258. Curry divides the total data on free black occupations into eight categories: unskilled; semiskilled; personal service; transportation; food service; artisan; entrepreneurial and mercantile; and professional managerial, artistic, clerical, or scientific. The ingenuity of free Black people (whose employments were limited) shows up in the over 350 different occupations, ranging from rag picker to merchant, and 17 unclassifiable occupations, including bones player, listed in city censuses from 1800 and 1850. "Wants to Know" columns in the flash press provide corroboration. *Flash*, Sept. 11,

1842, 2; *Whip and Satirist of New-York and Brooklyn*, Jan. 29, 1842, 6; "Cranberry," *Whip and Satirist*, Mar. 26, 1842, 3; "Columbiaville," *Flash*, Oct. 2, 1842, 3; *Flash*, Dec. 3, 1842, 4; *Whip*, Sept. 10, 1842, 2; *Flash*, Jan. 22, 1842, 3.

7. Curry, *Free Black in Urban America*, 24; Laurie A. Wilke, "Granny Midwives: Gender and Generational Mediators of the African American Community," in *Engendering African American Archeology: A Southern Perspective*, ed. Jillian E. Galle (University of Tennessee Press, 2004), 79; James Thomas, *From Tennessee Slave to St. Louis Entrepreneur: The Autobiography of James Thomas* (1904), ed. Loren Schweninger (University of Missouri Press, 1984), 67, 70.

8. Curry, *Free Black in Urban America*, 175; Darlene Clark Hine et al., *The African American Odyssey* (Pearson / Prentice Hall, 2008), 175.

9. *Whip*, Jan. 28, 1843, 6; Harris, *In the Shadow of Slavery*, 82.

10. Barnum, *Struggles and Triumphs*, 79.

11. Vincent DiGirolamo, *Crying the News: A History of the American Newsboy* (Oxford University Press, 2019), 7.

12. Abram Child Dayton, *Last Days of Knickerbocker Life in New York* (G. W. Harlan, 1882), 140.

13. Dayton, *Last Days*, 140; George C. D. Odell, *Annals of the New York Stage, Vol. IV: 1834–1843* (Columbia University Press, 1928), 433; "Vauxhall Gardens," *Evening Post* (New York), June 25, 26, 1840, 3.

14. Naomi J. Stubbs, *Cultivating National Identity Through Performance: American Pleasure Gardens and Entertainment* (Palgrave Macmillan, 2013), 135–137.

15. *Philadelphia History* (City History Society of Philadelphia, 1916), 2:366.

16. "Castle Garden . . . Stages run from Bowling Green until 11 o'clock," "Colonnade Garden . . . Fulton ferry boats run all night," and "Niblo's Garden . . . Omnibusses will run to and from the Garden during the evening," *Evening Post* (New York), July 24, 1840, 4; Cezar Joseph Del Valle, *The Brooklyn Theatre Index, Volume 1: Adams Street to Lorimer Street* (Theater Talks, 2010), 106.

17. Naomi Stubbs, "Pleasure Gardens of America: Anxieties of National Identity," in *The Pleasure Garden, from Vauxhall to Coney Island*, ed. Jonathan Conlin (University of Pennsylvania Press, 2013), 141–142; Marvin Edward McAllister, *White People Do Not Know How to Behave at Entertainments Designed for Ladies & Gentlemen of Colour* (University of North Carolina Press, 2003), 29; Stubbs, *Cultivating National Identity*, 88; Harris, *In the Shadow of Slavery*, 77–79.

18. Jonathan Dewberry, "The African Grove Theatre and Company," *Black American Literature Forum* 16, no. 4 (1982): 128–131; McAllister, *White People*, 30.

19. Ira Aldridge, *Anglo-African Magazine*, Jan. 1860, quoted in Dewberry, "The African Grove Theatre," 128.

20. "To the Public," *Evening Post* (New York), July 16, 17, 1829, 3.

21. *National Advocate*, Sept. 21, 1821, 2. Pleasure gardens mostly operated from mid-June to October and in winter were used for other purposes. "Equestrian Exchange—Vauxhall Garden," *Morning Herald* (New York), Oct. 3, 1839.

22. Dayton, *Last Days*, 140–141.

23. "Niblo's Garden," *Evening Post* (New York), Sept. 14, 1837, 2; "Niblo's Garden and New Saloon," *Evening Post*, Aug. 27, 1839, 3; Stubbs, "Pleasure Gardens of America," 144–145; Dayton, *Last Days*, 140.

24. "Vauxhall Garden Saloon, Bowery," *New York Herald*, July 14, 1845, 3; Odell, *Annals of the New York Stage*, 494, 434.

25. "Vauxhall Gardens," *Evening Post* (New York), July 22, 30, 31, and Aug. 3, 1840, 3; Odell, *Annals of the New York Stage*, 434.

26. "Vauxhall Gardens," *Morning Herald* (New York), July 18, 1840, 3; "Vauxhall Gardens," *Evening Post* (New York), July 20, 1840, 3; "Vauxhall Gardens," *Morning Herald*, July 24, 1840, 4.

27. "Rattling" and dances such as the "Rattlesnake Jig" became showpieces among nineteenth-century challenge dancers and twentieth-century tap dancers. "Ann Miller tapped 500 taps per minute in 1974" (Ollie Mae Ray, "Biographies of Selected Leaders in Tap Dance" [PhD diss., University of Utah Graduate School, 1976], 295).

28. Marion Hannah Winter, "Juba and American Minstrelsy," in *Chronicles of the American Dance*, ed. Paul Magriel (1948), 40; Pierre Swartenbroeckx, *Dictionnaire Kikongo et Kituba—Français: Vocabulaire comparé des langages Kongo traditionnels et véhiculaires* (CEEBA, 1973), 2:805, 521.

29. "VAUXHALL GARDENS," *New York Herald*, Aug. 31, 1840, 3.

30. Shane White, *Stories of Freedom in Black New York* (Harvard University Press, 2002), 141, 150; McAllister, *White People*, 32.

31. *New York Herald*, July 24, 1840, 3.

32. "Vauxhall Gardens," *Evening Post* (New York), July 27, 1840, 3.

33. Many thanks to Patricia Cline Cohen for advice on reading this document.

34. "Vauxhall Gardens," *New York Herald*, July 29, 1940, 3; *Evening Post* (New York), Aug. 1, 4, 1840, 3.

35. "Multiple News Items," *Morning Herald*, July 29, 1840.

36. "Vauxhall Gardens," *Evening Post* (New York), July 31, Aug. 1, 1840, 3.

37. "Vauxhall Gardens," *Morning Herald* (New York), July 29, Aug. 3, 1840.

38. "New Chatham Theatre" and "Vauxhall Gardens," *Morning Herald*, Aug. 3, 1840.

39. "THE DIAMOND," *New York Evening Tattler* quoted in the *Picayune* (New Orleans), Jan. 2, 1841, 2.

40. Martha Hodes, "The Mercurial Nature and Abiding Power of Race: A Transnational Family Story," *American Historical Review* 108, no. 1 (2003): 85.

41. "Vauxhall Gardens" and "New Chatham Theatre," *Morning Herald* (New York), Aug. 6, 7, 1840, 3; "Vauxhall Gardens," *Evening Post* (New York), Aug. 5, 6, 1840, 3.

42. "Vauxhall Gardens," *Morning Herald* (New York), Aug. 15, 12, 1840, 3.

43. "Vauxhall Gardens," *Evening Post*, Aug. 22, 27, 1840, 3.

44. "Vauxhall Gardens," *Evening Post*, Aug. 25, 1840, 3.

45. "Vauxhall Garden," *New York Herald*, Aug. 29, 1840, 2.

46. Stuart Thayer, *Annals of the American Circus, Vol. II: 1830–1847* (Peanut Butter Publishing, 1986), 15.

47. "Vauxhall Gardens," *Morning Herald* (New York), Sept. 5, 1840.

Chapter 5. North and South

1. "From the Loco Foco New Era of Saturday" quoted in "THE RIOT AND OUTRAGE," *New-York American for the Country,* published as *New-York American,* Aug. 17, 1840, 2, and reprinted in London's *Morning Chronicle,* Sept. 2, 1840.

2. "Fanny Elssler: Austrian Ballerina," https://www.britannica.com/biography/Fanny-Elssler.

3. "Folly," *North American and Daily Advertiser* (Philadelphia), May 21, 1840; "An Ass," *Morning Herald* (New York), May 25, 1840.

4. John Bach McMaster, *A History of the People of the United States: 1830–1841* (D. Appleton, 1906), 586.

5. F. Byrdsall, *The History of the Loco-Foco or Equal Rights Party, Its Movements, Conventions and Proceedings, with Short Sketches of its Prominent Men* (Clement and Packard, 1842), 107–108, 110.

6. The 1849 Astor Place riot included nativists and Irish immigrants who were against the British and Anglophile upper classes. Paul A. Gilje, *The Road to Mobocracy: Popular Disorder in New York City, 1763–1834* (University of North Carolina Press, 1987), 247.

7. "From the Loco Foco New Era, of Saturday," *Morning Chronicle* (London), Sept. 2, 1840.

8. *New-York American,* Aug. 17, 1840, 2; *New-York Express* quoted in *Virginia Free Press,* Aug. 20, 1840; Dale Cockrell, *Demons of Disorder: Early Blackface Minstrels and Their World* (Cambridge University Press, 1997), 127–128.

9. "More Serenading," *Public Ledger* (Philadelphia), Aug. 29, 1840, 2.

10. Gary B. Nash, *Forging Freedom: The Formation of Philadelphia's Black Community, 1720–1840* (Harvard University Press, 1988), 166, 168, 206, 249; "Letter from Philadelphia, Apr. 12, 1842," *Whip and Satirist of New-York and Brooklyn,* Apr. 16, 1842, 3; Dennis Clark, *The Irish in Philadelphia: Ten Generations of Urban Experience* (Temple University Press, 1982), 18–19, 41.

11. John Fanning Watson, *Annals of Philadelphia . . .* (1830), 244; John Thomas Scharf and Thompson Westcott, *History of Philadelphia, 1609–1884* (1884), 2:1012; *Philadelphia in 1830–1: or, A Brief Account of the Various Institutions and Public Objects in this Metropolis* (E. L. Carey and A. Hart, 1830), 224; Harry Kyriakodis, *Northern Liberties: The Story of a Philadelphia River Ward* (Arcadia Publishing, 2012), chap. 21; "Dancing for Eels," *The Flash,* Nov. 12, 1842, 1.

12. Nash, *Forging Freedom,* 216, 252.

13. Clark, *The Irish in Philadelphia,* 18–19.

14. Emma Jones Lapsansky, "'Since They Got Those Separate Churches': Afro-Americans and Racism in Jacksonian Philadelphia," *American Quarterly* 32, no. 1 (1980): 57, 62, 64; Leslie M. Harris, *In the Shadow of Slavery: African Americans in New York City, 1626–1863* (University of Chicago Press, 2003), 182.

15. *Public Ledger* (Philadelphia), Mar. 10, 1840, 2.

16. "The Anti-Railroad Meeting," *Public Ledger,* Aug. 4, 1840, 2.

17. *Philadelphia Inquirer,* Sept. 30, 1840, 2.

18. Stuart Thayer, *Traveling Showmen: The American Circus Before the Civil War* (Astley and Ricketts, 1997), 27, 23.

19. Frank Keeler, *Vagabond Adventures* (Field, Osgood and Company, 1870), 123, 125.

20. Solomon Northup, *Twelve Years a Slave* (1853; facsimile ed., Dover Publications, 1970), 23–32, 218; James Thomas, *From Tennessee Slave to St. Louis Entrepreneur: The Autobiography of James Thomas,* ed. Loren Schweninger (1904; University of Missouri Press, 1984), 44–45; Phil Jamison, *Hoedowns, Reels, and Frolics: Roots and Branches of Southern Appalachian Dance* (University of Illinois Press, 2015), 44–59; "Twenty Dollars Reward," *Mississippi Free Trader* (Natchez), Apr. 5, 1833, 3.

21. George G. Foster, "Philadelphia in Slices," *New-York Daily Tribune,* Nov. 17, 1848, reprinted in *Philadelphia Magazine of History and Biography* 93 (1969): 38–40.

22. Thayer, *Traveling Showmen,* 39.

23. Phineas T. Barnum, *The Life of P. T. Barnum* (Redfield, 1855), 211.

24. Noah Miller Ludlow, *Dramatic Life as I Found it: A Record of Personal Experience, with an Account of the Rise and Progress of the Drama in the West and South, with Anecdotes and Biographical Sketches of the Principal Actors and Actresses who Have at Times Appeared Upon the Stage in the Mississippi Valley* (G. I. Jones and Company, 1880), 195.

25. "Grand Concert and Comical Entertainment," *Cabinet* (Schenectady, NY), Sept. 8, 1840; "Chedell's Concert Room," *Auburn Journal,* Sept. 16, 1840; *Commercial Advertiser and Journal* (Buffalo), Oct. 9, 1840, 2; and "Eagle Street Theatre," *Commercial Advertiser and Journal,* Oct. 22, 1840, 6.

26. Thayer, *Traveling Showmen,* 26.

27. Barnum, *The Life,* 211; "Delany's Saloon," *Morning Courier* (Springfield, IL), Nov. 1, 1840; "A CHALLENGE FOR ONE HUNDRED DOLLARS," *Detroit Free Press,* Nov. 12, 1840, 2; Alfred Theodore Andreas, *History of Chicago, Volume I: Ending with the year 1857* (A. T. Andreas, 1884), 497.

28. P. T. Barnum, *Struggles and Triumphs* (1869; abridged ed., Penguin Classics, 1987), 91.

29. Charles Keemle to Noah Ludlow, Dec. 13, 1840, box 2, Ludlow-Field-Maury Family Papers, Missouri History Museum and Library, quoted in Nicole Berkin, "Antebellum Touring and the Culture of Deception: The Case of Master Diamond," *Theatre History Studies* 34 (2015): 45.

30. "Police Office. Sept. 12 . . . Somewhat Suspicious," *Morning Herald* (New York), Sept. 14, 1840, 1.

31. *New York Daily Express,* Sept. 14, 1840, quoted in Cockrell, *Demons of Disorder,* 88n109.

32. "From the New World Abuse of the Laws," *Emancipator and Free American* (London), Nov. 24, 1842, 120.

33. Harris, *In the Shadow of Slavery,* 208.

34. "How to Carry an Election," *Boston Courier,* Sept. 29, 1842.

35. "Vauxhall Garden," *Morning Herald,* Sept. 14, 1840, 3.

36. Thayer, *Traveling Showmen,* 98.

37. "Court of Sessions . . . James Hewlett, the negro tragedian," *New York Herald,* June 20, 1837, 1; "Police Office, June 7 . . . An Amalgamationist," *Evening Post* (New York), June 8, 1839, 2; "A Practical Amalgamationist," *New York Herald,* June 8, 1839, 2.

38. "A Fast Going Watch," *Weekly Picayune* (New Orleans), Feb. 22, 1841, 1.

39. Northup, *Twelve Years a Slave,* chap. 6; Walter Johnson, *Soul by Soul: Life Inside the Antebellum Slave Market* (Harvard University Press, 2001), chap. 4.

40. "Impudent Theft," "Mr. Ranger," and "Master Diamond," *Daily Picayune* (New Orleans), Jan. 2, 1841, 2.

41. File# 1840-0001, filename John Dimond, Article 17, Person and Property Guardianship Petition, Municipal Archives of New York City.

42. Barnum, *Struggles and Triumphs,* 91–92; Barnum, *The Life,* 211.

43. Ludlow, *Dramatic Life,* 553.

44. Solomon Smith, *Theatrical Management for Thirty Years with Anecdotal Sketches* (Harper and Brothers, 1868), 157, 155; "American Theatre," *Picayune* (New Orleans), Jan. 6, 1841, 3.

45. Sol Smith to E. Woolf, New Orleans, Feb. 7, 1841, quoted in Smith, *Theatrical Management,* 155; Ludlow, *Dramatic Life,* 540.

46. "St. Charles Theatre" and "American Theatre," *Times-Picayune* (New Orleans), Jan. 8–10, 1841.

47. William G. B. Carson, *Managers in Distress: The St. Louis Stage, 1840–1844* (Ayer Company, 1949), 145.

48. Paul Smith Hostetler, "James H. Caldwell: Theatre Manager" (PhD diss., Louisiana State University, 1964), iv–vi.

49. "MASTER DIAMOND," *Daily Picayune,* Jan. 12, 1841, 2.

50. *Daily Picayune,* Jan. 14, 1841, 3.

51. "Negro Dancers," *New York Sporting Whip,* Jan. 21, 1843, 2.

52. "Master Diamond," *Daily Picayune,* Jan. 3, 1841, 2; "Negro Dancers," *Whip,* Jan. 21, 1843, 2; Thomas L. Nichols, *Forty Years of American Life* (Longmans, Green and Company, 1864), 229.

53. "War in Texas!!!," *Daily Picayune,* Jan. 15, 1841, 2; and "St. Charles Theatre," *Daily Picayune,* Jan. 16, 1841, 3.

54. "Master Diamond," *Daily Picayune,* Jan. 2, 1841.

55. William J. Mahar, *Behind the Burnt Cork Mask: Early Blackface Minstrelsy and Antebellum American Popular Culture* (University of Illinois Press, 1999), 198, 200–201; W. T. Lhamon, *Jump Jim Crow: Lost Plays, Lyrics, and Street Prose of the First Atlantic Popular Culture* (Harvard University Press, 2003), 88.

56. Barnum, *The Life,* 211.

57. "Master Diamond," "Challenge Accepted," and "St. Charles," *Daily Picayune,* Jan. 17, 1841, 2.

58. *Daily Picayune,* Jan. 17, 1841, 2.

59. "Amusements. St. Charles Theatre," *Daily Picayune,* Jan. 19, 1841, 3; and "St. Charles," *Daily Picayune,* Jan. 19, 1841, 2.

60. Smith diary quoted in Berkin, "Antebellum Touring," 46.

61. "Sol Smith, City Hotel, Natchez, to N. M. Ludlow, Jany. 24, Sunday night, 1841," box 1, Solomon Franklin Smith Papers, Sol Smith Collections, Missouri History Museum Archives, St. Louis.

62. Barnum, *Struggles and Triumphs,* 92.
63. "THEATRE," *Vicksburg (MS) Daily Whig,* Jan. 28, 1841, 2; "The Omnibus" quoted in the *Daily Picayune,* Jan. 22, 1841, 2; *Daily Picayune,* Jan. 26, 1841, 2.
64. *Daily Picayune,* Jan. 22, 1841, 2.
65. The *Mobile Register* quoted in "Master Diamond at Mobile," *Daily Picayune,* Feb. 23, 1841, 2.
66. Barnum, *The Life,* 211–212.
67. *Vicksburg Tri-Weekly Sentinel,* Feb. 6, 1841, 2; *Daily Picayune,* Feb. 9, 1841, 2.
68. *Daily Picayune,* Feb. 9, 10, 1841, 2.
69. P. T. Barnum to "Messrs. Fogg & Stickney, Ludlow & Smith," Mobile, Feb. 27, 1841, box 4, Smith Papers.
70. Barnum, *The Life,* 211–212.
71. Roy Rosensweig, "The Rise of the Saloon," in *Rethinking Popular Culture,* ed. Chandra Mukerji and Michael Schudson (University of California Press, 1991), 143; "The Cake Dance," *Béaloideas: The Journal of the Folklore of Ireland Society* 11, no. 1/2 (1941): 131.
72. Barnum to "Messrs. Fogg & Stickney, Ludlow & Smith," Mobile, Feb. 27, 1841.
73. P. T. Barnum to Mr. S. Smith, New Orleans, Mar. 3 [1841], box 4, Smith Papers.
74. Hostetler, "James H. Caldwell," 478–481; *Daily Picayune,* Mar. 9, 1841, 2, 3.
75. Ludlow, *Dramatic Life,* 536–537; Smith, *Theatrical Management,* 155.
76. There are several accounts of this incident. In another of Barnum's versions, Jenkins asked R. W. Lindsay to sue Barnum for breach of promise, which Barnum claimed referred to some brandy he had promised Lindsay when he bought Joyce Heth off him in 1835. Another version, taken from court records, has Lindsay testifying that Barnum stole the stage name Master Diamond from "a negro boy" whom he had hired. See Barnum, *The Life,* 212–213; Barnum, *Struggles and Triumphs,* 92; J. W. F. White, "The Judiciary of Alleghany County," *Pennsylvania Magazine of History and Biography* 7 (1883): 176.
77. Matt Field to Cornelia Field, March 16, 1841, box 2, Ludlow-Field-Maury Family Papers; "CIRCUS," *Vicksburg (MS) Daily Whig,* Mar. 15, 1841, 2; Berkin, "Antebellum Touring," 51.
78. Barnum, *Struggles and Triumphs,* 109.
79. "Vauxhall Garden," *Evening Post,* Sept. 24, 1841, 3; "Arcadian Garden," *New-York Tribune,* Sept. 3, 1841, 3.
80. "Double Refined Humbug," *Sunday Flash,* Sept. 19, 1841, 3.
81. "Vauxhall Humbug Again," *Sunday Flash,* Sept. 26, 1841, 2.
82. Barnum, *Struggles and Triumphs,* 81–84; Leroy Ashby, *With Amusement for All: A History of American Popular Culture Since 1830* (University Press of Kentucky, 2006), 27–31.
83. Karen Halttunen, *Confidence Men and Painted Women: A Study of Middle-Class Culture in America, 1830–1870* (Yale University Press, 1982), xv, and see chaps. 1–4.
84. "Vauxhall Garden," *Evening Post,* Sept. 4, 1841, 3.
85. "VAUXHALL GARDEN," *Evening Post,* Sept. 9, 1841, 3; "VAUXHALL GARDEN . . . Old Phil's Benefit," *Evening Post,* Sept. 24, 1841, 3.

86. *Philadelphia Ledger,* Sept. 15, 16, 1840, 3; *Baltimore Sun,* Sept. 25, 1840, 2.

87. "New York Museum and Picture Gallery," *New York Herald,* Dec. 18, 24, 1842.

88. "Negro Dancers," *Whip,* Jan. 21, 1843, 2.

89. Lindsay had Barnum arrested on capias and thrown into jail in Pittsburgh. The argument went before Judge Robert C. Grier of Alleghany County, Pennsylvania, who saw no difference between the two "vagabond" impresarios and discharged Barnum. Lindsay's story was probably true. White managers did engage Black performers, and at least one circus employee remembered his company's agent riding ahead to cover up or change the dates on another company's posters. See White, "The Judiciary of Alleghany County," 176; P. A. Older, *The 1906 Barnum & Bailey Route Book,* 109, cited in Thayer, *Traveling Showmen,* 36.

90. "New Theatre" playbill, Mobile, Feb. 22, 1841, MS Thr 1848, box 10 (Diamond, Master), Houghton Library, Harvard University.

91. Ed. James, *Jig, Clog, and Breakdown Dancing Made Easy with Sketches of Noted Jig Dancers* (Ed. James, New York Clipper Building, 1873), 1–2; T. Allston Brown, "Early History of Negro Minstrelsy," *New York Clipper,* Feb. 24, 1912, 5.

92. "Theatricals," *Boston Daily Atlas,* Aug. 24, 1841, 2.

93. Robert A. Gross, "The Print Revolution," and John Nerone, "Journalism," *Encyclopedia of American Cultural and Intellectual History* (2001), 1:271–279, 423.

94. "Vauxhall Gardens," *New York Herald,* Sept. 1, 1841.

95. *Dramatic Mirror and Literary Companion* (New York and Philadelphia), Sept. 4, 1841.

96. "Vauxhall Garden," *Evening Post,* Sept. 6, 1841, 3.

97. "Vauxhall Garden," *Evening Post,* Sept. 7, 9, 10, 1841, 3.

98. "Every night was Vauxhall Garden crowded to witness Diamond's antics by anxious spectators . . . inveigled into an excitement which formerly could have been conjured up at the old Haymarket by the production of half a score of thoroughbred darkies, eager to dance . . . [for] the paltry trophy of a string of eels," wrote T. Allston Brown after seeing those ads ("Early History," 5).

99. Vincent DiGirolamo, *Crying the News: A History of the American Newsboy* (Oxford University Press, 2019), 22–24, 39.

100. Quoted from *New World,* July 1842, in Patricia Cline Cohen et al., *The Flash Press: Sporting Male Weeklies in 1840s New York* (University of Chicago Press, 2008), 17.

101. Cohen et al., *The Flash Press,* 18, 83.

102. "Vauxhall," *Evening Post,* Sept. 23, 1841, 3; Barnum, *Struggles and Triumphs,* 126.

103. "Vauxhall," *Evening Post,* Sept. 22, 1841, 3.

Chapter 6. Under Canvas

1. James Thomas, *From Tennessee Slave to St. Louis Entrepreneur: The Autobiography of James Thomas,* ed. Loren Schweninger (1904; University of Missouri Press, 1984), 52.

2. Loren Schweninger, introduction to Thomas, *From Tennessee Slave,* 3–7; and Schweninger, "Thriving Within the Lowest Caste: The Financial Activities of James P. Thomas in the Nineteenth-Century South," *Journal of Negro History* 63, no. 4 (1978): 353–364.

3. Camille Heung, "James P. Thomas (1827–1913)," *Black Past*, June 24, 2008, http://www.blackpast.org/aah/thomas-james-p-1827-1913.

4. Thomas, *From Tennessee Slave*, 48.

5. "Sol Smith, City Hotel, Natchez, to N. M. Ludlow, Jany. 24, Sunday night, 1841," box 1, Solomon Franklin Smith Papers, Sol Smith Collections, Missouri History Museum Archives, St. Louis.

6. "S[ol Smith], New Orleans, to N. M. Ludlow, Mobile, Sunday, 1 o'clock, Feb. 21, 1841," Smith Papers.

7. Solomon Smith letters, Feb. 23, 1841, and Apr. 23, 1841, Smith Papers; Stuart Thayer, *Traveling Showmen: The American Circus Before the Civil War* (Astley and Ricketts, 1997), 17, 20.

8. "S[ol Smith], New Orleans, to N. M. Ludlow, Mobile, Sunday, 1 o'clock, Feb. 21, 1841," Smith Papers.

9. "American Theatre" and "St. Charles Theatre," *Daily Picayune* (New Orleans), Apr. 7–10, 1841, 2, 3.

10. "S[ol Smith], New Orleans, to N. M. Ludlow, [St. Louis], Apr 23 1841," Smith Papers; Thayer, *Traveling Showmen*, 89.

11. "Sol Smith, New Orleans, to N. M. Ludlow [St. Louis], Apr 29 1841," Smith Papers.

12. "Sol Smith, City Hotel, Natchez, to N. M. Ludlow, Jany. 24, Sunday night, 1841," box 1, Smith Papers.

13. "S[ol Smith], New Orleans, to N. M. Ludlow [St. Louis], May 12, 1841," Smith Papers.

14. Sol. Smith, *Theatrical Management for Thirty Years with Anecdotal Sketches* (Harper and Brothers, 1868), 157.

15. William G. B. Carson, *Managers in Distress: The St. Louis Stage, 1840–1844* (St. Louis Historical Documents Foundation, 1949), 144–146.

16. Hugh Lindsay, *History of the Life, Travel and Incidents of Col. Hugh Lindsay, the Celebrated Comedian, for a Period of Thirty-seven Years* (O. P. Knauss, Book and Job Printer, 1883), 18.

17. Sol Smith letters, July 25 and Apr. 29, 1841, Smith Papers; Thayer, *Traveling Showmen*, 23, 46.

18. Sol Smith, Cincinnati, to N. M. Ludlow, St. Louis, Sunday, July 25, 1841, Smith Papers.

19. Smith to Ludlow, "Paris, July 28, Monday. 1841," Smith Papers.

20. Marcus Rediker, *Between the Devil and the Deep Blue Sea* (Cambridge University Press, 1993), 81–107.

21. Thayer, *Traveling Showmen*, 7–10.

22. Col. T. Allston Brown, "Early History of Negro Minstrelsy: Its Rise and Progress in the United States," *New York Clipper*, Feb. 24, 1912, 5.

23. Amy Varty, *Children and Theatre in Victorian Britain: "All Work, No Play"* (Palgrave Macmillan, 2008), 7.

24. Thayer, *Traveling Showmen*, 81.

25. Smith to Ludlow, "Paris, July 28, Monday. 1841," Smith Papers.

26. Thomas, *From Tennessee Slave*, 39.

27. Smith to Ludlow, "Paris, July 28, Monday. 1841," Smith Papers.

28. Thayer, *Traveling Showmen*, 18; "Sol Smith, New Orleans, to N. M. Ludlow [St. Louis], Apr 29 1841," Smith Papers.

29. Thayer, *Traveling Showmen*, 114.
30. Gilbert Robinson, *Old Wagon Show Days* (Brockwell, 1925), 31–32.
31. Thayer, *Traveling Showmen*, 25.
32. Phineas T. Barnum, *The Life of P. T. Barnum* (Redfield, 1855), 204.
33. Lindsay, *History of the Life*, 19.
34. George Conklin, *The Ways of the Circus, Being the Memories and Adventures of George Conklin, Tamer of Lions*, set down by Harvey W. Root (Harper and Brothers Publishers, 1921), 16.
35. Townsend Walsh, "Fifty Years a Trouper," *Billboard*, Dec. 13, 1924, 112.
36. Thayer, *Traveling Showmen*, 70.
37. Wording from Robinson, *Old Wagon Show Days*, 30–31.
38. Thayer, *Traveling Showmen*, 57, 45.
39. Thayer, *Traveling Showmen*, 64.
40. Robert White interview, *New-York Daily Tribune*, May 30, 1881.
41. "Now that has undergone a change," lamented Thomas fifty years later. "Three rings are not enough. . . . The circus that used to delight all, old and young, would now be a small affair" (*From Tennessee Slave*, 52).
42. "Home Affairs," *Holly Springs (MS) Gazette*, Nov. 4, 1841, image 2, Chronicling America, Library of Congress; Thayer, *Traveling Showmen*, 79; "American Circus," *The Tennessean* (Nashville), Sept. 14–30, 1841, 3.
43. J. S. Bratton, "Dancing a Hornpipe in Fetters," *Folk Music Journal* 6, no. 1 (1990): 68.
44. Thayer, *Traveling Showmen*, 79–80.
45. Thomas, *From Tennessee Slave*, 49.
46. Robinson, *Old Wagon Show Days*, 31; Thayer, *Traveling Showmen*, 77.
47. "American Circus," *Southern Banner* (Holly Springs, MS), Oct. 22, 1841.
48. "Home Affairs," *Holly Springs Gazette*, Nov. 4, 1841.
49. Lindsay, *History of the Life*, 19.
50. Thomas, *From Tennessee Slave*, 45n33; Rachel Gains quoted in *The American Slave: A Composite Autobiography*, ed. George P. Rawick (Greenwood Press, 1972–1979), 16:17.
51. Thomas, *From Tennessee Slave*, 41, 70.
52. Robert Ball Anderson, *From Slavery to Affluence: Memoirs of Robert Anderson, Ex-Slave*, ed. Daisy Anderson (Steamboat Springs Pilot, 1927), 30–31.
53. Alonzo M. Swann quoted in Thayer, *Traveling Showmen*, 73.
54. Thayer, *Traveling Showmen*, 75; "Circus. Amphitheatre of the Republic," *New York Herald*, Jan. 8, 1843; "Home Affairs," *Holly Springs Gazette*, Nov. 4, 1841.
55. Robert White interview, *New-York Daily Tribune*, May 30, 1881, quoted in Thayer, *Traveling Showmen*, 86.
56. Thayer, *Traveling Showmen*, 90–91.
57. All spelling has been reproduced as it appears in the original. "Home Affairs," *Holly Springs Gazette*, Oct. 28, 1841, 2.
58. John Glenroy, *Ins and Outs of Circus Life or Forty-Two Years Travel of John H. Glenroy, Bareback Rider, Through United States, Canada, South America and Cuba*, comp. Stephen Stanley Stanford (M. M. Wing and Company, 1885), 158–159.
59. Thayer, *Traveling Showmen*, 90; Lindsay, *History of the Life*, 54, 52, 34.

60. Lindsay, *History of the Life*, 31.
61. Lindsay, *History of the Life*, 41.
62. *Daily Picayune*, Nov. 25, 1841, 3.
63. Lindsay, *History of the Life*, 35–36, 39.
64. Glenroy, *Ins and Outs of Circus Life*, 73.
65. *Daily Picayune*, Nov. 28, 1841, 3; *Evening Journal* (Albany), Nov. 30, 1841.
66. *Daily Picayune*, Nov. 30, 1841, 2, 3; "A Diamond Set," *True Flash*, Dec. 4, 1841, 4; "A Brief History of the Recorder's Courts of New Orleans: 1840," Library Research Guides, Law Library of Louisiana, https://lasc.libguides.com/c.php?g=536548&p=3694768.
67. "A Diamond Set," *True Flash*, Dec. 4, 1841, 4; *Evening Journal*, Nov. 30, 1841, 2.
68. "News/Opinion," *Daily Picayune*, Dec. 15, 1841, 1.
69. *Dramatic Mirror, and Literary Companion, Devoted to the Stage and Fine Arts*, Dec. 4, 1841, 134, and Dec. 25, 1841, 158.
70. "Trotting in America," *Spirit of the Times*, Dec. 8, 1849, 501; "Louisville (KY.) Races—Last Day," *Spirit of the Times*, Oct. 22, 1853, 426; "Fine Cattle in Boone," *Valley Farmer: A Monthly Journal of Agriculture . . .* 6–7 (June 1854): 256; *Daily Picayune*, Jan. 8, 1842, 2.
71. *Daily Picayune*, Jan. 2, 1842.
72. *Daily Picayune*, Jan. 4, 1842, 2.

Chapter 7. A Sensation in Print

1. "A public ball," *Newark Daily Advertiser,* Apr. 20, 1842.
2. G. W. Putnam, "Part I: Four Months with Charles Dickens," *Atlantic Monthly* 26 (October 1870): 481, https://cdn.theatlantic.com/media/archives/1870/10/26-156/131867610.pdf.
3. Charles Dickens, *American Notes* (Chapman and Hall, 1842; edited ed., Penguin Classics, 2000), 90–91.
4. Dickens, *American Notes*, 94.
5. "Boz at Five Points," *Whip and Satirist of New-York and Brooklyn,* Mar. 12, 1842, 2; Dickens, *American Notes,* 101.
6. Dickens, *American Notes*, 101.
7. T. D. Rice had taken "Jim Crow" to England in the 1830s. Dickens, *American Notes,* 102.
8. Shane White and Graham White, *Stylin' African American Expressive Culture from Its Beginnings to the Zoot Suit* (Cornell University Press, 1998), 78–79; Constance Valance Hill, *Tap Dancing America: A Cultural History* (Oxford University Press, 2010), 17–18; Tyler Anbinder, *Five Points: The Nineteenth-Century New York Neighborhood* (Simon and Schuster, 2001), 172–175; Marian Hannah Winter, "Juba and American Minstrelsy," *Dance Index* 6, no. 2 (1947): 31; Lynne Fauley Emery, *Black Dance: From 1619 to Today* (Princeton Book Company, 1988), 185–189; James W. Cook, "Lane, William Henry [*performing name* Juba, Master Juba]," in *Oxford Dictionary of National Biography,* Oct. 3, 2013, 2, https://doi.org/10.1093/ref:odnb/100407.
9. Raymond Williams, *Writing in Society* (Verso, 1983), 87, 95, 161.
10. Dickens, *American Notes,* 99.

11. Ward McAllister, *Society as I Have Found It* (Cassell, 1890), 211–212; Pierce Egan, *Life in London, or The Day and Night Scenes of Jerry Hawthorne, Esq. and his Elegant Friend Corinthian Tom in their Rambles and Sprees through the Metropolis* (Sherwood, Neely and Jones, 1821), 199, 320.

12. "Fires," *Evening Post* (New York), Apr. 3, 1841, 2; *Weekly Messenger* (Boston), Apr. 7, 1841, 2.

13. "City Intelligences. Dickens on 'The Points,'" *New York Herald*, Mar. 6, 1842; "Boz at Five Points," *Whip and Satirist*, Mar. 12, 1842, 2.

14. "City Intelligence . . . Almack's Broken Up," *New York Herald*, Apr. 22, 1842.

15. City directories for 1843 and 1846 list Williams's place at 67 Orange Street. See James W. Cook, "Dancing Across the Color Line," *Common-Place* 4, no. 1 (2003), https://commonplace.online/article/dancing-across-the-color-line/.

16. Whortleberries or bilberries are a blueberry family variety. "City Intelligences. Dickens on 'The Points,'" *New York Herald*, Mar. 6, 1842.

17. Neither gender, race, nor class is a determiner of a person's virtue or corruption in Dickens's stories. Brian M. Flint, review of "Mary Poovey, *Making a Social Body: British Cultural Formation, 1830–1864*," *Forum: Journal of History* 1, no. 12 (2009): 112.

18. "City Intelligence," *New York Herald*, Mar. 6, 1842.

19. Judith R. Walkowitz, *City of Dreadful Delight: Narratives of Sexual Danger in Late-Victorian London* (University of Chicago Press, 1992), 21–22.

20. Patricia Ingham, introduction to Dickens, *American Notes*, xii.

21. "Boz at Five Points," *Whip and Satirist*, Mar. 12, 1842, 2.

22. "Police Office," *New York Aurora*, Apr. 22, 1842, 2.

23. Thomas Downing, a prosperous Black oyster cellar proprietor with many white patrons, was another *Aurora* target. "Meanness," *Whip and Satirist*, July 2, 1842, 2.

24. "Almack's Broken Up," *New York Herald*, Apr. 22, 1842.

25. *Compact Edition of the Oxford English Dictionary* (Oxford University Press, 1971), 269; John F. Szwed and Morton Marks, "The Afro-American Transformation of European Set Dances and Dance Suites," *Dance Research Journal* 20, no. 1 (1988): 29–36; "The Cake Dance," *Béaloideas: The Journal of the Folklore of Ireland Society* 11, no. 1/2 (1941): 127; *Dancing Between Two Worlds: Kongo-Angola Culture and the Americas*, ed. Robert Farris Thompson and C. Daniel Dawson (Caribbean Cultural Center, 1991), 8.

26. William Carleton, "The Country Dancing-Master, an Irish Sketch," *Irish Penny Journal*, Aug. 29, 1840, 69.

27. "Bowery Amphitheatre," *New York Herald*, Feb. 1, 1843.

28. Ned Buntline, *Mysteries and Miseries of New York: a story of real life* (W. F. Burgess, 1849), 82.

29. R. Shelton Mackenzie, *Bits of Blarney* (Redfield, 1854), 299.

30. Catherine E. Foley, *Step Dancing in Ireland: Culture and History* (Ashgate, 2013), 27.

31. Carleton, "The Country Dancing-Master," 69–70.

32. Judith R. Walkowitz, *Prostitution and Victorian Society: Women, Class and the State* (Cambridge University Press, 1980), 14–15; Christine Stansell, *City of Women: Sex and Class in New York, 1789–1860* (University of Illinois Press, 1987), 176, 42.

33. George G. Foster, *New York by Gas-Light* (Dewitt and Davenport, 1850), 73–74.

34. Thomas Butler Gunn, *The Physiology of New York Boardinghouses* (Mason Brothers, 1857), 280.
35. "Fanny Ellsler," *Flash,* Dec. 18, 1841, 2.
36. "A Boston Match Dance," *Whip and Satirist,* June 11, 1842, 2; *Boston Post,* May 28, 1842, 3, and May 30, 1842, 2; "A Boston Plug Muss. Or A Fight on the Common," *Whip and Satirist,* May 7, 1842, 2; "Tremont Theatre," *Boston Evening Transcript,* May 9, 1842, 2.
37. "Dance on Long Wharf—Boston," *Libertine,* June 15, 1842, 14.
38. Walkowitz, *Prostitution,* 15.
39. Charles J. Kickham, *Knocknagow, Or The Homes of Tipperary* (1879), 129.
40. "Dance on Long Wharf—Boston," *Libertine,* June 15, 1842, 14.
41. "Dance on Long Wharf—Boston," *Libertine,* June 15, 1842, 14.
42. Breandán Breathnach, *Folk Music and Dances of Ireland* (Mercier, 1971), 53.
43. "Dance on Long Wharf—Boston," *Libertine,* June 15, 1842, 14.
44. "A Boston Match Dance," *Whip and Satirist,* June 11, 1842, 2.
45. Dickens, *American Notes,* 3.
46. "American Notes for General Circulation," *Spirit of the Times,* Nov. 19, 1842, 447.
47. "Boz on Americans," *Flash,* Nov. 12, 1842, 2.
48. *Spirit of the Times,* Dec. 3, 1842, 469.
49. *Newark Daily Advertiser,* Apr. 20, 1842.
50. "African Notes for General Circulation," *Spirit of the Times,* Feb. 4, 1843, 579.
51. "Boz at Five Points," *Whip and Satirist,* Mar. 12, 1842, 2.
52. "From Our New York Correspondent. Monday, March 13, 1843," *Daily National Intelligencer* (Washington, DC), Mar. 16, 1843.
53. "From Our New York Correspondent. Monday, March 13, 1843," *Daily National Intelligencer* (Washington, DC), Mar. 16, 1843; "DICKENS' PLACE," *National Aegis* (Worchester, MA), Mar. 29, 1843, 1; Nathaniel P. Willis, *Complete Works* (J. S. Redfield, 1846), 582.
54. "Another Charge," *New York Herald,* Oct. 16, 1844, 2.
55. "Our Eleventh Walk About Town: OR, NIGHTS IN GOTHAM," *New York Sporting Whip,* Dec. 31, 1842, 2.
56. "Our Eleventh Walk About Town: OR, NIGHTS IN GOTHAM," *New York Sporting Whip,* Dec. 31, 1842, 2.
57. Michael Kaplan, "New York City Tavern Violence and the Creation of a Working-Class Male Identity," *Journal of the Early Republic* 15, no. 4 (1995): 611.
58. "Our Eleventh Walk About Town: OR, NIGHTS IN GOTHAM," *New York Sporting Whip,* Dec. 31, 1842, 2.
59. "American Theatre. Walnut Street," *Daily Pennsylvanian* (Philadelphia), June 16, 17, 1842, 3.
60. *Daily Picayune* (New Orleans), Jan. 4, 1842, 2; "The Money Market," *Public Ledger* (Philadelphia), Mar. 12, 1842, 2; "Great Excitement," *New York Herald,* May 29, 1842.
61. "Local Affairs. . . . Aid for Texas," *Public Ledger,* Apr. 13, 1842, 2; *Whip and Satirist,* Apr. 16, 1842, 3.
62. "The Negro Minstrels of the Nights Gone By," ca. 1875, HTC Clippings 13 (Bryant, Dan), Houghton Library, Harvard University.

63. *Evening Post* (New York), May 23, 31, 1842, 3; *New York Arena,* May 24, 27, 1842, 3; *New York Commercial Advertiser,* May 24–June 2, 1842, 3.

64. "Holiday at the Museum," *New York Herald,* June 4, 1842, 3.

65. "AMERICAN THEATRE," *Daily Pennsylvanian* (Philadelphia), June 11–17, 1842, 3.

66. Frank Dumont, "The Golden Days of Minstrelsy," *New York Clipper,* Dec. 19, 1914.

67. "Showboats" ranged from "very rudely built" affairs (basically a vessel with wooden staves supporting a roof) to steamboat decks to the "floating palaces" of later years. "*Philadelphia,* Aug. 10, 1842," *New York Herald,* Aug. 11, 1842; "Great Attractions, Masters Diamond, Sanders, and Reed," *Public Ledger,* Aug. 19, 1842, 3; John Hanners, *"It Was Play or Starve": Acting in the Nineteenth-Century American Popular Theatre* (Bowling Green State University Popular Press, 1993), 12–13.

68. Barney Williams was the stage name of Bernard O'Flaherty, the son of immigrants from Cork, Ireland. In 1833 he was one of the *New York Sun*'s first newsboys, and in 1836, at age twelve, he began playing blackface and Irish parts at Dinneford's Franklin Theatre for "$10 a week." "National Theatre," *Boston Daily Atlas,* Oct. 5, 1842, 3.

69. "National Theatre," *Boston Daily Atlas,* Oct. 7, 8, 12, 14, 1842, 3.

70. "Chatham Theatre," *New York Herald,* Oct. 22–29, 1842; "Theatre-Front Street," *Baltimore Sun,* Nov. 22–26, 1842, 3.

71. "Philadelphia, Sept. 20, 1842," *New York Herald,* Sept. 21, 1842; "Welch's Olympic Circus," *Public Ledger,* Oct. 20, 1842, 3.

72. *Public Ledger,* Dec. 24, 1842, 2.

73. "WELCH'S OLYMPIC CIRCUS," *New York Herald,* Jan. 3, 5, 6, 1843.

74. "Park Theatre Circus," *New York Herald,* Jan. 23, 1843, 2.

75. "The PARK," *Whip,* Dec. 24, 1842, 3.

76. "Welch's Olympic Circus," *New York Herald,* Jan. 7, 1843.

77. "Park Theatre Circus," *New York Herald,* Jan. 21, 22, 23, 27, 1843, 2.

78. "Park Olympic Circus," *New York Sporting Whip,* Jan. 28, 1843, 5.

79. Edward Ruggles, *A Picture of New York in 1848: with a short account of places in the vicinity: designed as a guide to citizens and strangers* (C. S. Francis, 1848), 63.

80. "General Sessions," *New York Herald,* Jan. 20, 1843.

81. "Pioneers of Minstrelsy," *New York Clipper,* Mar. 13, 1880.

82. "Excitement among the Sporting Community," *New York Sporting Whip,* Jan. 28, 1843, 4.

83. "Franklin," *Whip,* Jan. 21, 1843, 3.

84. Patricia Cline Cohen et al., *The Flash Press: Sporting Male Weeklies in 1840s New York* (University of Chicago Press, 2008), 41.

85. "Negro Dancers," *New York Sporting Whip,* Jan. 21, 1843, 2; "Burnt Cork," *Daily Alta Californian* (San Francisco), Apr. 6, 1885, 1.

86. Ralph Keeler, *Vagabond Adventures* (Fields, Osgood and Company, 1870), 113; Buntline, *Mysteries and Miseries,* 79.

87. "Juba" was both a euphemism for "slave" used by white people and a last name chosen by free Black people.

88. "Our Eleventh Walk About Town: OR, NIGHTS IN GOTHAM," *New York Sporting Whip*, Dec. 31, 1842, 2; "Excitement among the Sporting Community," *New York Sporting Whip*, Jan. 28, 1843, 4.

Chapter 8. Partners in Time

1. "Pioneers of Minstrelsy," *New York Clipper*, Mar. 13, 1880; "Park Theatre Circus," *New York Herald*, Jan. 23, 1843, 2; "The River," *New-York Daily Tribune*, Jan. 28, 1843, 2; "From our New York Correspondent. Monday, March 13, 1843," *Daily National Intelligencer* (Washington, DC), Mar. 16, 1843.

2. Nathaniel P. Willis, *The Complete Works of N. P. Willis* (J. S. Redfield, 1846), 582; Tyler Anbinder, *Five Points: The Nineteenth-Century New York Neighborhood* (Simon and Schuster, 2001), 26, 33–34; "Negro Minstrels and Their Dances," *New York Herald*, Aug. 11, 1895, fourth section, MS Thr 1848, boxes 20–21, Houghton Library, Harvard University; Carol Groneman Pernicone, "The 'Bloody Ould Sixth,' a Social Analysis of a New York City Working-Class Community in the Mid-Nineteenth Century" (PhD diss., University of Rochester, 1973), 197–198.

3. "The Negro Minstrels of the Nights Gone By—Shoo-Fly, Don't Bodder Me—Shakespeare and Dumas on Burnt Cork—The Old Time Banjo-Players—The Great Match-Dance—Barnum's Museum Against Pete Williams' Dance-House," ca. 1875, HTC Clippings 13 (Bryant, Dan), Houghton Library, Harvard University.

4. "The Negro Minstrels of the Nights Gone By."

5. Robert Farris Thompson, *African Art in Motion: Icon and Act in the Collection of Katherine Coryton White* (University of California Press, 1979), 16.

6. Frank Dumont, "The Golden Days of Minstrelsy," *New York Clipper*, Dec. 19, 1914.

7. "The Negro Minstrels of the Nights Gone By."

8. "The Negro Minstrels of the Nights Gone By"; "Our Eleventh Walk About Town: OR, NIGHTS IN GOTHAM," *New York Sporting Whip*, Dec. 31, 1842, 2; "Vauxhall," *Morning Post (London)*, Sept. 22, 1848; Charles Dickens, *American Notes* (Chapman and Hall, 1842; edited ed., Penguin Classics, 2000), 102.

9. "The Negro Minstrels of the Nights Gone By"; Dickens, *American Notes*, 102; Susan Eike Spalding, "Aesthetic Standards in Old Time Dancing in Southwest Virginia: African-American and European-American Threads" (EdD diss., Temple University, 1993), 73.

10. "The Negro Minstrels of the Nights Gone By."

11. "THE MECHANIC," *Flash*, Nov. 12, 1842, 2.

12. Roy Rosenzweig, *Eight Hours for What We Will: Workers & Leisure in an Industrial City, 1870–1920* (Cambridge University Press, 1983), 63; "The Negro Minstrels of the Nights Gone By."

13. "Franklin Theatre," *Morning Herald* (New York), Apr. 16–24, 1839; "New Theatre" playbill, Mobile, Feb. 22, 1841, MS Thr 1848, box 10 (Diamond, Master), Houghton Library, Harvard University; "Home Affairs," *Holly Springs (MS) Gazette*, Nov. 4, 1841; "Whitlock's Collection of Ethiopian Melodies," 1846, Sheet Music—Negro Minstrels, American Antiquarian Society, Worcester, MA.

14. "The Negro Minstrels of the Nights Gone By."
15. "The Negro Minstrels of the Nights Gone By."
16. "The Negro Minstrels of the Nights Gone By."
17. "The Davenport Assembly," *New York Sporting Whip*, Feb. 4, 1843, 5; Phil Jamison, *Hoedowns, Reels, and Frolics: Roots and Branches of Southern Appalachian Dance* (University of Illinois Press, 2015), 25.
18. "The Negro Minstrels of the Nights Gone By."
19. "Excitement among the Sporting community—Match between John Diamond and Juba," *New York Sporting Whip*, Jan. 28, 1843, 4.
20. Elliott J. Gorn, *The Manly Art: Bare-Knuckle Prize Fighting in America* (Cornell University Press, 1986), 45–46; Ann Fabian, *Card Sharps, Dream Books, & Bucket Shops: Gambling in 19th-Century America* (Cornell University Press, 1990), 40–41.
21. Rosenzweig, *Eight Hours*, 35–64.
22. Kevin R. Smith, *Black Genesis: The History of the Black Prizefighter 1760–1870* (iUniverse, 2003), 2.
23. "Excitement among the Sporting Community," *New York Sporting Whip*, Jan. 28, 1843, 4.
24. Rosenzweig, *Eight Hours*, 55.
25. "Missing," *Harper's New Monthly Magazine* 38 (Dec. 1868–May 1869): 504.
26. Gorn, *The Manly Art*, 46, 85, 137.
27. "Missing," 504.
28. Gorn, *The Manly Art*, 47.
29. Smith, *Black Genesis*, 19, 30, 95, 131.
30. *Boston Daily Advertiser*, May 9, 1835, 3; "BOSTON GYMNASIUM," *Daily Atlas* (Boston), Oct. 7–10, 1842, 3.
31. "Challenge to the World," *New York Herald*, July 1, 1844, 3.
32. James W. Cook, "Dancing Across the Color Line," *Common-Place* 4, no. 1 (2003), https://commonplace.online/article/dancing-across-the-color-line/.
33. Contemporary engravings of the Molineaux-Cribb match depict both women and men in the crowd of raucous spectators. Pierce Egan, *Boxiana, or Sketches of Ancient and Modern Pugilism* (Sherwood, Jones and Company, 1812), 401, 408; Gorn, *The Manly Art*, 19, 34–36; Thomas Rowlandson, "Rural Sports, a Milling Match," Thomas Tegg, publisher, Sept. 29, 1811, Elisha Whittelsey Collection, Elisha Whittelsey Fund, 1959, Metropolitan Museum of Art, New York.
34. Noel Ignatiev, *How the Irish Became White* (Routledge, 1995), 40–41.
35. "The Negro Minstrels of the Nights Gone By."
36. "The Negro Minstrels of the Nights Gone By."
37. "Old Time Minstrels. Billy Birch, in the New York Mail and Express," *Times-Picayune* (New Orleans), July 5, 1891, 10.
38. Cook, "Dancing Across the Color Line."
39. "Negro Minstrels and Their Dances."
40. *Spirit of the Times*, Feb. 11, 1843.
41. *Brooklyn Eagle*, Apr. 19, 20, 1843, 2.
42. "CIRCUS," *New York Herald*, Oct. 10, 23, 1843, 3, Nov. 1, 1843, 4.

43. *New York Herald*, May 3, 1843, 3.

44. P. T. Barnum, *Struggles and Triumphs* (1869; abridged ed., Penguin Classics, 1987), 133–137; "American Museum" and "New York Museum and Picture Gallery," *New York Herald*, Nov. 5–15, 1842, 3.

45. "PEALE'S NEW YORK MUSEUM AND PICTURE GALLERY," *New York Herald*, July 2–7, 1843, 3, 4; "Vauxhall Garden Saloon," *Evening Post* (New York), July 21, 1843.

46. "American Museum" and "Peale's Museum," *New York Herald*, Aug. 20, 1843.

47. "Chatham Theater," *New York Herald*, Dec. 15–20, 1843, 2; "Barney Williams," *New York Clipper*, May 6, 1876, 1; Chatham Theatre playbill, Dec. 16, 1843, in Joseph Norton Ireland, "Records of the New York Stage from 1750–1860," unpublished scrapbook, TS 939.5.3, Houghton Library, Harvard University.

48. "Chatham Theatre," *New York Herald*, Dec. 16, 1843, 2.

49. "Chatham Theatre," *New York Herald*, Dec. 19, 1843, 2.

50. "Poetry and Music," *New York Herald*, Dec. 19, 1843, 2.

51. "Musical Mania—Rival Concerts," *New York Herald*, Dec. 11, 1843, 2; "Poetry and Music," *New York Herald*, Dec. 19, 1843, 2.

52. "The great star in the musical firmament," *New York Herald*, Dec. 1, 1843, 2; "Ole Bull's Farewell Concert," *New York Herald*, Dec. 20, 1843, 2.

53. James Thomas, *From Tennessee Slave to St. Louis Entrepreneur: The Autobiography of James Thomas*, ed. Loren Schweninger (1904; University of Missouri Press, 1984), 43.

54. "Ole Bull v. Juba," *Boston Daily Bee*, Nov. 26, 1844, 2.

55. *New York Herald*, June 8, 11, 1844, 3.

56. "Knickerbocker Bowery Amphitheatre," *New York Herald*, June 28, 1844, 3.

57. "The Murder of Joe Smith, the Mormon Prophet," *New York Herald*, July 8, 1844, 2; "Dreadful Riot at Philadelphia," *New York Herald*, May 9, 1844; "Terrible State of Affairs in Philadelphia," *New York Herald*, July 9, 1844, 1–4; Ballard C. Campbell, *American Disasters: 201 Calamities That Shook the Nation* (Checkmark Books, 2008), 86–88.

58. "MORE TERRIBLE RIOTS IN PHILADELPHIA," *New York Herald*, July 8, 1844, 3; "GREAT PUBLIC CONTEST," *New York Herald*, July 8, 1844, 3.

59. Thank you, Kenneth Cohen, for identifying J.S.M.

60. "Challenge to the World," *New York Herald*, July 1, 2, 1844, 3.

61. "How it Was Done," *Clipper*, June 6, 1857, 52.

62. Patricia Cline Cohen et al., *The Flash Press: Sporting Male Weeklies in 1840s New York* (University of Chicago Press, 2008), 112.

63. Rosenzweig, *Eight Hours*, 53, 63.

64. "74 Chambers," in *Longworth's American Almanac, New-York Register and City Directory* (T. Longworth, 1842–1843), 471, 324; "Ottignon's Gymnasium," *New York Herald*, Apr. 9, 1845, 3.

65. The ad, entitled "Rational Amusement," was sandwiched between notices for a "Temperance Mass Meeting" and "Phrenology!" "Rational Amusement," *New York Herald*, July 4, 1844, 3.

66. "The Match Dance—Sliter vs. Brown," *New York Clipper*, Sept. 6, 1856, 156; "How It Was Done—The Late Dancing Match," *New York Clipper*, June 6, 1857, 52.

67. "The Match Dance—Sliter vs. Brown," *New York Clipper*, Sept. 6, 1856, 156.

68. "Great Public Contest," *New York Herald*, July 7, 8, 1844, 3; "Black Musicians and Early Ethiopian Minstrelsy," *Black Perspective in Music* 3, no. 1 (1975): 82.

69. Col. T. Allston Brown, "Early History of Negro Minstrelsy: Its Rise and Progress in the United States," *New York Clipper*, Feb. 29, 1912, 5; "Grand Concert by the Georgia Champions" playbills, June 18, 19, [1845], MS Thr 1848, box 14 (Juba, Master), Houghton Library, Harvard University.

Chapter 9. Gross Imitators

1. "Thus all great poets have been gross imitators. It is, however, a mere *non distributio medii* [fallacy of the undistributed middle] hence to infer, that all great imitators are poets" (Edgar Allan Poe, "Marginalia—part 06," in *The Collected Writings of Edgar Allan Poe—Vol. II: The Brevities*, ed. B. R. Pollin [1985], 270).

2. William J. Mahar, *Behind the Burnt Cork Mask: Early Blackface Minstrelsy and Antebellum American Popular Culture* (University of Illinois Press, 1999), 202–209.

3. [scrap: "One strong feature of the Sables was the dancing by Gray"] and [scrap: "7. After the Harmonists were organized . . . This Company had 3 champion Jig dancers, Ned Gray (colored man) known as the Boston Rattler, Master Juba and John Diamond (the original)"], in H. B. White, "The origin of Ethiopian minstrelsy: Reminiscences of its early history in Boston," autograph manuscript, undated, MS Thr 1848, box 22, Houghton Library, Harvard University; "Boylston Garden" playbill, June 8, [1845], MS Thr 1848, box 12 (Gray, Edward), Houghton Library, Harvard University.

4. Susan A. Glenn, "'Give an Imitation of Me': Vaudeville Mimics and the Play of the Self," *American Quarterly* 50, no. 1 (1998): 48–49.

5. James H. Hammond, "Letter to the Free Church of Glasgow, on the Subject of Slavery," June 21, 1844, in *Selections from the Letters and Speeches of the Hon. James H. Hammond, of South Carolina* (J. F. Trow and Company, 1866), 105–113; *Slavery Justified, by a Southerner* (Recorder Printing Office, 1850), in George Fitzhugh, *Sociology for the South, or, The Failure of Free Society* (A. Morris, 1854), 226–258.

6. Frederick Douglass, "The Hutchinson Family.—Hunkerism," *North Star*, Oct. 27, 1848, 2.

7. Frank Dumont, "The Golden Days of Minstrelsy," *New York Clipper*, Dec. 19, 1914.

8. James Thomas, *From Tennessee Slave to St. Louis Entrepreneur: The Autobiography of James Thomas*, ed. Loren Schweninger (1904; University of Missouri Press, 1984), 48–49.

9. Whitlock quoted in *Music in the USA: A Documentary Companion*, ed. Judith Tick and Paul Beaudoin (Oxford University Press, 2008), 116; Joseph Jackson, *Encyclopedia of Philadelphia*, cited in Charles Kelley Jones, *Francis Johnson, 1792–1844: Chronicle of a Black Musician in Early Nineteenth-Century Philadelphia* (Lehigh University Press, 2006), 226–227; "Pioneers of Minstrelsy," *New York Clipper*, Mar. 13, 1880.

10. "Bowery Amphitheatre," *New York Herald*, Feb. 1, 1843, 3.

11. Whitlock quoted in "Pioneers of Minstrelsy," *New York Clipper*, Mar. 13, 1880; *New York Herald*, Feb. 16–18, 1843; "AMERICAN THEATRICALS," *The Era* (London), Mar. 12, 1843.

12. Samuel S. Sanford, "Personal Reminiscences," manuscript p. [24], Minstrel Show Collection, 1831–1859, Harry Ransom Center, University of Texas at Austin; Dumont,

"The Golden Days of Minstrelsy"; M. B. Leavitt, *Fifty Years in Theatrical Management* (Broadway Publishing Company, 1912), 33–34.

13. Edw. Le Roy Rice, *Monarchs of Minstrelsy from "Daddy" Rice to Date* (Kenny Publishing Company, 1911), 19; Barton Atkins, *Modern Antiquities: Comprising Sketches of Early Buffalo and the Great Lakes, also sketches of Alaska* (Courier Company, 1898), 43–44; Col. T. Allston Brown, "Early History of Negro Minstrelsy: Its Rise and Progress in the United States," *New York Clipper*, Feb. 17, 1912, 13.

14. Joseph Mainzer, *Singing for the Million: A Practical Course of Musical Instruction* (Printed by the Author, 1842); Barnarr Rainbow, introduction to the facsimile reproduction of *Singing for the Million: A Practical Course of Musical Instruction* (1841), and "Singing for the Million," introduction to Joseph Mainzer, *Singing for the Million: A Practical Course of Musical Instruction* (1841), published online by Cambridge University Press, https://doi.org/10.1017/CBO9781107300019; Robert A. Marr, *Music for the People: A Retrospect of the Glasgow International Exhibition, 1888, with an Account of the Rise of Choral Societies in Scotland* (J. Menzies and Company, 1889), xc–xcii; *Musical World* 17 (1842): 102.

15. "Mr. Rice," *New York Herald*, Jan. 6, 1844, 2.

16. "Last and Greatest of all the Shilling Concerts," *Public Ledger* (Philadelphia), Apr. 17, 1844; Brian Roberts, *Blackface Nation: Race, Reform, and Identity in American Popular Music, 1812–1925* (University of Chicago Press, 2017), 5, 129, 130; Douglass, "The Hutchinson Family.—Hunkerism"; "Get Off the Track," sheet music, 1844, https://www.americanyawp.com/reader/the-market-revolution/.

17. "Shilling Concerts," *New York Herald*, Feb. 12, 1844, 2; "The Greatest Novelty of the Season," *New York Herald*, Nov. 21, 1844, 2; "Sable Sisters," *New York Herald*, Dec. 29, 30, 1844, 3; "Temperance Hall," *Public Ledger*, Mar. 4, 1845; "COLORED CONCERT," *New York Herald*, Sept. 30, 1845, 2; and "MUSIC FOR THE MILLION," *New York Herald*, Nov. 18, 1845, 2.

18. "Hartford, Nov. 8, 1845," *New York Herald*, Nov. 10, 1845.

19. Armory Hall playbill, Mar. 25, [1846], MS Thr 1848, box 24 (Brown, John, "tambourine player"), Houghton Library, Harvard University.

20. In the winter of 1843–1844, a half-dozen or so "bands" or "choirs" of minstrels gave "operatic concerts" at the Bowery Circus and Chatham Theatre. "Chatham Theatre," *New York Herald*, Jan. 23, 24, 1844; "Amusements," *Evening Post* (New York), Jan. 24, 1844, 3; *New York Herald*, Feb. 1, 1844; "Bowery Amphitheatre," *Evening Post*, Mar. 21, 1844, 3.

21. Wooldridge had been booking agent for Whitlock's Virginia Minstrels in Britain in 1843. "National Theatre," *Daily Atlas* (Boston), Apr. 2, 1844; *Salem Register*, Apr. 8, 1844, 3; "Songs of the Virginia Serenaders. Arranged for the piano forte by J. W. Turner," published in Boston and entered for copyright in 1844, Sheet Music—Negro Minstrels, American Antiquarian Society, Worcester, MA.

22. "Great Novelty," *Bangor (ME) Daily Whig and Courier*, May 2, 1844, 2; "Chatham," *New York Herald*, Apr. 28, 1844.

23. John Thomas Scharf, *History of Philadelphia, 1609–1884* (L. H. Everts and Company, 1884), 1091.

24. [scrap: "7. After the Harmonists were organized"].

25. White, "The origin of Ethiopian minstrelsy," 5.

26. Stuart Thayer, *Annals of the American Circus, Volume II, 1830–1847* (Peanut Butter Publishing, 1986), 324; *Boston Daily Bee*, Nov. 23, 26, 1844, 2; "New-York Museum, and Picture Gallery," *New-York Daily Tribune*, Sept. 2, 1844, 3.

27. "Melodeon," *Boston Evening Transcript*, Nov. 24–29, 1844, 3.

28. "OLE BULL vs. JUBA," *Boston Daily Bee*, Nov. 26, 1844, 2.

29. "Melodeon," *Boston Evening Transcript*, Nov. 29, 1844, 3.

30. "The Fair!," *The Liberator* (Boston), Nov. 29, 1844, 3; "Juba, the Great Dancer," *Boston Daily Bee*, Dec. 2, 4, 1844; and "The Splendid Dancer Juba," *Boston Daily Bee*, Dec. 11, 1844, 2.

31. "Benefit of the Great Juba," *Boston Daily Bee*, Dec. 13, 1844, 2.

32. Palmo's was the new name of the Concert Saloon on Broadway and Chambers where Juba had danced. Sanford, "Personal Reminiscences," manuscript p. [14]/12.

33. "Circus and Theatre," *American and Commercial Advertiser* (Baltimore), Nov. 7, 1844, 3.

34. Leavitt, *Fifty Years*, 33–34.

35. "THE GREAT ETHIOPIAN SERENADERS," *Public Ledger*, Nov. 29, 1844, 2.

36. Scharf, *History of Philadelphia*, 1091; "Commissioners Hall," *Public Ledger*, Nov. 29, 1844, 2; and "Temperance Hall," *Public Ledger*, Dec. 7, 1844, 2.

37. *Public Ledger*, Dec. 28, 31, 1844, 2.

38. "OLE BULL vs. JUBA," *Boston Daily Bee*, Nov. 26, 1844; *Salem (MA) Register*, Apr. 8, 1844, 3; "Melodeon," *Boston Evening Transcript*, Nov. 29, 1844, 3.

39. "Hartford," *New York Herald*, June 9, 1845, 1.

40. *Public Ledger*, Jan. 14–17, 1845, 3.

41. "A CARD," *Public Ledger*, Jan. 21, 1845, 2.

42. Pennsylvania Governor Francis R. Shunk (1845–1848) was inaugurated in Harrisburg on January 21, 1845. "From Harrisburgh," *Pittsburgh Weekly Gazette*, Jan. 31, 1845, 1; William Slout, "SANFORD'S (S.S.) MINSTRELS," 115–116, box 33.14 disbound scrapbook, 1848–1927 (3 of 4), Minstrel Show Collection, Harry Ransom Center, University of Texas at Austin.

43. Roy Rosensweig, "The Rise of the Saloon," in *Rethinking Popular Culture*, ed. Chandra Mukerji and Michael Schudson (University of California Press, 1991), 123.

44. The hall's name derived from its history as a second-floor drinking house bought by "the temperance people to purify it," fitted up as a theater seating five to six hundred, and reserved for temperance and antislavery society meetings and church worship services until 1844, when the building was leased to a theatrical manager. "Challenge Accepted—Temperance Hall," *Public Ledger*, Mar. 15, 1845, 3; John F. Watson, *Annals of Philadelphia and Pennsylvania, in the Olden Time* (Edwin S. Stuart, 1884), 3:376; Harry Kyriakodis, "Invisible NoLibs," *Hidden City: Exploring Philadelphia's Urban Landscape*, Nov. 9, 2011, https://hiddencityphila.org/2011/11/temperance-hall-a-northern-liberties-saga/.

45. "The Great Ethiopian Serenaders," *Public Ledger*, Apr. 15–16, 1845, 3.

46. "National Circus," *Daily National Pilot* (Buffalo), May 15, 1845, 2; "Circus," *Jamestown (NY) Journal*, July 25, 1845, 3.

47. "Theatricals," *New York Herald*, Jan. 11, 1845.

48. "Great Attraction! Master Juba!" playbill, [1845], MS Thr 1848, box 14, Houghton Library, Harvard University.

49. "Mechanic Hall," *Salem (MA) Register*, Jan. 16, 1845, 3; "The Georgia Champions," *Bangor (ME) Daily Whig and Courier*, Mar. 26, 1845, 2.

50. "Grand Concert by the Georgia Champions" playbills, June 18 and 19, [1845], MS Thr 1848, box 14 (Juba, Master), Houghton Library, Harvard University; "New Concert Saloon" (Weybossett Street, Providence, RI) playbill, July 4, 1845, reproduced in *New York Clipper*, 1873; Stuart Thayer, *Traveling Showmen: The American Circus Before the Civil War* (Astley and Ricketts, 1997), 28.

51. *South Carolina Gazette and Country Journal*, Mar. 4–18, 1766; Hugh F. Rankin, *The Colonial Theatre Its History and Operations*, Research Report Series 0057 (Colonial Williamsburg Foundation Library, 1955), 140, https://research.colonialwilliamsburg.org/DigitalLibrary/view/index.cfm?doc=ResearchReports%5CRR0057.xml&highlight=#p140.

52. "Grand Concert by the Georgia Champions" playbill, June 19, [1845], MS Thr 1848, box 14 (Juba, Master), Houghton Library, Harvard University.

53. *Boston Daily Bee*, Sept. 4, 1845, 2; "Great Attraction! Master Juba!" playbill, [1845], MS Thr 1848, box 14, Houghton Library, Harvard University.

54. "Vauxhall Garden Saloon," *New York Herald*, June 29 and July 11, 1845, 3.

55. Leavitt, *Fifty Years*, 33–34.

56. Brown, "Early History," June 15, 1912; "Theatricals," *New York Herald*, Sept. 3, 1845; "Vauxhall Garden Saloon . . . Benefit of the Manager, Mr. De Laree," *New York Herald*, July 14, 1845, 3; "Dan Bryant," in W. K. Gladding, *A Group of Theatrical Caricatures; being Twelve Plates*, n.s., no. 4 (Dunlap Society, 1897), 61–62.

57. White, "The origin of Ethiopian minstrelsy," 5.

58. Leavitt, *Fifty Years*, x, 29.

59. Thayer, *Annals*, 118, 320.

60. 1850 census, https://www2.census.gov/library/publications/decennial/1850/1850a/1850a-20.pdf; Sophie Hagen, "How Two Riots Made Providence a City," *Providence Monthly*, posted February 28, 2017, https://providenceonline.com/stories/snowtown-hardscrabble-riots-providence,22373.

61. "Ned" Gray was probably not Edward S. Gray [Grey], "the Boston Rattler" who worked with A. L. Thayer's minstrel troupes after 1848. See African American Trail Project, accessed July 2, 2020, https://africanamericantrailproject.tufts.edu/19th-century-sites.

62. Jay P. Dolan, *The Irish Americans: A History* (Bloomsbury Press, 2008), 38.

63. White, "The origin of Ethiopian minstrelsy," 5.

64. Seth Low, introduction to Archie Emerson Palmer, *The New York Public School; being a history of free education in the city of New York* (Macmillan and Company, 1905), xxiv–xxv.

65. Quoted in James W. Cook, "Master Juba, The King of All Dancers! A Story of Stardom and Struggle from the Dawn of the Transatlantic Culture Industry," *Discourses in Dance* 3, no. 2 (2006): 13–14.

66. "Editor's Table," *Knickerbocker or New-York Monthly Magazine* 21 (1843): 484–485.

67. "Grand Parade Through the Country," *New York Herald*, May 2, 1845, 2; "Welch, Mann & Delevan's National Circus," *Georgetown Advocate* (Washington, DC), Sept. 25, 1845, 3.

68. "The Town," *Chambersburg Times*, Oct. 13, 1845, 3; "LETTER FROM HARRISBURG," *Philadelphia Dollar Newspaper*, Oct. 1, 1845; Michele R. Wade, *Escapes from the Old Jail: Actual Accounts from Local Newspapers* (Franklin County Historical Society, n.d.), 11, 8.

69. Mahar, *Behind the Burnt Cork Mask*, 19, 133.

70. David H. Ela, "Hints to a Very Young Lady on Dancing," *Mother's Assistant and Young Lady's Friend* 8–9 (July 1846): 92–95; "Tendency of the Waltz," *Advocate of Moral Reform*, Nov. 15, 1838.

71. "Miss Ince, the dancer," *Boston Daily Atlas*, Sept. 5, 1845.

72. "Dancing as an Exercise," *North Star*, July 21, 1848; "The Western Reserve Synod," *Frederick Douglass' Paper*, Sept. 25, 1851.

73. "A CARD. To AMATEUR DANCERS," *Public Ledger*, Dec. 22–31, 1835, 3; *National Gazette* (Philadelphia), Jan. 23, 1836, 3.

74. "Circus, Welch, Mann & Delavan," *Jamestown (NY) Journal*, July 25, 1845, 3; and *Carlisle Herald and Expositor*, Aug. 27, 1845, 2; Bob Carlin, *Birth of the Banjo: Joel Walker Sweeney and Early Minstrelsy* (McFarland and Company, 2007), 46.

75. *Public Ledger*, Dec. 10, 1845, 3.

76. *American and Commercial Daily Advertiser* (Baltimore), Dec. 24, 27, 1845, 3.

77. White, "The origin of Ethiopian minstrelsy," 5.

78. "Washingtonian Hall," *Boston Daily Transcript*, Sept. 1–3, 1845, 2; *Boston Daily Bee*, Sept. 4, 1845, 2; "Theatricals," *New York Herald*, Sept. 4, 1845.

79. John Brown, John T. Brown, and John G. Brown were probably the same man. They all played tambourine and danced competitively. "Washingtonian Hall," *Daily Evening Transcript* (Boston), Sept. 4, 1845; *Boston Daily Bee*, Sept. 4, 1845, 2; "The American Chimers," *Boston Daily Bee*, Sept. 9, 1845, 2; "Amory Hall," *Boston Evening Transcript*, Sept. 12, 1845, 2; Rhett Krause, "Step Dancing on the Boston Stage: 1841–1869," *Country Dance and Song* 22 (June 1992): 8; "American Chimers and Juba the King of Dancers," *Boston Evening Transcript*, Nov. 10, 1845, 3.

80. "Music and Mirth for the Million," *Boston Daily Bee*, Sept. 11, 1845, 4; "To Lovers of Music and Dancing," *Springfield (MA) Republican*, Oct. 14, 1845, 3.

81. Ryder had been the Georgia Champions' violinist. "Original Guinea Minstrels" playbill, Apr. 10, 1846, MS Thr 1848, box 12, Houghton Library, Harvard University.

82. "Palmo's Opera House," *New-York Daily Tribune*, Mar. 25, 1846, 3; "Negro Minstrels and Their Dances," *New York Herald*, Aug. 11, 1895, fourth section, MS Thr 1848, boxes 20–21, Houghton Library, Harvard University; Thayer, *Traveling Showmen*, 71.

83. "Grand Match Dance, by Mast. Diamond" playbill, May 23, [1846], MS Thr 1848, box 10 (Diamond, Master), Houghton Library, Harvard University.

84. "Rival Darkies" was a minstrelsy version of T. D. Rice's blackface farce *Oh! Hush! Or, the Virginia Cupids: An Operatic Olio*. Mahar, *Behind the Burnt Cork Mask*, 102, 403n13.

85. "IMMENSE ATTRACTION—NOT TO BE BEAT," *Boston Post*, Apr. 9, 1846.

86. "Amusements," *Boston Daily Atlas*, June 20, 1846, 3.

87. "OLYMPIC," *Boston Bee*, Jan. 3, 1846.

88. "Amusements," *Boston Daily Atlas*, June 20, 1846, 3.

89. "Smoking Ladies in the Street," *Boston Post* quoted in the *Springfield (MA) Republican*, July 4, 1846, 2; "Assault on a Female," *Boston Daily Bee*, June 23, 1846, 2; *Boston Evening Transcript*, June 23, 1846, 2.

90. *The Times and Compiler* (Richmond, VA), June 27, 1846; "SERVED HIM RIGHT," *Hartford Courant*, June 26, 1846, 2; "Good," *Vermont Phoenix* (Brattleboro, VT), July 7, 1846, 1; "Good," *Newport (RI) Mercury*, July 11, 1846, 1.

91. "Police Court—Yesterday," *Boston Daily Bee*, Aug. 18, 1846, 2; *Reasons, Principally of a Public Nature, Against a New Bridge From Charlestown to Boston* (Wells and Lilly, 1825), 17; "City News. Veranda Affair," *Boston Herald*, Dec. 13, 1848.

92. "The Greenwich Theatre, 1846," in George C. D. Odell, *Annals of the New York Stage, Vol. V: 1843–1850* (Columbia University Press, 1931), 296.

93. "Music for the Million," *Southern Patriot* (Charleston, SC), Nov. 23–24, 26–28, 1846, 3.

94. "Music for the Million," *Daily Constitutional* (Augusta, GA), Dec. 3–5, 1846, 3.

95. *Boston Daily Bee*, Feb. 10–Mar. 6, 1847, 3.

96. Charles White, *Going for the cup; or, Old Mrs. Williams' dance. An Ethiopian interlude in one scene*, in *De Witt's Ethiopian and Comic Drama*, no. 20 (R. M. De Witt, 1874).

97. Odell, *Annals*, 308; "DRAMA IN BOWERY DAYS," *New York Times*, Dec. 13, 1896.

98. Odell, *Annals*, 162.

99. Charles Edward Ellis, *An Authentic History of the Benevolent and Protective Order of Elks* (Published by the Author, 1910), 138.

100. "Melodeon," *New York Herald*, Oct. 22, 27, 1847, Jan. 17, and Feb. 1, 1848, 2.

101. "The Beginnings of Negro Minstrelsy. By Tony Pastor," MS Thr 1848, boxes 20–21, Houghton Library, Harvard University.

102. "Records of the New York Stage. White's Melodeon, in the Bowery," *New York Clipper*, n.d., in *Negro Minstrelsy in New York*, vol. 2, MS Thr 1848, boxes 20–21, Houghton Library, Harvard University.

103. "BROADWAY ODEON," *Herald*, Jan. 19, 1848; Odell, *Annals*, 396–397.

104. *New York Herald*, Feb. 8, 1848.

105. "Old Time Minstrels. Billy Birch, in the New York Mail and Express," *Times-Picayune* (New Orleans), July 5, 1891, 10.

106. Brown, "Early History," Feb. 29, 1912, 5.

107. "National. Benefit of Mast. Diamond" playbill, Oct. 18, 1839, MS Thr 1848, box 10, Houghton Library, Harvard University; "Vauxhall Gardens," *Morning Post*, June 21, 1848, 6.

108. Frederick Douglass, "Gavitt's Original Ethiopian Serenaders," *North Star*, June 29, 1849, 2.

Chapter 10. Juba Abroad

1. "Vauxhall Garden," *The Times* (London), June 14, 1848, 5; David Coke and Alan Borg, "Vauxhall Gardens 1661–1859," May 30, 2015, http://www.vauxhallgardens.com/vauxhall_gardens_briefhistory_page.html; "The Vauxhall Pleasure Gardens Detailed History," Vauxhall, Kennington and the Oval, accessed Sept. 5, 2022, http://www.vauxhallandkennington.org.uk/sgdetail.shtml.

2. *Morning Chronicle* (London), June 13, 1848; *Morning Post* (London), June 16 and July 17, 1848, 1.

3. "Free-Trade Hall," *Manchester Guardian,* Oct. 18, 1848.

4. Douglas A. Lorimer, *Colour, Class and the Victorians: English Attitudes to the Negro in the Mid-Nineteenth Century* (Leicester University Press, 1978), 38; Alan J. Rice and Martin Crawford, "Triumphant Exile: Frederick Douglass in Britain, 1845–1847," in *Liberating Sojourn: Frederick Douglass & Transatlantic Reform,* ed. Alan J. Rice and Martin Crawford (University of Georgia Press, 1999), 5; and Sarah Meer, "Competing Representations: Douglass, the Ethiopian Serenaders, and Ethnic Exhibition in London," in Rice and Crawford, *Liberating Sojourn,* 141.

5. "Dumbleton's Ethiopian Serenaders," *New York Herald,* Jan. 29, 1848, 1.

6. Samuel S. Sanford, "Personal Reminiscences," manuscript pp. [21]/18 and [27]/24, Minstrel Show Collection, 1831–1859, Harry Ransom Center, University of Texas at Austin.

7. *Hampshire Telegraph and Sussex Chronicle* (Portsmouth), Dec. 18, 1847.

8. George Wilkes in "*The Pioneer* (California Magazine)," reproduced in "Publisher's Preface" to *Briggs' Banjo Instructor* (Oliver Ditson, 1855), 4.

9. "Maritime Intelligence," *New York Herald,* Apr. 26, 1848; "A MALICIOUS FABRICATION," *Belfast (Ireland) News-Letter,* Jan. 18, 1850.

10. Rice and Crawford, "Triumphant Exile," 2; Meer, "Competing Representations," 160.

11. "Foreign Artists & Managers," *The Era* (London), May 28, 1848, 11.

12. *Morning Post,* June 9, 1848, 1; *Morning Chronicle,* June 13, 1848; *The Era,* June 18, 1848; *The Times,* July 11, 1848, 1.

13. "Vauxhall Gardens," *The Era,* June 25, 1848, 11.

14. "BOZ'S 'JUBA' at VAUXHALL GARDENS," *Morning Post,* June 9, 10, 1848.

15. "VAUXHALL GARDENS," *The Times* (London), June 14, 1848, 5; "VAUXHALL GARDENS," *The Standard* (London), June 13, 1848; "Vauxhall Gardens," *The Era,* June 18, 1848.

16. "Boz's 'Juba' at Vauxhall," *Morning Chronicle,* June 13, 1848; "Vauxhall Gardens," *The Era,* June 25, 1848.

17. *Belfast News-Letter,* Jan. 22, 1850.

18. "Vauxhall Gardens," *The Era,* June 18, 1848; "Elementary Spirits," in *The Works of Heinrich Heine,* trans. Charles Godfrey Leland (William Heinemann, 1906), 6:138–139.

19. "Provincial Theatricals . . . Brighton," *The Era,* July 30, 1848; "Free-Trade Hall," *Manchester Guardian,* Oct. 18, 1848; "THE REAL ETHIOPIANS," *Birmingham Journal,* Dec. 16, 1848, 5.

20. *The Times,* July 15, 1848, 5; "Vauxhall," *Morning Chronicle,* July 7 and June 28, 1848; *The Era,* July 23, 1848.

21. "The Adelphi," *Caledonian Mercury* (Edinburgh), Aug. 23, 1849.

22. "Provincial Theatricals," *The Era,* July 30, 1848.

23. The cartoon "Juba and Pell" can be found on Alamy.com with no citation information.

24. "Provincial Theatricals," *The Era,* July 30, 1848.

25. "JUBA AT VAUXHALL," *Illustrated London News,* Aug. 5, 1848, 77–78.

26. "Vauxhall Gardens," *Morning Post,* June 21, 1848, 6.

27. "The Gardens of England. No. II.—Vauxhall," *The Puppet-Show* (London), Aug. 12, 1848, 172.

28. "Vauxhall Gardens," *Morning Post,* June 21, 1848, 6; William Collins, "The Passions: An Ode for Music," in *The Poetical Works of William Collins* (Leavitt, Trow and Company, 1848), 74–78.

29. *Bell's Life in London,* Aug. 13, 1848, 2; "The Gardens of England. No. II.—Vauxhall," *The Puppet-Show,* Aug. 12, 1848, 172.

30. "Brighton," *Morning Post,* July 27, 1848, 5; "Provincial Theatricals," *The Era,* July 30, 1848.

31. *Newcastle Courant* (Newcastle-upon-Tyne), Feb. 9, 1849; "Edinburgh Adelphi Theatre" playbills, Aug. 27 and 28, 1849, MS Thr 1848, box 14 (Juba, Master), Houghton Library, Harvard University.

32. *Sheffield & Rotherham Independent,* Oct. 28, 1848.

33. *Illustrated London News,* Aug. 5, 1848, 77–78.

34. Lorimer, *Colour, Class and the Victorians,* 70; J. S. Bratton, "English Ethiopians: British Audiences and Black-Face Acts, 1835–1865," *Yearbook of English Studies* 11 (1981): 128.

35. J. S. Bratton argues that British blackface performers and their audiences did not share with Americans "the personal need to feel that blacks were inferior" ("English Ethiopians," 131).

36. Lorimer, *Colour, Class and the Victorians,* 212–214, 42–43.

37. Lorimer, *Colour, Class and the Victorians,* 87; Bratton, "English Ethiopians," 128–133.

38. "MUSIC HALL," *Freeman's Journal and Daily Commercial Advertiser* (Dublin), July 9, 1849.

39. "Provincial Theatricals," *The Era,* July 30, 1848; *Newcastle Courant,* Feb. 23, 1849, 1; "Royal Sadler's Wells Theatre," *The Era,* June 3, 1849.

40. Pierce Egan, *Boxiana; Or, Sketches of Ancient and Modern Pugilism: From the days of the renowned Broughton and Slack, to the championship of Cribb* (George Virtue, 1830), 1:449, 360.

41. Lorimer, *Colour, Class and the Victorians,* 16.

42. *Caledonian Mercury,* Aug. 30, 1849, 3.

43. Lorimer, *Colour, Class and the Victorians,* 42–43.

44. *Sheffield & Rotherham Independent,* Oct. 28, 1848.

45. Bernth Lindfors, *Ira Aldridge: The Vagabond Years, 1833–1852* (University of Rochester Press, 2011), 1–2, 137–160, 135.

46. "Vauxhall," *Morning Post,* Sept. 22, 1848.

47. "Public Amusements," *Bell's Life in London,* Aug. 20, 1848, 2; "Vauxhall Gardens," *Morning Post,* Aug. 22, 1848, 1.

48. Lorimer, *Colour, Class and the Victorians,* 86; *Singing for the Million* (BIRT, Printer, 39, Great St. Andres Street, Seven Dials, London, n.d.).

49. "BOWERY AMPHITHEATRE," *New York Herald,* Jan. 17, 1842, 3; *Daily National Intelligencer* (Washington, DC), May 28, 1842, 4.

50. Bratton, "English Ethiopians," 136.
51. "Vauxhall Gardens," *The Standard,* Aug. 22, 1848.
52. "Free-Trade Hall," *Manchester Guardian,* Oct. 18, 1848.
53. "Vauxhall," *Morning Post,* Sept. 22, 1848.
54. "Vauxhall," *Morning Post,* Sept. 22, 1848.
55. "Juba," *Manchester Times and Manchester and Salford Advertiser and Chronicle,* Oct. 21, 1848.
56. "Vauxhall Gardens," *Morning Post,* Sept. 22 and Aug. 22, 1848, 1.
57. "Vauxhall Gardens," *Morning Post,* June 21, 1848, 6; playbill reproduced in *Sheffield & Rotherham Independent,* Oct. 28, 1848.
58. "Free-Trade Hall.—'Juba' and the Serenaders," *Manchester Guardian,* Oct. 18, 1848; "Juba.—The Ethiopian Serenaders," *Manchester Times and Manchester and Salford Advertiser and Chronicle,* Oct. 21, 1848, 5; "The Ethiopian Serenaders and the Inimitable Juba," *Manchester Examiner,* Oct. 17, 1848, 4.
59. "A Malicious Fabrication," *Belfast News-Letter,* Jan. 18, 1850.
60. "Ethiopian Serenaders," *Manchester Courier & Lancashire General Advertiser,* Oct. 18, 1848, 5.
61. "Free-Trade Hall," *Manchester Guardian,* Oct. 18, 1848.
62. "Ethiopian Serenaders," *Manchester Courier & Lancashire General Advertiser,* Oct. 18, 1848, 5.
63. "Juba.—The Ethiopian Serenaders," *Manchester Times,* Oct. 21, 1848, 5.
64. Lorimer, *Colour, Class and the Victorians,* 92.
65. "Juba.—The Ethiopian Serenaders," *Manchester Times,* Oct. 21, 1848, 5.
66. Dexter Gabriel, "A West Indian Jubilee in America: British Emancipation and the American Abolition Movement" (PhD diss., Stony Brook University, 2016), 75–83.
67. "Juba.—The Ethiopian Serenaders," *Manchester Times,* Oct. 21, 1848, 5.
68. "Free-Trade Hall," *Manchester Guardian,* Oct. 18, 1848.
69. E. P. Thompson, *The Making of the English Working Class* (Vintage Books, 1963), 26–27; Bratton, "English Ethiopians," 128, 133.
70. "Clog Dancing," *Bell's Life in London,* Sept. 28, 1856, 7.
71. "Juba.—The Ethiopian Serenaders," *Manchester Times,* Oct. 21, 1848, 5.
72. *Sheffield & Rotherham Independent,* Oct. 28, 1848.
73. "THE REAL ETHIOPIANS.—BOZ'S JUBA," *Birmingham Journal,* Dec. 16, 1848, 5.
74. Thompson, *Making of the English Working Class,* 319; *Manchester Examiner,* Oct. 10, 1848, 4.
75. Archibald Prentice, *History of the Anti-Corn-Law League* (W. and F. G. Cash, 1853), 2:1; Asa Briggs, *The Making of Modern England 1783–1867: The Age of Improvement* (Harper and Row, 1959), 314.
76. Bratton, "English Ethiopians," 128; Thompson, *Making of the English Working Class,* 26–27.
77. *Sheffield & Rotherham Independent,* Oct. 28, 1848.
78. Dagmar Kift, *The Victorian Music Hall: Culture, Class and Conflict* (Cambridge University Press, 1996), 19.

79. Peter Bailey, "Introduction: Making Sense of Music Hall," in *Music Hall: The Business of Pleasure,* ed. Peter Bailey (Open University Press, 1986), ix.

80. "Public Amusements," *Liverpool Mercury,* Nov. 17, 1848, 1; *Liverpool Courier,* Dec. 13, 1848; "THE REAL ETHIOPIANS," *Birmingham Journal,* Dec. 16, 1848, 5.

81. "THEATRE-ROYAL," *Liverpool Mercury,* Nov. 24, 28, 1848, 1.

82. "MR. PELL'S SERENADERS," *Liverpool Mercury,* Dec. 8, 1848, 2.

83. *Manchester Times,* Jan. 20, 1849; *Liverpool Mercury,* Feb. 13, 16, 1849, 1; *Newcastle Courant,* Feb. 23, 26, 1849, 1.

84. Clarissa Lablache Cheer, *The Great Lablache: Nineteenth Century Operatic Superstar His Life and His Times* (Xlibris Corporation, July 29, 2009), 643–644.

85. "Concert-Hall, Lord Nelson-Street" and "Collegiate Institution, Liverpool," *Liverpool Mercury,* Feb. 13, 1849, 1.

86. "Music Hall," *Newcastle Courant,* Feb. 9, 1849; "MUSIC HALL, GRAINGER STREET," *Newcastle Courant,* Feb. 23, 26, 1849, 1.

87. "THEATRES NORTH & SOUTH SHIELDS" and "MUSIC HALL, GRAINGER STREET," *Newcastle Courant,* Mar. 2, 1849, 1; *Birmingham & General Advertiser,* Mar. 22, 1849, 47.

88. "ROYAL SURREY THEATRE," *The Times,* Apr. 4, 1849, 4; "Surrey," *Morning Post,* Apr. 10, 1849, 5; "Royal Standard Theatre, Shoreditch," *Lloyd's Weekly Newspaper* (London), Apr. 29, 1849, 6; *The Era,* May 13, 1849; Sanford, "Personal Reminiscences," manuscript p. [67]/64.

89. "Provincial Theatres," *The Era,* June 3, 1849, 12; "Royal Sadler's Wells Theatre, *The Era,* June 3, 1849; Juba at Sadler's Wells playbill, London, June 7–9, 1849, TCS 63, box 289, Houghton Library, Harvard University.

90. John Earl, "Building the Halls," in Bailey, *Music Hall,* 3–5; and Bailey, "Introduction," ix–x; Laurence Senelick, introduction to *Tavern Singing in Early Victorian London: The Diaries of Charles Rice for 1840 and 1850* (Society for Theatre Research, 1997), xxvii; Martha Vicinus, *The Industrial Muse: A Study of Nineteenth Century British Working-Class Literature* (Croom Helm, 1974), 238; Annette Benoist, *The Music Halls of Newcastle upon Tyne* (Center for Continuing Education, 1993), n.p.

91. Frank Dumont says R. W. Pelham opened a public house after leaving the Virginia Minstrels. But in 1852 a printer to whom Pelham owed money identified him as "a cooper by trade." Richard "Dick" Pelham died in Liverpool in 1876.

92. *Yankee Smith's Nigger Melodist; or, Newest Collection of Nigger Songs, Dialogues, Stories, &c.: as given by him in his entertainments by Pell's Ethiopians, at Vauxhall, and other celebrated artists: no. 4* (W. Strange, 1849).

93. "Police Intelligence," *Morning Post,* May 31, 1849, 7.

94. "Police Intelligence," *Morning Post,* May 31, 1849, 7.

95. "Music Hall," *Freeman's Journal and Daily Commercial Advertiser,* June 15–20, 1849, 1.

96. "Private Boxes, £3 8s., £1 11s. 6d., £1 1s. 15s.; Dress Boxes, 4s.; Side Boxes, 2s.; Body of the Hall, 1s."

97. "Music Hall," *Freeman's Journal,* June 26, 1849, 1.

98. "The Bosjesmans," *Freeman's Journal*, Dec. 4, 1847, 1; *United Irishman* (Dublin), Apr. 1, 1848, 7.

99. *Freeman's Journal*, July 9, 1849, 1.

100. *Freeman's Journal*, July 3, 1849, 1.

101. *Freeman's Journal*, July 6, 7, 20, 21, 1849, 1.

102. "Adelphi Theatre," *Caledonian Mercury*, Aug. 30, 1849, 3.

103. "Provincial Theatres," *The Era*, Sept. 9, 1849, 11; *Dundee Courier* (Scotland), Sept. 19, 1849, 3–4; *Dundee Courier* quoted in *The Era*, Oct. 7, 1849.

104. "Harmonic Hall, Southwark Bridge Road," *The Era*, July 16, 1848; "New Royal Victoria Theatre," *Lloyd's Weekly Newspaper* (London), July 23, 1848; "Licensed Victuallers' School," *The Era*, Aug. 13, 1848; "Theatre Royal, Southampton," *Hampshire Advertiser & Salisbury Guardian* (Southampton, England), Sept. 16, 1848, 1.

105. "Provincial Theatres," *The Era*, Sept. 30 and Oct. 9, 1849, 11.

106. "Under the Patronage of the Queen," *Sheffield & Rotterham Independent*, Sept. 29, 1849, 1; "Local Intelligence," *Sheffield & Rotterham Independent*, Oct. 6, 1849, 5.

107. "A Regular Dodge," *Manchester Examiner and Times*, Nov. 24, 1849.

108. *Aberdeen Journal*, Oct. 10–24, 1849, 4; *Glasgow Herald*, Nov. 9, 30, 1849, and Jan. 4, 1850.

109. Sanford, "Personal Reminiscences," manuscript p. [67]/64; Meer, "Competing Representations," 147–148; David Coke and Alan Borg, *Vauxhall Gardens: A History* (Yale University Press, 2011), 333–334; *Morning Chronicle*, July 25, 1848.

110. "Trades' Hall," *Glasgow Herald*, Jan. 4, 1850; "MUSIC HALL BELFAST," *Belfast News-Letter*, Jan. 15, 1850.

111. "A MALICIOUS FABRICATION," *Belfast News-Letter*, Jan. 18, 1850 (includes *Banner of Ulster* review).

112. "THEATRE ROYAL, BELFAST," *Belfast News-Letter*, Jan. 22, 1850.

Chapter 11. Assertions of Independence

1. John Glenroy, *Ins and Outs of Circus Life or Forty-Two Years Travel of John H. Glenroy, Bareback Rider, Through United States, Canada, South America and Cuba*, comp. Stephen Stanley Stanford (M. M. Wing and Company, 1885), 70–71.

2. John T. Ford, "Reply to Mr. S. S. Sanford," *Baltimore Sun*, June 29, 1853, 2.

3. Col. T. Allston Brown, "Early History of Negro Minstrelsy: Its Rise and Progress in the United States," *New York Clipper*, Feb. 24, 1912, 5.

4. Richard Bruce Winders, *Mr. Polk's Army: The American Military Experience in the Mexican War* (Texas A&M University Press, 2001), 66–69, 114.

5. United States Mexican War Service Records, 1846–1848, https://www.archives.gov/research/military/mexican-war.

6. Daniel Walker Howe, *What Hath God Wrought: The Transformation of America, 1815–1848* (Oxford University Press, 2007), 705, 737, 739; Ethan Allen Hitchcock, *Fifty Years in Camp and Field*, ed. W. A. Croffut (G. P. Putnam's Sons, 1909), 213.

7. *Philadelphia History* (City History Society of Philadelphia, 1916), 2:260–261; *Public Ledger* (Philadelphia), Aug. 4, 1846, Apr. 3, 26, 1849; John D. McWilliams, "'Men of Colour':

Race, Riots, and Black Firefighters' Struggles for Equality from the AFA to the Valiants," *Journal of Social History* 41, no. 1 (2007): 110; Howe, *What Hath God Wrought*, 207.

8. Paul Foos, *A Short, Offhand, Killing Affair: Soldiers and Social Conflict During the Mexican-American War* (University of North Carolina Press, 2003), 87, 19–20; Winders, *Mr. Polk's Army*, 72; M. B. Leavitt, *Fifty Years in Theatrical Management* (Broadway Publishing Company, 1912), 37–38, 150.

9. Winders, *Mr. Polk's Army*, 113–114, 86.

10. Winders, *Mr. Polk's Army*, 176; Foos, *A Short, Offhand, Killing Affair*, 6, 110, 122–124; Samuel E. Chamberlain, *My Confession: The Recollections of a Rogue* (Harper and Brothers, 1956), 125.

11. *Public Ledger*, Jan. 6, 1847, 3.

12. "THE DEAD ALIVE AND THE LOST FOUND," *Louisville (KY) Daily Courier*, Oct. 6, 1848, 1.

13. "*Olympic*," *Daily Delta* (New Orleans), July 19, 1848, 3; "Olympic Theatre," *Picayune* (New Orleans), July 30, 1848; "Amusements," *New Orleans Crescent*, Aug. 7, 1848, 2; "*Olympic Theater*," *Daily Delta*, Aug. 29, 1848, 3.

14. "Stoppani Hall," *New York Herald*, Dec. 20, 1848, 3; Ernst C. Krohn, "Nelson Kneass: Minstrel Singer and Composer," *Anuario interamericano de investigación musical 7* (1971): 22; *Brooklyn Daily Eagle*, Apr. 13, 1848, 3; "Pittsburgh Theatre," *Pittsburgh Daily Post*, July 12, 1848, 2.

15. "Extraordinary Combination of Talent," *Louisville Daily Democrat*, Oct. 11, 1848, 3, and Oct. 13, 1848, 2; "Kneass' Burlesque Opera Troupe," *Cincinnati Inquirer*, Oct. 21, 1848, 3.

16. "Dan Rice Circus," *Washington (PA) Reporter*, May 16, 1849, 2; *Cabinet* (Schenectady, NY), July 24–31, 1849, 3; *Luzern Union* (Wilkes-Barre, PA), Aug. 29, 1849, 3; *Baltimore Sun*, Oct. 10–20, 1849, 3; David Carlyon, *Dan Rice: The Most Famous Man You've Never Heard Of* (Perseus Books Group, 2001), 94–97.

17. "Masonic Hall," *Cincinnati Enquirer*, Nov. 3, 1849, 2.

18. "Now For It!," *Cincinnati Enquirer*, Dec. 1, 1849, 2; "No Subterfuge," *Baltimore Sun*, June 27, 1853, 2.

19. "Lloyd's Sable Harmonists," *Louisville Daily Courier*, Dec. 22, 1849, 3; "Louisville Theater," *Louisville Daily Journal*, Dec. 28, 1849, 3.

20. "Lloyd's Sable Harmonists," *Louisville Daily Courier*, Dec. 29, 1849, 2, and Dec. 22, 1849, 3.

21. Brendan Breathnach, *Folk Music and Dances of Ireland* (Ossian Publications, 1996), 53.

22. Between 1841 and 1850 780,719 Irish people immigrated to the United States, and 914,119 immigrated between 1851 and 1860. Patrick J. Blessing, "Irish," in *Harvard Encyclopedia of American Ethnic Groups*, ed. Stephan Thermstrom (Belknap Press, 1980), 528.

23. John E. Kleiber, ed., *The Encyclopedia of Louisville* (University Press of Kentucky, 2001), 420–422.

24. *Public Ledger*, July 4, 1851, 3.

25. Charles L. Perdue Jr. et al., *Weevils in the Wheat: Interviews with Virginia Ex-Slaves* (University of Virginia Press, 1976), 316.

26. "Mr. Hill's Concerts," *Evening Star* (Washington, DC), Aug. 10, 1853, 3.

27. *Louisville Daily Courier*, Apr. 10, 1850, 2; *The Tennessean* (Nashville), Apr. 10, 1850, 3; *Picayune* (New Orleans), Apr. 22, 1850, 3.

28. "Criminal Court," *Nashville Daily Union,* Apr. 24, 1850, 3.

29. *Louisville Daily Courier,* May 17, 1850, 3; *Cincinnati Enquirer,* June 5–18, 1850, 3; *Louisville Daily Courier,* June 28, 1850, 2.

30. Kleiber, *Encyclopedia of Louisville,* 97; "Kentucky," *Seventh Census of the United States: 1850,* 612, https://www2.census.gov/library/publications/decennial/1850/1850a/1850a-39.pdf.

31. "Arrested," *Louisville Daily Courier,* Dec. 2, 1850, 2; "Police Court," *Louisville Daily Courier,* July 10, 1848, 1, and June 5, 1848, 3; "Arrested," *Louisville Daily Courier,* Oct. 31, 1850, 2.

32. *Louisville Daily Courier,* Aug. 8, 1850, 2, 3; Hurston C. Burkhart et al., "Who Is Committed to the Louisville Workhouse?" (1949), *Electronic Theses and Dissertations,* Paper 1918, https://doi.org/10.18297/etd/1918.

33. *Louisville Daily Journal,* Aug. 9, 1850, 3.

34. "Sporting Intelligence," *The Times* (London), Feb. 11, 1850, 8; *Newcastle Courant* (Newcastle-upon-Tyne), Feb. 22, 1850.

35. *Lloyd's Weekly Newspaper* (London), Mar. 24, 1850.

36. "Concert Hall," *Buffalo Daily Republican,* Oct. 30, 1851, 3.

37. *The Era* (London), Aug. 31, 1851; "CREMORNE," *Morning Post* (London), Sept. 2, 1851.

38. The Lion Hotel still stands in Warrington on the River Mersey, twenty miles east of Liverpool. "Town-Hall, Market-Place," *Liverpool Mercury,* Feb. 22, 1850, 1.

39. "MECHANICS' INSTITUTE," *Bradford Observer,* Mar. 7, 1850, 1; "Odd Fellows' Hall," *Bradford Observer,* Feb. 21, 1850, 1.

40. Timetables for the South Yorkshire Railway were published in the local papers. Leeds is only eight miles from Bradford, and market towns such as Pudsey and Shipley are even closer.

41. *Nottinghamshire Guardian and Midland Advertiser* (London), Mar. 21, 1850, 1, and Mar. 28, 1850, 2; *Sheffield & Rotterham Independent,* Mar. 23, 1850, 1.

42. "Athenaeum & Mechanics' Institute," *Sheffield & Rotterham Independent,* Mar. 30, 1850, 1.

43. "Sheffield Athenaeum & Mechanics' Institute," *Sheffield & Rotterham Independent,* Apr. 6, 1850; "Boz's Juba," *Sheffield & Rotterham Independent,* Apr. 13, 1850, 8.

44. *The Era,* May 5, 1850.

45. *Liverpool Mercury,* Apr. 12, 1850; "Local Intelligence," *Liverpool Mercury,* Apr. 19, 1850; "Concert Hall," *Liverpool Mercury,* Apr. 26, 1850.

46. "Music and the Drama at Liverpool," *The Era,* Apr. 21, 1850.

47. "The Casino," *Sheffield Times,* May 11, 1850, 8.

48. "The Casino," *Sheffield Times*, May 11, 1850, 8.

49. "Labour and the Poor. Liverpool. [From Our Special Correspondent.] The Amusement and Literature of the People. Letter XVI.," *Morning Chronicle* (London), Sept. 2, 1850, 5.

50. *Freeman's Journal and Daily Commercial Advertiser* (Dublin), Jan. 16, 1850.

51. "Labour and the Poor," 5.

52. "Labour and the Poor," 5.

53. "Provincial Theatricals," *The Era*, June 16, 1850; "Sheffield.—Royal Casino," *The Era*, July 7, 1850.

54. Dagmar Kift, *The Victorian Music Hall: Culture, Class and Conflict* (Cambridge University Press, 1991), 19–20.

55. J. S. Bratton, "English Ethiopians: British Audiences and Black-Face Acts, 1835–1865," *Yearbook of English Studies* 11 (1981): 139.

56. "Colosseum," *Theatrical Journal* (London), July 11, 1850, 2.

57. *Theatrical Journal*, Aug. 1, 1850, 2; "The African Roscius, Mr. John Aldridge," *Lloyd's Weekly Newspaper* (London), Mar. 24, 1850; Bernth Lindfors, *Ira Aldridge: The African Roscius* (University of Rochester Press, 2007), 110–111, 147, 151.

58. "The Colosseum," *The Era*, Aug. 4, 1859.

59. Samuel S. Sanford, "Personal Reminiscences," manuscript p. [67]/64, Minstrel Show Collection, 1831–1859, Harry Ransom Center, University of Texas at Austin.

60. "Labour and the Poor," 5.

61. "The Colosseum," *The Era*, Aug. 11, 1859.

62. James W. Cook interprets the *Era*'s warning as stemming from "racialized resentment in Manchester," where stage workers were complaining "about low salaries, poor job security, and a growing influx of 'foreign celebrities'" ("Master Juba, King of All Dancers!," *Discourses in Dance* 3, no. 2 [2006]: 17–18).

63. "BOZ'S JUBA IN TROUBLE," *Sheffield & Rotterham Independent*, Oct. 12, 1850, 3.

64. "SURREY MUSIC HALL, (late Casino,) Westbar," *Sheffield & Rotterham Independent*, Sept. 7, 1850, 4.

65. *Sheffield & Rotterham Independent*, Oct. 12, 1850, 3.

66. "MUSIC AND THE DRAMA . . . THE CASINO," *The Era*, May 18, 1851.

67. Brown, "Early History," 5.

68. "TOWN FACTS AND FANCIES," *Cincinnati Enquirer*, Jan. 19, 1851, 2; *Daily Scioto Gazette* (Chillicothe, OH), Jan. 27, 1851, 2; "Philosophical Society Lectures, No. 2," *Daily Scioto Gazette*, Jan. 30, 1851, 2.

69. *Pittsburgh Daily Post*, Apr. 19, 1851, 2, 3; "Dimond's [sic] Minstrels," *Pittsburgh Gazette*, Apr. 21, 1851, 3; "Lafayette Hall," *Pittsburgh Gazette*, Apr. 21, 1851, 4; "Gray's Warblers," *Buffalo Courier*, Apr. 21, 1851, 2.

70. "The Negro Minstrels of the Nights Gone By," ca. 1875, HTC Clippings 13 (Bryant, Dan), Houghton Library, Harvard University.

71. "Museum," *Albany Evening Journal*, May 20–26, 1851, 2.

72. "White's Melodeon," *New York Herald*, June 6, 1851, 1.

73. "National Theatre and Circus," *Public Ledger,* July 2, 3, 1851, 3.

74. Gary B. Nash, *First City: Philadelphia and the Forging of Historical Memory* (University of Pennsylvania Press, 2002), 168; Karen Halttunen, *Confidence Men and Painted Women: A Study of Middle-Class Culture in America, 1830–1870* (Yale University Press, 1982), xiii–xviii.

75. "Silver Goblet," *Brooklyn Eagle,* Oct. 6, 1851, 2; "CONCERT HALL," *Newark (NJ) Daily Advertiser,* Oct. 10, 13, 1851, 3; "Van Vechten Hall," *Albany Evening Journal,* Oct. 27–29, 1851, 3; "Apollo Hall" playbill, Oct. 31, 1851, MS Thr 1848, box 16 (New Orleans Serenaders), Houghton Library, Harvard University.

76. "Federal Street Theatre," *Boston Herald,* Dec. 6, 8, 9, 11, 1851, 3.

77. Gayle V. Fischer, *Pantaloons & Power: A Nineteenth-Century Dress Reform in the United States* (Kent State University Press, 2001), 79–80; *Hear Me Patiently: The Reform Speeches of Amelia Jenks Bloomer,* ed. Anne C. Coon (Greenwood Press, 1994), 9–12.

78. William J. Mahar, *Behind the Burnt Cork Mask: Early Blackface Minstrelsy and Antebellum American Popular Culture* (University of Illinois Press, 1999), 93–94.

79. "Federal Street Theatre," *Boston Herald,* Dec. 11, 1851, 3; "Harmony Hall. The Original John Diamond!" playbill, January 2, 1852, MS Thr 1848, box 16 (Ordways Aeolian Vocalists), Houghton Library, Harvard University; "Harmony Hall," *Boston Herald,* Dec. 29, 1851, 2.

80. "Harmony Hall," *Boston Herald,* Jan. 1, 1852, 2; "Mead's Euterpean vocalists," *Boston Bee,* Jan. 26, 1852, Feb. 1–9, 1852; "Mead's Euterpean Vocalists" playbill, Feb. 4, [1852], MS Thr 1848, box 15, Houghton Library, Harvard University.

81. "Ordway Hall," *Boston Herald,* Apr. 15, 1852, 2.

82. George C. D. Odell, *Annals of the New York Stage, Vol. VI: 1850–1857* (Columbia University Press, 1931), 173–174.

83. For Laura Gordon [Boon], see Odell, *Annals,* 244–245.

84. Mahar, *Behind the Burnt Cork Mask,* 365; "White's Melodeon . . . Mast. Marks, the Best Dancer of his age in the World" playbill, April 16, [1852], MS Thr 1848, box 20, Houghton Library, Harvard University; "The Beginnings of Negro Minstrelsy. By Tony Pastor," MS Thr 1848, boxes 20–21, Houghton Library, Harvard University.

85. "Negro Minstrels and Their Dances," *New York Herald,* Aug. 11, 1895, 4th sec., MS Thr 1848, boxes 20–21, Houghton Library, Harvard University.

86. "Lowerre's Minstrels!," *Public Ledger,* Nov. 1, 1852, 3.

87. "GRAND FESTIVAL," *Trenton State Gazette,* Jan. 1, 1853, 2; "LECTURE ROOM, CHINESE MUSEUM," *Public Ledger,* Apr. 15, 1853.

88. "Horticulture Hall," *Boston Bee,* Feb. 1–3, 1852; "City Hall, Charlestown," *Boston Bee,* Feb. 7–9, 1852; Brown, "Early History," 5.

89. *Huddersfield (England) Chronicle and West Yorkshire Advertiser,* Nov. 16, 1850, 4, Nov. 17, 1850, 2, and Nov. 30, 1850, 4.

90. "Provincial Theatricals. . . . Bradford," *The Era,* Dec. 15, 1850, 1.

91. Parliamentary Papers 1843 XIV, pp. E 37–39, quoted in Steven Burt and Kevin Grady, *The Illustrated History of Leeds* (Breedon Books, 1994), 158.

92. *The General Baptist Repository and Missionary Observer,* vol. 12, n.s. (Benjamin L. Green, 1850), 133.

93. "Provincial Theatricals," *The Era,* Dec. 15, 1850, 1.

94. *The Era,* Feb. 9, 1851, 12.

95. "Labour and the Poor," 5.

96. "DANCING," *Bell's Life in London and Sporting Chronicle*, Oct. 29, 1854, 7, and Feb. 25, 1855, 5.

97. "DANCING," *Bell's Life in London*, Dec. 7, 1856, 6; "Nigger Watson of Birmingham," *Bell's Life in London*, Mar. 19, 1854, 6; "Sparring at Public Houses Not Illegal," *Bell's Life in London*, Apr. 2, 1854, 7.

98. Brown, "Early History," 5.

99. "Mr and Mrs Dwight, Negro Melodists and Juba Dancers," *Theatrical Journal*, Mar. 27, 1851; "Dudley.—Concert-Room, Hall street," *The Era*, July 20, 1851, 13.

100. James W. Cook, "Master Juba, King of All Dancers!," *Discourses in Dance* 3, no. 2 (2006): 18.

101. "Provincial Theatricals," *The Era*, June 22, 1851, 11.

102. "THE REAL SABLE HARMONISTS," *The Era*, Sept. 19, 1852, 1; *Huddersfield Chronicle*, Nov. 5, 1853, 5.

103. *Narrative of Henry Box Brown, Who Escaped from Slavery Enclosed in a Box 3 Feet Long and 2 Wide, Written from a Statement of Facts Made by Himself, with Remarks upon the Remedy for Slavery, by Charles Stearns* (Brown and Stearns, 1849), https://publicdomainreview.org/collection/the-narrative-of-henry-box-brown-1849.

104. "Music Hall," *Freeman's Journal*, Jan. 1, 1852, 2; and "South Africans," *Freeman's Journal*, May 30, 1851, 1.

105. "Rattler and the Southern Delineators," *Liverpool Mercury*, Aug. 12, 1851; "Free Trade Hall," *Manchester Times*, Aug. 27, 1851.

106. Henry Mayhew, *London Labour and the London Poor*, 1st ed. (1851), 1:12–13.

107. "Provincial Theatricals," *The Era*, Aug. 17, 1851; "Dublin-City Tavern," *The Era*, Sept. 14, 1851, 11.

108. "MUSIC HALL," *Freeman's Journal*, Dec. 16, 17, 1851, 1.

109. For example, "D. Hodgson, the female Juba," *The Era*, Nov. 23, 1852.

110. Mahar, *Behind the Burnt Cork Mask*, 166, 390nn21, 22.

111. "Marylebone," *The Times*, Oct. 25, 1852, 4.

112. "PUBLIC AMUSEMENTS AT Liverpool," *The Era*, July 18, 1852, 10; "Fugitive Slave William Wells Brown in London," *Manchester Times* (supplement), Aug. 7, 1852, 1.

113. "Refugee from the United States," *Daily News* (London), Oct. 13, 1849; William Wells Brown, "Speech Delivered at the Town Hall, Manchester, England, 1 August 1854 and Speech Delivered at the Concert Rooms, Store Street, London, England, 27 September 1849," accessed Sept. 5, 2022, https://docsouth.unc.edu/neh/index.html.

114. Alan J. Rice and Martin Crawford, eds., *Liberating Sojourn: Frederick Douglass & Transatlantic Reform* (University of Georgia Press, 1999), 6, 141.

Chapter 12. Above All Puny Rivalry

1. John H. B. Latrobe Jr., *Picture of Baltimore* (Lucas Fielding Jr., 1832), 189; "Amusements," *Baltimore Sun*, May 20, 1853, 2; *American and Commercial Daily Advertiser* (Baltimore, MD), June 20, 1853, 3.

2. *Baltimore Sun*, June 27, 1853, 2.

3. John Ford Sollers, "The Theatrical Career of John T. Ford" (PhD diss., Stanford University, 1962), 13, 17, 32. 53.

4. Sollers, "The Theatrical Career," 52, 31, 32.

5. "Amusements," *Baltimore Sun*, May 20, 1853, 2, and May 21, 1853, 3; "Mr. John Diamond!," *American and Commercial Daily Advertiser*, May 25, 1853, 3; "Holliday Street Theatre," *Baltimore Sun*, May 26, 1853, 2.

6. *American and Commercial Daily Advertiser*, May 20–21, 1853, 3; "Mr. JOHN DIAMOND. THE INVINCIBLE DANCER," *Baltimore Sun*, May 27, 1853, 2; *Baltimore Sun*, May 28, 1853, 2.

7. "Ordway Hall! John Diamond" playbill, June 5, 1854, MS Thr 1848, box 16 (Ordway's Aeolian Vocalists), Houghton Library, Harvard University.

8. "Mr. JOHN DIAMOND," *Baltimore Sun*, May 23, 1853, and May 27, 1853, 2.

9. Sean Wilentz, *Chantz Democratic: New York City and the Rise of the American Working Class 1788–1850* (Oxford University Press, 1984), 327–328.

10. "CHALLENGE ACCEPTED!," *Baltimore Sun*, June 27, 1853, 2.

11. *Baltimore Sun*, June 13, 14, 20, 1853, 3.

12. "Holliday Street Theatre," *American and Commercial Daily Advertiser*, June 20, 1853, 3; Frank Dumont, "The Golden Days of Minstrelsy," *New York Clipper*, Dec. 19, 1914.

13. "TRUTH IS MIGHTY AND WILL PREVAIL," *Baltimore Sun*, June 28, 1853, 2.

14. "To the Editor of the Clipper," *New York Clipper*, Jan. 2, 1858, 294.

15. "NO SUBTERFUGE!," *Baltimore Sun*, June 27, 1853, 2.

16. "To Delineators," *New York Sporting Whip*, July 16, 1842, 3.

17. "Bendigo's Benefit," *Spirit of the Times* (New York), July 9, 1842, 223.

18. "National Theatre," *Boston Post*, June 5, 9, 1862, [3].

19. *Baltimore Sun*, May 30, 1853, 2.

20. John T. Ford, "REPLY TO MR. S. S. SANFORD," *Baltimore Sun*, June 29, 1853, 2.

21. "To the Editor of the Clipper," *New York Clipper*, Jan. 2, 1858, 294; *New York Clipper*, June 12, 1858, 63.

22. "That Dancing Challenge," *New York Clipper*, Mar. 28, 1857, 387.

23. "CARD," *Baltimore Sun*, June 28, 1853, 2.

24. "To MR. SAMUEL S. SANFORD," *Baltimore Sun*, June 28, 1853, 2.

25. Ford, "REPLY TO MR. S. S. SANFORD," 2.

26. "Have you seen the Opera," *Baltimore Sun*, June 28, 1853, 2.

27. "R. H. Sliter's Empire Minstrels," *Mississippi Free Trader* (Natchez), Dec. 28, 1850, 2.

28. "Buffalo Museum," *Buffalo Commercial*, Apr. 29, 1851, 3; "Local Intelligence," *Buffalo Daily Republic*, May 13, 1851, 2.

29. *New York Clipper*, Apr. 10, 1858, 402.

30. *New York Clipper*, May 8, 1858, 23.

31. "Ordway Hall! John Diamond" playbill, June 5, 1854; "Ordway Hall," *Boston Herald*, June 8, 1854, 2.

32. "Look Out for Fun," *Illinois State Journal* (Springfield), Oct. 4, 1856, 2; Col. T. Allston Brown, "Early History of Negro Minstrelsy: Its Rise and Progress in the United States," *New York Clipper*, June 15, 1912.

33. "Dancing.—A CHALLENGE TO THE AMERICAN CHAMPION," *Bell's Life in London*, Aug. 30, 1857, 7.

34. *Evening Star* (Washington, DC), Aug. 9, 1853, 2, and Aug. 10–11, 1853, 3.

35. In 1853 Philadelphia music publisher Septimus Winner nestled "four of John Diamond's jigs" into a collection of violin music scores for the parlor that contained "Ladies' Polka Quadrilles," a set of "Negro Cotillions," and other dance tunes. *New York Clipper*, Jan. 7, 1854, 7; *Boston Investigator*, June 14, 1854, col. B; *Boston Herald*, May 24, 1854, 2; "Purdy's National Theatre," *Evening Post* (New York), Aug. 7, 1854, 3; "Violin Music.—Winner's Collection, No. 7," *Public Ledger* (Philadelphia), Apr. 6, 1853, 2.

36. *Newark (NJ) Daily Advertiser*, Jan. 23–Feb. 1, 1854, 2.

37. "Ordway Hall," *Boston Investigator*, May 24, 1854, col. A; *Boston Herald*, July 8, 1854, 2; *Briggs' Banjo Instructor* (Oliver Ditson, 1855), 4.

38. "Howard Athenaeum," *Boston Herald*, Nov. 10, 1854.

39. P. T. Barnum to Moses, "American Museum, Sept. 26, 1843, http://lostmuseum.cuny.edu/archive/iowa-indians-at-the-american-museum, courtesy Boston Athenaeum Library.

40. "Indian Entertainment," *Wooster (OH) Republican*, May 25, 1854, 2; "Indian Entertainment," *Sunbury (PA) American*, June 11, 1853, 2.

41. "The Indians from Southern Oregon," *Daily Constitutionalist and Republican* (Augusta, GA), Dec. 2, 1853; "The 'Monasco Troupe' of Indian Actors and Actresses," *St. Albans (VT) Messenger*, Mar. 8, 1855, 4; Cassandra Tate, "Cayuse Indians," posted Apr. 3, 2013, https://www.historylink.org/file/10365.

42. Tara Browner, *Heartbeat of the People: Music and Dance of the Northern Pow-Wow* (University of Illinois Press, 2002), 20, 52.

43. William R. Seaburg, ed., *Pitch Woman and Other Stories: The Oral Traditions of Coquelle Thompson, Upper Coquille Athabaskan Indian*, comp. Elizabeth Derr Jacobs (University of Nebraska Press, 2007), 38–39; "Environmental Histories Project," accessed Dec. 7, 2022, https://darkwing.uoregon.edu/~ecostudy/elp/ehistory/kalapuya.htm.

44. Matthew W. Wittman, "Empire of Culture: U.S. Entertainers and the Making of the Pacific Circuit, 1850–1890" (PhD diss., University of Michigan, 2010), 122, 134.

45. *Boston Herald*, Nov. 10, 1854, 2.

46. Browner, *Heartbeat of the People*, 21, 23.

47. Journals of the Lewis and Clark Expedition, January 1, 1805, [Clark], https://lewisandclarkjournals.unl.edu/item/lc.jrn.1805-01-01#lc.jrn.1805-01-01.01.

48. Chaney Mack interviewed by WPA worker Mrs. Judith Wulph, location and date unknown, WPA Slave Narrative Project, Mississippi Narratives, reproduced in *Black Indian Slave Narratives*, ed. Patrick Minges (John F. Blair, 2004), 150–153.

49. After Boston, the "Indian Troupe" toured New England. "Howard Athenaeum," *Boston Herald*, Nov. 14, 1854, 2; "ONE MORE CHANCE!," *Salem (MA) Register*, Nov. 29, 1854, 2; *St. Albans Messenger*, Mar. 8, 1855, 4.

50. George C. D. Odell, *Annals of the New York Stage, Vol. VI: 1850–1857* (Columbia University Press, 1931), 368.

51. "J.B.," *New York Clipper*, Jan. 7, 1854, 7.

52. Odell, *Annals*, 408, 375; "Things Theatrical," *Spirit of the Times* (New York), Apr. 14, 1855, 108; "White's Opera House," *New York Herald*, May 16, 1855, 7.

53. "Circus at the Bowery," in Odell, *Annals*, 371; "Purdy's National Theatre," *New York Times*, July 27, 1855, 8; T. Allston Brown, *A History of the New York Stage from the First Performance in 1732 to 1901* (Dodd, Mead, 1903), 1:320; "Williamsburgh [sic], 1854–1855," Odell, *Annals*, 423.

54. Edward Le Roy Rice, *Monarchs of Minstrelsy* (Kenny Publishing Company, 1911), 23–24. A few days after his death, a spurious account of Sanford's demise, ridiculing his fast life and fastidiousness in dress, appeared in the press. "James Sanford," *Springfield (MA) Republican*, Sept. 8, 1855, 8.

55. "Sanford's Opera House," *Public Ledger*, Sept. 20–21, 1855, 3; "Sanford's American Opera House," *Public Ledger*, Sept. 24, 1855, 3; "Philadelphia Theatricals," *Spirit of the Times*, Sept. 29, 1855, 396.

56. "Second Street Hall," *Public Ledger*, Oct. 25–30, 1855; "Southwark Opera House," *Public Ledger*, Nov. 26–Dec. 10, 1855, 3.

57. "Challenge to Jig Dancers," *New York Clipper*, Mar. 25, 1854.

58. "Baltimore Museum," *Baltimore Sun*, July 3, 1855, 2.

59. "To DICK SLITER," *New York Clipper*, Aug. 30, 1856, 151.

60. *Public Ledger*, Nov. 26, 1855, 3.

61. "Answer to Correspondents," *New York Clipper*, Mar. 1, 1856, 2.

62. "MATHIAS RUSK'S SPARRING EXHIBITION," *Public Ledger*, Feb. 20, 1856, 3.

63. *New York Herald*, Apr. 26, 27, 1857, 7; *New York Clipper*, May 15, 1858, 31.

64. "Jig Dancing—Buffalo," *Clipper*, Oct. 18, 1857, 215; Hunter M. Claypatch, "'Tough Little Specimens of the Light-Weight Order': The Establishment of Lightweight Prize-Fighting in the United States During the 1850s," International Boxing Research Organization, 2016, 2–3, https://www.ibroresearch.com/wp-content/uploads/2016/12/Tough-Specimens-of-the-Lightweight-Order.pdf.

65. "Benefit of Mr. J. E. Taylor," *New York Clipper*, June 24, 1854, 3; "GYMNASTIC EXHIBITION.—Worcester, Mass., July 6, 1856," *New York Clipper*, July 19, 1856, 97; "Barney Aaron's Sparring Exhibition," *New York Herald*, Apr. 28, 1859, 5.

66. *New York Clipper*, Feb. 21, 1857, 348.

67. Ed. James, *Jig, Clog, and Breakdown Dancing Made Easy with Sketches of Noted Jig Dancers* (Ed. James, 1873), 2.

68. "Special Card," *Baltimore Sun*, Apr. 11, 1856, 2; "Benefit of the Independent Fire Company," *Baltimore Sun*, Apr. 5, 1856, 2.

69. Steven Riess, *City Games: The Evolution of American Urban Society and the Rise of Sports* (University of Illinois Press, 1989), 15.

70. April F. Masten, "Man and Money Ready: Challenge Dancing in Antebellum America," in *The Oxford Handbook of Dance and Competition*, ed. Sherril Dodds (Oxford University Press, 2019), 614–615.

71. "$500 CHALLENGE! Miss Julia Morgan," *Boston Herald*, May 29, 1862, 3.

72. "National Theatre . . . CHALLENGE ACCEPTED," *Boston Post*, June 5, 1862, 3; "Canterbury Hall," *Evening Star* (Washington, DC), May 25, 1865, 1; *Boston Herald*, June 17–23, 1862, 3; "Jigs," *Sacramento Daily Union*, Aug. 12, 1862.

73. "The Beginnings of Negro Minstrelsy. By Tony Pastor," MS Thr 1848, boxes 20–21, Houghton Library, Harvard University.

74. Odell, *Annals*, 587; Chas. White, "Origin of Negro Minstrelsy," *New York Clipper*, June 24, 1854, 2. The minstrelsy chronicle published after White's excluded Diamond. "Negro Minstrelsy—Its History and Influences," *New York Clipper*, Feb. 21, 1857, 348.

75. *New York Herald*, June 27, 1856, 7, and July 11, 1856, 7.

76. *New York Herald*, Oct. 5, 1856, 8, and Oct. 7, 1856, 12.

77. "DRAMA IN BOWERY DAYS," *New York Times*, Dec. 13, 1896, 6.

78. Lawrence W. Levine, *Highbrow/Lowbrow: The Emergence of Cultural Hierarchy in America* (Harvard University Press, 1990), 77.

79. David R. Roediger, *The Wages of Whiteness: Race and the Making of the American Working Class* (Verso, 1991), 154, 127, 148.

80. *New York Clipper*, Oct. 17, 1857, 207; "Mechanics' Hall. Bryant's Minstrels" playbill, Jan. 18, 1859, MS Thr 1848, box 24, and "Bryant and Mallory's Campbell Minstrels" playbill, [Oct. 30, 1856], box 8, Houghton Library, Harvard University.

81. Henry Llewellyn Williams, *Challenge Dance* (18--), 38–46.

82. "Charley White's Opera House," *New York Herald*, Oct. 19–20, 1856, 7.

83. "NATIONAL CIRCUS . . . Yorkshire Clog Dance," *Public Ledger*, Apr. 6, 1857, 3; "Fred. Wilson . . . Yorkshire Clog Dance," *Bangor (ME) Daily Whig and Courier*, Aug. 18, 1858, 1; "Thomas Opera House . . . Lancashire Clog Dance," *Public Ledger*, Jan. 27, 1858, 3; Phil Jamison, *Hoedowns, Reels, and Frolics: Roots and Branches of Southern Appalachian Dance* (University of Illinois Press, 2015), 129, 147–149.

84. "Charley White's Opera House," *New York Herald*, Oct. 20–23, 1856, 7.

85. Charles W. Calomiris and Larry Schweikart, "The Panic of 1857: Origins, Transmission, and Containment," *Journal of Economic History* 51, no. 4 (1991): 808; "AMUSEMENTS," *New York Clipper*, Oct. 17, 1857, 203.

86. "Records of the New York Stage. White's Melodeon, in the Bowery," *New York Clipper*, n.d., in *Negro Minstrelsy in New York*, vol. 2, MS Thr 1848, boxes 20–21, Houghton Library, Harvard University.

87. "Answers to Correspondents," *New York Clipper*, Mar. 14, 1857, 370; "Mickey Warren and John Diamond," *New York Clipper*, Mar. 21, 1857, 379; "MELODEON," *Public Ledger*, Mar. 14, 1857, 4.

88. "National Circus," *Public Ledger*, Apr. 6, 1857, 3.

89. "Military Hall," *Public Ledger*, Apr. 18, 1857, 1, Apr. 24, 1857, 3, and Apr. 25, 1857, 4.

90. "Answers to Correspondents," *New York Clipper*, May 23, 1857, 2, Oct. 3, 1857, 186, and Oct. 17, 1857, 202.

Conclusion

1. "Bois Juba," no. 237, Feb. 3, 1854, register of deaths in the district of Mount Pleasant Liverpool, General Register Office, Liverpool, County of Lancaster; "Bois Juba," no. 1067, Feb. 6, 1854, p. 104, register of burials at the Free Parochial Cemetery of St. Martin in the Fields, Liverpool, County of Lancaster. Both records have been reproduced in Walter Dean Myers, *Juba! A Novel* (Amistad, 2015), 195, 196. Also see James W. Cook, "Lane, William Henry [performing name Juba, Master Juba]," in *Oxford Dictionary of National Biography*, Oct. 3, 2013, 2, https://doi.org/10.1093/ref:odnb/100407.

2. Diamond was buried in a lot owned by someone named Patrick Wood alongside a family named Mooney. "Deaths," *The Press* (Philadelphia), Oct. 30, 1857, 2; "Death of John Diamond," *New York Clipper,* Nov. 7, 1857, 226; Ollie Mae Ray, "Biographies of Selected Leaders in Tap Dance" (PhD diss., University of Utah, 1976), 49.

3. James Higgins, "Infectious Diseases and Epidemics," in *The Encyclopedia of Greater Philadelphia* (Rutgers University, 2016), https://philadelphiaencyclopedia.org/archive/infectious-diseases-and-epidemics/.

4. Charles E. Rosenberg, *The Care of Strangers: The Rise of America's Hospital System* (Basic Books, 1987), 22–30.

5. Col. T. Allston Brown, "Early History of Negro Minstrelsy: Its Rise and Progress in the United States," *New York Clipper,* Feb. 24, 1912, 5, and Feb. 29, 1912.

6. Brown, "Early History," Mar. 2, 1912, 3 (under "Richard Ward Pelham").

7. Samuel S. Sanford, "Personal Reminiscences," manuscript p. [67]/64, Minstrel Show Collection, 1831–1859, Harry Ransom Center, University of Texas at Austin.

8. "Death of John Diamond," *New York Clipper,* Nov. 7, 1857, 226.

9. "The First Negro Minstrels [from the San Francisco Alta-California]," *New Haven Daily Morning Journal and Courier,* May 28, 1885, 3; "The First Negro Minstrels," *Otago Witness* (Dunedin, Otago, New Zealand), Dec. 19, 1885, 26.

10. Edward Le Roy Rice, *Monarchs of Minstrelsy* (Kenny Publishing Company, 1911), 48, 40–41.

11. "Modern Jig Dancing," *Morning Republican* (Little Rock, AR), Apr. 22, 1873, 2.

12. Helen Tangires, *Public Markets and Civic Culture in Nineteenth-Century America* (Johns Hopkins University Press, 2003), 18, 98–106, 134–135.

13. Vincent DiGirolamo, *Crying the News: A History of America's Newsboys* (Oxford University Press, 2019), 7, 78–79, 162–175; Christine Stansell, "Women, Children, and the Uses of the Streets: Class and Gender Conflict in New York City, 1850–1860," *Feminist Studies* 8, no. 2 (1982): 309–335.

14. Roy Rosenzweig, *Eight Hours for What We Will* (Cambridge University Press, 1983), 131–146.

15. Walter Johnson, *The Broken Heart of America* (Basic Books, 2021), 2; April F. Masten, *Art Work: Women Artists and Democracy in Mid-Nineteenth-Century New York* (University of Pennsylvania Press, 2008), 108.

16. "At Toledo," *Santa Fe (NM) Weekly Post,* Aug. 2, 1862, 2.

17. Lawrence Levine, *Highbrow/Lowbrow: The Emergence of Cultural Hierarchy in America* (Harvard University Press, 1990), 68–69.

18. Wesley Morris, "Music," in *The 1619 Project,* created by Nikole Hannah-Jones (One World, 2021), 375–376; William T. Lhamon Jr., *Jump Jim Crow: Lost Plays, Lyrics, and Street Prose of the First Atlantic Popular Culture* (Harvard University Press, 2003), ix. For African American minstrel parties, see *Old Slack's Reminiscence and Pocket History of the Colored Profession from 1865 to 1891. By Ike Simond, Banjo Comique* ([Chicago], 1891).

19. Helen Brennan, *The Story of Irish Dance* (Roberts Rinehart, 2001), 28.

20. Robin D. G. Kelley, *Yo' Mama's DisFUNKtional! Fighting the Culture Wars in Urban America* (Beacon Press, 1997), 67–69.

INDEX

Aaron, Barney, 286
Aaron, Johnny, 286
absconding apprentices, 74–75, 100, 110–112
African American dancing, 30–31, 41–42, 97
African dance, 24, 29–30, 42
Albertine, Miss, 261
Aldridge, Ira, 83, 228–229, 257–259
Allen, A. J., 37
Almack, William, 147
Almack's, 144, 146–148, 150–151, 159–160; All-Max's, 149
American Circus, 126–137
American Notes, 146–151, 173, 195; American reception of, 152, 159–161, 192–193
Amistad case, 48
Anderson, Robert Ball, 136
Anson, John W., 241
antislavery activity, 7, 48, 196, 227–228, 270, 289
Artôt, Joseph, 182
Auber, Daniel, 46
Augusta, M'lle, 72, 318n57

Bailey, J. P., 127, 129
ballet dancing, 46–50, 93, 111–112, 120, 155, 164
Bancker, James W., 90, 101, 180, 205
Baresford, B., 209
Barnum, P. T., 3, 5, 31, 45, 51, 69, 180; accusations of dark transactions at Vauxhall and, 113–118; American Museum and, 162, 180; circuses and, 54–55; consequences of humbug contest for, 108, 110–113; contract with Diamond in 1840, 86–87; Diamond as disgruntled apprentice of, 74–75; early professional life of, 13–14; managing style of, 55, 58, 62–67, 72–73; in New Orleans, 102–110; new show with Diamond and Lane, 88; return to New York City without John Diamond, 112–113; theaters and, 33–35; traveling troupe including Diamond and Black fiddler, 97–100; Vauxhall Gardens and, 76, 78, 81–90, 113–115, 118–120; work with Black performers, 80, 85–86, 98
Barron, James, 140
Battas, Joe, 177
Bell's Life in London, 268, 280
Bennie, Mr. and Mrs., 62, 85
Bennett, Henry, 180
Bennett, James Gordon, 187
Benson, John C., 248, 269–271
Bertus, Paul, 141
Birch, Billy, 179, 212
Black employment: child, 80; conflicts in Philadelphia over, 96–97; as entrepreneurs, 79–80, 122–123; in the North, 78–81; in professional careers, 78–79; women, 80, 102
Black entertainers: as actors, 83–85, 228–229, 257; as dancers, 4, 78, 80, 85, 89, 187; in England, 218, 257–260, 269–271; as fiddlers, 98–100; in precarious situations, 78, 100–102; social scrutiny of, 85–86, 204–205, 259
blackface minstrelsy, 2, 6–8, 192–194; burlesque of challenge dancing, 289–291; imitation dancing and, 189, 191, 212–213;

358 · INDEX

blackface minstrelsy (*continued*): jig dancing and, 191–192, 201–203, 211–212, 289–291; Juba and Diamond and, 192–196; musicians of, 8, 192–195; in the United Kingdom, 218–221, 227–228, 256–257, 269; work with champion dancers, 8, 191–192, 201
blackface performance, 1, 38–40, 45, 89; costumes of, 37–38; "Negro" delineators, 34, 54, 88, 164, 220, 242, 254, 269, 270; racist characterizations and sexist stereotypes in, 40, 192, 229, 297, 306n15
Black fiddlers, 26, 61, 98–100, 145, 157, 170
Black-Irish relations, 4, 14–15, 22–25, 96–97, 144–145, 151–152, 296–298; racist characterizations and sexist stereotypes of, 6, 150–151; in taverns, 18
Black prizefighters, 174–179
Black Schooner or the Pirate Slaver Armistad!, The, 48
Boston Rattler, 189, 202, 336n3. *See also* Gray, Edward
Bowers, E., 288
Bowery Amphitheatre, 53; challenge dance at, 185; circuses at, 54, 164, 180, 193
boxing, 7, 50, 74, 174–179, 185, 203, 277, 286–287
Bratton, J. S., 133
breakdowns, 4, 13, 27, 151, 290
Briggs, Thomas F. (Fluter), 195, 209, 217, 219–220, 240, 252, 281–282
Brower, Frank, 167, 189, 192–193, 202
Brown, Henry Box, 270
Brown, Joe, 187, 201, 211, 280
Brown, John, 194, 201, 205, 206
Brown, T. Allston, 73, 128, 212, 244, 260, 269, 295
Brown, William Alexander, 82–83
Brown, William Wells, 197, 218, 271–272
Bryant, Dan, 201, 289–290
Bryant, Jerry, 201, 236, 264, 294
Bryant, Suse, 155–158, 163
Bull, John, 227
Bull, Ole, 181–182, 196
Buntline, Ned, 152
burlesque, 70, 248, 289–291
busking, 22

Cadwallader, George, 52, 55, 163
cake dances, 23–25
Caldwell, James Henry, 105–106, 111
camp town, 97; "Camp Town" hornpipe, 42, 54, 96
Carleton, William, 29, 151, 153
Carlisle, Dick, 74, 75

Carroll, Richard M. (Master Marks), 31, 211, 265, 288
Carroll, Thomas, 259
Carter, James P., 229
Catholic Church, 30, 183, 247
casino, 254
Catron, John, 122
Cavanaugh, Luke, 31
Céleste, Céline, 49, 50, 72, 108
challenge dancing, 2–5; as American sport, 167, 275–276; children, 3, 4, 7, 19, 25, 31, 71, 265, 296, 298; ballet version of, 49–50; Boylston Garden tournament, 201–203; compared to boxing matches, 174–179; as creolized form of jig dancing, 3–4; dancing masters teaching, 28–31; demographics of participants in, 4; 1844 challenge by Juba to Diamond, 183–188; in England, 268–269; first recorded match between Juba and Diamond, 169–173; first staged, 56–58; humbug matches, 67, 108–110; intersection with blackface minstrelsy, 8; journalistic record on, 5–6; Long Island, 26–27; making a match, 65, 173–174, 183–186, 268–269, 277–278, 285; mock challenges, 118–120; Native Americans and, 282–284; at New Chatham Theatre, 56–58, 62; newspaper coverage of, 117–120; prizes for, 23–25, 209, 277–278; as speculation, 7, 57, 184, 279; at street markets, 19, 21, 24–26; trial of skill, 62, 67, 69, 199, 206; wagers on, 56, 62–66, 165–168; at Walnut Street Theatre, 64–66; by women, 4, 7, 16, 27, 152–153, 155–158, 278, 287–288, 298; in working-class taverns, 16–19, 31, 61, 153, 170–173. *See also* dancers
champion belts, 273, 277–278, 280, 281
Chanfrau, Frank, 164, 261, 265
"characteristic" dances, 40, 42
child entertainers, 7, 35; in circuses, 54, 105, 128; cross-dressing by, 71; exploitation of, 78, 86; jig dancing by, 4, 13; labor arrangements for, 54–55, 86; learning to dance, 28–31; in markets, 19–21; in taverns, 18, 31
child labor, 7, 19, 21, 31, 33, 51, 54, 56, 78, 80, 103, 128, 142, 153
Christy, Edwin P., 193
Cinquez, Joe, 48, 50–51
circuses, 51–54, 122–124; advertising for, 132–133; American Circus, 126–137; Broadway Circus, 51–53; caravans of, 131–132; community objections to, 135, 137, 138–139; crew of, 127; fighting and swearing among men of, 129, 137–140; Fogg & Stickney's,

105, 112, 124–126; impact on local economies, 137–138; John Diamond's jig dancing with, 51, 97–100, 128–129, 163, 204, 205; long journeys of, 131–135; music at, 133–135; provision of food and housing for employees, 129; reaction of Southern audiences to, 135–137; segregated seating by, 136–137; spectators of, 133, 135, 136–137; traveling by steamboat, 103–104, 126–137; women in, 52, 127–128, 139
Clementine, Miss, 88, 89, 101
Clinton, De Witt, 203
clog dancing, 174, 233–234, 288, 290
Coleman, Thomas, 54, 74, 162, 202, 248
Comic Almanack, 44
concert rooms, 98, 232, 234, 236, 237, 254
Conner, Edmond S., 32
Cook, Alderman Joel, 75
costumes, 7, 29, 37–38, 71, 94, 229, 287
counter challenge, 276, 278
cracovienne dance, 40–41, 120; "cracover-again," 160
Cribb, Tom, 176, 177–178
cross-dressing, 7, 46, 49, 71, 229–231, 262–264, 276
Cruikshank, George, 44, 149
Cunningham, Michael (Albany Fat Boy), 286

dancers: ballet, 49–50, 93, 155, 318n57; burlesque, 70, 248, 264, 289–291; champion belts awarded to, 273–274, 277–278; clothes worn by champions, 170; costumes worn by, 37–38, 94, 221–222, 287; cross-dressing, 7, 49, 71, 229–231, 262–264; 276; female, 4, 7, 27, 151–158; health and deaths of, 293–294; imitation, 189–191, 198, 200; jig, 3–4, 116, 128–129, 171; "jig, reel, and trial," 173; as laborers, 7, 33, 78, 128, 294; Kentucky, 108, 136; Long Island, 22, 26–27; Million movement, 193–195; Nashville, 136; Native American, 282–284; "Negro," 14, 16, 21–26, 40–45, 135, 164, 165, 167; newspaper coverage of, 117–120; reputations of, 167, 172, 211, 288, 294–295; social scrutiny of, 204–205; stage names of, 8, 35–36, 78, 85, 89, 113, 116, 119, 180, 288. *See also* challenge dancing
dancing masters, 28–31, 136, 157
Daniels, John, 165, 167, 193
danseuse, 49
Darby, Rapsay, 113–115
Davenport, Eliza, 173
Davenport, Jean Margaret, 70–73
Davenport, Thomas D., 72–73
Davis, Louis, 89, 90, 100–102, 144

decanter jig, 249–250, 286
Democrat Party, 94–95
Deverna, William S., 181, 182
De Voe, Thomas, 21, 22
Diamond, Elizabeth, 22
Diamond, Frank, 189, 202, 205. *See also* Francis Lynch
Diamond, John, 1–3; announcement of first challenge match between Juba and, 168, 173–174; arrested as an absconding apprentice, 75; arrested for smoking in the street, 207–208; arrested for stabbing, 140–142; arrests in the Midwest, 250–251; awarded champion belt, 273–274, 277–278, 280; Band of Sable Melodists of, 260; biography in the *New York Clipper*, 117; in blackface, 37–40; Black fiddlers and, 97–100; in Boston, 45, 73–74, 163, 202–203, 206–208, 282; called best of the white "Negro dancers," 167; called the Philadelphia negro dancer, 97; circuses and, 51–54, 123–142, 163, 204, 205; consequences of humbug contest and, 110–113; contrasted with Fanny Elssler, 93–94, 96; costumes of, 37–38, 170; death of, 293; Dick Sliter and, 193, 249, 273, 276–280; as disgruntled apprentice, 74–75; disregard for social rank and self-preservation of, 204; dual identity as artiste-athlete, 280–282; early death of, 5; early life of, 2; economic hardships during the 1856 recession, 291–292; extravaganzas of, 43–45; first dancing match against Juba at Pete Williams' tavern, 169–173; at Ford's Holliday Street Theatre, 274–276; friendship with James Sanford, 68–69; hired by P. T. Barnum, 13–14; immigration of family of, 22; impersonation of a woman by, 46, 262–264; income of, 86; James Thomas on, 123–124; Joseph W. Harrison as guardian of, 86–87, in *La Bayadere in Ole Kentuck!*, 45–51; lack of social mobility of, 295–296; legacy of, 298–300; as Master Diamond, 33, 34–38, 73; military service of, 244–247; minstrelsy and, 38–40, 192–195; Music for the Million and, 208–209; music played for minstrel bands by, 196, 206; Native American opponents of, 282–284; in New Orleans, 102–103, 110, 140–142; in Philadelphia, 64–69, 74–75, 96–97, 162, 285, 292; press coverage of, 56–57, 117–118, 141–142, 167–168; promotion of 1844 challenge by Juba to, 183–188; reaction of Southern audiences to, 108–109, 135; return to dancing after the Mexican-American War, 248–249; return to the North, 161–165;

Diamond, John (*continued*): salary of, 69, 73, 104, 129, 162, 211; scholarship on, 6; shows with Lane, 88–89; social scrutiny of, 204–205; solo act of, 260–261; stage debut of, 32–33; stardom of, 4; theater acts of, 69–74; travel of, 69–70, 97–100, 126–137, 140, 161–165; types of "Negro dancing" and, 40–42; called "unrivalled" and "unequaled," 126; Vauxhall Gardens and, 88–90; as young performer, 7
Diamond, John, Sr., 22
Dickens, Charles, 4, 5, 173, 217; American reception of *American Notes* by, 159–161; arrival in New York, 143; description of Almack's in Five Points, 146–151, 167, 195–196; description of Juba's dancing, 151–152; observations of dancing, 145–146; visit to Black-run tavern, 144–146; walking tour of New York, 143–144
Dickson, Tom, 251
Dimond, John, 86. *See also* Diamond, John
Dimond, Nicholas, 22
Dinneford, William, 33–34, 35, 70
Douglass, Frederick, 191, 212–213, 218
Dubois, Sylvia, 30
Dudley, Bob, 287
Dumbolton, James A., 218–219, 221
Durang, Charles, 64
Durang, John, 38, 42, 64

Edwards, Bob, 195, 197, 205, 265–266, 285
Egan, Pierre, 148–149, 178, 268
1840 presidential election, 95
Elssler, Fanny, 41, 93–96, 111–112, 125, 155, 226
Emmett, Dan, 192, 209
entr'acte work, 33–34
equestrians, 109, 125–126, 130–131
"Ethiopian dancer," 33, 40–42, 117, 180, 200
Ethiopian Minstrels, 194, 206–207, 208–209
Ethiopian Serenaders (Pell's), 218–232; at humble venues in England, 236–237; in Ireland, 239–241; travel around England, Ireland, and Scotland, 232–235
Eversell, J., 127
Everton, J. H., 220, 238
extravaganzas, 43–45

fiddlers, 26, 28, 53, 61, 69, 97, 98–100, 106, 135, 145, 157, 162, 170, 181–182, 186, 192, 196
Field, Matt, 125
Fitzwilliam, Mrs. (née Fanny Elizabeth Copeland), 112
flash press, 5, 114, 120, 155, 165, 220

"flaxed out," 57–58, 62
Fluter, T. *See* Briggs, Thomas F. (Fluter)
Flynn, Thomas, 58, 61
Fogg, Jeremiah P., 105, 109
Fogg and Stickney's circus (Fogg & Stickney), 105, 109, 112, 124–126, 135
Foley, Catherine, 30
Ford, John T., 244, 274–275, 279
Ford's Theatre (Holliday Street), 273–276, 287
Foreign Airs and Native Graces, 112
Foster, George, 61, 154
Frazer, John, 148
Free Nigger of New York, The, 45
Fuller, William, 177

gag bills, 66–67
Gains, Rachel, 136
gallery seats, 8, 56, 58, 59, 60, 196, 234, 254, 289; "colored," 61, 205; "gods," 241, 266
Gannon, Mary Ann, 34, 120–121
Gannon, Phil, 285, 286–287
Gardner, Dan, 88, 89, 101
Garretts, J. L., 85, 86, 88
Garrison, William Lloyd, 197
Garson, Angeline, 194
Garson, Annette, 194
Garson, Pauline, 194
Garson, Rosina, 194
Georgia Champions, 195–196, 199–200, 202
Gibbs, Mrs., 56
Glenroy, John, 52, 55, 138, 140, 163, 244
Going for the Cup, 209–210, 257
Gordon, Lora, 265
Gray, Edward (Ned), 189–191, 202. *See also* Boston Rattler
Gunn, Thomas B., 154

Hall, Neil, 209
Hallett, John, 98, 113, 209
Harper, Edmund R. "Ned," 44–45
Harrington, William "Liverhead," 170, 172, 174–175, 207
Harrison, Joseph W., 86
Harrison, Miss, 281
Harrison, William Henry, 95
Hedden, William, 211
Heth, Joyce, 85, 114–115, 325n76
Hewlett, James, 83, 84, 85, 102
Holmes, Nance, 155–158, 163
Hook, Theodore Edward, 163
Horn, Eph, 281–282
Howe, Nathan, 164, 193
Hudson, J., 177

humbug contest, 67, 108–110; consequences of, 110–113

imitation dancing, 112, 185, 189–191, 196–202
impersonators and imposters, 2, 112, 116–118, 141, 192, 196–200, 229–231, 241–242, 261, 271, 291
Ince, Emma, 34, 49–50, 74, 204
Ince, Fanny, 74
indenture, 5, 27, 33, 75, 80, 86, 98, 202
interracial marriage in England, 150, 269
Irish immigrants, 14, 18, 22, 96–97, 161, 202, 247, 251, 285, 289, 322n6
Irwin, J. H., 220, 238

Jackson, Andrew, 49, 64, 94, 105
Jenkins, Charles, 97, 100, 112, 211, 266
Jerome, Louise, 265
jig dancing, 3–4, 8, 30, 40, 43, 80, 97, 128–129, 171–172, 179, 202, 262, 276, 285, 288; decanter jig, 249–250, 286; "jigs, reels, and hornpipes," 4, 8, 30, 31, 43, 186, 276; minstrelsy and, 193, 201–203, 212–213, 289–291; polite society's opinions of, 204–205; promoted as betting sport, 165–168, 174, 185–187, 280; by women (*see* women dancers)
Johnson, Francis, 79, 205
Johnson, Miss, 105
Jones, Bradford, 76
Jones, Ruthven, 183
Josaline, Miss, 181
Juba. *See* Lane, William Henry (Juba)

Kay, T. Belcher, 207
Kean, Miss, 89
Kent, Frank, 117, 162, 167
Kickham, Charles, 156
King, Lizetta, 288
Kirby, J. Hudson, 45–46, 48, 50, 89
Kneass, Nelson, 248
Know-Nothings, 95

La bayadère amoureuse, 46. *See* women dancers: ballet
La Bayadere in Ole Kentuck!, 45–51
labor history of challenge dancing, 8–9
Laforest, Mrs., 162
Lamertine, Miss, 266
Lane, Pete, 211, 291, 294
Lane, William Henry (Juba), 1–3; American Serenaders of, 252–254; announcement of first challenge match between Diamond and, 168, 173–174; appeal in United Kingdom, 227–228;

arrest in Sheffield, 259; arrest of Louis Davis and, 100–102; arrival in England, 217–218; becoming known as Juba, 114, 121; career path as competitive jig dancer, 116–117; as celebrity, 4, 179–180, 203, 218, 251–252, 295; as celebrity in England, 235–236; Charles Dickens and (*see* Dickens, Charles); cultural importance of, 6; dancing performances by, 85, 118–119, 151–152, 179–181; 229, 231–232; death of, 293; departure for England, 220; Dicken's observation of dancing by, 145–146, 151–152; early death of, 5; early life of, 2; family of, 22; female dancing partners of, 120–121, 146, 151–152, 160–161; first dancing match against Diamond at Pete Williams' tavern, 169–173; going solo in concert rooms in England, 251, 254–257; as imitation dancer, 189–190; imitation dancing by, 199–200, 201–202; impersonation of a woman by, 229–231; income of, 78, 80, 258–259; jump away from the Colosseum, 259–260; lack of social mobility of, 295–296; legacy of, 298–300; managing his own bookings and troupe in the United Kingdom, 252–254; marriage of, 269; as Master Champion, 181, as Master Diamond, 116–118, 120; as Master Rattler, 77, 82, 85, 88–89, 90, 113–114, 180; match at the Olympic Saloon, 206–207; at the Melodeon in Boston, 195–196; minstrelsy and, 192–193, 195–196; in new show with Diamond, 88–89; at the original Vauxhall, London, 220–226; performances at humble venues in England, 236–239, 266–268; performances in Ireland, 239–241, 271; performances in Scotland, 240–241; pleasure gardens and, 82; press coverage of, 167–168, 225–226, 232–233; promotion of, in England, 226–229; promotion of 1844 challenge with Diamond, 183–188; public reception of, in London, 226–232; scholarship on, 6; settlement in Liverpool, 272; significant performance of, 179–180; social scrutiny of, 204–205; stardom of, 4; travel around England, 232–235; at Vauxhall Gardens in New York, 76–78, 81–90, 113–121; at White's Melodeon, 211–212; work with four Ethiopian minstrel companies around Boston, 205–206; as young performer, 7, 78, 233
Lea, George, 264
Leavitt, Michael B., 201, 202, 203
Lee, Mary Ann, 49–50, 65, 78, 120, 155, 163
Lent, L. B., 132
Leroy, Miss, 211
Leslie, Emma, 208–209

362 · INDEX

Letton, V. M. W., 127, 129
Lewis, Dan, 291
Lewis, Jim, 291–292
Life in London, 148–149
Life in London and Sporting Guide, 268
lighting: circus, 133; theater, 36–37, 106
Lilly, Chris, 175, 177
Lindsay, Hugh, 126, 139
Lindsay, R. W., 117, 325n76, 326n89
Lloyd, William A., 249, 250–251
locomotive dance, 51, 53, 198, 200, 206, 250, 260, 261
Long Island dancing, 26–27, 57
Loomis, Martha, 279
Lossing, Benson, 35
Lottery Ticket, The, 70
Lowe, "Uncle Jim," 22
"Lucy Long," 158, 162, 229, 243, 262, 263, 276
Ludlow, M. C., 220, 238
Ludlow, Noah, 104–105, 112, 124, 125, 127
Lynch, Francis (Frank Diamond), 98, 100, 112, 189, 202, 205

Macarte, Marie, 226, 227
Macready, Mrs., 232
Macready, William Charles, 232
Mainzer, Joseph, 193–194
Mallory, Ben, 289–290, 294
Manager's Daughter, The, 70–71, 72
Manager's Son, Or-The Five Disappointments, 70, 71–72
Manning, Henry, 86
M'Arann's Garden, 74, 81, 319n64
markets, 15, 19–21; "Negro dancing" in, 21–26, 28
masculinity, 130, 156, 171
"Master" and "Miss" or "Mlle," 35–36
Marriotte, Signor, 97, 100
Mason, Hank, 277, 280, 286, 288
Masset, J. S., 183, 185
Master Diamond, 13, 33, 88, 116–117, 181. *See also* Diamond, John
Master F. Diamond, 116, 117, 167, 181
Master Hawk Diamond, 116
Master Rattler, 77, 82, 85, 88, 180–181, 183. *See also* Lane, William Henry (Juba)
McCabe, Francis, 150
McCoy, Thomas, 175, 177
McGowan, Jordan, 136
McLane, Andrew, 175
Melodeon: in Boston, 195–196; in New York, 211–212, 264; in Philadelphia, 291–292
Merchant of Venice, The, 70

Mexican-American War, 2, 244–247, 248, 261–262, 279
Miles, Joe (Master Miles), 118, 119, 165, 167, 171, 201, 211
Military Garden: in New York, 83; in Brooklyn, 85, 180
Miller, Mrs., 89
Millicent, John, 241, 259
Million movement ("Music for the Million"), 193–195, 205
Mitchell, John, 220
Mitchell, William 32, 70
mock challenges, 113, 118–120
Molineaux, Aaron, 286
Molineaux, Algernon, 176
Molineaux, Tom, 176, 177–178, 228, 334n33
Moncrieff, William Thomas, 148
Morgan, Julia, 278, 288
Moxley, Tom (Master Floyd), 276
Murphy, Ann, 161
Music for the Million (ensemble), 208–209
Myers, F. S., 194, 199
Myers, Richard (Ole Bull), 162, 163, 182, 192, 195, 198–199

Native American dancers, 27–28, 282–284
nativism, 95–96, 159, 183, 262, 276, 322n6
"Negro dancing," 4, 16, 21–26, 66, 95, 108–109, 135; extravaganzas, 43–45; jigs as, 95; types of, 40–43
Negro Plantation, 70
New Chatham Theatre, 58–60, 117, 181; challenge dance in, 56–58, 62
New Era, 93–95
New Orleans levee, 102–110
newsboys, 38–39, 45, 60, 120, 296
newspaper coverage, 5, 117–120, 233; of Diamond in New Orleans, 108; of Diamond's first staged match, 56; of 1844 match between Juba and Diamond, 183–188; flash press, 5, 114, 120, 155, 165; of Juba in Dublin, 239–240; of Juba in London, 225–226; of women dancers, 4, 150, 155–158;
New York Clipper, 280; dancers in, 117, 278, 281, 284, 285–287, 291, 292, 295
New York Sporting Whip, 1–2, 106, 120, 160–161, 165–168; announcement of match between Juba and Diamond, 168, 173–174
Nichols, Thomas, 151, 155
Nick of the Woods, 32–33, 284

O'Connell, James, 62–63, 194
Okatewaula, 282–284

INDEX · 363

Olympic Circus (Welch's), 163
Olympic Saloon (Graham's), 155, 207
Olympic Theatre: New York, 60, 70; New Orleans, 248
Ordway's, 263, 264, 281
Ottignon, Charles F., 176–177, 185

Paddy O' Rafferty, 70
Page, Col. James, 75
Panic of 1837, 35
Parrish, Frank, 122
Peel, Tommy, 287, 288, 294
Pelham, Richard Ward, 56–57, 61, 62, 64, 167–168, 189, 192–193, 202, 219, 238–239, 242–243, 254, 271, 345n91
Pell, Gilbert Ward, 218–220, 225, 226, 232, 234, 235–238, 240, 252, 254
Perkins, John, 193
Perkins, Samuel H., 75
Pierce, Earl, 163, 200, 201, 294
pit benches, 8, 32, 56, 59–60, 289; as "bleachers," 52, 133
pleasure gardens, 5, 76, 81–86. *See also* Vauxhall Gardens
popular culture, 3–5
port cities, 3, 7, 13, 14–15, 249, 298; markets in, 19–21, 22, 25, 28
Porter, Naomi, 278, 288
Porter, William T., 56
prize concerts, 260, 281
prizefighting, 7, 174–179, 255, 277. *See also* boxing
prostitutes, 4, 60, 149, 150, 153–156, 267
Puppet-Show, The, 225–226
Putnam, G. W., 143

Queen, Frank, 278, 280
Queen Victoria, 147, 236
Quinn, Billy, 211, 290, 294

racial mingling, 1, 15, 18, 22–23; in prizefighting, 173–179
Rainer's New Orleans Serenaders, 262, 279
Read, Tom, 148, 150–151, 173
Reed, Margaret, 22, 80
Reed, Zachary, 22, 80
Rees, James, 118
remunerative labor, 3, 8–9, 78, 154, 300
reputation, 110, 112, 139, 167, 172, 211, 259, 271
Rice, Dan, 244, 248–249
Rice, T. D., 43, 70, 211, 284
Richard III, 70, 84
Richardson, B., 213

Richardson, Mrs., 142
Richmond, Bill, 176, 287
Roache, John, 18
Robinson, Jimmy (Juan Hernandez), 105
Robinson, John P., 105, 124, 125–126, 127, 129, 130–131, 135, 139
Robinson, Lenite, 208
Rockwell, Henry, 53–54, 130, 163
Rosley, Miss, 155
rowdies, 138–139, 160
Royal Casino, England, 254–257, 259
Ryder, H., 199, 206, 340n81

Sanders, Mick, 107, 124, 125
Sanford, James (Sandford), 62, 67, 75, 158, 162, 189, 195, 202, 205, 261, 317n30, 354n54; Barnum and, 65; death of, 284; friendship with Diamond, 68–69, 74; match with Diamond, 65–66, 96; at the St. Charles Theater, 142; Walnut Street Theater and, 65–67
Sanford, James (pugilist), 175, 317n30
Sanford, Samuel S., 196–199, 219, 236, 258, 273, 278–279, 295; Philadelphia burlesque opera house of, 284–285
Schlim, C. L., 85, 113, 118
"Science against Strength," 50; "Art and Science," 185
Scott, James C., 40
Scribe, Eugène, 46
Sefton, Mrs., 65
Seward, William, 101
shared public culture, 46
Sheppard, Bob, 285
Sheridan, John, 176–177, 185
"shines," 135, 141, 251
Shore, S. G., 76
Silvers, John, 37
Singing for the Million, 193, 229
Sliter, Dick (R. H.), 187, 193, 249, 260, 264, 273, 276–280, 285, 294
Smith, A. M. C., 144
Smith, C. L., 238–239
Smith, Dan (Young Bendigo), 286–287
Smith, G. W., 205
Smith, Hugh, 286
Smith, John Washington, 33, 54, 74, 158, 189, 202
Smith, Joseph, 183
Smith, R. W., 209
Smith, Sol, 104–106, 108, 110, 112, 124–127, 129
Sparks, William, 286, 287
Spoiled Child, 70
stage names, 8, 36, 78, 85, 89, 113, 116, 119, 180, 182, 288

St. Charles Theatre, 105–108, 110, 111–112, 125, 142
Stephens, William H., 144, 150, 159
Stevens, Ephraim, 100–101
Stickney, John, 248
Stickney, Samuel P., 105, 109, 248
Strange Gentleman, The, 161–162
Strolling Country Actors; or, The Manager's Son, 71
structure of opportunity, 3, 9
Sweeney, Joel, 53, 54, 66, 162, 229
Sweetman, Johnny, 286

Taglioni, Marie, 48, 231, 314n57; travestied as Taglioni-rina, 48–51, 72
Taglioni, Paul and Anna, 48
tailor's leap, 157, 186
Taryon, Rose, 266
taverns, 16–19, 144–146, 185; in England, 232, 254–257, 269
Taylor, J. E., 286
Thayer, A. L., 206
theaters, in the United States, 33–37, 45, 59, 95, 274, 284, 291; African American seating in, 60–61, 289; children's attendance at, 60; in England, 232, 234–235, first staged challenge dance in, 56–58; increased attendance of women at, 60; New Orleans, 104–105; in Scotland, 241
Thomas, James, 41–42, 132, 135, 182, 192; early life of, 122–123; observations on John Diamond's dancing, 123–124
Thomas, Sally, 122
Thompson, William (Bendigo), 277
Thorne, Charles R., 58
timekeeping, 161, 186, 234, 236
Tom and Jerry, 89, 148, 161
travel, 69–70, 73, 97–98
travesty, 46, 48
trials of skill, 1, 7, 19, 29, 49–50, 58, 62, 86, 108–109, 118–119, 156, 168, 176, 181, 201, 249, 278, 290
tuberculosis, 293
Turnbull, Julia, 49–50, 155, 163
Turner, J. S., 281
Turning the Tables, 33
Tyrolean Brothers, 76

Valintine, J. W., 220, 238
Van Buren, Martin, 95
variety shows, 70, 84–85
Vauxhall Gardens, NY, 76–78, 81–90, 113, 201; dark transactions at, 113–118; Diamond and Lane's first show at, 88–89; managed by Bancker, 90, 101; newspaper coverage of, 118–120
Vauxhall Gardens, London, 81, 223–224, 242; Rotunda Theatre in, 217, 220–221, 226–227; successors of Juba at, 270. *See also* Ethiopian Serenaders
Vieuxtemps, Heinrich, 181

wagers, 56, 62, 64, 66, 107, 165, 174–175, 182–184, 277; fake, 66–67, 107–108, 111, 114
Wallace, Vincent, 182
Walnut Street Theatre (American Theatre), 64–66, 96, 161; gag bills and, 66–67
Walsh, Mike, 275
Ward, Jem, 177
Warren, Mickey, 211, 277, 284, 285, 286, 291
watchmen, 74, 83, 95, 144, 199, 208
Welch, Rufus, 53–54, 163, 193
Wemyss, Francis Courtney, 64, 66–67, 69
West, Johnny (Young America), 286
West African dancing traditions, 24, 29–30
Wheatly, Sarah, 163
Whig Party, 93–95, 101, 245
White, Charles, 209–212, 257, 264, 265, 284, 288
White, Robert, 133, 137, 206
Whitlock, William M., 69, 70, 74, 88, 162, 186, 192–193
Whitlock's Collection of Ethiopian Melodies, 37
Williams, Barney, 158, 162, 163, 181
Williams, Nancy, 250
Williams, Pete, 2, 148, 150, 169–170, 172, 173, 174, 179–180, 206
Williams, W. H., 70
Wilson, T., 248
Winnemore, A. F., 195, 205, 241
women dancers, 4, 7, 42, 93–96, 111–112, 125, 151–158, 161, 165, 179, 194, 288, 298; ballet, 49, 85, 120, 155, 222; champions, 158, 278, 288; indigenous, 28, 282; on stage, 36, 61, 184, 291; in taverns, 17–18, 27, 147, 149, 150–155, 160
women's rights, 262–263
Wooldridge, George B., 2, 5, 165, 184, 195, 337n21
working-class audiences, 8, 35, 44, 56–57, 60–61, 67, 191, 223, 234, 245, 252, 266, 290; Lane and Diamond as popular with, 296
working-class life, 4, 7–8, 31, 96–97, 245–246; culture of reciprocity in, 110–111, 174; military service and, 245–247; racial integration in, 288, 296–298; taverns in, 14, 16–19, 154, 173, 185

xenophobia, 95, 183, 228

APRIL F. MASTEN is a professor of American history at the State University of New York at Stony Brook. She is the author of *Art Work: Women Artists and Democracy in Mid-Nineteenth-Century New York*.

The University of Illinois Press
is a founding member of the
Association of University Presses.

Composed in 10.5/13 Minion Pro
with Bauer Bodoni Std 1 display
by Lisa Connery
at the University of Illinois Press
Manufactured by Versa Press, Inc.

University of Illinois Press
1325 South Oak Street
Champaign, IL 61820-6903
www.press.uillinois.edu